Monetary Policy, Taxation, and International Investment Strategy

MONETARY POLICY, TAXATION, AND INTERNATIONAL INVESTMENT STRATEGY

EDITED BY
Victor A. Canto and Arthur B. Laffer

Q

QUORUM BOOKS

New York • Westport, Connecticut • London

Library of Congress Cataloging-in-Publication Data

Monetary policy, taxation, and international investment strategy /
   edited by Victor A. Canto and Arthur B. Laffer.
      p. cm.
    ISBN 0–89930–534–2 (lib. bdg. : alk. paper)
    1. Monetary policy. 2. Taxation. 3. Investments, Foreign.
  I. Canto, Victor A. II. Laffer, Arthur B.
  HG230.3.M638 1990
  332.4′6—dc20   90–30017

British Library Cataloguing in Publication Data is available.

Library of Congress Catalog Card Number: 90–30017
ISBN: 0–89930–534–2

First published in 1990

Quorum Books, 88 Post Road West, Westport, CT 06881
An imprint of Greenwood Publishing Group, Inc.

Printed in the United States of America

The paper used in this book complies with the
Permanent Paper Standard issued by the National
Information Standards Organization (Z39.48–1984).

10 9 8 7 6 5 4 3 2 1

TP

Contents

PART FOUR. PORTFOLIO STRATEGIES

Figures

Tables

Introduction

Victor A. Canto and Arthur B. Laffer

Most economics books that focus on the policy implications of government actions analyze those implications in the context of whether they offer the appropriate solution to the problem in question. Seldom does the analysis consider the practical implications and strategies that are vital to business managers, financial analysts, and investors in general.

In this book we attempt to take that extra step. We try to illustrate how incentives and disincentives affect economic behavior and the performance of the economy. In addition, we present a top-down approach that shows the reader how to trace the impact of government policies through the economy and thereby discover investment implications that will be helpful to investors and policymakers alike, from portfolio managers and financial analysts to corporate strategists and government officials.

MONETARY POLICY

The first section of the book focuses on monetary issues. Since the inflation potential of the economy depends, in large part, on the organization of the monetary market, particular attention must be paid to the likely intervention mechanisms, as well as to discussing the relevant monetary aggregate.

The first chapter discusses a common macroeconomic view that the press has attributed to some members of the Fed. The view postulates that sustained increases in overall economic activity eventually strain capacity and lead to higher prices. Conversely, a decline in capacity utilization is viewed as relieving inflationary pressures in the economy. The empirical implications of this view are quite clear: increases in capacity utilization result in higher prices. Conversely, a reduction in capacity utilization will result in lower prices. If the monetary authorities subscribe to this view, then the policy implications are that whenever capacity utilization rises, attempts would be made to slow the economy, an undesirable choice, or that through monetary actions, the rate of price increase should be slowed.

In a monetary model, the rise in the inflation rate will be slowed through slower growth of the monetary aggregates. Thus the authorities must also choose the relevant aggregate to implement their policy of achieving slower inflation. Thus the implementation of monetary policy must rest on a number of critical relations: first, the assumed relation between capacity utilization and inflation. Alternative theoretical frameworks yield different implications. Whether the monetary framework is relevant or not is an empirical issue. The second relation is that between the monetary aggregates and inflation, and the third is the monetary authorities' ability to control and thus select the relevant aggregate. Before examining the empirical evidence it is worthwhile to review the alternative monetary framework of analysis.

The alternative framework of analysis is based on a "general equilibrium" analysis where inflation is defined as a monetary phenomenon of too much money chasing too few goods. Thus, the general equilibrium analysis postulates a negative relation between inflation and real economic activity. The general equilibrium monetary analysis implies that, holding monetary policy constant, acceleration in capacity utilization will be associated with a lower, not higher, inflation rate. A decline in capacity utilization will be associated with higher, not lower, prices. However, since we view inflation as a monetary phenomenon, the correlation between capacity utilization and inflation depends on the monetary response. If monetary policy accommodates the expansion of capacity utilization (i.e., the increase in the demand for money), the price level need not change and inflation will be unrelated to changes in capacity utilization.

The empirical results reported in Chapter 1 stand directly at odds with received doctrine. The international evidence does not support the popular view that the international increase in inflation rates is the result of increases in capacity utilization. The evidence suggests that the Phillips curve does not provide a clear-cut explanation of inflationary pressure. The data point to a better alternative, a monetary explanation of inflation.

The belief that higher economic growth and increases and acceleration in capacity utilization result in higher inflation is deeply embedded. Stated another way, some would have us believe that slower growth and declines in capacity utilization result in lower inflation. This fallacy is dangerous to the welfare of the nation and to the world economy. Policies intended to slow economic activity and capacity utilization (i.e., cooling-off the economy) will result in higher inflation, not lower inflation. Declines in capacity utilization are harbingers of rising inflationary pressure.

The empirical evidence suggests that a monetary framework provides a more adequate explanation of inflation. However, considerable disagreement exists as to the relevant quantities of money and goods that determine inflation and as to who controls those quantities. Thus, empirically, one must distinguish between variables that help explain inflation and those that cause it. If monetary policy is to be successful in curbing inflation, the selection of a monetary variable under the control of the monetary authorities is a must. Otherwise the monetary authorities' actions will be inconsequential. Two major variants of the monetarist model are considered in Chapters 2 and 3. One, the local view, argues that the relevant concepts of money and output are the national (local) quantities. The other, the global view, argues that the relevant concepts of money and output in their relationship with inflation and the world quantities are the world quantities. Even within the local and global view, variants exist as to the relevant quantities of money. Variants of local monetarists focus on the monetary base, M1 and M2. In turn, variants of the global monetarism focus on the global counterparts: world base, world M1, and world M2.

The local monetarist model takes narrowly defined measures of either M1 or M2 as the relevant empirical counterpart to the concept of money. By virtue of the fact that the Fed, alone, controls the money supply, growth in the monetary aggregate represents shifts in that supply. Real GNP growth represents shifts in the demand for money.

Global monetarism represents the most aggregative form of the monetarist models. Global monetarism argues that money is, after all, one of the easiest commodities to move across national boundaries. Therefore, if people can transact in one anothers' area, it would be misleading not to aggregate both areas.

Eurodollars and money market funds play a somewhat special role in the American financial system. Eurodollars play a similar role at the international level. To the extent that Eurodollars and money market funds pay a competitive interest rate, they are indexed and do not suffer an inflation tax. As inflation increases, holders of money balances will tend to shift their balances toward this kind of money.

The evidence of the last three decades presented in Chapter 2 is supportive of the global monetarist view. There is a close relationship between the excess of the world money supply over world real GNP growth lagged two years and U.S. inflation.

The empirical results reported in Chapter 3 simply do not support the M1 monetarist model. Expanding the definition of money to include M2 in the equation does not improve the monetarist's case. A combination of the facts that monetary aggregates are not statistically significant in explaining long-run inflation and that the most significant variable is lagged inflation is damaging to the local and global monetarist models. One plausible explanation for these results is that both M1 and world money are endogenous. However, the nature of the endogeneity is quite different for the two monies.

Imperfect substitutability among the monetary aggregates provides a mechanism by which the monetary authorities may influence, but perhaps not control, the overall quantity of money. Our choice of a proxy for the supply shifts is the growth in the monetary base. The reason for this simply is that the Federal Reserve totally controls and only controls the monetary base. We have argued that changes in the equilibrium quantity of money are the result of both shifts in the demand for and supply of money. Thus, if we are able to identify shifts in the supply of money (i.e., growth in the monetary base) and to know that the quantity of money reflects both demand and supply, then netting the supply component would have M1 growth as a total proxy for money demand.

Money market funds represent a viable substitute for narrowly defined transaction balances. Similarly, Eurocurrencies represent a viable substitute for domestic monies. Suppliers (banks) often have a choice of producing local currency denominated balances or participating in nonlocal currency deposit taking and lending. Likewise, demanders (depositors) can often choose deposits in the country of origin or in the Eurocurrency market. Profit considerations imply that as the costs of local currency balances rise, Eurocurrency alternatives become more attractive. The ability of Eurocurrencies and money market funds to substitute for checking accounts implies that monetary policy initiatives by domestic authorities are potentially offset.

Chapter 4 provides a framework of analysis that is consistent with the empirical results reported in the earlier chapters. The basic premise of the analysis presented is that the confusion and controversy in interpreting the empirical results arise from trying to infer how the demand curve has shifted vis-à-vis the supply curve from changes in the equilibrium quantity of money and changes in the price level.

Money possesses characteristics similar to all other commodities. When the supply curve for money is shifted outward and the demand curve is stationary, the new equilibrium will occur at a greater quantity and a lower unit value. Since the value of a unit of money is the quantity of goods and services for which it can be exchanged, a decrease in the value of money is equivalent to an increase in the general price level (i.e., inflation).

Alternatively, if the demand for money is shifted outward, the new equilibrium also will be at a greater quantity but at a greater value per unit. An increase in the value of money is equivalent to a decline in the price level (i.e., deflation). In the absence of other changes, inward shifts of supply will result in lessened quantities and deflation, and inward shifts of demand will result in lessened quantities and inflation.

The important point is that knowledge about changes in the quantity of money alone is not sufficient to determine whether prices will rise or fall. If an increase in the quantity of money is the result of a shift in the demand for money, then this will lower inflation, lower interest rates, and raise the value of the currency in the foreign exchanges. Conversely, if an increase in the quantity of money is the consequence of a shift in the supply of money, then inflationary pressures will be heightened, resulting in higher interest rates and a weaker currency. All in all, no one can say that increases or decreases in the quantity of money are "inflationary" or "deflationary" or whether the policies that precipitated these changes were "loose" or "tight." Knowledge of the origin of each disturbance, that is, whether the demand curve or supply curve shifted, is necessary to determine its impact.

The evidence that inflation and higher interest rates are the products of excess money growth supports the position that the role of monetary policy should be to provide stable prices. Price stability is achieved whenever shifts in the supply of money equal shifts in the demand for money. The policy implication is quite clear: monetary policy conducted in accordance with a price rule will insure that the supply of money automatically accommodates shifts in the demand for money.

A commitment to use monetary policy solely for the purpose of stabilizing prices, and not to finance government expenditures, provides the basis for a successful and sustainable monetary system that would insure price stability for years to come. If the purchasing power of the dollar literally was assured indefinitely, nearly everyone would hold dollars rather than gold or other inflation hedges. Likewise, if interest rates were low because of the reduction of inflationary anticipations, far wider use of dollar money balances would occur. The use of foreign currencies to support international transactions or simply as stores of value also would diminish. A successful monetary policy would expand the demand for money and necessitate an increase in the dollar money supply.

Financial economists are interested in anticipating movements in financial variables. If able to do so, a portfolio strategy can be designed to take advantage of the anticipated changes. Crucial to the strategy is the development of a framework which will anticipate changes in key monetary indicators and market expectations, and will determine their potential impact on interest rates and inflation.

Chapter 5 provides such a framework. The key policy indicators derived from the analysis are the growth rate of the monetary base, which is a variable under the control of the monetary authorities and thus a proxy for shifts in the money supply function, and excess base over M1 growth, which is a proxy for the excess supply of money.

In addition to the policy variables, market expectations also play a significant role in the development of the portfolio strategy. For example, more often than not, a declining dollar and a rise in interest rates are harbingers of mounting inflationary pressures. However, these variables can also change for reasons other than changes in expected inflation. When gold prices, the foreign exchange value of the dollar, and interest rates move in different directions, they yield conflicting signals about the inflation outlook. The resolution of such conflicting signals is a major challenge. The problem faced by most managers is that prices reflect joint information regarding inflation and real effects. Therefore, they must exercise care in distinguishing between inflation and real effects.

The most important development from the efficient market/rational expectations debate is a consensus that market data reflect expectations as to what will occur in the future. This is not to say that what the market expects to occur *will* occur, only that current market data contain a forecast of the future. A direct implication of this analysis is that financial prices such as interest rates, the slope of the yield curve, gold prices, the foreign exchange value of the dollar, and stock price indices may collectively contain the market's implicit forecast of the future path of interest and inflation rates. Policy variables under the influence of the monetary authorities may also affect the economy's inflation rate and the market's expectations about the future.

Through careful analysis of market data and the policy variables, asset managers can develop insights as to what the market collectively anticipates. In this way they can utilize the collective wisdom of the markets to see events more clearly and to differentiate their own views from the views of the market.

Policy actions may also result in an interrelationship between the financial variables. A preannounced increase in the monetary base is likely to simultaneously result in an upward revision of inflation expectations, interest rates, gold prices, and a depreciation of the dollar. These, in turn, through their effect on bracket creep, may affect stock prices. Similarly, a tax rate cut will result in lower inflation, lower interest rates, lower gold prices, a stronger dollar, and a higher stock market. In short, it is fairly clear that policy changes will induce a multitude of interconnections in the movements of the financial variables. Therefore, interpreting the movement and the interrelationship among the variables may yield an accurate forecast of the path of financial variables several periods into the future.

The empirical approach followed in this chapter initially includes all of the above-mentioned policy and price variables. Vector autoregression (VAR) has proven a successful technique for forecasting systems of interrelated time series variables. Vector autoregression is also frequently used, although with considerable controversy, for analyzing the dynamic impact on system variables of different types of random disturbances and controls.

An empirical model that combines short-term interest rates, the slope of the yield curve, the foreign exchange value of the dollar, stock prices, base growth, and excess base growth does quite well in explaining the inflation rate and changes in the three-month T-bill. Given that the empirical specification of the model only uses quarterly values of financial prices and that monetary aggregates lagged from one to five quarters, the estimated equation may be used to forecast changes in interest rates and inflation one step ahead (i.e., one quarter). For the sample considered, the model correctly forecasts the direction of change in interest rates approximately 75 percent of the time. The results are encouraging enough to suggest the possible use of the model in forecasting interest rates.

Monetary policy also has a significant effect on financial markets. The implications for the financial markets and the economy resulting from an inverted yield curve are discussed in Chapter 6. The historical record of inverted yield curves reveals a clear pattern. First, during a fiat standard period, a rise in short-term interest rates accompanied by an inverted yield curve has been associated with subsequent rising inflation and slower economic growth. In contrast, under a price rule, an inverted yield curve has been accompanied by a subsequent fall in long rates and an expanding economy.

The problem faced by investors and economists is to determine whether the monetary authorities are pursuing a price rule or some other framework. The task becomes difficult in light of the monetary authorities' reluctance to fully disclose their monetary policy and the standard under which they operate. During the inversion period, the stock market rose whenever the Fed was on a price rule and declined when the Fed was on a fiat standard. Thus, the financial markets appear to contain information regarding their assessment of the Fed's monetary standard. The behavior of the stock market during 1989 strongly suggests that U.S. monetary policy is being conducted within the price rule framework. The implications for the financial markets is one of a continued secular decline in interest rates.

FISCAL ISSUES

Supply-side economics is little more than a new label for standard neoclassical economics. The essential tenet of classical economic analysis is that people alter their behavior when economic incentives change. If the incentives for doing an activity increase relative to alternative activities, more of the attractive activity will be done. Likewise, if impediments are imposed on an activity, less of the activity will be forthcoming.

Basically, people face both time and resource constraints in their quest for self-fulfillment. With limited resources and time, the attainment of objectives necessitates prudent management within the structure of constraints imposed by nature and humanity. Government, with its full power of enforcement, has the ability to alter the constraints encountered by the vast array of economic factors. Changes in the structure of governmentally imposed constraints alter the economy's behavior.

The forms of constraint emanating from government are virtually unlimited. Taxes, subsidies, regulations, restrictions, and requirements are but a few of the endless series of possible government actions in the area of economics. The composition as well as the magnitude of government spending will also affect private activity, as will the methods of government financing. The general precepts of classical economics are founded on the role played by incentives and on the effect government actions have on those incentives.

The perennial cry from redistributionists, whether liberal or conservative, is to slow the growth of government spending and postpone any tax cut. Tax rate reductions are held out as the far-distant carrot to induce the electorate to select this program of economic austerity. Such programs, however, have shown themselves time and again to be bankrupt. They are poorly founded on both conceptual and empirical grounds. The method most successful in reducing government incursions in the private sector is to precede any reductions in government spending by major reductions in tax rates.

It is axiomatic that much of what the government spends is wasted. Each one of us could name program after program that should either be eliminated or scaled down. Every president and presidential contender has waxed eloquent with promises to reduce waste and increase the efficiency of government. Almost all have failed. The simple reason is that each failed to understand the central role of government.

The constellation of economic incentives is the moving force in the goods market, and changes in marginal tax rates are as important a factor affecting incentives as can be found. People and businesses work and produce to earn after-tax income. As a general rule, they do not work and produce because they like to pay taxes. As tax rates increase, after-tax rewards from engaging in market activities decline. The consequences are less output and less employ-ment.

Conversely, as tax rates decline, alternatives to market activities become less attractive. Individuals and businesses commit more effort to market activities. Therefore, as tax rates decline, more labor and capital enter the market, and output expands. Slow output growth is just as inflationary as rapid money growth. The slower the growth in output, the higher will be the rate of inflation.

The case put forth by the tax cut detractors has several elements. Their argu-ments encompass the following: Tax cut antagonists argue that across-the-board tax rate reductions will not materially increase equity values, economic growth, or savings. In addition, those opposed to tax rate reductions argue that across-the-board income tax rate cuts will lead to higher inflation and greater deficits, and will hurt the poor.

Chapter 7 illustrates that, historically, periods of rapid growth, low inflation, and rising stock markets frequently have been periods of lower tax rates. Perhaps given the close association between higher tax rates, lower real growth, and lower savings and capital formation, it should be obvious that equity values and rates of taxation also are closely related. They are!

From 1916 to 1918 the highest marginal tax rate on income rose from a mere 7 percent to 73 percent. Other changes in the rates of taxation were consistent with the enormous rise in the rate at the highest bracket. Equity values tumbled. With Harding's overwhelming defeat of Cox in 1920 (Harding received over 60 per-cent of the total vote), an era of rapid and deep tax rate cuts commenced.

From 1919 to 1929, the highest marginal rate fell from 77 percent to 24 percent. The lowest rate was reduced from 6 percent to ⅜ of one percent. Real GNP grew at a 2.7 annual rate, the inflation rate declined to a 0.36 percent annual rate, and equity values rose in what was to be called the Roaring Twen-ties. The S&P 500 rose at a 9.5 percent annual rate.

In 1929 an era of tax rate increases began in earnest. In an exceptionally detailed analysis, Jude Wanniski documented the parallel movements of the political effort to pass the Smoot-Hawley Tariff Act and the Great Crash.[1] The thirties saw the highest rate of taxation rise from 24 percent in 1929 to 81.1 percent in 1940. During the 1930–35 period, real GNP declined at an annual rate of 3.1 percent, and the stock market declined precipitously—at an annual rate of 8.3 percent.

During the Kennedy and Johnson administrations, the pace of economic activity accelerated as tax rates were cut. During the 1964–67 period, real GNP grew at an annual rate of almost 5 percent per year. The S&P 500 grew at 6.3 percent per annum. The Reagan administration inherited an economy badly in need of repair after the damage done during the prior 12 years. Tax rates were lowered, energy prices decontrolled, industries were deregulated, and monetary stability was restored.

To one recording the history of the early 1980s, as important as any feature of the tax/legislative nexus is the observation that anticipated changes in tax rates also can have a profound impact on the path of the economy. In the 1981 tax bill, the tax rate cuts were phased in. Supposedly, there was a 5 percent cut on October 1, 1981; a 10 percent cut on July 1, 1982; and a final 10 percent cut on July 1, 1983.

The flaw in this phased-in approach to tax rate cuts was to ignore the role of incentives on individual behavior. Common sense tells us that people don't shop at a store the week before that store has a widely advertised discount sale. Prospects of lower tax rates in future years created incentives for individuals and businesses to reduce their income during 1981 and 1982 when tax rates were high, in order to realize that income in 1983 and 1984 when tax rates would be lower. The economy slowed, unemployment rose, and the deficit swelled (Figure 7.4). Ironically, the attempt to stave off deficits by delaying tax cuts, in reality, caused those very deficits to soar.

What appears truly astounding is the rapidity with which the economy responds to incentives. Virtually on January 1, 1983, when the bulk of the tax cuts became effective, the economy began to recover. The recovery, true to supply-side logic, did not foster the "roaring inflation" so confidently predicted by Walter Heller, but it robustly provided jobs, higher capacity utilization, and increased productivity. Even subtle differences in incentives appear to work. The fourth-quarter-1983 slowdown was followed by a first-quarter-1984 rebound in exact conformance with the anticipation and then the realization of the final 5 percent cut in tax rates.

In January 1983, total civilian employment stood at 99,161,000 people, and in January 1988, employment had reached 114,129,000. That is an increase of over 15 percent in five years. The Reagan/supply-side job machine really worked. Real GNP measured in 1982 dollars went from a low of $3166 billion in 1982 to $4024 billion in 1988, a 27 percent increase in real GNP.

With the Jarvis-Steiger-Reagan revolution, the balance of political power has been dramatically changed. Supply-side Republicans were able to effectuate a metamorphosis. They transformed themselves from the tax collectors for the welfare state to the tax cutters for the opportunity society. The political response has been overwhelming. Voters latched on to the tax issue with a vengeance. The new income tax rates that came into effect on January 1, 1988 are extremely conducive to economic growth. The highest federal marginal tax rates on personal and corporate incomes will be 28 percent and 34 percent respectively. The tax structure beginning in 1988 is the most pro-production structure the United States has experienced since the Harding and Coolidge administrations reduced the highest marginal tax rate on personal income to 25 percent from 73 percent.

If the past is a guide to the future, the tax rate reductions of 1988 portend continued strong growth over the coming years, a rising stock market, and a corresponding lid on inflation. There are some major initiatives on horizons near and far that, if implemented, could make the 1990s exceptional.

The United States does not need another visionary; Ronald Reagan did his job. A new era is at hand. What is needed now is good management to change Reagan's revolutionary ideas into the conventional wisdom. A consolidation phase to make the Reagan gains permanent is what is required. President Bush is the right person for the job.

There has been a fundamental shift in personality from Reagan to Bush. Whereas President Reagan was more confrontational, President Bush is more a consensus builder. His strategy has been to find a position behind the Democrats' position which leaves them two choices: an all-out fight or to fall back to President Bush's position. The minimum wage and capital gains legislation are two examples. President Bush won on the minimum wage.

Productivity, savings, and investment are the catchwords of the Bush team's view of economics. Those policies that would increase any or all of those three concepts will be favored policies.

One dream of tax reform had always been to reduce the perceived immorality of the tax codes. By lowering individual and business tax rates, so the logic proceeded, the benefits of evading taxes would be reduced and yet the penalties for evading taxes would remain unchanged. Thus, we argued that the calculus of income tax evasion would be sufficiently rearranged that heretofore income churning in the underground economy would resurface as legitimate, above-ground taxable income. How wrong we were.

No one believed that the component of income skulking in the underground economy that was derived from illicit activities would expose itself to the light of federal auditors. But there was a firmly held view that large amounts of underground income resulted exclusively from the straightforward motive to evade tax payments. The government took too much. And, when the government's take diminished, vast amounts of income would now be reported: this does not appear to have been the case.

The mistake made long ago and far away was to underestimate the enormous power of precedence in conjunction with fear. People who have cheated on their taxes historically find it impossible to fess up and pay now even if they never would begin to cheat under the current tax codes. Reporting income for the first time is seen as a sure trigger to receive a federal audit. Past tax anomalies under the cold, bright light of the IRS would sooner or later lead to criminal negligence charges and God-knows-what. Better that attention should not be drawn and that unprofitable tax evasion continue.

The tax increase advocated in Chapter 8 is a genuine tax increase that could raise anywhere from $25 to $40 billion in its initial years and lesser amounts on an ongoing basis. The rather astounding features of this immodest proposal are twofold. The specific payers of this tax will, by their own admission, be better off than they would be if they were not to pay the tax, and—without arcane doublethink and convoluted chains of economic illogic—output, unemployment, and production will literally rise as a consequence of the tax increase. This proposal encompasses a federal tax amnesty program, in cooperation with the individual states, coupled with a massive effort for the government to enter into contractual agreements with taxpayers for the compromising of tax liabilities and the collection of tax through installment agreements.

The debate about capital gains taxation has been reopened by President George Bush. Chapters 9 through 12 discuss several issues relative to capital gains tax rate legislation. During the presidential campaign Bush stated that the maximum tax rate on capital gains on assets held for over one year should be lowered to 15 percent from the current 28 percent rate. He argued that, over time, the reduction in the capital gains tax rate would raise investment, national income, labor productivity, the capital stock, and the overall standard of living. Bush believes that the proposed tax rate reduction might even increase federal tax revenue. It has been reported that such a two-tiered tax rate reduction would also reduce volatility in the stock market.

Historically, capital gains tax receipts have comprised 5 percent of personal income tax receipts and less than 2 percent of all federal revenue. Moreover, capital gains on stock transactions have accounted for only one-third of total capital gains. Thus, looking at the capital gains tax on a static revenue basis or in terms of its average impact on the economy, it appears that a capital gains tax reduction will have minor impact on the economy. Thus, if the rate reduction is to have the desired effect on the economy, it must, through the increased incentives, have a profound effect on economic behavior.

The proposed reduction in the top capital gains tax rate to 15 percent from 28 percent would have numerous beneficial effects on the economy: It will reduce the hurdle rate of return required by investors, leading to higher investment and higher valuation of the current profit (capital gains) stream. This will tend to increase the value of stocks as well as the taxable base. In the long run, it will increase capital gains tax revenues. Indexing the capital gains tax code and adopting a domestic price rule that reduces the inflation rate will have an even stronger beneficial impact on the U.S. economy. The effect of such action will be to reduce the hurdle rate of return for new investments, thus setting the stage for increased investment, productivity, and a higher standard of living.

A capital gains tax rate cut from the current 28 percent to 15 percent without indexing should be preferred over pure indexing if the real return on the investment exceeded the rate of inflation. With inflation higher than the real return, the preference would be for indexing. At a 20 percent capital gains tax rate, the breakpoint occurs when inflation is 40 percent the size of the real yield. This explains why people who are after "the big kill" prefer almost any rate reduction over indexing.

We should never let the best become the enemy of the good. Any cut in the capital gains tax should, in and of itself, raise the real value of existing assets and thus the stock market. Two questions arise. First, what would the magnitude of the rise be under the different proposals? Second, how much of the expected rise is already in the market? With regard to the second question, our belief is that we've experienced about half of the effect to date.

With inflation assumed at 4 percent and investors requiring a 3 percent real yield after all taxes, then the after-all-tax yield to shareholders has to be 7 percent. For corporations, a dividend yield of 3 percent paid by corporations would, after the 28 percent personal income tax, be equivalent to 2.2 percent to the shareholders. This leaves 4.8 percent to be generated by after-all-tax nominal capital gains. With a capital gains tax of 28 percent, the pretax capital gains would have to be 6.7 percent to yield a 4.8 percent after-all-tax return to the shareholders. Putting it all together, a corporation would have to pay share-holders 3 percent in dividends and 6.7 percent in capital gains for a total 9.7 percent pretax (to the shareholders) for the shareholders to receive 7 percent after all taxes. With the corporate tax at 34 percent, then the pre–corporate/pre–personal tax yield on the assets would have to be 14.7 percent.

The Bush proposal anticipates lowering the capital gains tax rate for individuals only from 28 percent to 15 percent for long-term capital gains. Short-term gains would still be taxed at the 28 percent rate, and even for long-term gains the cut would not apply to all assets. Nonetheless, if all capital gains tax rates were cut from 28 percent to 15 percent—clearly a big exaggeration of the Bush proposal—we could calculate the overall effects rather easily. Pre–corporate tax yields would have to be 13 percent instead of the 14.7 percent required with a 28 percent tax rate. Assuming nothing else changed save asset valuations, then there would be a 13 percent appreciation in all asset values. In terms of the Dow Jones Industrial Average (DJIA), that would come out to about 250 points. Recognizing the exaggeration effect somewhere between 100 points and 150 points seems reasonable for the Bush proposal.

Doing all the same calculations for indexing—mindless, boring, and dull as they are—would give a pre–corporate tax yield of 12.3 percent instead of the 14.7 percent without indexing. Assuming nothing else changed save assets valuation, there would be an initial appreciation of asset values by some 19.5 percent or, in DJIA equivalents, around 500 points. The exaggeration effect for indexing is not as large as it is for cutting the tax rates à la Bush. Best guess on indexing would be a 300 to 400 point effect on the DJIA.

On Friday the thirteenth of October, the Senate killed the capital gains tax cut. The fact that it was Friday the thirteenth of October had nothing to do with the fall. George Mitchell deserves full credit for that. The decline in the stock market is due to the fact that, in a forward-looking market, events alter investors' perceptions and thereby equity valuations. In our own analysis, we estimated that passage of the capital gains legislation would add between 400 to 500 points to the market. We also estimated that approximately half of the gain was already incorporated in the market. Thus, if capital gains legislation did not materialize, the market would have to decline 200 to 250 points.

Chapter 12 discusses the explosion of leveraged buyouts and corporate take-overs as natural by-products of the tax rate cuts enacted during the Reagan years. With the Reagan tax revolution of the 1980s, corporate and personal tax rates were altered dramatically. Inadvertently, so was the relative advantage of corporate debt versus corporate equity. The incentive to shift from equity to debt financing from the differential tax treatment increased to 24 cents on the dollar in 1988 from 14 cents on the dollar in 1980. It should come as no surprise that the markets saw this and reacted to the change in incentives. Corporate debt financing exploded.

Congressional worries with present levels of debt will likely lead to measures making debt capital less attractive and equity capital more attractive. The static thinkers, in spite of the last six-plus years, appear to occupy center stage today. Balancing even is an option. We propose the following revenue-neutral plan to eliminate the tax differences between debt and equity without any static tax revenue consequences: a reduction of taxation on what is now called corporate income balanced with a rise in the taxation at the corporate level of corporate interest disbursements.

The correct balance would be struck when the tax structure on corporate income is identical to the tax structure on interest disbursements (e.g., when corporate income plus corporate interest disbursements could be aggregated fully and taxed as an entity). The only reason we recommend such a practice is that the proposal inextricably ties the lowering of taxation on corporate income to the rise in taxation of corporate interest payments—an even greater good offsetting the evil. From the standpoint of economics, there should be no taxation of either corporate income or corporate interest payments. The ideal solution would be to constructively impute the income a corporation earns to its shareholders and have them liable for any and all taxation. The calculation suggests that a tax rate of 15 percent will, on a static revenue basis, generate slightly higher revenue than the current structure.

Corporate takeovers provided the mechanism through which the returns created by this increased incentive were realized. The differential tax treatment that has allowed this tax arbitrage to occur can very efficiently be rectified through our proposal. The new tax will be neutral with respect to financing choice (i.e., debt versus equity). Therefore, when considering new investment projects, corporate America will now focus on the merits of the project and not on the relative tax consequences. Choice of financing, debt versus equity, will now be irrelevant and will not determine the investment decision. An implication of this analysis is that the proposed reduction in the top capital gains tax rate to 15 percent, while increasing incentives to invest in new ventures, will also reduce takeovers.

Consumer debt is discussed in Chapter 13. A good deal was written in the mid- to late-1950s about the problem of consumer debt growing out of control. Curiously enough, the rapid growth of consumer debt in the mid-1980s parallels the growth spurt of the 1950s. For both periods, consumers began the period with low debt levels. Prior to both periods, government regulation depressed consumer credit usage. Credit controls during the period of the Korean War artificially limited consumers' ability to borrow. With the removal of restrictions after the war, the growth rate of consumer credit soared.

The early 1980s saw the growth in consumer credit limited by credit controls and usury laws. High nominal interest rates bumped into old nominal interest rate ceilings. But with economic recovery, deregulation, and the end of formal controls came rapid growth in consumer debt. The lesson of the study of consumer debt is that debt itself is not the issue but could become the issue as debt could create a constraint on economic flexibility when high debt levels are combined with sudden, unexpected economic shocks (such as a stock market crash).

The recognition that there exists a moving limit is especially useful when a person is looking at the peaks of the business cycle. The peaks of the debt limit correspond to the peaks of the business cycle. The sensitivity of borrowing reflects the willingness of households to take on debt, over the course of the business cycle, as proxied by the rate of growth of debt. It appears that this willingness to take on debt is endogenous to the business cycle itself. That is, the growth of consumer debt itself is a reflection of the state of the business cycle and may not be the independent factor affecting consumer spending that some analysts claim.

The usefulness of the commonly reported debt-to-income ratio is diminished by the Tax Reform Act of 1986. Home equity loans are a new factor affecting the interpretation of all measures of consumer debt since the Tax Reform Act of 1986 eliminated the interest cost deduction for consumer installment debt but retained it for home mortgage loan interest. To measure total consumer indebtedness, home equity loans must be removed from mortgage debt outstanding and added back into the consumer installment debt series.

A lower debt service burden, in terms of monthly payment, is the result of changing the form of debt from installment to home equity loans. In addition, the consumer benefits from a lower after-tax interest rate than the traditional installment loan. This will also tend to lower the monthly interest payment on a home equity loan compared to an installment loan of a similar size.

Rising consumer debt does not necessarily indicate economic evil. When consumer spending is moving the economy forward, consumer debt will increase. This is a positive indicator of economic expansion. Consumer debt is an economic good enabling consumers to take advantage of rising expected income for the purchase of consumer durables.

Chapter 14 discusses the U.S. savings rate. The Keynesian and supply-side views of savings are compared and contrasted. To Keynesians of old, an increase in savings was exactly the same as a reduction in consumption and therefore in total demand. With lower aggregate demand, a slowdown was sure to follow. They didn't even discuss inflation back then. Therefore, to keep the economy as recession-proof as possible, the idea was to keep consumption as high as possible and savings as low as possible. Keynesian policies developed into a set of distinctly antisavings actions that we all know and hate so well today.

Today's mainstream economists are as rabid in their anti-Keynesian focus as the Keynesians of old were pro-Keynes. Both Keynesians and anti-Keynesians live in a world where savings and consumption reign supreme. One group hates savings and loves consumption, while the other loves savings and hates consumption. We of the classical persuasion observe their frenetic machinations in alternating states of amusement and terror.

To the new anti-Keynesians, the share of income saved must be increased above what it otherwise would have been. With income growth a direct result of savings and the level of income determined by the existing capital stock, anything that can be done to discourage consumption and encourage savings is worthwhile. The more people save and the more productive the capital stock, the faster the economy will grow. How to encourage savings, investment, and productivity is the central question. The low U.S. savings rate is a legacy of misguided Keynesian policies directly linked or related to tax policies, government deficits, and social insurance.

In the Keynesian view, the Reagan tax cuts caused two things: huge budget deficits (e.g., government dissavings) and a consumption binge on the part of consumers. A reversal of these negative effects would clearly lead to an increase in the savings rate. The flexible freeze and other spending restraints will go a long way toward eliminating the public sector's dissaving to increase private savings. They would devise a consumption tax that optimally would not affect, in a detrimental way, private savings.

Classical or supply-side economics treats savings as a normal byproduct of the choice between labor and leisure and future versus current consumption. No great importance is attached to savings per se from the perspective of public policy. If people work to consume, that's fine. If people work to save, that's fine, too. To a classical economist, the focus is on work and not on savings or consumption.

From a supply-sider's viewpoint, a far more complete approach would increase the total value of human capital. Focusing on productivity alone or on new capital (i.e., investment) misses a major source of growth stressed by supply-side economics. The low tax rate environment increases incentives to use old and new machinery alike. Similarly, it increases the incentives to work for young and old people alike, without discriminating by age of individual or machinery. Focusing on new machinery ignores the increase in output from existing productive capacity that is used more effectively under the new tax system. The implications of including human capital are truly fundamental—not merely a refinement.

The issues surrounding health care policy are extremely important to the future of our country. These are discussed in Chapter 15. We must deal with the problem of health care spending in order to maintain our competitive standing in the world. The United States now spends a larger proportion of its GNP on health care than any other country. American business is now devoting 50 percent of its corporate operating profit to health care for its employees and retirees. These hidden liabilities, by one estimate one trillion dollars, now exceed all other liabilities on the balance sheets of American corporations.

As if the sheer size of the overall health care problem and its rapid growth were not enough for American business, the accounting profession is now considering instituting a further burden: reserves for unfunded liabilities. The effect on American business would be devastating. The required reserve for current retirees of American business is about $200 billion. Including the liability for the employees currently working brings the estimate to $2 trillion. These liabilities for health benefits will exceed all the liabilities on the balance sheet of American business—a gigantic economic problem.

A confluence of events and opinions is forming among health care constituents that may push lawmakers and bureaucrats into establishing national health insurance. Many Americans are dissatisfied with their public or private health care plan (or their lack of one) and want something better; business is faced with a humongous unfunded liability problem, and it will welcome a global solution. Certainly small business would be reluctant to pick up its share of the 37 million uncovered persons. Hospitals are going bankrupt at the rate of 300 per year and are ready for a different funding mechanism. The National Medical Association has already endorsed a national health insurance program. It is a long way from the NMA to the AMA but the frustration level is rising, even among doctors. It remains to be seen if the long-term solution to our health care will involve the private sector or if it will become a national health insurance program.

INTERNATIONAL ECONOMIC ISSUES

The third section of the book discusses a supply-side view of selected international economic issues. For example, Chapter 16 discusses a subtle but important distinction that is being neglected in current discussions of the foreign exchange value of the U.S. dollar. It is true that monetary disturbances, such as a deliberate devaluation of a country's currency, will lead to roughly offsetting inflation. It also is true that under a regime of floating exchange rates, differential inflation rates resulting from monetary disturbances will lead to a roughly offsetting change in exchange rates. These relations reflect what is commonly referred to as purchasing power parity.

However, saying that monetary disturbances result in differential inflation rates and in offsetting exchange rate changes does not preclude other factors from also affecting exchange rates. Under a domestic price rule with floating exchange rates, real disturbances, such as fiscal policy changes or shifts in the terms of trade, can cause dramatic changes in exchange rates without the slightest pressure for offsetting inflation.

The reduction in the top personal income tax rate in the United States to 50 percent from 70 percent resulted in an increase in after-tax take home pay in the United States to 50 cents from 30 cents on the dollar for those in the top bracket: a 66 percent increase in after-tax returns. If the United States and its trading partners were truly on a price rule, exchange rate changes would reflect a fluctuation in the terms of trade. Because of absent tax rate reductions by our trading partners, the foreign exchange value of the U.S. dollar was expected to increase 66 percent.

The tax rate reductions generated a gradual capital inflow which, in the long run, arbitraged the international differences in after-tax rates of return. On a GNP weighted basis, the foreign exchange value of the dollar increased 60.7 percent from 1980 through the end of 1984. The dollar appreciation peaked during the first quarter of 1985, when it started a sustained decline lasting more than two years. The experiences of the U.S. dollar are consistent with our analysis.

The Tax Reform Act of 1986 goes a long way to explain the surge in the dollar during 1988. Tax reform resulted in a reduction of the top marginal personal income tax rate to 28 percent in 1988 from 50 percent two years prior. The increase in the after-tax rate of return took place over a two-year period. However, during 1988, our trading partners enacted tax rate reductions that will increase the after-tax rate of return in the rest of the world by approximately the same amount as in the United States. Therefore, only the 1987 installment of the tax rate reduction was not matched by our trading partners. The implications of this analysis are that the appreciation of the dollar will peak at approximately 23 percent and will subsequently decline.

The basic premise presented in Chapter 17 that trade deficits are a symptom of misguided policies is simply not correct. The fact that this premise alone is false is more than sufficient to negate the entire panoply of policy analysis and prescriptions being proffered today. Views expressed so eloquently by neomercantilists are granted total credence even to the point where alternative interpretations are provided scarcely any exposure. When put to the test, neomerchantilists' ideas fail.

There is also good reason to expect, and even welcome, trade deficits when an economy experiences a renaissance of performance as has been the case for the United States since 1983. As a consequence of the rejuvenation of the American economy, foreigners have more than willingly provided the United States with the real resources to increase our output, employment, and productivity. Far from being a problem, the United States trade deficit was a solution. Both the foreign lenders and the American borrowers were better off with the deficit than they would have been had trade been balanced or in a U.S. surplus position. Since the commencement of our trade deficit in the first quarter of 1983 when the Reagan tax rate cuts became effective, the United States has created over fifteen million jobs. Our foreign deficit has not cost jobs, but instead has provided the resources to facilitate our labor force's surge toward full employment.

The neomercantilist analysis of late despairs over the observation that the United States has become a net debtor nation of incredible and increasing magnitude. International assets are, however, book value data and most likely unrelated to market values. In 1987, the United States had a surplus of investment income which would seem to imply that U.S. assets abroad are sufficiently undervalued relative to foreign assets in the United States that the United States is, in reality, not a net debtor nation in market value terms. Whether the United States is or is not a net debtor nation is beside the point. The relevant point is whether the United States is better off as a consequence of its debt position. Reliance on the number zero is no defense against the market's assessment of what should be. The essence of international trade as a discipline is that trade in goods and assets improves welfare.

If economic policies were to change such that the long-term investment horizon of the United States were to worsen, then foreigners might wish to take some of their capital back out of the United States. This would precipitate a sequence of unpleasant events. American investors, however, would also want their capital out of the United States, and if foreigners did not beat them to the punch, they would precipitate the ominous consequences first. It is unreasonable to assume that somehow foreigners are any different from Americans. In matters of the pocketbook, nationality does not count for much. Therefore, whether foreigners have a large or small involvement in the U.S. economy is really of little importance. Bad economic policies will cause capital flight for both domestic and foreign capital.

No policy that we can think of is more generically disruptive to investors than a tax increase. Given the current political milieu, tax increases show a total inability of governments to control their spending, and, in addition, they illustrate a failure of the body politic to control government. The tax side of a proposal to eliminate the budget deficit is, in my view, the sine qua non of the debacle neomercantilists so earnestly wish to avoid.

Chapter 18 examines the United Kingdom's version of the supply-side revolution. In contrast to the United States, where interest rates and inflation have declined, high interest rates and high inflation seem in the eyes of British voters to have more than offset the euphoria of lower taxes. Margaret Thatcher, now serving her fourth term as prime minister, can still pull it out, but, to date, she doesn't seem to have any intention of doing so.

During the early days, much like in the United States, the stated monetary policy of the Thatcher government was based on monetarist principles of targeting the monetary aggregates. The experience of Great Britain was similar to that of the United States when the Federal Reserve experimented with the targeting of monetary aggregates.

Disappointed with the monetarist experiment, the monetary authorities of both countries shifted from quantity targeting. The United States shifted to a price rule, a monetary policy based on domestic prices and interest rates. The United Kingdom shifted to a policy based on exchange rates and exchange rate stability. Under these new operating procedures, the U.S. money supply would be allowed to expand to accommodate interest in the demand for money.

The monetary objective of the British government appears to be a policy of stabilizing the foreign exchange value of the pound, a position supported by most supply-side economists. Our analysis suggests that British tax reform will result in an appreciation of the pound vis-à-vis other currencies. Thus, a policy of exchange rate stability will result in an excessive monetary expansion in order to prevent the rise in the pound. The tendency for the pound to rise will present a policy dilemma for British monetary authorities. They will have to choose between exchange rate or interest/inflation rate stability.

The battle lines have been drawn among British cabinet members. Early in 1989, Thatcher said the British would not intervene to prevent the rise in the pound. She correctly argued that exchange rate intervention to prevent the rise would lead to excess money growth and hence a rise in inflation. This position was reaffirmed by Lawson when he unveiled the tax reform package. He made it clear that he had shifted his monetary policy to focus on interest rates rather than exchange rate stability as the chief weapon for fighting inflation. In our view, this was the proper and correct policy response.

Largely as a result of gyrations in the foreign exchange value of the dollar, proponents of exchange rate stability have now focused on maintaining the pound/mark exchange rate. The prime minister remains true to her original position of letting the pound fluctuate. In contrast, Lawson now appears to favor stabilizing the pound/mark exchange rate, and he has been joined by Robin Leigh-Pemberton, Governor of the Bank of England. It appears that, for now, Lawson has won the dispute. The chancellor won the right to publicly restate his commitment to keep the pound stable against the West German mark. However, if this policy is pursued, large scale currency intervention will be required. These interventions will fuel a potentially inflationary growth in the British money supply.

The most recent data for the United Kingdom show just how serious is the plight for Margaret Thatcher. British gilts have a yield a smidgeon below 10 percent as compared to long-term Treasury bond yields in the United States of a little less than 8 percent. Short-term Treasury securities in the United Kingdom are yielding about 14 percent whereas their U.S. counterparts have a yield less than 8 percent. Individual consumer loans in the United Kingdom cost as much as 22 percent annually. The British pound has been soft against the U.S. dollar of late and has been holding its own against other European currencies. U.K. inflation is high and rising.

The Labour party has been bolstered by the virtual demise of all third parties. These third parties had siphoned votes away from Labour in earlier elections. In addition, Labour under the stewardship of Neil Kinnock appears and probably is somewhat less radical than before. No longer does the articulate Fabian socialist Wedgwood Benn hold sway. And Michael Foote is also out of the picture. Labour, while still far to the left, does not appear nearly so dogmatic to the average U.K. voter.

Lastly, and probably illogically, people are simply tired of the sameness and would like change for change's sake: Margaret Thatcher has been in office a long, long time. Her very dominant personality has afforded no opportunity for a successor to be groomed. Flowers rarely grow in trampled fields.

What is more, government officials in the United Kingdom look embarrassed whenever they discuss tax cuts. While they may recognize the enormous political and even macroeconomic appeal of tax cuts, they just don't feel good talking about lower tax rates. They feel guilty as though somehow the years and years of imprinted liberal ideology make them ashamed of what they are saying. Those who advocate tax cuts are considered selfish, unfeeling, and just plain bad. They can't help it; they were raised that way. To them, the Kennedy ideas that the best form of welfare is a good, high-paying job, or the concept of the rising tide are simply not part of the British psyche. The ideas are foreign to them. In the long run, Britain will have a very hard time living with low taxes.

PORTFOLIO STRATEGIES

The last section of the book discusses the portfolio strategies that are derived from our analysis. Theory and common experience postulate that general economic factors impact stock prices in the aggregate. These same factors can also have substantially different effects depending upon the industry group being considered. The finance literature of the past several decades has taken a different tack. Industry performances have been relegated to a minor role in modern finance.

Scientific rigor requires an ability to discriminate among alternatives. Modern finance, with its statistical sophistication, in conjunction with high-speed computers, demonstrably increased our abilities to discriminate. All the while, the theory of profit maximization, carried forward as it was in the finance field, did much to alter the way we all view the world. The straightforward question, "If you can see it, why doesn't everybody else see it?" was carried to new importance. A number of the earlier filter rules were quite rightly relegated to the domain of discarded thought and were seen for what they were, ill-conceived notions impeding intellectual progress.

A sequence of questions relating to the essential features of modern finance has arisen over the past several years but no question is more in keeping with intellectual pursuits than why a given asset has a specific Beta. Quite simply, it is not sufficient to respond with an empirical answer. Just how an asset acquires a specific value for its Beta depends upon production technologies, resource availability, governmental policies, and human tastes. Economics has advanced considerably in the theories of both individuals and firms and how these, in turn, mesh to form a general equilibrium framework. To ignore all of this does not make sense and is tantamount to an inefficient intellectual market.

The Capital Assets Tax Sensitivity (CATS) approach discussed in Chapters 19 and 20 redresses several of modern finance's more serious shortcomings. It proceeds directly from the theory of the firm and the household to establish the principle as to how any market returns to equilibrium following a macroeconomic shock. In principle, equilibrium is restored by some combination of price and quantity adjustment. Whether the alteration in the market operates through the industry's demand schedule or supply schedule, price and quantity will be the rebalancers. Quite clearly, from the standpoint of any specific firm within an industry, the greater the impact of macroeconomic shocks and the greater the role played by price in the adjustment process, the greater will be the sensitivity of that industry's profits and stock value.

While rooted in economic theory, both the conception and the measurement of equity responses to macroeconomic events are straightforward. Pillaging data from the more recent past has allowed us to establish links between macroeconomic events and the returns of equities by industry. From all we are able to uncover, the market's reassessment of equity values is far from haphazard. There are distinct patterns that emerge. Some are focused with great resolution, while others are only dimly visible through the vast array of numbers. The CATS strategy overlays the vector of more traditional macroeconomic events on the matrix of asset relatives. If data patterns recumbent in our past observances can be presumed to extend into the future, then knowledge of what is to be for the economy can readily be translated into what is to be for stock returns. As a guide for asset managers, such linkages may prove quite valuable. Asset managers are one group with the curse to be always fully committed. Whether in or out of the market, their performance is continuously at risk. They have no choice.

Over the past decade, research at A. B. Laffer, V. A. Canto & Associates has focused on measuring the effects of macroeconomic shocks on specific industry stock returns. Our CATS strategy predicts the relative performances of individual industry stocks in the aftermath of economic shocks.

Development of the CATS strategy came as a direct consequence of Reaganomics, Proposition 13, the Steiger-Hansen capital gains tax rate reduction, and the like. It was our view then, as it is now, that such a radical change in economic policy would have widely divergent effects by industry. Given what we thought would occur, it was a natural extension of our supply-side perspective to address the issue of relative asset yields. Patterns of synchronous stock price movements as they relate to factors other than tax cuts may also exist. Precipitous changes in interest rates or rates of inflation may well be associated with systematic patterns in the equity markets. Likewise, changes in exchange rates or changes in the price of oil appear to be reasonable candidates for similar patterns in the stock market.

However, in spite of the similarities, the impact by industry resulting from a decline in interest rates is far from identical to an income tax rate reduction. The differences in behavior between the CATS classification and rising and falling interest rates add substantially to our knowledge about the behavior of equity returns. The final factor that currently plays a role in our CATS strategy is the degree to which an industry's products are traded internationally. Along with tax cut and interest rate sensitivity, responsiveness to both exchange rate movements and trade restrictions appears to have a substantial and an independent impact on the returns to individual equities.

Identification of how macroeconomic shocks impact industry relatives is a necessary, but may not be a sufficient, condition to ensure superior portfolio performance. Under certain circumstances, one must also know how to forecast the economic environment. A superior portfolio strategy is the joint result of the quality of the macroeconomic forecast and the validity of the incidence models.

In order to capture as closely as possible the Reagan bull market (i.e., trough to peak), we have calculated the performance of the different portfolios from January 1981 through August 1987. The results reported clearly indicate a wide variation in the behavior of different portfolios. The differences in behavior provide evidence that, on average, the CATS strategy has been able to identify the incidence of the different macroeconomic shocks. The evidence clearly indicates that the correct identification of the economic environment yields the highest returns. This result supports our view that the driving force behind the Reagan bull market was the tax rate reduction. Thus, the most important screen in the analysis would be the CATS classification.

Another logical step in the framework development is to extend the analysis to take advantage of the differences in economic policies across economic boundaries. Strategies designated to take advantage of differences in economic policies across political jurisdictions are considered in the next two chapters. One strategy, discussed in Chapter 21, focuses on the United States. The strategy attempts to exploit differences in state and local fiscal policies among the various states. In Chapter 22, the analysis is extended to the world economy, thereby focusing on differences in fiscal and monetary policies across international boundaries.

When a state's tax burden falls relative to tax burdens in other states, that state is likely to experience economic growth. Conversely, when a state's relative tax burden rises, it is likely to suffer an economic slowdown. Due to the connection between state and local tax policy and economic performance, the values of assets located in states that alter their tax policies will fluctuate in predictable directions. Assets will tend to become more valuable in states cutting tax rates, while tax rate increases will tend to depress asset values.

The investment implications of these observations are straightforward: buy the stocks of companies located in states lowering tax rates and sell the stocks of companies in states raising tax rates. Results over the period December 1, 1988 to November 7, 1989 are promising. The stocks of small-cap companies based in states with falling relative and absolute tax burdens outperformed the stocks of small-cap companies headquartered in states with rising relative and absolute tax burdens. Stocks located in states with falling tax burdens outperformed the S&P 500 during most of the period examined. The performance of a state-based portfolio strategy may be enhanced by taking into consideration the January effect. Regardless of their performance over the entire year, small-cap stocks have been winning in every January since 1963.

Gains in relative economic performance are expected in states with declining relative tax burdens. Recent tax changes point to Hawaii, Maine, Maryland, Texas, Utah, and Wisconsin as the states most likely to gain in competitiveness this year. A state that has raised its tax burden above the national average will find it more difficult to retain existing facilities and to attract new businesses. Recent tax changes point to Alaska, Arizona, Connecticut, Georgia, Illinois,

Massachusetts, Montana, Nevada, New York, North Carolina, North Dakota, Ohio, Pennsylvania, Rhode Island, Tennessee, Vermont, and West Virginia as the states most likely to become less competitive.

State tax policy also has political implications. States that lower their relative tax burden will gain population and, as a consequence, congressional seats. Similarly, states raising their tax burden will lose population and hence representation. Changes in relative tax burden may be helpful in projecting the reapportionment of congressional seats after the 1990 census.

For example, in California, taxes have fallen with a vengeance since 1978. In 1978, California ranked as the fourth highest tax rate state in the nation. Then along came Proposition 13 and the accompanying tax cuts. By 1987, California had fallen to the 16th highest tax rate state. California could pick up as many as six congressional seats. Conversely, because of its rising tax rates, New York could lose three or four congressional seats as a result of the 1990 census.

Conceptually, extension of the portfolio strategy to an international setting is fairly straightforward. The only major difference is that in contrast to the states, the different countries may choose to pursue an independent monetary policy. Therefore, care must be exercised in distinguishing between nominal and real fluctuations.

Much like the states' economies during the last two decades, the world economy has been subjected to major economic shocks that have significantly affected the differential performance of national economies. The shocks include major fluctuations in gold prices and three oil shocks. Evidence of changes in the national economies' competitive position will be reflected in deviations from purchasing power parity. During the 1970–87 period, significant fluctuations were observed in the real exchange rate between the United States and its trading partners.

Consider the effect of an increase in the U.S. real exchange rate. An appreciation of the real exchange rate means that every unit of a domestic good is now capable of acquiring more foreign goods than before. This implies that the real rate of return of domestically located assets will increase relative to assets in the rest of the world. The higher real rate of return in the U.S. economy will increase productive activity in the United States relative to the rest of the world. Domestic asset values will increase relative to asset values in the rest of the world, and the United States will experience an inflow of capital. Given a floating exchange rate system, the balance of payments is always zero, and the trade balance mirrors the capital account. Thus, the deterioration in the trade balance will mean an improvement in the capital account. The U.S. experience of the 1980s is entirely within this view.

Preliminary results over the period 1971–88 indicate systematic patterns of relative stock return performance. In addition to a contemporaneous response, changes in the real exchange rate between the United States and its trading partners appear to lead the relative stock market performance.

Although one cannot claim to anticipate all of the changes in terms of trade

Introduction

between the United States and its trading partners, there are some discrete events, such as tax rate reductions, that will have substantial impact on the real exchange rate and can be analyzed before implementation. Other events such as oil shocks may not be easily predictable. Once they occur, however, they could be immediately analyzed and incorporated in the portfolio.

The decision rule for this portfolio strategy is quite simple: If the U.S. real exchange rate appreciates vis-à-vis one of our trading partners, for example, Germany, then the U.S. stock market will outperform the German stock market. As a consequence, German stocks will be excluded from the portfolio. If the real exchange rate depreciates, German stocks will be included in the portfolio.

NOTE

1. Jude Wanniski, *The Way the World Works* (Morristown, N.J.: Polyconomics, Inc., 1978), p. 36.

PART ONE
MONETARY POLICY

1

Capacity Utilization and Inflation

Victor A. Canto

A widely accepted proposition in macroeconomic analysis is that a sustained increase in overall economic activity eventually strains capacity and leads to higher prices. The proposition has been applied not only to the United States, but also internationally:

To the extent that misery enjoys company, Americans concerned over accelerating inflation at home may derive some comfort from the fact that inflation is speeding up abroad as well. This speedup abroad has received relatively little notice amid much recent worrying about the U.S. inflation outlook. But prices are rising appreciably faster than a year ago in most major industrial nations, as well as in the newly industrial nations of Asia and most poorer Third World countries.[1]

The pattern, by and large, reflects developments similar to what underlies the U.S. price speedup: a sustained rise in overall business that eventually strains economic capacity and leads to higher prices.

This "partial equilibrium" analysis yields the result that, in the short run, increases in production eventually strain production capacity (i.e., reduce the supply elasticity) and ultimately result in price increases—rationing excess demand through price increases. Conversely, a decline in capacity utilization is viewed as relieving inflationary pressure in the economy.

The empirical implications are quite clear:

- Increases in capacity utilization will result in higher prices

- Decreases in capacity utilization will result in lower prices
- Since adjustment is costly, the rate of the price increase may also be affected by the levels and rate of change in capacity utilization

An alternative proposition is based on a "general equilibrium" analysis where inflation is defined as a monetary phenomenon of too much money chasing too few goods. Thus, the general equilibrium analysis postulates a negative relation between inflation and real GNP growth.[2] Since economic activity and capacity utilization are positively related, increases in GNP and increases in capacity utilization will tend to move together. Therefore, increases in the U.S. growth rate should also be highly correlated to increases in the growth rate in capacity utilization. Alternatively stated, acceleration of economic growth will be positively related to acceleration in capacity utilization.

The general equilibrium monetary analysis implies that, holding monetary policy constant, acceleration in capacity utilization will be associated with a lower, not higher, inflation rate. A decline in capacity utilization will be associated with higher, not lower, prices. However, since we view inflation as a monetary phenomenon, the correlation between capacity utilization and inflation depends on the monetary response. If monetary policy accommodates the expansion of capacity utilization (i.e., the increase in the demand for money), the price level need not change and inflation will be unrelated to changes in capacity utilization.

INFLATION AND CAPACITY UTILIZATION: INTERNATIONAL EVIDENCE

The regression analysis uncovers some empirical regularities (Table 1.1). The coefficients for percent changes and acceleration in capacity utilization are not statistically significant.[3] The only exception is the equation for the United States where percentage changes in capacity utilization show a positive and marginally significant coefficient while the acceleration coefficient is negative and statistically significant.

The U.S. results are consistent with the view that acceleration of the pace of economic activity (i.e., real GNP, capacity utilization) is associated with slower inflation. A decline in economic activity will be associated with higher prices. In the remaining countries, capacity utilization does not appear to have any significant correlation with inflation.

INFLATION AND THE OVERHEATED ECONOMY: THE PARTIAL EQUILIBRIUM VIEW

The reasoning behind the proposition that increases in capacity utilization result in higher inflation is based on the presumption that what is true for an individual commodity is true for the economy as a whole. Applying the indi-

Table 1.1
Inflation and Capacity Utilization* (t-Statistics in Parentheses)

Dependent Variable Inflation Rate in:	Constant	Changes in Inflation Rate Lagged 1 Year	Percent Changes in Capacity Utilization	Acceleration in Capacity Utilization	R^2	SE	DW	F
Belgium	1.75 (0.73)	0.70 (1.96)	0.07 (0.19)	-0.12 (-0.56)	0.25	2.99	1.75	2.56
Canada	1.94 (0.89)	0.74 (2.53)	0.01 (0.04)	-0.12 (-1.19)	0.49	2.04	1.50	5.54
France	2.07 (0.83)	0.74 (2.71)	-0.01 (-0.02)	-0.13 (-0.64)	0.38	2.72	2.08	3.83
West Germany	0.77 (0.73)	0.73 (3.06)	-0.08 (-0.46)	0.05 (0.48)	0.48	1.62	2.00	5.30
Italy	9.15 (1.64)	0.29 (0.72)	-0.11 (-0.16)	-0.00 (-0.01)	-0.11	5.62	2.07	0.55
Spain	2.65 (0.77)	0.79 (3.13)	0.36 (0.62)	-0.39 (-1.08)	0.33	3.73	1.54	3.34
Sweden	1.16 (0.75)	0.64 (1.88)	0.15 (0.45)	-0.12 (-0.63)	0.17	2.75	1.97	1.95
United States	0.53 (0.29)	0.93 (3.42)	0.34 (1.60)	-0.33 (-2.66)	0.55	2.37	1.61	6.62

* Percent changes are fourth quarter over fourth quarter.

vidual commodity analysis to the overall economy suggests that a higher demand for all goods and services will increase both the quantity of goods and services produced and their prices. The individual commodity analysis assumes *all other prices to remain unchanged;* thus an increase in the demand for a product will, *all else the same,* result in an excess demand for the product (Figure 1.1). In economic parlance, the analysis amounts to a partial equilibrium analysis where all other things are held constant.

How the excess demand is satisfied depends on the supply elasticity of the commodity. If the supply is perfectly elastic, then production is flexible and will change to accommodate the increase in demand without the slightest increase in the price of the product *relative to all other commodities* (Figure 1.2). If, on the other hand, the supply is perfectly inelastic, then production plans will be inflexible and the excess demand will be satisfied by increases in prices, and production will remain unchanged (Figure 1.3).

The supply elasticity depends, in part, on the time horizon considered. In the short run, firms may be able to increase production by using their facilities and resources more intensively (i.e., increasing capacity utilization, paying overtime.) Therefore, short-term increases in production will elicit increases in the marginal cost, resulting in an upward-sloping supply curve. Under these general conditions, the initial excess demand (*AB* in Figure 1.1) will be satisfied by a combination of a price increase (from P_{old} to P_{new}). The higher price will elicit an increase in supply from Q_o to Q_e (or a movement along the supply curve from *a* to *d*). The higher price will also induce some of the initial demanders to pull out of the market (from Q_d to Q_e). This represents a movement along the demand curve from *b* to *d*.

When the analysis is extended to the economy as a whole, ignoring the basic assumptions of the partial equilibrium analysis of a single commodity yields a trade-off between growth and inflation. The balance between output growth and inflation, it is argued, is determined by the amount of utilized labor and capital. If sufficient quantities of capital and labor are present, then higher demand will yield a disproportionately greater amount of real output and little inflation. The supply curve for goods, in other words, will be more elastic when there is higher unemployment and excess capacity.

Symmetrically, when unemployment rates are low and capacity utilization is high, increases in aggregate demand will yield little by way of real growth and instead will produce inflation. In the instance of tight labor and capital markets, increases in aggregate demand are inflationary because the supply curve for goods is relatively inelastic.

TOWARD A MORE GENERAL VIEW

Extending the analysis of a specific market to the overall economy (i.e., going from a partial equilibrium to a general equilibrium analysis) is a little trickier than would, at first glance, appear to be the case. In a partial equilibrium analysis

Figure 1.1
The Effects of Increases in Demand When Supply Is Neither Perfectly Elastic nor Perfectly Inelastic

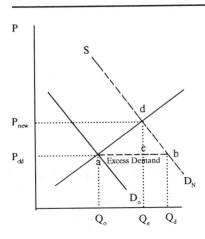

Figure 1.2
The Effects of Increases in Demand When Supply Is Perfectly Elastic

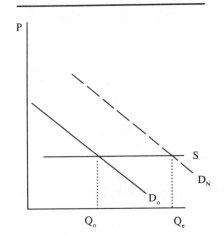

Figure 1.3
The Effects of Increases in Demand When Supply Is Perfectly Inelastic

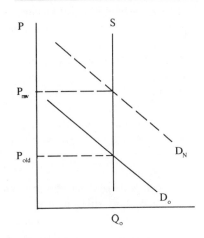

of an individual commodity, the general value of income is taken to be a constant. Therefore, by implication, any change in the price of the commodity is presumed to be a change in the price of that commodity vis-à-vis all other commodities. By lowering or raising the price of a specific commodity in relation to all other commodities, incentives are changed such that producers and consumers will tend to substitute into or away from the commodity in question.

When the partial equilibrium analysis is extended to the overall economy, the framework breaks down. Although supposed experts do it all the time, it is silly in the extreme to conjure up an image of a change in the price of all commodities relative to all commodities. There is no place into which or out of which producers and consumers can substitute. Thus, the analogy of a specific market, when projected to the overall economy, is neither straightforward nor obvious. In fact, the analogy to specific markets is grotesquely misused as a matter of common practice in discussions of aggregate inflation.

In any general equilibrium analysis market system, a transaction price is literally the ratio of two commodities in the process of market exchange. When we talk about the consumer price index (CPI), for example, we are referring to the price of one specific bundle of goods measured in terms of dollars. By the precise method of measurement these are goods being exchanged between retail sellers and customers for U.S. dollars at a single moment of time. CPI inflation, therefore, is a comparison of the number of dollars that are exchanged for this bundle of goods now versus some time in the past.

The phrase "real wage" is used to describe the exchange value of a unit of labor for a composite bundle of goods and services. The "real interest rate" is the exchange value of a bundle of goods and services offered now for a bundle of goods and services received at some prespecified date in the future. The "exchange rate" is the price of one dollar transacted in the market place in terms of foreign currency.

The importance of reiterating exactly the meaning of these price measures is to recognize that all prices represent the exchange of one commodity for another. There has to be the quid pro quo. With this exchange notion firmly in hand, a number of commonplace errors in the interpretation of overall inflation can easily be avoided.

The price of one product measured in terms of another will rise whenever there is an excess demand for the first product relative to the second. Saying that there is an excess demand for the first product in terms of the second is identical to saying there is an excess supply of the second product in terms of the first. In either description, it should be clear that the price of the first product must rise in relation to the second product for a new equilibrium to be established.

The purpose here is neither to obfuscate nor to confuse, but merely to make the point that whenever prices or inflation are discussed, they must be discussed in the context of two items: the first commodity and the second commodity. A rise in the price of one thing in terms of another means that there has to have been an excess demand for the former in terms of the latter. In discussing the more popular measures of inflation, the first commodity is goods and the second commodity is money. Higher prices, in this instance, reflect an excess supply of money matched by an excess demand for goods.

The fallacy of the partial equilibrium here is really quite subtle for one accustomed to thinking in microeconomic terms. To illustrate, an increase in the demand for rubber gloves surely will affect both the price for those gloves and how many are produced. If the glove factories are close to capacity and have depleted their potential labor pools, then prices will rise and few additional pairs will be forthcoming.

In the goods market as a whole, any increase in aggregate demand has to be defined in terms of where the excess supply takes place. In microeconomics, the second part of the question is swept under the rug by assumption. Tight labor and capital markets, quite simply, mean that there is an excess demand for labor and capital and an excess supply of goods and services. As such, bringing the system back into equilibrium does require a rise in wages for workers and returns to capital, but not in money terms. The rise in wages and returns on capital have to be measured in units of output, not money. Real wages and real yields have to go up, and, at the same time, nothing is known about money wages or money returns on capital. During the low unemployment/rapid growth periods of the 1950s and 1960s, real wage increases were accompanied by low inflation.

The desire to increase production per se is not inflationary. In addition, the desire to increase production is not inflationary even when labor and capital markets are tight. When the dust settles and the smoke clears, there simply is not any straightforward relationship between either inflation and capacity utilization or inflation and the rate of unemployment.

What is true, however, is that real wages and the real returns to capital are related to capacity utilization and unemployment. Both capacity utilization and the rate of unemployment measure the excess demand for both labor and capital relative to goods and services. Absolutely nothing has been specified between the goods market and the money market and therefore nothing can be said about inflation. The higher the demand for labor and capital relative to goods and services, the greater will be the price of both labor and capital measured in units of goods and services. Also, the greater will be the supply of labor and capital provided to the overall market.

RANGING INFLATION

Inflation, as commonly referenced, is the percentage change in the price of goods measured in terms of money. As such, inflation arises out of an ongoing imbalance between the goods market and the money market. It is an incipient excess demand for goods matched by an excess supply of money. The numerous measures that have been developed for inflation, from the consumer and wholesale price indexes to the GNP price deflator to the sensitive commodity index, only reflect our obsession with the consequences of too much money chasing too few goods.[4]

Any additions to the supply of money or reductions in the demand for money will result in an incipient excess supply of money, other factors remaining unchanged. With too much money as with too much of anything, the value people assign to money, that is, the price of money, will fall. In the case of money, if there is too much money and too few goods, the price of money in terms of goods will fall. Alternatively stated, the price of goods in terms of money will rise. If the excess supply of money is anticipated to continue, then higher nominal interest rates will coincide with lower real interest rates.

Allowing our attention to focus exclusively on the money market for a moment, we notice that adding an unrequested sum to the supply of money tends to have the following consequences:

- higher prices (inflation)
- higher nominal interest rates
- lower real interest rates

Perhaps, the single best indicator of a net shift in the supply of money is the difference between changes in the monetary base and changes in M1.[5] The monetary base is comprised of bank deposits at the Federal Reserve plus bank holdings of currency and currency in circulation. M1 is the sum of all demand deposits held at banks plus currency in circulation.

While arguments can and have been made that even the monetary base can be influenced by demand factors, it is nonetheless clear that the monetary base also reflects independent exogenous movements in the supply of money. The same cannot be said of M1. The case for demand influences on M1 is exceptionally strong and clearly much stronger than the case for demand influences on the monetary base. As such, M1 is not an appropriate measure for shifts in the supply of money, nor is it an appropriate indicator of an excess supply of money. The difference between the growth of the monetary base and the growth of M1 (i.e., excess base growth) is therefore an appropriate measure of the net shift in the supply of money.

IMPLICATIONS

The empirical results stand directly at odds with received doctrine. The belief that higher economic growth and increases and acceleration in capacity utilization result in higher inflation is deeply embedded. Stated another way, some would have us believe that slower growth and declines in capacity utilization result in lower inflation. This fallacy is dangerous to the welfare of the nation and to the world economy. Policies intended to slow economic activity and capacity utilization (i.e., cooling-off the economy) will result in higher inflation, not lower inflation. Declines in capacity utilization are harbingers of rising inflationary pressure.

The international evidence does not support the popular view that the international increase in inflation rates is the result of increases in capacity utilization. An alternative explanation is that the rise in inflation may be the direct result of coordination of international monetary policies intended to maintain the foreign exchange value of the dollar in a trading range. If foreign central banks intervene to support the dollar, they will, in effect, adopt U.S. monetary policy.

NOTES

1. Alfred L. Malabre, Jr., "Rising Inflation Is a Global Trend," *Wall Street Journal,* March 27, 1989, p. 1.

2. Arthur B. Laffer, "The Phillip's Buster Filibuster," A. B. Laffer Associates, August 4, 1988.

3. Acceleration in capacity utilization is defined as the changes in capacity utilization.

4. Victor A. Canto, "The Quality of Inflation Indicators," A. B. Laffer Associates, March 31, 1989.

5. See Chapter 4.

2

World Money and U.S. Inflation: Part I

Victor A. Canto and Alex Winters

The ubiquitous nature of inflation and recession across countries in various degrees in recent years justifies labeling the phenomenon global rather than national.[1] While talk of economic "interdependence" is widespread, economic policy is still perceived as national in scope. Economic policy initiatives proceed on the premise that economies of different nations are, at best, only loosely connected.

This isolationist frame of mind has been most notable in the design of policies to control inflation. Experience, however, lends credence to the notion that domestic factors alone are not sufficient to explain domestic inflation. Moreover, policy implications that emanate from a worldwide view of inflation are very different from those resulting from a closed economy perspective.

Whether true or not, one can imagine that the monetary authorities could control a closed economy's money supply—say, demand deposits plus currency. In the world economy, however, control, as a practical matter, borders on inconceivable. The role of any one country's monetary authority—such as the U.S. Federal Reserve Board—wanes dramatically in the perspective of the world.

Money is, after all, one of the easiest commodities to move across national borders. Banks and other financial institutions operate in numerous U.S. and foreign locations. Even when the foreign operations are not direct subsidiaries, correspondent relationships and other close associations have been developed. Money markets, not only within the United States but also in the world economy, are closely interrelated by this vast financial network.[2] The advent of floating exchange rates has not led to the dissolution of integrated money markets. With spot and forward foreign exchange markets, floating rates, at most, have only added somewhat to the cost of operating in those markets.

Considerable disagreement exists as to the relevant quantities of money and goods that determine the inflation rate in a given locality or country. The local view argues that the relevant concepts of money and output are the national (local) quantities.[3] The global view argues that the relevant concepts of money and output in their relationship with inflation are the world quantities.

This paper presents a "global monetarist" view of inflation and money. It incorporates into the analysis a worldwide integration of money and product markets. In contrast to the local monetarist view, U.S. money and U.S. production are considered to be only a fraction of their global counterparts. Global money and global production are the relevant dimensions for examining inflation, be it global inflation or inflation in a specific country such as the United States.[4] The evidence during the last three decades is supportive of the global monetarist view. There is a close relationship between the excess of the world money supply over world real GNP growth lagged two years and U.S. inflation (Figure 2.1).

SOURCES OF GLOBAL PRODUCTION

Money is not the exclusive source of changes in the world price level. In addition to growth in the quantity of world money, the growth in the quantity of world production is related to inflation. Inflation is frequently defined as too much money chasing too few goods. That is, all else the same, an increase in the growth rate of money is associated with a higher inflation rate. Similarly, an increase in the growth rate of output reduces the rate of inflation. From a global monetarist perspective, the relevant quantities of money and output are the world measures. Increases in the growth rate of world money raise global inflation. Symmetrically, declining production growth raises the rate of global inflation.

The growth rate of world production adjusted for inflation is divided into two components: growth attributable to U.S. production and that attributable to the rest-of-world production. During the 1970s, the world real GNP growth rate remained approximately the same as that of the previous decade (Table 2.1). The one difference was that the U.S. contribution to world production declined. During the 1960s, the United States accounted for 1.88 percentage points of the world's 4.40 growth rate. In the seventies, it only accounted for 1.10 percentage points of the worlds 4.46 growth rate.

The U.S. growth rate declined relative to the rest of the world. The decline continued during the 1980–84 period and appears to have been arrested during the 1985–88 period. The resurgence of U.S. economic growth relative to the rest of the world is largely attributable to the Reagan tax rate cuts which became fully effective in January 1984.

Figure 2.1
World Excess Money Growth Lagged Two Years and U.S. Inflation

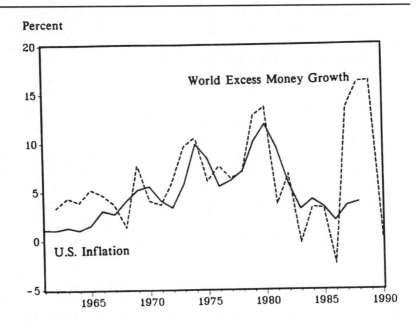

Sources: *BIS Annual Report; International Financial Statistics; Survey of Current Business*, Department of Commerce.

Table 2.1
Sources of World Production Growth

Years	Total World Production	U.S. Production	Rest of The World Production
1960–69	4.40	1.88	2.52
1970–79	4.46	1.10	3.36
1980–84	2.11	0.72	1.39
1985–88	3.22	1.28	1.94
1960–88	3.83	1.33	2.50

SOURCES OF WORLD MONEY

Money knows no national boundaries. To money, the political subdivisions of the world are little different from the San Diego city limits or the California state line. The only relevant domain for money is the world itself. While the debate over which aggregate corresponds to domestic money is likely to continue, the measures of domestic money selected for this paper are "money" and "money plus quasi money" as reported in *International Financial Statistics*. These measures of money correspond closely to M1 and M2 while allowing for differences among countries.[5]

For analytic purposes, each domestic component of world money must be expressed in a single numeraire in order to permit aggregation. Just as the world production of oil can be expressed in U.S. gallons, barrels also provide a common unit of measure. The U.S. dollar has been chosen as the unit of measure of world money.[6]

The measure of world money used here is the dollar value of domestic monies of 11 major countries plus net Eurodollar deposits.[7] United States M2 is expressed in dollars. The M2s of the rest of the world are reported in their respective domestic currency units. These quantities then are converted into dollar amounts using the appropriate prevailing dollar exchange rates.

World M2 money in dollars, inclusive of Eurodollars, increased nearly 23 fold during the 29 years ending in 1988. That is an annual average rate of growth of 10 percent. In 1959, world money is estimated to have been $451 billion. By 1970, world money totaled $1224 billion and almost quadrupled to $4775 billion in 1980. By the end of 1988, the dollar value of world money reached $10 trillion.

The most striking feature of the sources of world money is the decline in the importance of U.S. money. In 1950, U.S. money constituted 66 percent of world money. By 1979, less than 34 percent of world money was located in the United States. During the first Reagan administration, the trend was temporarily arrested and the U.S. share of world money increased to almost 44 percent in 1984. Since then, it declined to 29 percent in 1988 (Figure 2.2).

U.S. Money Growth

The contribution of U.S. money to the growth rate in world money diminished during the 29-year period. A comparison of the average annual growth rates of each component of world money growth during the decades of the 1960s, 1970s and 1980s is provided in Table 2.2. Over the three decades, the importance of U.S. money as a source of world money growth declined sharply relative to other sources (Figure 2.2).

Rest-of-World Domestic Money

The domestic monies of the rest of the world are by far the most important source of world money growth and are increasingly so as the decades pass.

Figure 2.2
U.S. Money as a Fraction of World Money

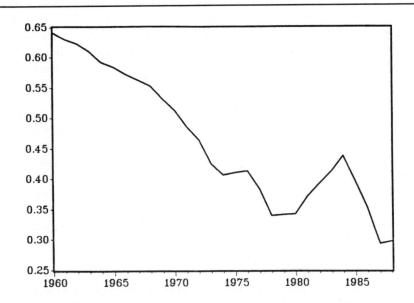

During the 1960s and 1970s, while the contribution of U.S. money to world money growth remained virtually unchanged, the rest-of-the-world contribution increased substantially (Table 2.2). In turn, during the 1980–84 period, the rest-of-the-world contribution declined to less than 1 percent and rose to double digits during the 1985–88 period. The data suggest that fluctuations in the world money supply are largely attributable to fluctuations in the rest-of-the-world money growth.

The changes in relative importance of the rest-of-the-world money growth are a mirror image of the foreign exchange value of the dollar. On average, the dollar

Table 2.2
Sources of World Money Growth

Years	Total World Money Growth	U.S. Money Growth	Rest of The World Money Growth
1960–69	8.59	3.89	4.70
1970–79	12.79	3.74	9.05
1980–84	3.99	3.40	0.59
1985–88	14.72	2.18	12.54
1960–88	10.1	3.52	6.58

appreciated against its trading partners during the 1960s. The rate of appreciation came to a halt during the 1970s, resumed with a vengeance during the 1980–84 period, and was completely reversed during the 1985–88 period.

Effect of Exchange Rate Changes on World Money

The currency exchange rate effect depends solely on the specific currency selected as numeraire for world money. To illustrate, imagine that there are 200 Deutsche marks and the exchange rate is four marks per U.S. dollar. The dollar value of the German money is $50. Suppose the dollar devalues to a new exchange rate of two marks to the dollar. The dollar value of the 200 marks is now $100. Thus, even though the quantity of marks is stable, German money contributes twice as much to the stock of world money measured in dollars following depreciation of the dollar. Depreciation of the dollar relative to other currencies implies an increase in the dollar denominated world money aggregate. Conversely, if a different numeraire had been selected, dollar devaluation implies a reduction in the foreign currency value of world money. If measured in a generally appreciating currency, say the Swiss franc, world money growth would be slower. In addition, the currency depreciation will induce a substitution effect away from using the depreciating currency as payment mechanisms. The substitution effects may also be induced by government restrictions, such as capital and credit controls.[8] The currency substitution effects will exacerbate the incipient relative inflation rates. In addition, the inflation effect will feed back and induce further substitutions, in which case, the fluctuations in the exchange rate could very well exceed the incipient relative excess money growth.

In the 1950s and 1960s, when the Bretton Woods fixed exchange rates were in force, changes in exchange rates were largely the result of our trading partners devaluing against U.S. currencies. During these two decades, the average effect of exchange rates was a reduction in the growth rate of world money (Table 2.3).

Table 2.3
Sources of Rest of the World Money Growth

Years	Rest of World Money Growth	Exchange Rate	Foreign Money Growth	Eurodollars
1960–69	4.68	-5.16	9.25	0.65
1970–79	9.05	-0.75	8.32	1.48
1980–84	0.59	-11.67	11.15	1.26
1985–88	12.54	16.55	-5.68	1.68
1960–88	6.57	-1.79	7.11	1.25

But during the 1970s, as Bretton Woods was dismantled, the dominating effect exchange rates had on the rest of the world money supply disappeared. Exchange rate changes contributed both positively and negatively to world money growth in recent years. The average effect of exchange rate changes during the early 1980s, when the Reagan tax rate cuts and Paul Volcker's price rule were implemented, was to cause the dollar to appreciate substantially and to reduce the relative importance of foreign money.[9] However, as the terms of trade effects wore off, the dollar depreciated and increased the contribution of foreign monies to the world money supply.

Relative Money Growth and Exchange Rates

During the last three decades, the U.S. contribution to the world money supply steadily declined (Table 2.2). However, the difference between U.S. money growth net of U.S. real GNP growth, and foreign domestic money creation net of foreign real GNP growth explains the fluctuations in the exchange rate.

Under a fixed exchange rate system, such as Bretton Woods with dollar convertibility, the quantities of money would be demand determined and, hence, would not be a cause for inflation. Hence, it is only during floating exchange rate periods when the dollar is nonconvertible that the quantity of money may reflect supply conditions.

During the 1970s, the excess foreign money growth relative to the U.S. excess money growth was 2.30 percent, and the dollar appreciated at a 0.75 percent average annual rate (Table 2.4). In turn, during the 1980–84 period, the excess foreign growth increased to 7.40 percent from 2.30 percent during the 1970s. As

Table 2.4
Sources of Exchange Rate Growth

Years	Exchange Rate	U.S. Money Growth	U.S. GNP Growth	Foreign Money Growth Net of Exchange Rate Reductions	Foreign GNP Growth	Excess Money Creation in the U.S. Relative to The Rest of The World
1960-69	5.16	3.89	1.88	6.14	2.52	1.61
1970-79	0.75	3.74	1.10	7.97	3.36	2.07
1980-84	11.67	3.42	0.70	6.46	1.39	2.35
1985-88	-16.55	2.18	1.28	0	1.94	1.52
1960-88	0.59	3.52	1.33	4.97	1.17	1.61

Source: International Monetary Fund, *International Financial Statistics.*

a result, the dollar rate of appreciation increased to 11.57 percent from 0.75 percent. Since 1985, foreign money has grown slower than U.S. money and, as a consequence, the dollar depreciated 16.55 percent per annum.

THE USES AND LIMITATIONS OF THE WORLD MONEY CONCEPT AS AN INDICATOR OF INFLATIONARY PRESSURES

Eurodollars and money market funds play a somewhat special role in the American financial system. Eurodollars play a similar role at the international level.

To the extent Eurodollars and money market funds pay a competitive interest rate, they are indexed and do not suffer an inflation tax. As inflation increases, holders of money balances will tend to shift their balances toward this kind of money.[10]

Increases in the inflation rate, holding everything else the same, will induce money holders to substitute away from non–interest bearing currency and demand deposits into interest bearing forms of money such as Eurodollars and money market funds. This substitution effect will lead to a secular increase in the velocity of the non–interest bearing money. The substitution effect away from M1 to other forms of money will tend to leave unchanged the overall quantity of broadly defined money and thus velocity. In fact, since 1950, the velocity of U.S. M1, and world M1, has increased while the velocity of M2 has remained relatively constant, and the velocity of world money, including Eurodollars, has trended downwards (Figure 2.3).

Eurodollars may partially offset changes in domestic money growth—thus making the quantity of money partially endogenous. The negative relationship between growth in the U.S. money and Eurodollars since 1960 indicates that the Eurodollar market has provided a partial offset to U.S. domestic monetary policy (Figure 2.4).

Money market funds represent a viable substitute for narrowly defined transaction balances. Similarly, Eurocurrencies represent a viable substitute for domestic monies. Suppliers (banks) often have a choice of producing local currency denominated balances or participating in nonlocal currency deposit taking and lending. Likewise, demanders (depositors) can often choose deposits in the country of origin or in the Eurocurrency market. Profit considerations imply that as the costs of local currency balances rise, Eurocurrency alternatives become more attractive.

The ability of Eurocurrencies and money market funds to substitute for checking accounts implies that monetary policy initiatives by domestic authorities are potentially offset. Changes in reserve requirements, the discount rate, and open market operations affect the costs of the domestic banking system, while the Eurocurrency system and money market funds are relatively free from those regulations.[11] If a monetary authority implements policies which would have the

Figure 2.3
U.S. and World Velocity of Money

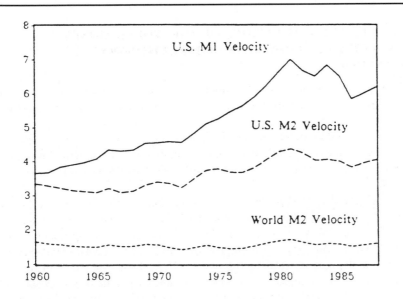

Figure 2.4
The Effect of Eurodollar Growth on U.S. Money Growth

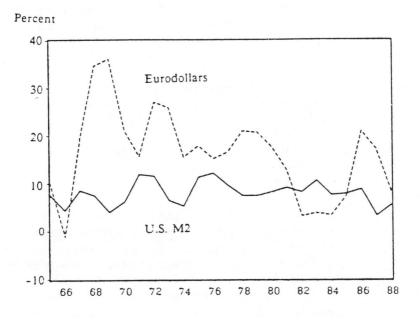

effect of contracting domestic money, the Eurocurrency and money markets become relatively less costly and can expand to absorb the excess demand for money.

NOTES

1. See Arthur B. Laffer, "The Phenomenon of Worldwide Inflation: A Study in Market Integration," in *The Phenomenon of Worldwide Inflation,* ed. Arthur B. Laffer and David Meiselman (Washington, D.C.: American Enterprise Institute, 1975).

2. See Tamir Agmon, "International Money in a Multiple Currency World: The Internationalization of the Yen" (Manuscript, University of Southern California, November 1980); Victor A. Canto, "Monetary Policy, 'Dollarization,' and Parallel Market Exchange Rates: The Case of the Dominican Republic," in *Economic Reform and Stabilization in Latin America,* ed. Michael Connolly and Claudio Gonzalez-Vega (New York: Praeger, 1987); Victor A. Canto and Marc A. Miles, "Exchange Rates in a Global Monetary Model with Currency Substitutions and Rational Expectations," in *Economic Interdependence and Flexible Exchange Rates,* ed. Jagdeep Bhandari and Bludford Putnam (Cambridge, Mass.: MIT Press, 1983); Richard N. Cooper, *The Economics of Interdependence* (New York: McGraw-Hill, 1968); Richard N. Cooper, "Macroeconomic Policy Adjustment in Interdependent Economies," *Quarterly Journal of Economics* 83, no. 1 (February 1969); Paul Evans and Arthur B. Laffer, "Demand Substitutability across Currencies" (Manuscript, Stanford University and University of Southern California, 1977); Lance Girton and Don Roper, "Theory and Implications of Currency Substitution," *Journal of Money, Credit, and Banking* 12, no. 1 (February 1981); Marc A. Miles, "Currency Substitution, Flexible Exchange Rates, and Monetary Independence," *American Economic Review* 68, no. 3 (June 1978); Don E. Roper, "Macroeconomic Policies and the Distribution of the World Money Supply," *Quarterly Journal of Economics* 85, no. 1 (February 1971).

3. See Milton Friedman and Anna Jacobson Schwartz, *A Monetary History of the United States, 1867–1960* (Princeton, N.J.: Princeton University Press, 1963); Milton Friedman and Anna Jacobson Schwartz, *Monetary Statistics of the United States* (Washington, D.C.: National Bureau of Economic Research, 1970).

4. For the earlier research and origin of the global monetarist concept, see Arthur B. Laffer, "The Practical Implications of Global Monetarism" (Boston: H. C. Wainwright & Co., May 23, 1977); Jude Wanniski, "The Mundell–Laffer Hypothesis—A New View of the World Economy," *The Public Interest,* no. 39 (Spring 1975); Arthur B. Laffer, "Global Money Growth and Inflation," *Wall Street Journal* (September 23, 1976); Arthur B. Laffer and James C. Turney, "World Inflation," A. B. Laffer Associates (May 10, 1982).

5. See *International Financial Statistics* (Washington, D.C.: International Monetary Fund), Introduction.

6. The value of the dollar, of course, is not currently fixed over time as is the exchange ratio of gallons to liters or gallons to barrels.

7. The 11 countries included in this study are Belgium, Canada, France, Germany, Italy, Japan, the Netherlands, Sweden, Switzerland, the United Kingdom, and the United States. Eurodollar data encompass only the eight European countries reporting to the BIS, excluding Canada and Japan.

8. Arthur B. Laffer, "Substitution of Monies in Demand: The Case of Mexico" (Boston: H. C. Wainwright & Co., May 27, 1977); Victor A. Canto, "Monetary Policy, 'Dollarization,' and Parallel Market Exchange Rates: The Case of the Dominican Republic," in *Economic Reform and Stabilization in Latin America*, ed. Michael Connolly and Claudio Gonzalez-Vega (New York: Praeger, 1987); Victor A. Canto, "Monetary Policy 'Dollarization' and Parallel Market Exchange Rates: The Case of the Dominican Republic," *Journal of International Money and Finance* 20, no. 1 (December 1985); Victor A. Canto and Gerald Nickelsberg, *Currency Substitution: Theory and Evidence from Latin America* (Boston: Kluwer Academic Publishing, 1987); Victor A. Canto, "Tax Rates Move Currencies, and There's No Easy Fix," *Wall Street Journal* (September 22, 1988), p. 36.

9. See Chapter 16.

10. See Chapter 4.

11. Reserve requirements and the discount rate are nothing more than a tax on domestic banking activity. See Charles W. Kadlec and Arthur B. Laffer, "The Monetary Crisis: A Classical Perspective," A. B. Laffer Associates (November 12, 1979).

3

Alternative Monetary
Theories of Inflation: Part II

Victor A. Canto and Arthur B. Laffer

Legend contends that once upon a time a big man in acceptable physical condition, but most of all a New Yorker, was confronted by four toughs on his way home after an evening on the town. Choosing discretion over valor, he ran like the blazes with his four assailants in hot pursuit. One by one, his pursuers flagged and dropped out of the macabre chase until only one remained. At this point, the New Yorker stopped, turned around, and retraced his steps, confronting each assailant one by one and beating the living daylights out of each of them.

Arguments for monetarism also are numerous and, on their surface, seem invincible. However, when confronted openly and explicitly, one by one, each of the arguments collapses under its own weight. This paper is the second in our monetary series and focuses on different variants of a common theme: M1 monetarism, M2 monetarism, and global monetarism.

The past has more influence on our analysis than any of us would care to admit. As in dominoes, we all build on what is rather than what should be. Errors, once introduced, persist. Each time a subject is broadened, the errors of the past must once again be convincingly put to rest—and put to rest to the satisfaction of the skeptics.

Virtually everyone holds to the view that money matters and most people believe that money matters a lot. Monetarists distinguish themselves from others who also believe that money matters a lot by postulating that for all practical purposes (1) the quantity of money supplied to the economy is controlled by government, and (2) the demand for money is sufficiently stable such that changes in the measured quantity of money reflect changes in supply.

From these two premises and a basic understanding of markets, the policy implications follow pari passu. Slower money growth will reduce inflation. By supplying less money to a marketplace, where the demand for money is stable, the value of each unit of money will rise, that is, prices will fall. Some versions of monetarism go so far as to argue that less money will be accommodated by lessened output initially, and only after a period of time will prices fall and output return to where it otherwise would have been.

For all of its seeming precision, at least as it is described in textbooks, monetarism—as well as every view where money matters—is embroiled in voluminous controversies at every level of abstraction. Just finding the appropriate empirical counterpart to the concept of money or trying to measure to what the demand for money is stably related are hair-pulling dilemmas.

Without confronting these great unknowns, the conceptual enigmas virtually guarantee a compounding of our ignorance. What if the Fed cannot control money—whatever money may be? Or, if the demand for money were not stable, where would we go for solace and guidance? This chapter is not a hedgehog and therefore does not answer the great questions. This chapter does postulate three alternative empirical versions of monetarism, and for lack of a better moniker, a more general money model. After describing each version, data are compared to describe the efficiency of the model as described. The specific models were selected because of their respective popularity. One local monetarist model uses M1 as money while the other local monetarist model uses M2. The other monetarist model goes beyond the territorial confines of the United States and uses the concept of world money as the key to global monetarism. The more general money model juxtaposes money demand and money supply in a nonmonetarist monetary framework.

LOCAL MONETARISM

Local monetarism argues that, as the name suggests, inflation is a country by country phenomenon and therefore national inflation can best be explained by national variables. The Fed is presumed to maintain strict control over the monetary base (the reserve deposits of depository institutions held by Federal Reserve banks plus currency in circulation). Because of its power to set minimum reserve requirements, monetarism also maintains that the Fed controls what is known as the "money multiplier," that is, the ratio of the quantity of money to the monetary base. Therefore, in theory, the money supply is perfectly inelastic to market forces and totally under the control of the monetary authorities.

Shifts in the supply of money will only result from actions of the monetary authorities. When the supply of money is increased, the new equilibrium will occur at a greater quantity of money and a lower unit value. Since the value of a unit of money is the quantity of goods and services for which that unit can be exchanged, a decrease in the value of money is equivalent to an increase in the general price level. Holding the demand for money constant, as is central to monetarism, an increase in the supply of money will result in greater money growth and higher inflation.

The local monetarist model takes narrowly defined measures of either M1 or M2 as the relevant empirical counterpart to the concept of money. Implicitly, monetary analysis assumes that the components that make up the narrow aggregate are perfect substitutes for each other, and those elements that are excluded from the definition of money are not money substitutes. To the extent that money substitutes are important, fluctuations in the demand for money and/or velocity will be outside the purview of this model.

By virtue of the fact that the Fed, alone, controls the money supply, growth in the monetary aggregate represents shifts in that supply. Real GNP growth represents shifts in the demand for money. By explicit omission, local monetarist forecasts will miss shifts in the demand for money. When demand shifts are important, local monetarists will incorrectly forecast inflation and recommend inappropriate policy responses. During the Reagan years, as confidence in the economy increased, the demand for money shifted accordingly, and thus the velocity of narrowly defined money decreased. The higher than normal money growth did not result in higher inflation, but instead was absorbed by increased money holdings per unit of GNP. The opposite occurred during the Korean War.

Substitution Effects: Shifts in the Demand for Money

Money market funds and Eurodollars may play a special role in the overall financial system and especially in the implementation of monetary theory. Money market funds and Eurodollars pay explicit interest to their holders and have many of the characteristics usually attributed to money. Because holders earn interest, they do not suffer an inflation tax. As inflation increases, holders of money balances will tend to shift their balances away from non–interest bearing monies toward interest bearing money forms.

In addition, money market funds as well as Eurodollars are not subject to explicit reserve requirements. All things considered, a reasonable case could be made that money market funds represent a viable substitute for narrowly defined money balances. Similarly, Eurocurrencies would seem to represent a viable substitute for domestic monies. Banks often do have the choice of producing local currency denominated balances or participating in a nonlocal currency deposit market. Some money holders may also be able to choose deposits in various currencies and in alternative locations. If the costs of local currency balances rise for whatever reason, be it inflation or regulations, Eurocurrency alternatives become more attractive. The substitution effects from non–interest bearing, reserve-intensive deposits to interest-bearing, non-reserve intensive deposits may well be quite large.

If inflationary expectations are highly sensitive, a catch–22 situation could be the result. Inflationary expectations could well induce a substitution in money demand out of narrowly defined non–interest bearing debt into near monies that do pay interest. Defined in terms of narrowly measured money, this substitution would be an increase in velocity resulting from higher inflationary expectations. The higher velocity could push prices higher, justifying the higher inflationary expectations. This self-fulfilling prophesy could result in substantial instability. Substitution effects provide a reasonable explanation for a negative relationship between money growth and inflation if inflationary expectations move counter to money growth. At the very least, these substitution effects will confuse the effects of money growth on inflation.

GLOBAL MONETARISM

Global monetarism represents the most aggregative form of the monetarist models. It argues that money is, after all, one of the easiest commodities to move across national boundaries. Therefore, if people can transact in one anothers' area, it would be misleading not to aggregate both areas.

There are substitution effects across regional dimensions as well as across different forms of debt. Instead of using some interest bearing domestic money substitute, some money holders may prefer to hold foreign currency money balances. World money does not suffer from regional substitution effects since a shift away from U.S. money into any of the other country's aggregates will be captured in the world measure. Therefore, the global monetarist view argues that the relevant concepts of money and output, even when focusing exclusively on U.S. inflation, are world quantities.

Global money will effectively capture cross currency shifts in the demand for money. However, as a policy matter, things become very complex because control of inflation requires control of world money, and that is no simple task.

During the fixed exchange rate period under the rules of Bretton Woods, when the United States exercised significant control over world money. U.S. trading partners were committed to maintaining fixed exchange rates to the dollar. In doing so, foreign central banks subjugated their domestic monetary policies to the United States. Dollars and foreign currencies were perfect substitutes. Because foreign central banks relinquished their power over money, the major source of world money growth was the United States. The United States was the world's central banker, and fixed exchange rates eliminated geographical substitution effects. These are the precise conditions under which global monetarism would be the relevant framework. Empirically, that was the case. Global monetarism explained inflation prior to the 1970s.[1]

The dismantling of Bretton Woods eliminated geographical perfect substitutability and thereby gave rise to varying degrees of currency substitution. Concurrent with the dismantling of Bretton Woods, the high inflation of the 1970s and financial deregulation encouraged the expansion of minimally regulated near-monies (i.e., money market funds and Eurodollars). Minimal regulation of anything other than narrowly defined monies increased the availability of money substitutes and reduced the power of monetary authorities to control world money.

The broader world measure of the quantity of money includes aggregates such as money market funds and Eurodollars which are determined by the private sector. Since Eurodollars and money market funds pay market interest, periods of rising expectations of inflation will induce a substitution effect away from non–interest bearing money into interest bearing deposits. Eurodollars and money market funds can be expected to expand as inflation increases, making world money largely endogenous. Empirically, the interest bearing components of domestic and world money are the aggregates most closely and positively related to the inflation rate.

THE EVIDENCE

Inflation and M1 Growth

Our statistical analysis relates the importance of changes in U.S. GNP growth, a proxy for demand shifts in the monetarist model, and U.S. M1 growth, a proxy for supply shifts, to U.S. inflation. To bypass a lot of hemming and hawing, the empirical results simply do not support the M1 monetarist model. Contrary to the hypothesis, contemporaneous increases in M1 growth are negatively, not positively, related to the inflation rate (Table 3.1). If they could be taken at face value, the results indicate that a 1 percent increase in M1 growth is associated with a 0.26 percent reduction in the inflation rate.

After one year, a 1 percent increase in M1 switches effects and then is associated with a 0.22 percent increase in the inflation rate. Since the contemporaneous and one-year lag approximately cancel each other, the statistical results suggest there is no significant long-run relationship between M1 growth and inflation.

The statistical results reported in Table 3.1 indicate that the most significant correlation is between current inflation and past inflation.[2] In fact, the estimated coefficient between current and lagged one-year inflation is not statistically different from one. If we could presume the coefficients to be one, then this result suggests that inflation is basically a random walk. The best predictor of inflation could well be past inflation if the process truly were a random walk.

Inflation and M2 Growth

Expanding the definition of money to include M2 in the equation does not improve the monetarist's case. As in the M1 equation, the contemporaneous growth in M2 is negatively related to inflation, while the one-year lag in M2 growth is positively related to inflation. As before, the two coefficients roughly cancel each other out, suggesting no significant long-run relationship.

There are differences between the M1 equation and the M2 equation. The

Table 3.1

U.S. Inflation: The Local Monetarist View (*t*-Statistics in Parentheses), Sample 1960–88

Variable	Equation 1	Equation 2
Constant	-0.024	-0.006
	(1.33)	(0.27)
GUSGNP	-0.076	-0.072
	(0.42)	(0.321)
GUSGNP(-1)	0.52	0.058
	(3.25)	(0.248)
GUSGNP(-2)	0.131	0.008
	(0.57)	(0.04)
GM1	-0.260	--
	(2.23)	
GM1(-1)	0.221	--
	(1.86)	
GM1(-2)	0.057	--
	(0.52)	
GM2	--	-0.268
		(1.65)
GM2(-1)	--	0.316
		(1.56)
GM2(-2)	--	0.179
		(1.06)
INF(-1)	1.17	1.31
	(4.86)	(5.97)
INF(-2)	-0.15	-0.56
	(0.49)	(1.98)
Adj. R^2	0.803	0.783
SE	0.0147	0.0155
D-W	1.84	1.99
F	14.29	12.76

GUSGNP	= Year-over-year percent change in real US GNP
GUSGNP(-1)	= Year-over-year percent change in real US GNP lagged one year
GUSGNP(-2)	= Year-over-year percent change in real US GNP lagged two years
GM1	= December-over-December growth in M1
GM1(-1)	= December-over-December growth in M1 lagged one year
GM1(-2)	= December-over-December growth in M1 lagged two years
GM2	= December-over-December growth in M2
GM2(-1)	= December-over-December growth in M2 lagged one year
GM2(-2)	= December-over-December growth in M2 lagged two years
INF(-1)	= Inflation rate lagged one year.
INF(-2)	= Inflation rate lagged two years.

statistical significance of the coefficient of M2 growth (equation 2) is much lower than that of M1 growth (equation 1). A possible explanation for the short-run negative relationship and its subsequent biasing when M2 is used is that the rise in inflation expectations induces a substitution effect away from non–interest bearing money (M1) into interest bearing money (i.e., money market funds). The increase in the interest bearing component of M2 will tend to offset the reduction in non-interest bearing M1, thereby leaving M2 relatively less changed.

However, to the extent that the interest bearing component of M2 does not encompass all the interest bearing near-money substitutes, the reduction in M1 will be greater than the increase in the interest bearing component of M2. Therefore, a weak relationship will still be observed. Once the substitution away from non–interest bearing money has taken place, the nominal quantity should increase at the same rate as the inflation rate. The fact that the coefficient for the one-year lag in money growth is smaller than one, suggests that there is still something else going on.

Inflation and World Money

The empirical results relating world money output and world money growth to U.S. inflation are qualitatively similar to those of the local monetarist model.[3] The coefficient for the contemporaneous world money growth is negative while those of world money growth lagged one and two years are positive (Table 3.2). A marginally statistically significant relationship between world money growth and inflation is present. However, as with the local monetarist model, the coefficient for the lagged inflation variable is the most significant and, again, not statistically significantly different from one. This suggests that the best single predictor of current inflation is past inflation. Empirically, the global monetarist model also cannot reject the hypothesis that inflation is a random walk.

THE FAILURE OF LOCAL AND GLOBAL MONETARIST MODELS: AN EXPLANATION

A combination of the facts that monetary aggregates are not statistically significant in explaining long-run inflation and that the most significant variable is lagged inflation is damaging to the local and global monetarist models. One plausible explanation for these results is that both M1 and world money are endogenous. However, the nature of the endogeneity is quite different for the two monies.

The source of endogeneity of M1 and M2 was the substitution in demand. For M1 the endogeneity results form a substitution effect across various forms of debt instruments—substitution effects away from non–interest bearing money to interest bearing money. On the other hand, the endogeneity of the world aggregate results from a substitution of monies across currency boundaries.

Table 3.2
U.S. Inflation: The Global Monetarist View (*t*-Statistics in Parentheses), Sample 1960–88

Variable	Equation
Constant	-0.015
	(0.86)
GWGNP	-0.072
	(0.34)
GWGNP(-1)	0.296
	(1.48)
GWGNP(-2)	0.027
	(0.113)
GWM2E	-0.039
	(0.63)
GWM2E(-1)	0.035
	(0.48)
GWM2E(-2)	0.16
	(1.96)
INF(-1)	0.86
	(3.08)
INF(-2)	-0.09
	(0.41)
Adj. R^2	0.762
SE	0.0102
D-W	1.55
F	11.41

GWGNP	= Year-over-year change in world real GNP
GWGNP(-1)	= Year-over-year change in world real GNP lagged one year
GWGNP(-2)	= Year-over-year change in world real GNP lagged two years
GWM2E	= December-over-December growth in world M2
GWM2E(-1)	= December-over-December growth in world M2 lagged one year
GWM2E(-2)	= December-over-December growth in world M2 lagged two years
INF(-1)	= Inflation rate lagged one year
INF(-2)	= Inflation rate lagged two years

Table 3.3
U.S. Inflation: The Imperfect Substitution View (*t*-Statistics in Parentheses), Sample 1960–88

Variable	Equation 1	Equation 2
Constant	-0.28 (2.26)	-0.0253 (2.17)
GB	1.09 (2.79)	1.22 (4.85)
GB(-1)	0.297 (0.71)	--
GB(-2)	-0.123 (0.32)	--
GM1	-0.58 (3.49)	-0.607 (4.43)
GM1(-1)	-0.002 (0.10)	--
GM1(-2)	-0.05 (0.28)	--
INF(-1)	1.13 (5.35)	1.10 (0.50)
INF(-2)	-0.52 (3.05)	-0.50 (3.62)
Adj. R^2	0.819	0.842
SE	0.0138	0.0132
D-W	1.94	1.80
F	16.76	35.56

GB = December-over-December percent change in the monetary base
GB(-1) = December-over-December percent change in the monetary base lagged one year
GB(-2) = December-over-December percent change in the monetary base lagged two years
GM1 = December-over-December growth in M1
GM1(-1) = December-over-December growth in M1 lagged one year
GM1(-2) = December-over-December growth in M1 lagged two years
INF(-1) = Inflation rate lagged one year.
INF(-2) = Inflation rate lagged two years.

A MORE GENERAL THEORY: IMPERFECT
SUBSTITUTABILITY AMONG MONETARY AGGREGATES

Imperfect substitutability among the monetary aggregates provides a mechanism by which the monetary authorities may influence, but perhaps not control,
the overall quantity of money. Within this framework, attempts by the monetary
authorities to create money will result in a substitution in demand away from
non–interest bearing money into interest bearing money. However, since the
aggregates are imperfect substitutes in demand and supply (i.e., inflation avoidance is costly), the currency flight will not be complete.

Our choice of a proxy for the supply shifts is the growth in the monetary base.
The reason for this simply is that the Federal Reserve totally controls and only
controls the monetary base. The proxy for demand shifts is somewhat more
difficult to determine. While it is true that increases in real GNP growth encompass a source of money demand, such a measure does not include fluctuations in
demand resulting from any number of other factors. We have argued that changes
in the equilibrium quantity of money are the result of both shifts in the demand
for and supply of money. Thus, if we are able to identify shifts in the supply of
money (i.e., growth in the monetary base) and to have the full knowledge that the
quantity of money reflects both demand and supply, then netting the supply
component would have M1 growth as a *total* proxy for money demand.

Increases in base growth are associated with a positive and statistically significant effect on U.S. inflation (Table 3.3). Only the contemporaneous coefficient
for the growth in the monetary base appears to be statistically significant. Taken
at face value, a 1 percent increase in the monetary base is associated with a 1.1
percent increase in the inflation rate. This estimate, however, is not statistically
significantly different from unity.

In line with our expectations, changes in M1 growth are associated with a
negative and statistically significant effect on U.S. inflation. Again, only the
contemporaneous coefficient appears to be statistically significant. Taken at face
value, the results indicate that a 1 percent increase in M1 growth is associated
with a 0.60 percent reduction in the inflation rate.

The empirical results suggest that the estimated equation adequately captures
supply shifts (i.e., growth in the monetary base) as well as demand shifts (i.e.,
growth in the quantity of money). Thus, in order to forecast inflation, shifts in
the supply of money (i.e., growth in the base) and shifts in the demand for money
have to be forecasted first.

NOTES

1. Arthur B. Laffer, "Global Money Growth and Inflation," *Wall Street Journal,*
September 23, 1976.

2. Ibid.

3. See Chapter 2.

4

Money, Interest Rates, and Inflation: A Classical View

Victor A. Canto and Arthur B. Laffer

ERRANT DOGMA

Monetary policy and its consequences are seen as virtually one jingoism after another:

- Slow growth of money means monetary policy is tight
- Tight money is reflected by higher interest rates
- High interest rates reduce economic growth
- Higher interest rates strengthen the dollar in the foreign exchanges
- Slow growth in money lowers inflation
- Slow growth in output lowers inflation
- High interest rates stop inflation

It is hard to imagine a set of beliefs more at odds with reality. With the single exception that in the long run higher interest rates do slow economic growth—but only in the long run—every single statement listed above is both illogical and factually incorrect. Adherence to the dictates of this dogma has put the U.S. economy on the brink.

Figure 4.1
The Foreign Exchange Value of the Dollar and the Three-Month Treasury Bill Yield, 1970–88

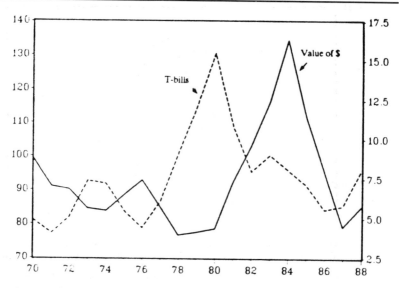

Sources: *International Financial Statistics; Selected Interest Rates,* Federal Reserve; *Economic Report of the President; Wall Street Journal.*
A.B. Laffer Associates

Figure 4.2
Inflation Rate and M1 Growth Rate

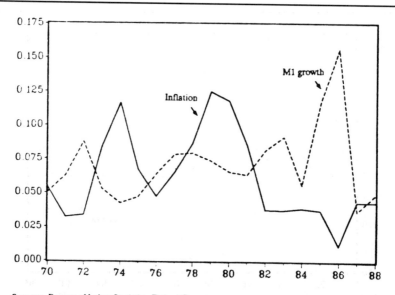

Sources: Bureau of Labor Statistics; Federal Reserve.
A.B Laffer Associates

Figure 4.3
Real GNP Growth and Inflation Rate

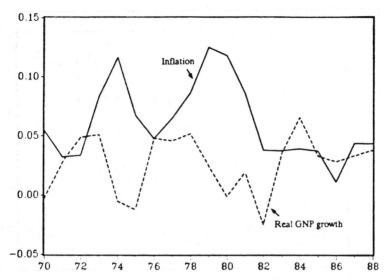

Sources: Bureau of Labor Statistics; *Economic Report of the President, 1989*; Department of Commerce.
A.B. Laffer Associates

Figure 4.4
Excess Base Growth and Interest Rates

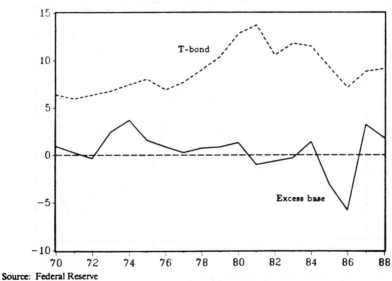

Source: Federal Reserve
A.B. Laffer Associates

Figure 4.5
Inflation and Three-Month T-Bills

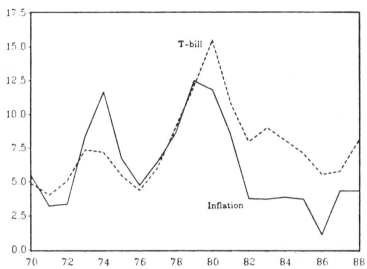

Sources: Bureau of Labor Statistics; Federal Reserve.
A.B. Laffer Associates

In Figures 4.1 through 4.5, three of the more obvious fallacies are illustrated with annual data from the past two decades:

- High interest rates are not associated with a high foreign exchange value of the dollar (Figure 4.1)[1]
- More rapid growth in money is not associated with higher inflation (Figure 4.2)[2]
- High real GNP growth is not associated with high inflation (Figure 4.3)[3]
- Excess base growth (i.e., easy money) is not associated with low interest rates (Figure 4.4)[4]
- High interest rates do not stop inflation (Figure 4.5)

If anything, in each instance the data show the converse proposition more likely to be true.

THE ROLE OF MONETARY POLICY

Imagine what would happen if the Fed were to announce that there would be no increase in the monetary base for the next decade. Interest rates, which are the best indicators of what markets foresee, would fall and probably fall sharply. The dollar would skyrocket in the foreign exchanges. Inflation would fade away, and goodness knows just how high the stock market would go.

On the other hand, if the Fed were to have a preannounced policy of expanding the monetary base at, say, 50 percent per annum for the next decade, interest rates would rise and the dollar would collapse in the foreign exchanges. In addition, inflation would pick up and the financial markets would tumble. Higher interest rates are proof positive that monetary policy has eased and that Fed policies are expansive. The faster the growth of the monetary base, the easier monetary policy is, and vice versa.

Just on this intuitive level, it is extraordinary that anyone could argue that higher interest rates are a sure sign that the Fed is tightening, let alone that these higher interest rates will dampen inflation or strengthen the dollar in the world's bourses. If raising interest rates dampened inflation, surely Brazil would have price stability by now and Japanese inflation would be out of control. If high interest rates made for a strong currency, the Mexican peso would be one of the benchmark currencies and the Swiss franc would have gone down the tubes long ago.[5]

Confronted by these admitted anecdotes, the guardians of the mythology retort that they were referring all along to real interest rates. It is true that higher real rates of interest could well mean that Fed policy is tighter and will both dampen inflation and strengthen the domestic currency. But such an answer is disingenuous within the experience of the recent past.

Higher nominal interest rates of the past several decades were not the result of higher real interest rates. Indexed bonds have extraordinarily low yields and these yields have virtually no volatility. In the 1950s and early 1960s, when inflationary expectations were arguably low and constant, an annual change in interest rates could be far less than one percent and still be considered large.

Changes in nominal interest rates today predominantly reflect changes in inflationary expectations. They do not reflect changes in the real rate of interest. To postulate theory on the presumption that changes in interest rates are one and the same as changes in real rates of interest is misleading.[6]

MONETARY POLICY: A CLASSICAL VIEW

There is considerable disagreement as to what constitutes tight or loose monetary policy. There is little unanimity even as to what monetary variables should be used—interest rates, the money supply, free reserves, or the base. The confusion and controversy arise from trying to infer from changes in the equilibrium quantity of money and changes in the price level how the demand curve has shifted vis-à-vis the supply curve.

Money possesses characteristics similar to all other commodities. When the supply curve for money is shifted outward and the demand curve is stationary, the new equilibrium will occur at a greater quantity and a lower unit value (Figure 4.6). Since the value of a unit of money is the quantity of goods and services it can be exchanged for, a decrease in the value of money is equivalent to an increase in the general price level (i.e., inflation).

Figure 4.6
The Effects of an Increase in the
Supply of Money

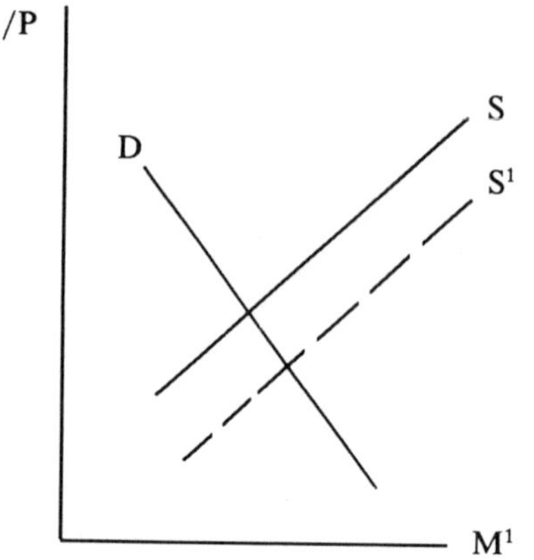

Figure 4.7
The Effects of an Increase in the
Demand for Money

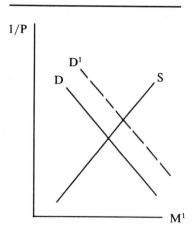

A.B. Laffer Associates

Alternatively, if the demand for money is shifted outward, the new equilibrium also will be at a greater quantity but at a greater value per unit (Figure 4.7). An increase in the value of money is equivalent to a decline in the price level (i.e., deflation). In the absence of other changes, inward shifts of supply will result in lessened quantities and deflation, and inward shifts of demand will result in lessened quantities and inflation.[7]

The important point is that knowledge about changes in the quantity of money alone is not sufficient to determine whether prices will rise or fall. If an increase in the quantity of money is the result of a shift in the demand for money, then this will lower inflation, lower interest rates, and raise the value of the currency in the foreign exchanges. Conversely, if an increase in the quantity of money is the consequence of a shift in the supply of money, then inflationary pressures will be heightened resulting in higher interest rates and a weaker currency. All in all, no one can say that increases or decreases in the quantity of money are "inflationary" or "deflationary" or whether the policies that precipitated these changes were "loose" or "tight." Knowledge of the origin of each disturbance, that is, whether the demand curve or supply curve shifted, is necessary to determine its impact.

THE ELASTICITIES OF MONEY DEMAND AND SUPPLY

If the demand for money is perfectly elastic, the monetary authorities have no power to change the price level (Figure 4.8). In this case, changes in the quantity of money are due to changes in supply conditions exclusively. The demand for

Figure 4.8
The Effects of Changes in the Money Supply When Money Demand Is Perfectly Elastic

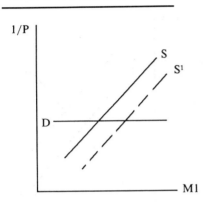

Figure 4.9
The Effects of Money Demand Shifts When the Money Supply Is Perfectly Inelastic

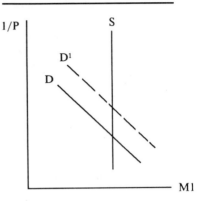

money could be nearly perfectly elastic if near-money substitutes were readily available at little or no additional cost. The availability of money market funds, trade credit, and other near monies increases substitutability and makes the demand curve for money more elastic.[8] However, the government, through legal tender requirements, limits the degree of substitutability and prevents money demand from being perfectly elastic.[9] Thus, the demand for money is somewhat less than perfectly elastic.

Traditional analysis assumes that the Fed maintains strict control of the monetary base: the reserve deposits of depository institutions held by Federal Reserve Banks plus currency in circulation. Because of its power to set minimum reserve requirements, textbooks also maintain that the Fed controls what is known as the "money multiplier," that is, the ratio of the quantity of money to the monetary base. Therefore, in theory, the money supply is perfectly inelastic and invariant to changes in market conditions. Shifts in demand cause changes in the price level, but the quantity of money remains constant (Figure 4.9).

The traditional textbook view is incorrect. While the Fed can *influence* the interaction between the banking system and the private sector, it cannot *control* that interaction. Insofar as market conditions influence private sector behavior, the money multiplier is not under the complete control of the Fed. In the extreme, if the multiplier is determined entirely by the private sector, changes in the multiplier conceivably can offset changes in the base. Under such circumstances, the money supply would be perfectly elastic. The quantity of money would then be demand-determined, and the price level would remain constant (Figure 4.10).

If the private sector cannot completely offset the Fed's actions, then the money supply will not be perfectly elastic. Given the nature of our money markets, the

Figure 4.10
The Effects of Money Demand
Shifts When the Money Supply Is
Perfectly Elastic

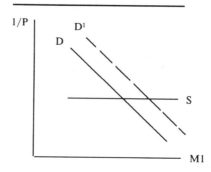

Figure 4.11
Equilibrium in the Money Market
When Demand Shifts Exceed Sup-
ply Shifts

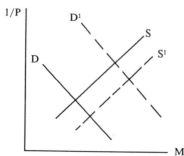

Figure 4.12
Equilibrium in the Money Market
When Supply Shifts Exceed De-
mand Shifts

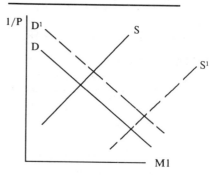

A.B. Laffer Associates

money supply is neither perfectly elastic nor perfectly inelastic. Everything else the same, increases in the demand for money will result in increases in the quantity of money and in lower prices (Figure 4.7). Similarly, increases in the supply of money will result in increases in the quantity of money and in higher prices (Figure 4.6).

EQUILIBRIUM IN THE MONEY MARKET

In spite of the weight placed by many economists on monetary policy, considerable disagreement remains as to what constitutes tight or loose monetary policy. The confusion or controversy arises from trying to infer from changes in the equilibrium quantity of money alone how the demand curve has shifted vis-à-vis the supply curve. A change in the quantity of money reflects the combined effects of shifts in both demand and supply, and, by itself, it sheds no light on the relative impact each has. In fact, any change in the quantity of money is a weighted average of shifts in demand and supply.

A change in the quantity of money becomes important once any information is known about either the demand or the supply of money. Changes in the quantity of money, if known to be greater than changes in the supply of money, imply that demand shifts were greater than supply shifts (Figure 4.11). Likewise, if changes in the quantity of money are less than changes in supply, then it follows that demand shifts were less than supply shifts (Figure 4.12). All in all, while money stock numbers taken in a vacuum mean little they become extraordinarily important when taken in conjunction with other information.

What perfect knowledge of either the supply of money or the demand for money would be ideal, less-than-perfect knowledge can be also valuable. To determine the inflationary or deflationary implications of money market developments, some way of discriminating between shifts in the demand for money and shifts in the supply of money is required. The development of operational measures for shifts in the demand for and supply of money is especially important for financial decisions and as a guide for evaluating Federal Reserve policy.

A PROXY FOR SUPPLY SHIFTS

Shifts in the supply of money to a substantial extent result from Federal Reserve actions. These actions are best summarized by changes in the monetary base.[10] Whether operating through changes in loans to depository institutions or open market operations, Federal Reserve actions have a predictable impact on the monetary base. Therefore, changes in the monetary base are an important factor in shifts in the overall supply of money.

Outward shifts in the supply of money will, all else the same, result in a higher price level. In a dynamic context, a sustained acceleration of the growth rate of the monetary base will result in a higher inflation rate.

When the inflation rate is regressed on the contemporaneous and 11 lagged values of the growth rate of the monetary base, the contemporaneous relationship is negative but not statistically significant (Table 4.1). However, all 11 lagged coefficients are positive, and the sum of the contemporaneous and lagged values taken together is positive and statistically significant. This should come as no surprise to anyone familiar with monetary theory.

SOURCES OF MONEY DEMAND

Inflation is often described by the old saw as "too much money chasing too few goods." If true, then the more goods, the lower the inflation. Historical

Table 4.1
Monthly Inflation and Base Growth,* 1970.01–1989.02

Lag	Base Growth
0	-0.108
	(-1.046)
1	0.078
	(0.736)
2	-0.108
	(-1.027)
3	0.133
	(1.228)
4	0.091
	(0.839)
5	0.264
	(2.443)
6	-0.021
	(-0.201)
7	0.022
	(0.207)
8	0.022
	(0.207)
9	-0.044
	(-0.426)
10	0.092
	(0.912)
11	0.071
	(0.701)
SUM	0.491
	(1.99)

* t-statistics in parentheses.

periods of rapid economic growth frequently have been periods of low inflation (Figure 4.3). The rationale for this relation is quite simple. Increases in real economic activity result in increases in the demand for money. All else the same, increases in money demand result in lower inflation.

Clearly, any simple depiction of the relationship between the goods markets and inflation will miss the important contributions of the money market. In addition to increased real economic activity, falling interest rates and lower expectations of inflation increase the demand for money. Heightened money demand induces an increase in the quantity of money as the monetary system moves outward along the supply curve. The velocity of money and the inflation rate will decline.

If demand shifts are the dominant factors producing changes in the money markets, then inflation and M1 growth will be inversely related:

- An increase in anticipated inflation results in higher interest rates. Because certain components of M1 do not earn interest (e.g., currency and certain demand deposits), higher interest rates encourage economic agents to substitute out of M1 into interest bearing assets. This substitution will tend to retard the growth of M1 as the expected rate of inflation rises.

- Increases in real economic activity increase the demand for money. Increased money demand produces both an increase in the quantity of money and lower inflation. As a result, the relationships between M1 growth and inflation and between real GNP growth and inflation will be negative.

A PROXY FOR DEMAND SHIFTS

If changes in M1 are due largely to shifts in the demand for money, the relation between M1 growth and inflation will be negative. When the monthly inflation rate is regressed on the contemporaneous and 11 lagged values of the annual differences in the growth rate of M1, the contemporaneous relationship is negative and significant (Table 4.2). Collectively, the contemporaneous and lagged values are significantly different from zero. These results suggest that fluctuations in M1 capture, albeit imperfectly, shifts in the money demand function.

A PROXY FOR EXCESS MONEY GROWTH

The appropriate depiction of the relationship between money markets and inflation requires a variable that reflects the net effects of shifts in the demand for and supply of money. Changes in the monetary base indicate shifts in the money supply curve. Changes in M1 indicate shifts in the demand curve. Thus, an approximate measure of excess money growth is the difference between the growth rates of the base and M1.

Since the breakdown of the Bretton Woods agreement in 1971, the relationship between inflation and this measure of excess money growth has been close (Figure 4.13). The excess growth of the base over M1 exhibits a positive and significant contemporaneous relationship with inflation (Table 4.3). The sum of the contemporaneous and 11 lagged coefficients is positive and statistically significant.

The estimated relationship reported in Table 4.3 forces the coefficient for M1 growth and base growth to be equal in magnitude and opposite in sign. In order to allow for the possibility that the coefficients for the two variables may be different in magnitude, the relationship between inflation, base growth, and M1 growth was estimated directly. The results reported in Table 4.4 indicate that,

Table 4.2
Monthly Inflation and M1 Growth,* 1970.01–1989.02

Lag	M1 Growth
0	-0.121
	(-2.56)
1	-0.023
	(-0.469)
2	-0.056
	(-1.10)
3	-0.002
	(-0.044)
4	-0.063
	(-1.224)
5	0.013
	(0.245)
6	0.014
	(0.262)
7	-0.062
	(-1.211)
8	-0.020
	(-0.403)
9	0.054
	(1.069)
10	-0.003
	(-0.058)
11	-0.022
	(-0.169)
SUM	-0.292
>	(-2.766)

* t-statistics in parentheses.

consistent with our earlier results, the sum of the coefficients for base growth is positive and statistically significant.[11] The sum of the coefficients for M1 growth is negative and statistically significant. The results also indicate that the magnitude of the long-run impact (i.e., sum of the coefficients) appears to be different in magnitude for base and M1 growth.

Care must be exercised in interpreting the correlation among the different variables.[12] If our interpretation is correct, the monetary base will be exogenous to the inflation rate. Thus, increases in base growth will result in a higher inflation rate which, in turn, will reduce the demand for narrowly defined money.

Figure 4.13
Excess Base Growth versus Inflation

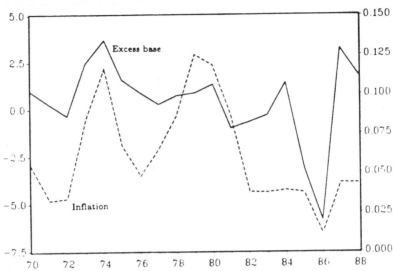

Sources: Bureau of Labor Statistics; Federal Reserve.
A.B. Laffer Associates

The decline in demand for money will then feed back and result in a higher inflation rate.

Econometricians have developed alternative statistical procedures to investigate the causal structure (i.e., temporal precedence) among economic variables. One such test, developed by Granger, is used here. The test is designed to investigate what effect, if any, changes in base growth, money growth, and excess base growth have on interest rates and inflation.[13] The test is as follows. Past value of inflation rates and excess base growth are regressed on current inflation rates. If, given past values of the inflation rate, past values of base growth have a significant explanatory power of current inflation rate, then base growth is said to cause the inflation rate.

The results of the Granger test on inflation and 10-year Treasury bond yields are reported in Table 4.5 and 4.6. The empirical results indicate that past values of base growth, in conjunction with past values of the inflation rate, are superior at predicting the current inflation rate to just past values of the inflation rates. Thus, in the Granger sense, base growth causes inflation. Again, this result should not be surprising to anyone familiar with monetary policy.

The results also indicate that past values of M1 growth, in conjunction with past inflation, do not increase the predictive power of the regression that uses only past values of the inflation rate. Therefore, in a Granger sense, M1 growth does not cause inflation. While at the usual significance level (i.e., 10 percent),

Table 4.3
Monthly Inflation and Excess Base Growth,* 1970.01–1989.02

Lag	Excess Base Growth
0	0.124
	(2.529)
1	0.810
	(1.614)
2	0.068
	(1.342)
3	0.043
	(0.857)
4	0.099
	(1.93)
5	0.073
	(1.43)
6	-0.013
	(-0.252)
7	0.089
	(1.74)
8	0.045
	(0.903)
9	-0.052
	(-1.033)
10	0.030
	(0.601)
11	0.049
	(0.942)
SUM	0.634
	(4.784)

* t-statistics in parentheses.

the empirical results do not indicate that inflation causes M1 growth, the results reported in Table 4.5 indicate that M1 growth is more likely to be caused by inflation than base growth. Taken together, the results are consistent with our description of the process equilibrating the money market.

The interest rate results reported in Table 4.6 indicate that M1 growth causes changes in interest rates while changes in the base are marginally significant. In turn, changes in interest rates appear to cause changes in base and M1 growth. The linkage from interest rates to the base may be induced by the Fed policy

Table 4.4
Monthly Inflation, Monetary Base Growth, and M1 Growth,* 1970.01–1989.02

Lag	Base Growth	M1 Growth
0	0.45	–.13
	(0.38)	(–2.68)
1	.22	0.54
	(1.85)	(–1.02)
2	0.12	–0.92
	(1.05)	(–1.74)
3	0.23	–0.37
	(1.99)	(–0.70)
4	0.26	–0.12
	(2.24)	(–2.31)
5	0.41	–0.94
	(3.62)	(–1.75)
6	0.06	–0.05
	(.49)	(–0.90)
7	0.15	–0.11
	(1.33)	(–1.94)
8	0.46	–0.07
	(0.41)	(–1.25)
9	–0.04	0.04
	(–0.37)	(0.81)
10	0.16	–0.06
	(1.46)	(–1.01)
11	0.09	–.07
	(.89)	(–1.33)
SUM	1.75	–0.84
	(5.31)	(–5.91)

* t-statistics in parentheses.

responses to changes in the level of interest rates. Similarly, changes in expectations about opportunity cost of holding money will also induce a change in M1 growth.

Taken together, the results are consistent with the interpretation that changes in base growth result in a higher inflation rate. In turn, monetary disturbances will affect overall monetary equilibrium M1 growth. The base over M1 growth captures the excess money supply thereby resulting in changes in interest rates and inflation. In turn, changes in interest rates and inflation alter the monetary equilibrium thereby causing changes in excess base growth.

Table 4.5
Inflation Rate Granger Test: Joint Significance of Independent Variables

Y	X (Forcing Variable)	F (12,205)	Significance
Inflation rate	Base growth	2.52	.004
Inflation rate	M1 growth	.85	.59
Inflation rate	Excess base	1.47	.12
Base growth	Inflation rate	.64	.80
M1 growth	Inflation rate	1.11	.35
Excess base	Inflation rate	1.13	.33

Table 4.6
10-Year Treasury Bond Yields Granger Test: Joint Significance of Independent Variables

Y	X (Forcing Variable)	F (12,205)	Significance
Interest rate	Base growth	1.39	0.16
Interest rate	M1 growth	2.09	0.18
Interest rate	Excess base	1.48	0.12
Base growth	Interest rate	2.11	0.03
M1 growth	Interest rate	4.57	0.00001
Excess base	Interest rate	4.11	0.0001

RELATIONSHIP BETWEEN EXCESS BASE GROWTH, INFLATION, AND TREASURY BOND YIELDS

All in all, excess base growth provides a better explanation of the monthly inflation rate than either base growth or M1 growth separately. The results indicate that past values of excess base growth have a significant impact on the monthly inflation rate.

The next step in the analysis is to investigate the strength of the contemporaneous relationship as the frequency of the series is reduced from monthly intervals to quarterly, semiannual, and annual intervals. The presumption is that, as the frequency of the series is reduced, the significance level of the contemporaneous coefficient will increase and the importance of lagged variables will decline.

Empirical studies investigating the annual relationship among variables usually focus on either December-over-December changes or year-over-year changes. However, it is equally valid to examine annual relationships by looking at January-over-January changes. A priori, there is no reason to preclude from the analysis even the February-over-February changes. In order to allow for possible distinct seasonal patterns in the series, we constructed twelve annual series, one for each month in the year. The annual changes were calculated by taking the change in one month over that level of the variable twelve months prior.

For the 1970–88 period, a statistically significant relationship exists between the annual inflation rate and excess base growth (Table 4.7). The magnitude of the estimated coefficient ranges from a low of .26 to a high of .81. This suggests that, in spite of, or perhaps as a result of the seasonal adjustment of the monetary aggregates, seasonal patterns remain. The estimated relationship does not appear to be statistically significant for the April-over-April and May-over-May annual series. On average, the magnitude of the coefficient is not much different than the estimated relationship between contemporaneous and eleven month lag changes in the excess base and monthly inflation rate reported in Table 4.3. The magnitude of the coefficient in Table 4.3 is .63.

Six semiannual series were constructed. One series starts in January and July, a second one starts in February and August, and so on. The relationship between semiannual changes in the two variables is also statistically significant. However, the magnitude of the estimated coefficient is smaller. Once again, seasonal patterns are evident in the data. This is reflected by the variations in the magnitude of the estimated coefficient (Table 4.8).

The first quarterly series begins with the months of January, April, July, and October. For the second series, the quarter begins in February, May, August, and November. The third series' quarters start in March, June, September, and December. The relationship between the quarterly changes in excess base growth and inflation is positive and statistically significant (Table 4.9). In line with the earlier results, seasonal differences as reflected by the magnitude of the coefficient are clearly evident. In addition, the magnitude of the coefficient is clearly lower than those of the semiannual and annual series.

Finally, over a period of a month a statistically significant relationship is uncovered between excess base growth over M1 and changes in the inflation rate (Table 4.10). The coefficient is smaller than those estimated using a longer frequency of the data. Taken at face value, the results indicate that 1 percent excess base growth will result in a .083 percent increase in the inflation rate.

Taken together, the empirical results indicate a positive and statistically significant relationship between excess base growth and inflation. The results also indicate that the magnitude of the estimated coefficient is inversely related to the frequency of the estimation interval. The decline in the estimated coefficient as one moves from the lower frequency (annual) to the higher frequency data is consistent with our basic hypothesis that, as the frequency estimation interval is increased, the regression estimates capture the instantaneous or contempo-

Table 4.7
Relationship between Annual Inflation and Excess Base Growth, 1970–88

Dependent Variable	Constant	Excess Base Growth	MA1	R2	SE	DW	F	Month
Inflation Rate	0.058 (10.07)	0.702 (2.59)	0.572 (2.13)	0.417	0.024	1.52	7.44	Jan
Inflation Rate	0.057 (11.77)	0.665 (2.73)	0.905 (3.45)	0.577	0.021	1.65	13.26	Feb
Inflation Rate	0.058 (12.00)	0.515 (2.08)	0.915 (3.30)	0.565	0.020	1.50	12.70	Mar
Inflation Rate	0.058 (11.01)	0.262 (1.09)	0.888 (2.81)	0.449	0.023	1.69	8.35	Apr
Inflation Rate	0.058 (10.88)	0.360 (1.38)	0.853 (2.58)	0.439	0.023	1.71	8.04	May
Inflation Rate	0.058 (10.68)	0.598 (2.09)	0.619 (2.00)	0.455	0.023	1.76	8.52	Jun
Inflation Rate	0.058 (9.94)	0.561 (1.87)	0.566 (1.92)	0.386	0.025	1.83	6.66	Jul
Inflation Rate	0.058 (10.10)	0.521 (1.65)	0.626 (2.12)	0.373	0.024	1.85	6.36	Aug
Inflation Rate	0.057 (10.00)	0.715 (2.33)	0.548 (2.00)	0.407	0.024	1.56	7.18	Sep
Inflation Rate	0.057 (10.67)	0.793 (2.91)	0.756 (2.64)	0.497	0.022	1.42	9.90	Oct
Inflation Rate	0.057 (10.98)	0.815 (2.95)	0.768 (2.92)	0.533	0.022	1.45	11.27	Nov
Inflation Rate	0.057 (10.37)	0.759 (2.95)	0.665 (2.64)	0.478	0.024	1.71	9.25	Dec

Table 4.8
Relationship between Semiannual Inflation Rate and Semiannual Excess Base Growth, 1970–88

Dependent Variable	Constant	Excess Base Growth	MA1	R2	SE	DW	F	Intervals
Inflation Rate	0.029 (13.40)	0.478 (2.82)	0.527 (3.10)	0.348	0.014	1.98	11.12	Jan to Jun / Jul to Dec
Inflation Rate	0.029 (13.97)	0.510 (2.77)	0.557 (3.25)	0.374	0.013	1.93	12.34	Feb to Jul / Aug to Jan
Inflation Rate	0.030 (12.37)	0.208 (1.05)	0.413 (2.27)	0.196	0.015	1.89	5.64	Mar to Aug / Sep to Feb
Inflation Rate	0.030 (12.94)	0.299 (1.89)	0.458 (2.65)	0.264	0.014	1.92	7.81	Apr to Sep / Oct to Mar
Inflation Rate	0.030 (14.52)	0.301 (2.24)	0.585 (3.45)	0.399	0.013	1.72	13.59	May to Oct / Nov to Apr
Inflation Rate	0.029 (13.71)	0.526 (3.44)	0.558 (3.29)	0.412	0.013	1.90	14.32	Jun to Nov / Dec to May

A.B. Laffer Associates

Table 4.9
Relationship between Quarterly Inflation Rate and Quarterly Excess Base Growth, 1970–88*

Dependent Variable	Constant	Excess Base Growth	MA1	R2	SE	DW	F
Inflation Rate	0.015 (16.49)	0.285 (2.97)	0.456 (3.87)	0.290	0.008	1.84	16.27
Inflation Rate	0.015 (19.50)	0.143 (1.71)	0.799 (6.60)	0.419	0.007	2.01	28.07
Inflation Rate	0.015 (16.43)	0.282 (2.84)	0.519 (4.34)	0.306	0.008	1.86	17.51

*   The first quarterly series begins with the months of January, April, July, and October. For the second series, the quarter begins in February, May, August, and November. The third series's quarters start in March, June, September, and December.

A.B. Laffer Associates

Table 4.10
Relationship between Monthly Inflation Rate and Monthly Excess Base Growth, 1970–88

Dependent Variable	Constant	Excess Base Growth	MA1	R^2	SE	DW	F
Inflation Rate	0.005	0.083	0.469	0.212	0.003	1.847	31.51
	(23.69)	(1.83)	(6.91)				

A.B. Laffer Associates

Table 4.11
Relationship between Monthly 10-Year Treasury Bond Yield and Monthly Excess Base Growth, 1970–88

Dependent Variable	Constant	Excess Base Growth	R2	SE	DW	F
Inflation	0.011	-15.625	0.034	0.447	1.74	6.38
Rate	(0.376)	(-2.526)				

A.B. Laffer Associates

raneous effect as opposed to the long-run effect. If adjustment is costly, the long-run impact of excess base growth will be larger than the short-run/instantaneous impact. The data are consistent with this interpretation.

The estimated relationship between base over M1 growth and interest rates is consistent with our view that over time the inflation rate increases and inflationary expectations are revised upward. Taken at face value, the monthly regression results suggest that 1 percent excess base growth results in a 15.62 basis point decline in the 10-year Treasury bond rate (Table 4.11).

Empirically, the quarterly regression fails to uncover a statistically significant relationship between excess base growth and changes in interest rates (Table 4.12). Although a seasonal pattern is evident in the data, the semiannual regressions suggest that, over longer intervals (i.e., six months), the excess base over M1 growth is associated with a rise in interest rates of approximately 25 basis points (Table 4.13). The annual regression result indicates that 1 percent excess base growth is associated with an increase of approximately 32 basis points in the 10-year Treasury bond rate (Table 4.14).

Part of the explanation for the decline in explanatory power as the frequency of the estimation interval increases is the quality and reliability of the data or the information they reveal, or both. Absent a preannounced and believable policy, markets must extract information regarding long-run policy from changes in short-run data. Market participants must develop a way of separating the true signal regarding the long-term behavior of the aggregate from the "noise" resulting from reversible month-to-month variations in the data.

If there were no "noise" in the system, the month to month changes in excess base growth would reflect long-term market trends, in which case, the variable would provide a perfect signal. On the other hand, if month to month variations were totally unrelated to and far larger than the long-term trend, the excess base growth would be all "noise" and would not provide a signal regarding the status of monetary policy. However, if at longer intervals, the random monthly fluctuations cancel out, then the longer the interval, the more the information provided

Table 4.12
Relationship between Quarterly Changes in the 10-Year Treasury Bond Yield and Quarterly Excess Base Growth, 1970–88*

Dependent Variable	Constant	Excess Base Growth	R2	SE	DW	F	Interval
Changes in 10-yr T-bond	0.018 (0.219)	3.366 (0.386)	-0.011	0.722	1.93	0.149	Jan to Jun Jul to Dec
Changes in 10-yr T-bond	0.036 (0.359)	-11.751 (-1.126)	0.004	0.867	2.09	1.27	Feb to Jul Aug to Jan
Changes in 10-yr T-bond	0.012 (0.120)	4.558 (0.410)	-0.011	0.892	2.21	0.168	Mar to Aug Sep to Feb

* The first quarterly series begins with the months of January, April, July, and October. For the second series, the quarter begins in February, May, August, and November. The third series's quarters start in March, June, September, and December.

A.B. Laffer Associates

Table 4.13

Relationship between Semiannual Changes in the 10-Year Treasury Bond Yield and Semiannual Excess Base Growth, 1970–88

Dependent Variable	Constant	Excess Base Growth	R2	SE	DW	F	Intervals
Changes in 10-yr T-bond	0.12 (0.09)	27.59 (2.25)	0.096	1.01	2.14	5.06	Jan to Jun / Jul to Dec
Changes in 10-yr T-bond	-0.0004 (-0.019)	35.13 (2.19)	0.091	1.15	2.24	4.80	Feb to Jul / Aug to Jan
Changes in 10-yr T-bond	-0.010 (-0.053)	30.75 (2.16)	0.088	1.17	2.00	4.66	Mar to Aug / Sep to Fev
Changes in 10-yr T-bond	0.053 (0.316)	4.61 (0.420)	-0.022	1.02	1.31	0.176	Apr to Sep / Oct to Mar
Changes in 10-yr T-bond	0.045 (0.255)	8.341 (0.739)	-0.012	1.08	2.04	0.547	May to Oct / Nov to Apr
Changes in 10-yr T-bond	-0.003 (-0.015)	27.87 (2.18)	0.090	1.12	2.05	4.75	Jun to Nov / Dec to May

A.B. Laffer Associates

regarding the status of monetary policy. A signal could be extracted from the behavior of excess base growth during the longer-term interval.

The results are consistent with the view that expectations of inflation and the price level will be little affected by monthly fluctuations in the excess growth of the base over M1 due to the "noise" in the series. However, at longer intervals, say quarterly, if the excess base growth persists, the "noise" is reduced and the "signal" is increased. Market participants then increase their assessment of excess money creation and revise their expectations of inflation and money holdings accordingly. The end result is a rise in inflation and interest rates.

If the trend continues, as the interval is further increased, say to six months, and the "signal" becomes clearer, the expectations are further revised and the impact of excess base growth on inflation and interest rates will also increase. If money is neutral and excess money creation is correctly measured, inflation will increase by the full amount of the excess money creation, in which case, a 1 percent increase in excess base growth will be associated with a 1 percent increase in the inflation rate.

The magnitude of the impact of excess base on the inflation rate includes and approaches the theoretically expected coefficient of a 1 percent excess base growth resulting in a 1 percent increase in the inflation rate. The smaller-than-one coefficient may be due to the noise in the data or to the fact that the excess base over M1 growth is only an approximate measure of excess money creation.

THE FORMATION OF EXPECTATIONS

The estimated coefficients between excess money growth and interest rates and inflation are interpreted in terms of how markets form inflationary expectations. Markets form their expectations, in part, on objective information. As additional information becomes available, those expectations are revised. In fact, this process occurs on virtually a continuous basis. Therefore, we have focused on ever shorter intervals of reported excess base growth in an attempt to measure just how expectations are formed.

The tests were carried out on annual changes in interest rates versus semiannual excess base growth, as well as quarterly changes in interest rates versus monthly excess base growth. By far the most informative results of how new information on the excess of base over M1 growth affects the level of interest rates occurred using inflation and interest rates on a quarterly basis and excess money growth on a monthly basis (Table 4.15). The result of note for the annual basis tests is that the sum of the coefficients turns out to be approximately equal to one hundred basis points. That means if excess base growth increases by 1 percent, in due course, prices will rise by almost exactly 1 percent.

The quarterly tests on both interest rates and inflation provide exceptional insight into the formation of expectations. In precise terms, *quarterly* changes in interest rates (inflation) were correlated with the *monthly* changes in excess base growth of all three months contained in the quarter.[14] In addition, monthly

Table 4.14

Relationship between Annual Changes in the 10-Year Treasury Bond Yield and Annual Excess Base Growth, 1970–88

Dependent Variable	Constant	Excess Base Growth	R2	SE	DW	F	Period
Changes in 10-yr T-bond	-0.013 (-0.041)	28.68 (1.903)	0.127	1.36	2.27	3.62	Jan
Changes in 10-yr T-bond	-0.070 (-0.194)	38.41 (2.110)	0.161	1.534	2.34	4.45	Feb
Changes in 10-yr T-bond	-0.079 (-0.209)	42.942 (2.256)	0.185	1.60	2.48	5.09	Mar
Changes in 10-yr T-bond	0.089 (0.206)	11.73 (0.675)	-0.031	1.86	2.357	0.456	Apr
Changes in 10-yr T-bond	0.060 (0.144)	17.946 (1.023)	0.003	1.776	2.528	1.046	May

Changes in 10-yr T-bond	-0.028 (-0.067)	32.664 (1.669)	0.090	1.82	2.53	2.784	Jun
Changes in 10-yr T-bond	-0.035 (-0.101)	35.494 (2.261)	1.186	1.455	2.270	5.112	Jul
Changes in 10-yr T-bond	-0.040 (-0.105)	38.81 (2.075)	0.155	1.615	2.337	4.307	Aug
Changes in 10-yr T-bond	-0.073 (-0.172)	34.719 (1.567)	0.075	1.809	2.463	2.454	Sep
Changes in 10-yr T-bond	-0.085 (-0.247)	37.724 (2.125)	0.163	1.459	2.544	4.516	Oct
Changes in 10-yr T-bond	-0.087 (-0.323)	41.676 (2.918)	0.294	1.138	1.818	8.512	Nov
Changes in 10-yr T-bond	-0.080 (-0.25)	35.445 (2.382)	0.206	1.369	2.283	5.673	Dec

A.B. Laffer Associates

Table 4.15
Relationship between Quarterly Changes in Treasury Bond Yields and the Month-by-Month Changes in Excess Base Growth

Dependent Variable	Constant	Month1	Month2	Month3	L2	L3	R2	SE	F
Quarterly* Changes in 10-Yr. T-Bond	-0.017 (-0.346)	14.83 (1.37)	52.77 (4.75)	41.10 (3.82)	--	--	0.190	0.745	18.38
Quarterly* Changes in 10-Yr. T-Bond	-0.005 (-0.109)	18.88 (1.72)	54.27 (4.92)	39.70 (3.69)	-21.16 (-1.97)	-14.96 (-1.36)	0.209	0.736	12.78

* For the specific dependent variable listed there are three overlapping quarterly series. The first quarterly series begins with the months of January, April, July, and October. For the second series, the quarter begins in February, May, August, and November. The third series's quarters start in March, June, September, and December. The three series were then "pooled" in chronological order according to the date at the beginning of their respective quarters. The end result is 12 overlapping quarterly changes in Treasury bond yields during any given year. To think of the dependent variable in another way to see the series intuitively is to describe it as a three-month moving total of the changes in 10-year T-bond yields.

** The variable M1 denotes the excess growth of the base over money during the first month in the quarter. For example, for the January-March quarter, Month 1 denotes the excess base over M1 growth during January. Month 2 denotes the excess base over M1 growth during February. Month 3 denotes the excess of base over M1 growth in March.

*** The variable L2 represents the excess of base over money of the second month in the previous quarter.

A.B. Laffer Associates

changes in excess base growth were also lagged one and two months behind the quarter in question.

Changes in excess base growth are closely correlated with changes in interest rates. Interest rates seem to pick up information when it first appears. Looking at excess base growth, the last month of the quarter appears to be the most significant statistically, dropping to close to zero for the coefficient of the first month in the quarter.

There is a large body of accepted wisdom that the initial impact of increasing base growth, the liquidity effect, would be to drive interest rates down. That could not be found. Interest rates rise, not fall, when excess base growth first is observed. A key point here is that we were unable to find any liquidity effect whatsoever. As soon as excess base growth appears, interest rates rise. In fact, they rise the most the instant the excess base growth is known.

CONTRASTING THE 1970S AND 1980S

The experiences of the last two decades demonstrate the importance of distinguishing between supply and demand shocks in the money markets. Whenever money supply growth exceeds money demand growth, money is too loose. Inflation will increase, interest rates will rise, and the dollar will weaken. In contrast, when money demand growth exceeds money supply growth, money is tight. Inflation will subside, interest rates will fall and the dollar will strengthen relation to foreign currencies.

Throughout the 1970s, the monetary base grew more rapidly than M1. Fed policy was too loose, and inflation and interest rates rose while the dollar declined against many foreign currencies (Figures 4.1, 4.4, and 4.13). During the 1980s, with the exception of 1983, M1 grew faster than the base. Fed policy was relatively tight resulting in a decline in inflation and interest rates and a strengthening of the dollar (Figures 4.1, 4.4, and 4.14).

THE MOVE TO FULLY DISCRETIONARY MONETARY POLICY

The breakdown of the Bretton Woods system and the closing of the gold window in 1971 removed the one remaining link that forced the U.S. monetary authorities to provide the amount of money that would equilibrate the money market at a constant price level. If the growth of the U.S. monetary base was excessive, the United States would suffer a balance of payments deficit. Foreign central bankers would accumulate dollars that could be converted into gold. By converting their international reserves into gold, foreign central banks could force the Fed to reduce the supply of dollars (i.e., the monetary base). During the 1960s, France, under the leadership of Charles de Gaulle, made frequent use of this provision of the system.[15]

After the gold window was shut by the United States in 1971, there no longer

Figure 4.14
Monetary Base Growth versus M1 Growth

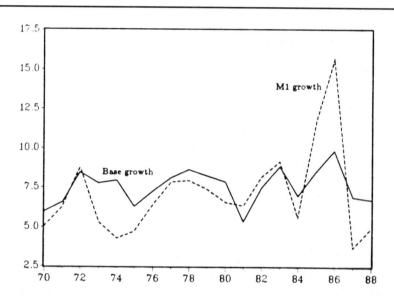

Source: Federal Reserve.

A.B. Laffer Associates

was a mechanism to force the U.S. monetary authorities to accommodate fluctuations in the demand for the monetary base. The United States moved to unconstrained, discretionary changes in the monetary base. In part to finance the Vietnam War, the growth of the monetary base accelerated, resulting in an outward shift of the supply of money. Simultaneously, the decline in real economic activity and the increased expectations of inflation resulted in an inward shift of the demand for money. The joint effect of these shifts in the demand for and supply of money was an excess supply of money. During the 1969–80 period, the monetary base grew faster than M1 in every year except 1972 (Figure 4.14). With the exception of 1972, inflation increased throughout this period.

THE MONETARIST EXPERIMENT

On October 6, 1979, the Federal Reserve began a policy of targeting monetary aggregates such as M1 and M2. Insofar as the Fed was successful in controlling the supply of money, fluctuations in demand resulted in fluctuations in the price level (Figure 4.7).

Since fluctuations in the demand for money are important in determining equilibrium in the money market, the Fed lacked the ability to control the quantities of monetary aggregates. As a result, attempts to target monetary aggregates resulted in increased volatility in both M1 growth and interest rates during 1980–81.[16]

AFTER MONETARISM

From 1981 to the time of Paul Volcker's resignation, the Fed de-emphasized targeting the growth rate of money. Instead, it monitored various indicators of economic activity and inflation, including sensitive commodity prices. The decline in interest rates, the rise in equity values, and the fall in the relative price of gold in the wake of this policy change were remarkable. The economy in 1983 and 1984 posted the strongest expansion since 1951. Yet, contrary to the forecasts of most leading economists, this surge in real economic growth was accompanied by lower inflation and falling interest rates (Figure 4.3).

While money growth during the Reagan administration was high by historical standards, the rate of growth of the monetary base was generally less than the growth rate of the money supply. This means that the Fed released money into the economy in response to growth in the demand for money. Since 1987, however, base growth has exceeded M1 growth. This suggests that the Fed has been creating money in excess of growth in the demand for money (Figure 4.14).

During October 1987, unfortunate events occurred. Apparently, our trading partners grew weary of supporting the dollar and inflating along with the United States. As a result, they abandoned their dollar support operations. Treasury Secretary James Baker, upset by this development, threatened to let the dollar fall against major currencies. This threat signaled the willingness of the United States to inflate and to undertake beggar-thy-neighbor policies to improve its perceived trade problems. Panic selling in world equity markets followed. The crisis led to a flight out of stocks and into bonds and to a surge in money demand.[17]

The surge in money demand led to a decline in interest rates and a temporary shortage of reserves. The Fed acted promptly to provide reserves to the financial system. However, as market participants regained confidence and returned to the stock market, the demand for money declined. At that point, the Fed should have pulled reserves out of the banking system. It did not, and the excess supply of money resulted in increased expectations of inflation and in rising interest rates.

CONCLUSIONS

The evidence that inflation and higher interest rates are the products of excess money growth supports the position that the role of monetary policy should be to provide stable prices. Price stability is achieved whenever shifts in the supply of money equal shifts in the demand for money. Monetary policy conducted in accordance with a price rule will insure that the supply of money automatically accommodates shifts in the demand for money.

A commitment to use monetary policy solely for the purpose of stabilizing prices, and not to finance government expenditures, provides the basis for a successful and sustainable monetary system that would insure price stability for years to come. If the purchasing power of the dollar literally was assured indefinitely, nearly everyone would hold dollars rather than gold or some other inflation hedge. Likewise, if interest rates were low due to the reduction of inflationary anticipations, far wider use of dollar money balances would occur. The use of foreign currencies to support international transactions or simply as stores of value also would diminish. A successful monetary policy would expand the demand for money and necessitate an increase in the dollar money supply.

Adoption of a price rule will result in an inflation rate of approximately zero. A price rule will also reduce volatility in the price level and in interest rates. The lower volatility of interest rates will reduce required risk premia and thereby lower longer term interest rates. The reduction in long-term rates will increase real economic activity. Thus, adoption of a price rule would ultimately lead to higher U.S. equity values.

APPENDIX A

A Classical Model

The model can be described in simplest form in terms of the following two equations:

$$EM^s = EB + \epsilon^s \pi \tag{1}$$

and

$$EM^d = ED - \epsilon^d \pi \tag{2}$$

where

$E =$ the dlog operator
$M^s =$ the money supply function
$B =$ the monetary base
$\pi =$ the inflation rate
$D =$ the real variable affecting the level of demand (i.e., income effects)
$\epsilon^s =$ the elasticity of the money supply with respect to the inflation rate
$\epsilon^d =$ the elasticity of the money demand with respect to the inflation rate

The first equation describes the money supply process. It postulates that the growth in the supply of money is the product of two variables: exogenous shifts in the monetary base (*EB*) and changes in the money multiplier in response to changes in expected inflation ($\epsilon^\tau \pi$). The latter relationship is assumed to be positive.

The second equation describes the demand for money. It postulates that the growth in the demand for money is the product of two factors: scale or income effects (i.e., demand shifts), and changes in the nominal demand for money in response to changes in anticipated inflation.

Money Market Equilibrium

Combining equations 1 and 2, one can easily solve for the equilibrium inflation rate:

$$\pi = \frac{EB - ED}{\epsilon^s + \epsilon^d} \tag{3}$$

The expression for equilibrium inflation rate yields the following propositions:

Proposition 1: *Increases in the growth rate of the monetary base will result in increases in the inflation rate.*

Proposition 2: *Increases in the growth rate of real income (i.e., money demand) will result in a lower inflation rate.*

The Equilibrium Quantity of Money

Substituting the equilibrium inflation rate (equation 3) into the money supply function (equation 2), one can solve for the equilibrium supply of money:

$$EM = (1+\alpha)\ EB - \alpha\ ED \tag{4}$$

where

$$\alpha = \frac{\epsilon^s}{\epsilon^s + \epsilon^d} \tag{5}$$

Equations 4 and 5 can be used to establish a number of propositions:

Proposition 3: *The equilibrium quantity of money is a weighted average of supply shocks (the EB term) and demand shocks (the ED term).*

Proposition 4: *The contributions (i.e., weights) of demand and supply shifts depend on the magnitude of demand and supply elasticities (i.e., the slope of the demand and supply curves).*

If the demand for money is perfectly elastic ($\epsilon^d = \infty$), then the expression for the equilibrium inflation rate (equation 3) and equilibrium quantity of money (equations 4, 5) simplify to:

$$E\pi = 0 \tag{3'}$$

In which case, the monetary authority will have no influence on the price level.

The equilibrium quantity of money equation will simplify to:

$$EM = EB \tag{4'}$$

$$\alpha = 0 \tag{5'}$$

The quantity of narrowly-defined money (M1) will be supply determined.

Proposition 5: *If the demand for money is perfectly elastic, the monetary authorities have no power to change the price level. In this case, changes in the quantity of money are due to changes in supply conditions.*

If the supply of money is perfectly elastic ($\epsilon^s = 0$), then the expression for the equilibrium inflation and quantity of money simplify to:

$$p = \frac{EB - ED}{\epsilon\delta} \qquad (3'')$$

$$EM = EB \qquad (4'')$$

$$\alpha = 0 \qquad (5'')$$

Traditional analysis assumes that the Fed maintains strict control of the monetary base: the reserve deposits of depository institutions held by Federal Reserve Banks plus currency in circulation. Because of its power to set minimum reserve requirements, textbooks also maintain that the Fed controls what is known as the "money multiplier," that is, the ratio of the quantity of money to the monetary base.

If the money supply is perfectly elastic ($\epsilon^s = \infty$), then the expression for the equilibrium quantity of money and inflation rates simplifies to:

$$\pi = 0 \qquad (3''')$$

$$EM = ED \qquad (4''')$$

$$\alpha = 1 \qquad (5''')$$

Proposition 6: *If the money supply is perfectly inelastic and invariant to changes in market conditions, shifts in demand cause changes in the price level, but the quantity of money remains constant. The quantity of money would then be demand-determined, and the price level would remain constant.*

The Relation between Excess Base Growth and Inflation

An expression for excess base growth is easily obtained by substituting the equilibrium quantity of money from base growth:

$$EB - EM = -\alpha (EB - ED) \qquad (6)$$

Proposition 7: *Excess base money is proportional to the excess money supply.*

After some manipulation, the previous equation may be written as:

$$EB - EM = \epsilon^s\pi \qquad (7)$$

Proposition 8: *Excess base growth will capture the net of the supply and demand shifts (i.e., the excess money supply) that must be eliminated through changes in the price of money in terms of goods (i.e., the inflation rate).*

Proposition 9: *In the context of a regression analysis, the coefficient for the inflation rate will be an estimate of the elasticity of the money supply with respect to the inflation rate.*

APPENDIX B

Short-Run versus Long-Run Correlation between Inflation and M1 Growth

The empirical results identify a negative relationship going from inflation to M1 growth. This result is at odds with received monetary theory. However, part of the explanation lies in the fact that the negative relationship identified empirically is a short-run relationship induced by substitution effects. In turn, the positive relationship between M1 growth and inflation postulated by monetarist models is a long-run relationship developed from macroeconomic models. Therefore, the apparent differences are not necessarily inconsistent with each other. While the long-run relationship between M1 growth and inflation may be a positive one, over the short run, substitution effects and other money demand shocks could induce a negative correlation. An empirical analysis that does not account for the possibility may dismiss the short-run relationship because it does not conform to the a priori long-run implications of the theoretical model. In doing so, the analyst may be excluding useful information from the analysis.

However, the fact that the negative correlation is the result of short-run relationships that may be different than the long-run relationship will make difficult the interpretation of the reduced form coefficients regarding the impact of lagged values of base and money growth and inflation reported in Table 4.4.

One possible way to disentangle the effects would be to, following Sims, estimate a larger form model, such as the one reported in Appendix A, using vector autoregression analysis. The estimated equation can then be used to analyze the many interactions between the different variables.[18] This is done by simulating the system where each of the variables is shocked, and then one traces out from the shock how the shock is propagated through the system. Following Geweke, one can construct measures of feedback of forecasted inflation rate and money growth generated by the series of shocks to each of the policy variables.[19] The Geweke measures of association can be used to examine the association for the entire series and for the series decomposed into different frequencies. These are time-dimensional measures of correlation. The magnitude of the measure, which is always non-negative due to squaring in computations is akin to Granger's strength of causality measure. The Geweke measures can be used for analyzing the entire time series and for the frequency domain component of the series. Associating high frequencies with the short-run and low frequencies with the long run, one can investigate the relationship among different economic series.

This approach has been used successfully in the past to examine the short- and long-run relationship between interest rates and inflation. The analysis uncovered a negative short-run relationship between interest rates and inflation and a positive long-run relationship between interest rates and inflation (i.e., the Fisher equation).[20]

NOTES

1. For a more detailed explanation of our view on the relationship between interest rates, inflation, and the foreign exchange value of the dollar see Arthur B. Laffer, "How Quickly We Forget: Must the Mistakes of the '70s Be Repeated?" A. B. Laffer Associates, November 20, 1987.

2. On this issue see Victor A. Canto and Arthur B. Laffer, "And Paul Volcker Smiles," A. B. Laffer Associates, October 30, 1987; and Victor A. Canto and Arthur B. Laffer, "Excess Base Growth and Interest Rates," A. B. Laffer Associates, February 25, 1988.

3. See Arthur B. Laffer, "The Phillip's Buster Filibuster," A. B. Laffer Associates, August 4, 1988.

4. Canto and Laffer, "And Paul Volcker Smiles"; Canto and Laffer, "Excess Base Growth and Interest Rates."

5. Laffer, "How Quickly We Forget."

6. Arthur B. Laffer and J. Richard Zecher, "Some Evidence of the Formation, Efficiency and Accuracy of Anticipations of Nominal Yields," *Journal of Monetary Economics* 1, no. 3 (July 1975); Arthur B. Laffer and R. David Ranson, "Some Practical Applications of the Efficient-Market Concept," *Financial Management* 7, no. 2 (1978), pp. 63–75; Victor A. Canto and Arthur B. Laffer, "The Measurement of Expectations in an Efficient Market," in *Expectations and the Economy: Hearings before the Joint Economic Committee, Congress of the United States* (Washington, D.C.: U.S. Government Printing Office, December 11, 1981), pp. 70–93.

7. A formal description of the relationship between money growth and inflation, base growth and inflation, and excess base growth and inflation is presented in Appendix A.

8. On these issues see "Trade Credit and Other Forms of Inside Money," ed. Ronald I. McKinnon, presented at the Stanford Conference honoring Edward Shaw, April 1974; Arthur B. Laffer, "Trade Credit and the Money Market," *Journal of Political Economy*, March–April 1970; Arthur B. Laffer, "Substitution of Monies in Demand: The Theory and Cases of Mexico, Chile, and Brazil," presented at the *International Monetary Conference*, Santiago, Chile, March 18, 1977.

9. For an example of how legal tender and monetary controls affect monetary equilibrium see Victor A. Canto and Gerald Nickelsburg, "Currency Crisis and Exchange Rate Instability," in *Dynamic Modeling and Control of National Economies*, ed. T. Basar and L. F. Pau (Elmsford, N.Y.: Pergamon Press, 1984), pp. 7–18; Victor A. Canto, "Monetary Policy 'Dollarization' and Parallel Market Exchange Rates: The Case of the Dominican Republic," *Journal of International Money and Finance* 4, no. 4 (December 1985), pp. 507–22.

10. While the Federal Reserve can affect the money multiplier by altering reserve requirements, this power is rarely exercised.

11. Victor A. Canto, M. Chapman Findlay, and Marc R. Reinganum, "Inflation, Money and Stock Prices: An Alternative Interpretation," *Financial Review* 20, No. 1 (February 1985), pp. 95–105.

12. See the description in Appendix B.

13. C. W. J. Granger, "Investigating Causal Relations of Econometric Models and Cross Spectral Methods, *Econometrica,* July 1969, pp. 424–38.

14. The results reported in the text are for the "pooled" quarterly series which consists of a three-month moving total of the changes in 10-year T-bond yields.

15. Arthur B. Laffer, "Monetary Policy and the Balance of Payments," *Journal of Money, Credit and Banking,* February 1972; Arthur B. Laffer, "The United States Balance of Payments—A Financial Center View," *Journal of Law and Contemporary Problems,* August 1969.

16. See Paul D. Evans, "What Monetarism Has Done to Us," A. B. Laffer Associates, February 3, 1984.

17. Victor A. Canto and Arthur B. Laffer, "Monetary Policy Caused the Crash," *Wall Street Journal,* October 22, 1987, p. 35.

18. Christopher Sims, "Macroeconomics and Reality," *Econometrica,* January 1980, pp. 1–35.

19. John Geweke, "Measures of Linear Dependence and Feedback Between Multiple Time Series," *Journal of the American Statistical Association,* June 1982, pp. 304–13.

20. Victor A. Canto, Paul Rizos, and Gerald Nickelsburg, "The Effect of Fiscal Policy on the Short-Run Relation Between Nominal Interest Rates and Inflation," *Economic Inquiry* 25, no. 1 (January 1987), pp. 27–43.

5

The Quality of Inflation Indicators: Part III

Victor A. Canto and Arthur B. Laffer

A key element in any portfolio strategy is the anticipation of changes in interest rates and inflation rates. Also crucial is the development of a framework which will anticipate changes in key monetary indicators and market expectations, and will determine their potential impact on interest rates and inflation.

The most important development from the efficient market/rational expectations debate is a consensus that market data reflect expectations as to what will occur in the future.[1] This is not to say that what the market expects to occur *will* occur, only that current market data contain a forecast of the future. A direct implication of this analysis is that financial prices such as interest rates, the slope of the yield curve, gold prices, the foreign exchange value of the dollar, and stock price indices may collectively contain the market's implicit forecast of the future path of interest and inflation rates. Policy variables under the influence of the monetary authorities may also affect the economy's inflation rate and the market's expectations about the future.

Through careful analysis of market data and the policy variables, the asset managers can develop insights as to what the market collectively anticipates. In this way they can utilize the collective wisdom of the markets to see events more clearly and to differentiate their own views from the views of the market.

NATURE OF INFORMATION CONTAINED
IN FINANCIAL PRICES

More often than not, a rise in the price of gold, a declining dollar, and a rise in interest rates are harbingers of mounting inflationary pressures. However, these variables can also change for reasons other than changes in expected inflation. When gold prices, the foreign exchange value of the dollar, and interest rates move in different directions, they yield conflicting signals about the inflation outlook. The resolution of such conflicting signals is a major challenge. The problem faced by most managers is that prices reflect joint information regarding inflation and real effects.

Interest Rates

Interest rates contain a forecast of the market's expectations of the inflation and real interest rates during the maturity of the instruments. In the past we have argued that changes in tax rates result in changes in real rates. Thus, during periods of tax rate changes, the accuracy of interest rates as predictors of inflation is likely to decline. The U.S. experience during the 1970s and 1980s is consistent with our view. During the 1970s when there were no abrupt and dramatic personal income tax rate changes, interest rates were very good indicators of inflation.[2] During the Reagan tax cut years, the accuracy declined. Directionally, however, interest rates still reflected the trend in inflation.

Slope of the Yield Curve

The slope of the yield curve has been suggested as a possible harbinger of inflation. The presumption is that a rise in the slope of the yield curve is a reflection of rising inflationary expectations. Symmetrically, a decline in the slope of the yield curve reflects a decline in inflationary expectations. This interpretation ignores the fact that a rise in future real rates relative to current real rates could also result in an increase in the slope of the yield curve. Conversely, a decline in future real rates could result in a decline in the slope of the yield curve. Therefore, during periods of abrupt fluctuations in future real rates relative to present real rates, the slope of the yield curve may not provide a clear inflationary signal.[3]

Exchange Rate Changes

While changes in the foreign exchange value of the dollar may reflect changes in the U.S. inflation rate vis-à-vis its trading partners, they are not the only cause of exchange rate fluctuations: Changes in the terms of trade can also cause changes in the exchange rate without any change in the relative inflation rate.

The terms of trade change reflect the real rate of return of U.S.-located assets relative to the rest of the world. The U.S. experience during the 1969–80 period is consistent with this interpretation.

Gold and Oil

Throughout the years, precious metals and, more recently, oil, have been used as inflation indicators.[4] However, in order to accurately use these commodities as a proxy for inflation, one must determine the appropriate base price. Increases or decreases around the base level may reflect changes in inflationary expectations, technological changes, or regulatory and tax rate changes altering the real return, and hence the base price, of the commodity in question.[5] Tax rate reductions and changes in the real rate will clearly affect the return, and hence the attractiveness, of gold as an inflation hedge.

Stock Market

In an efficient market, the value of an asset approximates the discounted present value of expected cash flows. Stock prices reflect the market's forecast of net after-tax corporate profits accruing to current shares in the future.[6]

The after-tax corporate profit forecasts by the marketplace are of true economic profits and not necessarily profits reported by accountants. For example, the relevant depreciation figure is based on the market value of a company's plant and equipment rather than on historical cost. In other words, it is expensed in terms of today's dollars. The relevant figure for cost of goods is likewise evaluated at replacement or market price and not historical cost.

In times of high inflation, accounting conventions use historical cost for depreciation to overstate economic profit substantially, thereby resulting in excessive taxation of true economic profits. Therefore, rising inflation rates will have a negative impact on stock prices.

INFLATION FORECAST AND MARKET PRICES

The three-month T-bill contains a short-term forecast (Table 5.1). The stock market contains a short- and long-term forecast. The slope of the yield curve contains a forecast of short-term versus long-term inflation expectations. The foreign exchange value of the dollar contains information regarding U.S. inflation relative to the rest of the world. Collectively, these price variables contain information regarding the path of inflation expectations. In addition, each of the variables contains information regarding real effects. Thus, the problem faced by the asset manager is how to extract the relevant inflation information from the price indexes.

Table 5.1
Nature of Inflation and Real Rate Information Contained in Financial Data

	Nominal Effects	Real Effects
Interest rates	Short term inflation	Short term real rate
Slope of the yield curve	Difference in current versus future inflation	Differences in current versus future real rate
Exchange rate	Current inflation relative to foreign	Current real return versus foreign
Stock market	Short and long term real rates	Short and long term inflation

EXPECTATION-INDUCED INTERRELATION AMONG THE VARIABLES

A preannounced increase in the monetary base is likely to simultaneously result in an upward revision of inflation expectations, interest rates, and gold prices, and in a depreciation of the dollar. These, in turn, through their effect on bracket creep, may affect stock prices. Similarly, a tax rate cut will result in lower inflation, lower interest rates, lower gold prices, a stronger dollar, and a higher stock market. In short, it is fairly clear that policy changes will induce a multitude of interconnections in the movements of the financial variables. Therefore, interpreting the movement and the interrelationship among the variables may yield an accurate forecast of the path of financial variables several periods into the future.

POLICY-INDUCED INTERRELATION AMONG THE VARIABLES

Federal Reserve Governor Johnson has argued that dollar depreciation, a rise in the slope of the yield curve, and a rise in gold prices are indications of inflationary pressure. Under these circumstances, a slowdown of the monetary aggregate may be appropriate. However, Governor Johnson has never specified which component of the aggregates should be reduced. Federal Reserve Governor Wayne Angell advocates adjusting M1 growth in response to fluctuations in commodity prices. Finally, Fed Chairman Alan Greenspan has stated a belief both in the Phillips' curve (i.e., strong growth may increase inflationary pressures), as well as the monetarist view.[7] If the Keynesian view dominates, with rising capacity utilization and strong economic growth, the likely policy response would be an attempt to reduce M1 growth. However, if the monetarist view dominates, higher real growth will result in higher monetary growth.

To the extent that Johnson, Angell, or Greenspan influences monetary policy, the monetary base will respond to changing "inflationary" indicators. Over the longer term, inflation indicators will influence monetary policy and vice versa. The policy response will depend on which of the views expressed by the governors dominates monetary policy, although one cannot establish, with certainty, the true operating model. The relationship between inflation and the monetary aggregate may be estimated empirically.

THE EMPIRICAL LINKAGES AMONG THE VARIABLES

The empirical approach followed in this study initially includes all of the above-mentioned variables. The final analysis excludes those that do not contribute to the forecasting nor to the explanation of the behavior of interest rates and inflation. However, care must be used in the empirical specification so that possible channels of influence or interconnections among the different variables are not excluded from the analysis. Vector autoregression (VAR) has proven a successful technique for forecasting systems of interrelated time series variables. Vector autoregression is also frequently used, although with considerable controversy, for analyzing the dynamic impact on system variables of different types of random disturbances and controls.

A vector autoregression is a system of equations that makes each endogenous variable a function of its own past and the past of other endogenous variables in the system. A detailed description of the empirical analysis is reported in Appendix A. We have devised a very compact way to illustrate the various channels of influence. Three types of relationship are identified:

- A one-way causal relationship. For example, the effect of the foreign exchange value of the dollar on the inflation rate is denoted by an arrow.
- A two-way causal relationship. A feedback relationship is uncovered. That is, past values of inflation help predict the three-month T-bill and vice versa. This is denoted by the arrows with two heads.
- An absence of a causal relationship. In this case, no arrow is drawn.

Figure 5.1 reports the empirically identified channels of influence. The diagram identifies many familiar linkages.

- The stock market is useful for forecasting interest rates.[8]
- The foreign exchange value of the dollar is useful in forecasting inflation and interest rates.[9]
- Interest rates are useful in forecasting the inflation rate and vice versa.[10]

Figure 5.1
Channels of Influence among Financial Variables

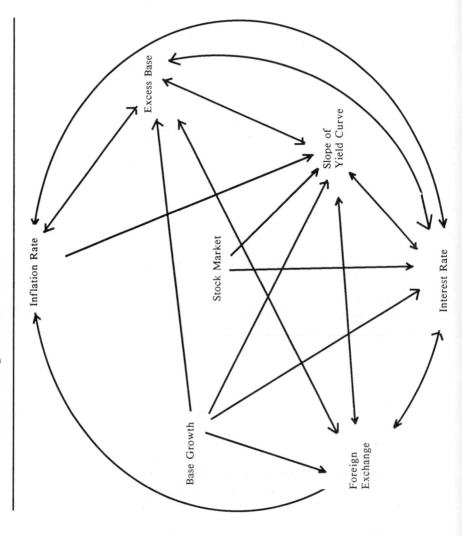

Figure 5.2
Quarterly Percent Change at Annual Rates in the Consumer Price Index, Actual versus Forecast

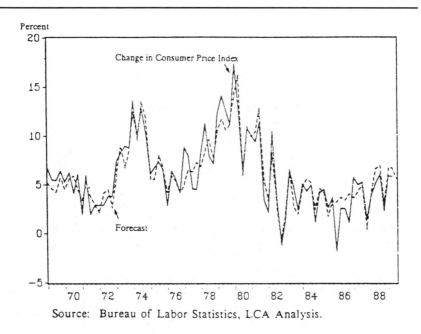

Source: Bureau of Labor Statistics, LCA Analysis.

Figure 5.3
Quarterly Changes in the Three-Month T-Bill, Actual versus Forecast

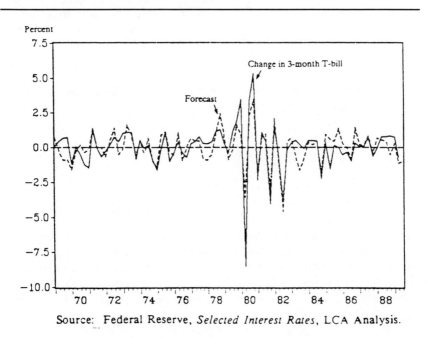

Source: Federal Reserve, *Selected Interest Rates*, LCA Analysis.

- While not useful in predicting future inflation, the slope of the yield curve is useful in predicting changes in interest rates.
- Commodity prices (i.e., gold and oil) do not appear to contribute any additional information to that contained in the other variables included in the analysis.
- Base growth is useful in forecasting interest rates.
- Excess base growth is useful in forecasting interest rates and inflation, and vice versa.

THE ONE-QUARTER-AHEAD FORECAST: THE SHORT RUN

The result of a model that combines financial prices, base growth, and excess base growth does quite well in explaining the inflation rate and changes in the three-month T-bill (Figures 5.2 and 5.3). Given that the empirical specification of the model uses only quarterly values of financial prices and that monetary aggregates lagged from one to five quarters, the estimated equation may be used to forecast one step ahead (i.e., one quarter) changes in interest rates and inflation. For the sample considered, the model correctly forecasts the direction of change in interest rates approximately 75 percent of the time. The projections for 1989 are equally encouraging.[11]

During the first quarter of 1989, the three-month T-bill rose 75 basis points. The model projected a 30 basis point rise. In the second quarter the model projected a 116 basis point decline. The three-month T-bill declined 67 basis points. For the third quarter, the model projects a 96 basis point decline. As of September 1, the three-month T-bill had declined 29 basis points.

The inflation forecasts are just as encouraging. During the first and second quarters, the model projected a 5.7 percent inflation rate which was close to the realized inflation rate. For the third quarter the model projects a decline in the inflation rate to 4.5 percent.

APPENDIX A

The formulation of the empirical analysis assumes that expectations regarding the different endogenous variables are formed rationally in the sense that, given the current available information, participants in each market use the structure of the economy to form optimal forecasts. Furthermore, actions based on these forecasts do, in fact, generate the economic structure. Our approach to estimating the relationship is to estimate a vector autoregression model of the series in question. The vector autoregression technique is based on the work of Sims and consists of a system of equations, one for each of the variables included in the analysis.[12]

Each of the equations contains the same set of explanatory variables. Originally, the empirical investigation included real GNP growth, the budget deficit as a percent of GNP, the three-month T-bill, the slope of the yield curve, the inflation rate, the foreign exchange value of the dollar, the S&P 500, the price of oil, the price of gold, M1, and base and excess base growth. Variables that did not contribute to the forecast or the explanation were excluded from the analysis. These variables were real GNP growth, the deficit as a percent of GNP, M1 growth, and oil and gold prices.

Another issue was the lag length of the variables used in the regression analysis. Initially, we estimated the model with six quarterly lags and gradually reduced the length. If no loss of information occurred, the lag length was reduced by one quarter. The result of this procedure yielded an optimal lag length of five quarters.

The final model included an explanatory variable for each of the equation's five lags of each of the following variables: base growth, excess base growth, changes in the three-month T-bill, changes in the slope of the yield curve, percent change in the S&P 500, and the percent change in the foreign exchange value of the dollar. The estimated equations are available on request.

The Long-Run Interrelationship among the Variables

The estimated coefficients of a vector autoregression are difficult to interpret. As a result, one commonly looks at the impulse response function and variance decomposition of the system to draw implications about a vector autoregression. An impulse response function traces the response of the endogenous variables in the system to shocks in the innovation. The estimated relationships are useful in understanding not only the short-run effects of unanticipated changes in any of the variables but also the long-run dynamic responses and interrelationships.

One possible way to ascertain how much one of the variables affects the others is to decompose and allocate the variance of the variable in question into the fraction attributable or explained by the remaining variables. By construction, the sum fraction of the variance explained has to add to 100 percent. Therefore, the variable decomposition may be quite sensitive to the variables included. If the variables included (e.g., S&P 500) are unrelated to (i.e., do not influence) the variables that one is trying to explain (e.g., inflation), then the bulk of the variations in inflation may be explained by inflation itself. If no variable explains inflation, then inflation is said to be an exogenous variable. In turn, if a variable (e.g., interest rates) explains a large fraction of inflation (i.e., 80 percent), then inflation is said to be an endogenous variable. Variable decomposition analysis can clearly be used to identify the most endogenous variables, in other words, those variables whose variance is largely explained by other variables.

The fact that a large fraction of the variance is explained by its own behavior may be the result of one of two possibilities. First, the variable may be truly exogenous. Second, other variables not included in the analysis may cause fluctuations in the variance in question. The results of the variance decomposition are reported in Tables 5A.1 through 5A.7. The analysis is as follows: Initially, when a disturbance or unanticipated change in a variable (e.g., the inflation rate) occurs, 100 percent of the variation in the variable will be due to the disturbance (Table 5A.1, column 6, row 1). Over time, the shock will propagate through the system. For example, after four steps, only 44.83 percent of the variation in the inflation rate is due to its own innovation or unanticipated shock (Table 5A.1, column 6, row 2). This clearly suggests that, over the long run, the inflation rate is not truly exogenous.

Innovations in the value of the dollar, the stock market, base growth, and excess base growth have little or no effect on the inflation rate. In contrast, innovations in the T-bill and the slope of the yield curve are quickly reflected in the inflation rate. After four periods, the two variables account for better than 20 percent of the variance of monetary base growth. However, over time, say after 32 quarters, together the two variables account for more than 50 percent of the variation in base growth.

The variance decomposition for the remaining variables tells a similar story. With the exception of the S&P 500, the innovations in interest rates and the slope of the yield curve account for better than 50 percent of the variation in the variables. In the case of the S&P 500, the percentage drops to 40 percent, a significant amount.[13] The empirical results support Federal Reserve Board Governor Manuel Johnson's proposition that the foreign exchange value of the dollar and the slope of the yield curve contain information regarding inflationary expectations. The results are also consistent with the view that, in addition to the financial prices, the monetary base and excess base growth contribute additional information useful in forecasting the inflation rate and interest rates. Taken together, the results suggest that the policy variables under control of the monetary authorities (i.e., the monetary base) are adjusted in response to changing inflation and interest rates. Over the longer term, the key variable appears to be interest rates.

Table 5.A1
Variance Decomposition Analysis for Changes in the Inflation Rate

Step	Base* Growth	Foreign* Exchange Value of $	S&P* 500	3-Month** T-Bill	Slope**	Inflation*	Excess* Base Growth
1	0	0	0	0	0	100	0
4	13.59	7.07	7.24	8.72	7.79	44.83	5.76
12	8.93	12.52	3.79	32.52	14.71	23.39	4.13
32	8.17	11.64	2.86	35.30	17.53	20.53	3.93

*   Percent change in variable.
**   Percentage-point change in variable

Table 5.A2
Variance Decomposition Analysis for Changes in the Three-Month T-Bill

Step	Base* Growth	Foreign* Exchange Value of $	S&P* 500	3-Month** T-Bill	Slope**	Inflation*	Excess* Base Growth
1	0	0	0	100	0	0	0
4	5.10	2.99	8.17	52.88	12.87	13.19	5.18
12	6.44	3.40	8.93	42.26	17.22	15.60	6.12
32	6.45	4.29	7.65	41.56	18.19	15.61	6.25

Table 5.A3
Variance Decomposition Analysis for Percent Changes in the Foreign Exchange Value of the Dollar

Step	Base* Growth	Foreign* Exchange Value of $	S&P* 500	3-Month** T-Bill	Slope**	Inflation*	Excess* Base Growth
1	0	100	0	0	0	0	0
4	2.22	75.69	5.08	3.98	0.72	3.74	8.57
12	7.58	32.05	4.68	22.42	23.13	4.67	5.45
32	7.35	26.74	4.16	27.23	22.03	7.55	4.80

Table 5.A4
Variance Decomposition Analysis for Percent Changes in the S&P 500

Step	Base* Growth	Foreign* Exchange Value of $	S&P* 500	3-Month** T-Bill	Slope**	Inflation*	Excess* Base Growth
1	0	0	100	0	0	0	0
4	2.59	0.78	57.37	24.19	11.59	1.66	1.81
12	5.99	5.82	41.89	25.64	14.29	2.88	3.49
32	8.36	5.98	37.14	26.28	14.40	4.20	3.64

*   Percent change in variable.
**   Percentage-point change in variable

Table 5.A5
Variance Decomposition Analysis for Changes in the Slope of the Yield Curve

Step	Base* Growth	Foreign* Exchange Value of $	S&P* 500	3-Month** T-Bill	Slope**	Inflation*	Excess* Base Growth
1	0	0	0	0	100	0	0
4	5.90	7.14	4.12	6.80	58.61	14.23	3.18
12	4.72	4.65	4.59	24.19	40.15	16.72	4.98
32	5.58	5.34	4.35	26.10	36.62	16.62	5.38

Table 5.A6
Variance Decomposition Analysis for Changes in Base Growth

Step	Base* Growth	Foreign* Exchange Value of $	S&P* 500	3-Month** T-Bill	Slope**	Inflation*	Excess* Base Growth
1	100	0	0	0	0	0	0
4	38.99	1.06	2.82	27.73	27.62	1.27	0.48
12	30.75	3.62	4.59	29.24	27.51	2.45	1.82
32	26.94	4.08	4.27	31.92	26.35	4.50	1.95

Table 5.A7
Variance Decomposition Analysis for Changes in Excess Base Growth

Step	Base* Growth	Foreign* Exchange Value of $	S&P* 500	3-Month** T-Bill	Slope**	Inflation*	Excess* Base Growth
1	100	0	0	0	0	0	0
4	0.85	2.11	1.42	46.14	30.65	5.76	13.06
12	3.44	2.90	1.54	45.33	25.90	10.46	10.36
32	3.97	3.82	1.76	44.57	24.94	11.62	9.32

*   Percent change in variable.
** Percentage-point change in variable

NOTES

1. A sequence of developments referred to as rational expectations was evolving at the same time at the same universities as efficient markets. While the focus of the two was slightly different, on a conceptual level they were virtually identical. See, for example, J. F. Muth, "Rational Expectations and the Theory of Price Movements," *Econometrica* 29 (July 1961), pp. 315–35; and R. E. Lucas, "An Equilibrium Model of the Business Cycle," *Journal of Political Economy* 83, no. 6, pp. 1113–44; R. E. Lucas, "Expectations and Neutrality of Money," *Journal of Economic Theory* 4 (April 1972), pp. 103–24; T. J. Sargent, "Rational Expectations, the Real Rate of Interest and the Natural Rate of Unemployment," *Brookings Paper of Economic Activity* 2 (1973); R. J. Barro, "Rational Expectations and the Role of Monetary Policy," *Journal of Monetary Economics* 2 (January 1976), pp. 1–32.

2. The inflation rate pushed people into higher tax brackets. This bracket creep had secondary effects which reduced the real rate and increased the inflation rate, thereby inducing a negative relationship between inflation and real rates. See Victor A. Canto, Douglas H. Joines, and Robert I. Webb, "Taxation, Rational Expectations, and the Neutrality of Money," *Journal of Macroeconomics* 6, no. 1 (Winter 1984), pp. 69–78; Victor A. Canto and Arthur B. Laffer, "The Measurement of Expectations in an Efficient Market," in *Expectations and the Economy: Hearings before the Joint Economic Committee, Congress of the United States* (Washington, D.C.: U.S. Government Printing Office, (December 11, 1981), pp. 70–93.

3. See Chapter 6.

4. James C. Turney, "Gold," A. B. Laffer Associates, January 25, 1980.

5. For an analysis of the impact of oil decontrol on oil prices, see Gerald Bollman, Victor A. Canto, and Kevin Melich, "Oil Decontrol, the Power of Incentives," A. B. Laffer Associates, June 12, 1981; Victor A. Canto and Charles W. Kadlec, "The Shape of Energy Markets to Come," A. B. Laffer Associates, October 4, 1985.

6. Arthur B. Laffer and R. David Ranson, "Inflation, Taxes and Equity Values," H. C. Wainwright & Co., September 20, 1979.

7. A widely accepted proposition in macroeconomic analysis associated with the Keynesian framework is that a sustained increase in overall economic activity eventually strains capacity and leads to higher prices. This is nothing more than the Phillips' curve. Conversely, a decline in capacity utilization (i.e., an economic slowdown) is viewed as relieving inflationary pressures in the economy. The empirical implications of this view are quite clear: Increases in capacity utilization or real GNP growth (or both) will result in higher prices; decreases in capacity utilization or lower real GNP growth will result in lower prices.[14]

An alternative proposition defines inflation as too much money chasing too few goods. Thus, the alternative proposition postulates a negative relation between real GNP and inflation. The monetary view of the world postulates inflation as an excess supply of money. An empirical implementation of this view requires a proxy for excess money supply. Several possible alternatives are clearly evident. In past research we have argued that the monetary base is under the complete control of the Fed. Therefore, increases in the monetary base may be rightfully interpreted as shifts in the supply of money; hence, increases in the growth of the monetary base will be associated with increases in the inflation rate. To illustrate, if the Fed were to have a preannounced policy of expanding the monetary base at, say, 50 percent per annum for the next decade, interest rates and inflation would rise and the dollar would collapse in the foreign exchange markets.

Monetarist economists would make a similar argument regarding M1 growth. However, in earlier reports we have argued that M1 is an equilibrium quantity that reflects the interaction of demand and supply. To the extent that fluctuations in M1 are dominated by demand shifts, the relation between inflation and M1 growth will be the opposite of the monetarist models. Furthermore, our approach argues that a better proxy for excess money growth is excess base over money.[15] The empirical implications of the different frameworks regarding macroeconomic policy and inflation are discussed in Chapters 2 and 3.

8. Canto, Joines, and Webb, "Taxation, Rational Expectations, and the Neutrality of Money."

9. Arthur B. Laffer, "How Quickly We Forget: Must the Mistakes of the '70s Be Repeated?" A. B. Laffer Associates, November 20, 1987.

10. Canto, Joines, and Webb, "Taxation, Rational Expectations, and the Neutrality of Money."

11. The forecast model correctly predicts changes in interest rates in approximately 75 percent of the sample. The quarters where the interest rate forecast missed the direction of the changes are:

69.2	72.4	83.2
69.3	73.1	84.4
69.4	77.4	85.2
70.2	78.1	86.1
71.3	78.2	86.2
71.4	79.3	88.1

12. Christopher Sims, "Macroeconomics and Reality," *Econometrica* (January 1980), pp. 1–35.

13. The errors are orthogonalized by a Cholesky decomposition so that the covariance matrix of the resulting innovations is lower triangular. While the Cholesky decomposition is widely used, it is a rather arbitrary method of attributing common effects. Changing the order of the equations can dramatically change the impulse response, and care should be given to interpreting the impulse response functions. Listing the base first will tend to bias the results in favor of the monetary base. The fact that the contribution of the base declines is consistent with the endogenous view stated in the text.

14. See Chapter 1 and Arthur B. Laffer, "The Phillip's Buster Filibuster," A. B. Laffer Associates, August 4, 1988.

15. See Chapters 3 and 4.

6

The Yield Curve: The Long and Short of It

Victor A. Canto and Arthur B. Laffer

Of late, analysts have busied themselves discussing the significance of an inverted yield curve. For the first time since 1982, the yield curve is literally on the verge of inverting. As it is told in the ancient book, when the yield curve inverts, a downturn follows.

To determine whether any systematic patterns can be uncovered and, specifically, whether there is any validity to the claim that inverted yield curves are precursors of recessions, we have chosen to examine the historical record of the United States during this century. For the purposes of this paper, the yield curve is said to be inverted when the short end of the yield curve (the three-month yield) exceeds the long end yields on bonds of 20 or 30 years. Since 1920, the short end of the yield curve has exceeded the long end of the curve in 10 instances (Figure 6.1). The length of the inversions ranged from one month to 24 months, with an average duration of 14.5 months (Table 6.1).

THE FRAMEWORK

Nominal interest rates on government securities reflect market participants' joint forecasts of inflation and real interest rates over the maturity length of the security in question. In turn, the slope of the yield curve reflects the market's forecasts of joint changes in inflation rates and real interest rate expectations.

An inversion in the yield curve indicates that the market believes nominal yields in the future will decline relative to the present. Such a change in expecta-

Figure 6.1
Slope of the Yield Curve: Long-Term Minus Short-Term Interest Rates (Monthly)

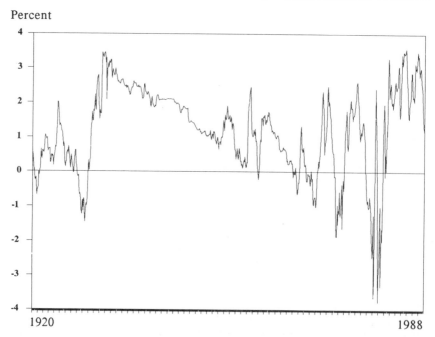

Percent

Sources: Federal Reserve System, *Banking and Monetary Statistics 1914-1941, 1941-1970;* Federal Reserve System, *Selected Interest Rates;* Department of Commerce, *Business Statistics 1984; Wall Street Journal.*

A.B. Laffer Associates

tions contains information about the future path of inflation, economic activity, and stock prices. Whether the inversion signals a decline in the inflation rate or a slowdown in the economy depends on the nature of the disturbance or policy change that brought about the inversion.

Generally, a yield curve can become inverted because short rates rise or because long rates fall. This may happen one of two ways: differential changes in inflation expectations, or differential changes in expected real rates of return.

- If long rates fall because future expected inflation falls, then equity values may well rise as a consequence of the inversion. If, on the other hand, the inversion results from higher current inflationary expectations, then equity values would be expected to fall.

- If the inversion were a result of temporary higher anticipated short-term real yields, as the economy adjusts to its long-run equilibrium, short-term real yields will exceed long-term real yields. During the transition to long-run equilibrium, equity values will rise.

Table 6.1
Inverted Yield Curve Episodes since 1920

Beginning	End	CPI*		Real S&P*		Real GNP*		Average Monthly Changes**	
		Year Before	Year After	Year Before	Year After	Year Before	Year After	Short	Long
June 1920	March 1921	23.67	-8.74	-37.72	21.22	-4.37	15.81	-1.20	-3.10
April 1927	May 1927	-3.35	-1.15	27.13	37.20	-0.11	0.58	6.50	-3.00
January 1928	November 1929	-1.14	-5.20	31.96	-14.04	0.58	-9.87	1.30	.78
November 1959	December 1959	1.38	1.36	7.63	-5.19	3.62	0.58	22.00	8.00
January 1966	February 1967	1.92	3.95	6.44	-0.07	7.58	3.89	-.25	.25
April 1968	March 1970	3.93	4.71	1.25	7.64	5.13	2.78	6.08	4.17
April 1973	December 1974	5.06	6.94	-3.68	25.31	5.92	2.19	5.05	2.76
September 1978	April 1980	8.31	10.00	-0.34	20.49	4.55	3.44	34.85	14.80
October 1980	September 1981	12.77	5.04	11.83	-1.58	-0.77	-2.96	38.58	26.67
February 1982	February 1982	7.62	3.49	-18.45	24.72	-1.98	0.51	137.00	-10.00

* Percent changes
** Basis Points

Sources: Bureau of Labor Statistics; Standard and Poors Security Price Index Record; Department of Commerce, Historical Statistics of the United States; Federal Reserve System, Banking and Monetary Statistics 1914-1941; Department of Commerce, Business Statistics, 1984.

A.B. Laffer Associates

However the inversion occurs, production plans will also change. In general, a yield curve inversion may result in either heightened economic expansion or a slow down. In order to trade on the possible effects of the inverted yield curve, it is necessary to develop a mechanism for discerning changes in inflationary expectations from changes in real rates. The organization of the monetary system provides the starting point for such a mechanism.

MONETARY DISTURBANCES

The inflationary potential of an economy depends on the organization of the monetary system. Holding the quantity of money constant, increases in real economic activity will result in an increase in the demand for money. The excess demand for money would indicate a decline in the inflation rate and thereby inflationary expectations. This effect is simply another rendition of too little money chasing too many goods.

Increased inflation, however, is the converse: too much money chasing too few goods. A rise in inflation will result in higher marginal tax rates and slower economic activity, and an inverted Phillips' curve relation between the inflation rate and economic activity will be observed. Rising inflationary expectations will be associated with weaker future economic activity.

An inverted yield curve due to changes in monetary policy should result in a negative relationship between the inflation rate and real economic activity. Under a forward-looking stock market, a projected economic slowdown will be reflected in a decline in stock prices during the inversion period.

Fiat Standard

Based on our interpretation of the historical events, a fiat standard monetary system existed from the mid-1960s through 1980. During all other periods, variants of a price rule system were in effect.

Under a fiat standard, rising interest rates are a harbinger of rising inflation and inflationary expectations and a slower economy. During periods of a fiat standard, the empirical evidence suggests that short-term interest rates may be better predictors of inflation over the near future than changes in long-term interest rates. The implications of our analysis are borne out by the data. During the four inversions that occurred between January 1966 and April 1980:

- The rise in short-term interest rates was a harbinger of inflation.
- The inflation rate was higher in the year following the inversion than in the year prior to the inversion (Table 6.1).
- Real GNP growth was slower in the year following the inversion than in the year prior to the inversion.

- Higher inflation was associated with slower growth. The relationship between inflation and real GNP was opposite of the Phillips' curve.
- In all cases, the S&P 500 declined in real terms during the inversion period.

Price Rule

During periods under which variants of the price rule were in effect (the pre–World War II gold standard, Bretton-Woods, the price rule of the 1980s), some empirical regularities were also evident:

- The inflation rate was lower in the year after the inversion than in the year prior to the inversion (Table 6.1). The exception is the 1927 inversion.
- The stock market increased in real terms during the inversion period.
- No systematic pattern is evident for real GNP growth during the year prior to and the year after the inversion.

That no systematic pattern emerges using a monetary perspective, however, does not rule out the presence of systematic patterns arising from real disturbances.

REAL DISTURBANCES

Real economic shocks will have different impacts on real rates of return. For example, tax rate reductions will temporarily increase real after-tax rates of return. The lower tax rates and higher real returns will increase incentives to produce and invest. Over time, the economy will adjust to its long-term interest rate and real GNP growth path. Therefore, during the early stages because of the rise in real returns, short-term interest rates will rise relative to long-term rates.

In the period immediate to tax rate cuts taking effect, real rates will be the highest. Similarly, during the expansion path, real rates will decline. The implications of this analysis are that under a price rule, long-term interest rates may be a good predictor of future economic activity. Rising real rates signal an expanding economy and declining real rates are associated with a slowdown in economic activity.

The empirical evidence is consistent with the model's predictions. During the price rule periods, there were two episodes in which the inverted yield curve was accompanied by an overall rise in interest rates. In the January 1928 to November 1929 and the October 1980 to September 1981 periods, real economic activity and real stock prices declined during the year after the inversion occurred.

During the June 1920 to March 1921 period, both the short and long rates fell. The economy expanded and stock prices rose during the year after the inversion was reversed. Similar results were observed during the two incidents when the

long rates declined and short rates increased, in April 1927 to May 1927 and in
February 1982.

THE YIELD CURVE IN 1988–89

Throughout 1988, short-term interest rates steadily increased. In turn, long
rates declined during the fourth quarter but now appear to be rising steadily,
although more slowly than the short rates (Figure 6.2). This suggests that if an
inversion occurs soon, it will be the result of short rates rising faster than long
rates.

Under a fiat standard, inversions accompanied by a rise in short-term interest
rates signal a rise in inflationary expectations and slower economic activity (i.e.,
an inverted Phillips curve). During the inversion period, the stock market will
decline in real terms. In contrast, under a price rule an inverted yield curve
accompanied by a fall in long rates signals an expanding economy in the future.
During the inversion period, equity values will rise in real terms.

Figure 6.2
Long-Term and Short-Term Interest Rates, 1988 (Monthly)

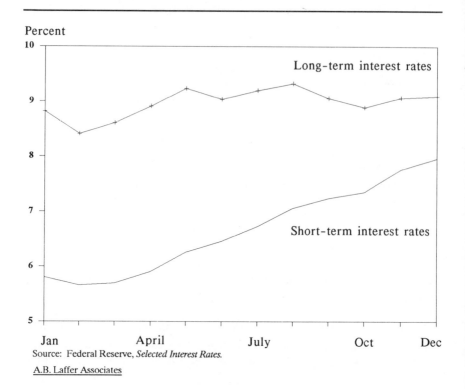

Source: Federal Reserve, *Selected Interest Rates.*
A.B. Laffer Associates

PART TWO

FISCAL POLICY

7

Bush's Economic Agenda within a Supply-Side Framework

VICTOR A. CANTO AND ARTHUR B. LAFFER

To a significant extent because of the efforts of Congressman Jack Kemp, the era of income and capital tax cuts is here and now. While the critics of lowered tax rates have always made claims against such cuts, their arguments now take on an additional sense of urgency. If the critics' case were to be convincing, the enormous momentum to cut tax rates could be postponed or even stopped. The American renaissance stands in the balance.

If Congressman Kemp has his way, the highest marginal tax rate on any form of income will be 36 percent by the end of 1984 with a maximum tax rate on capital gains of 14 percent. I personally feel quite confident that the momentum toward growthist economics will not falter and that, in historical perspective, the 1980s will be viewed in the same light as the roaring 20s and early 60s.

In all, tax rates and equity values move closely in opposite directions. A sense of the depressed state of today's equity market is also given with the more familiar Dow Jones industrial average. The Dow currently stands at roughly 960. If adjusted for inflation alone, the peak attained in 1965 (approximately 1000) would be 2640 today; if the current Dow were relative to total GNP, what it was in 1965, it would be approximately 4000.

Arthur B. Laffer, "Testimony before the House Ways and Means Committee" (March 4, 1981).

The perennial cry from redistributionists, whether liberal or conservative, is to slow the growth of government spending and postpone any tax cut. Tax rate reductions are held out as the far-distant carrot to induce the electorate to select this program of economic austerity. Such programs, however, have shown themselves time and again to be bankrupt. They are poorly founded on both conceptual and empirical grounds. The method most successful in reducing government incursions in the private sector is to precede any reductions in government spending by major reductions in tax rates.

It is axiomatic that much of what the government spends is wasted. Each one of us could name program after program that should either be eliminated or scaled down. Every president and presidential contender has waxed eloquent in his promises to reduce waste and increase the efficiency of government. Almost all have failed. The simple reason is that each failed to understand the central role of government.

The constellation of economic incentives is the moving force in the goods market, and changes in marginal tax rates are as important a factor affecting incentives as can be found. People and businesses work and produce to earn after-tax income. As a general rule, they do not work and produce because they like to pay taxes. As tax rates increase, after-tax rewards from engaging in market activities decline. The consequences are less output and less employment.

Conversely, as tax rates decline, alternatives to market activities become less attractive. Individuals and businesses commit more effort to market activities. Therefore, as tax rates decline, more labor and capital enter the market, and output expands. Slow output growth is just as inflationary as rapid money growth. The slower the growth in output, the higher will be the rate of inflation.

The case put forth by the tax cut detractors has several elements. Their arguments encompass the following: Tax cut antagonists argue that across-the-board tax rate reductions will not materially increase equity values, economic growth, or savings. In addition, those opposed to tax rate reductions argue that across-the-board income tax rate cuts will lead to higher inflation and greater deficits, and will hurt the poor.

TAXATION, ECONOMIC GROWTH, AND EQUITY VALUES

Historically, periods of rapid growth, low inflation, and rising stock markets frequently have been periods of lower tax rates. Perhaps given the close association between higher tax rates, lower real growth, and lower savings and capital formation, it should be obvious that equity values and rates of taxation also are closely related. They are!

What is surprising is just how closely related tax rates and economic indexation are. In the charts below, the annual rate of growth of real GNP and the annual rate of growth of Standard and Poor's index of 500 stocks are computed to the highest marginal rate of taxation on income in the United States. The period covered is from 1919 to 1989 (Figures 7.1 and 7.2).

Even with as crude an index of taxation as changes in the highest marginal

Figure 7.1
Equity Values and the Highest Income Tax Rate, 1919–89

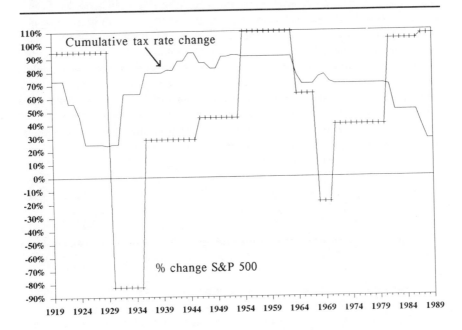

Figure 7.2
Economic Growth and the Highest Income Tax Rate, 1919–89

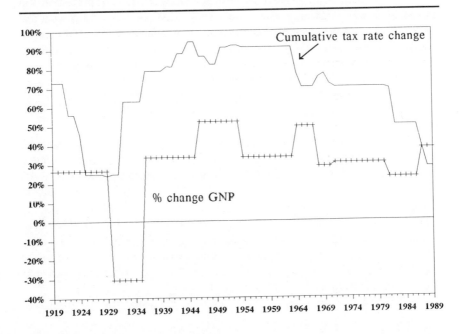

income tax rate, the association is remarkably close. From 1916 to 1918, the highest marginal tax rate on income rose from a mere 7 percent to 73 percent. Other changes in the rates of taxation were consistent with the enormous rise in the rate at the highest bracket. Equity values tumbled. With Harding's overwhelming defeat of Cox in 1920 (Harding received over 60 percent of the total vote), an era of rapid and deep tax rate cuts commenced.

From 1919 to 1929, the highest marginal rate fell from 77 percent to 24 percent. The lowest rate was reduced from 6 percent to ⅜ of one percent. Real GNP grew at a 2.7 percent annual rate, the inflation rate declined to a 0.36 percent annual rate, and equity values rose in what was to be called the Roaring Twenties. The S&P 500 rose at a 9.5 percent annual rate.

In 1929 an era of tax rate increases began in earnest. In an exceptionally detailed analysis, Jude Wanniski documented the parallel movements of the political effort to pass the Smoot-Hawley Tariff Act and the Great Crash. The thirties saw the highest rate of taxation rise from 24 percent in 1929 to 81.1 percent in 1940. During the 1930–35 period, real GNP declined at an annual rate of 3.6 percent, and the stock market declined precipitously—at an annual rate of 8.3 percent.

The early forties witnessed the highest marginal tax rate rising even further. The lowest marginal rate rose from 4.4 percent in 1940 to 23 percent in 1945. The stock market in nominal terms rose at an annual rate of 10.5 percent during this period. Inflation, however, ate away most of the appreciation in equity values by rising at approximately a 5.1 percent annual rate.

Tax rates dropped somewhat right after the war. The period from 1953 to 1963 was a period of sustained economic growth and rapid equity appreciation and almost no change in tax rates. During the period, GNP averaged 3.4 percent real GNP growth, and the stock market increased at an annual rate of 10.9 percent. The modest growth of the Eisenhower era witnessed some mild tax rate increases. From the standpoint of inflation and interest rates, the Eisenhower presidency was uneventful. Over the 1953–60 period, the Treasury bill rate rose to 2.25 percent from 2.09 percent, long-term Treasury bond yields rose to 3.88 percent from 2.75 percent, and the average rate of inflation measured by consumer prices was less than 1.4 percent per year.

During the Kennedy and Johnson administrations, the pace of economic activity accelerated as tax rates were cut. During the 1964–67 period, real GNP grew at an annual rate of almost 5 percent per year. The S&P 500 grew at 6.3 percent per annum. The Kennedy tax cuts are highly visible, as is the surge in real growth. Since the end of the Kennedy era, tax rates have climbed steadily (although the highest statutory rates have not). Between 1961 and 1968, consumer prices rose an average of 2.2 percent per year. The T-bill rate climbed to 5.96 percent from 2.25 percent, and long-term government bond yields rose to 5.65 percent from 3.88 percent. Growth was modest. The evidence is as clear as it can be in economics. Taxes inhibit growth.

The Nixon-Ford-Carter years were marked by a sequence of disastrous economic policies. The dollar was unhinged from gold, wage and price controls were imposed, federal government spending surged, and effective tax rates were increased by inflation-induced bracket creep. The economy sputtered while inflation soared.

Between 1971 and 1980, the S&P 500 increased at an annual rate of 3.9 percent. However, the consumer price index climbed an average 7.7 percent per year. Thus, inflation more than offset the rise in nominal stock prices. The price of a barrel of oil increased more than 19-fold from $1.80 to over $34. Gold's price hit $850 per ounce in January 1980—up more than 1900 percent from its early 1968 price of $42.

Interest rates climbed too. The T-bill rate increased to 15.49 percent from 5.96 percent, and long-term Treasury bond yields rose to 11.89 percent from 5.65 percent. Similarly, between 1968 and 1980, the prime rate shot up to 21.5 percent from 6.60 percent, while home mortgage rates rose to 12.53 percent from 6.90 percent.

The Reagan administration inherited an economy badly in need of repair after the damage done during the prior 12 years. Tax rates were lowered, energy prices were decontrolled, industries were deregulated, and monetary stability was restored.

To one recording the history of the early 1980s, as important as any feature of the tax/legislative nexus is the observation that anticipated changes in tax rates also can have a profound impact on the path of the economy. In the 1981 tax bill, the tax rate cuts were phased in. Supposedly, there was a 5 percent cut on October 1, 1981; a 10 percent cut on July 1, 1982; and a final 10 percent cut on July 1, 1983.

In truth, there is no such thing as an intra-year tax rate cut. The IRS simply cannot discriminate between income earned in January or the following December because most taxpayers report income on a calendar-year basis. As a result, the intra-year "tax cuts" were prorated across the entire year. In 1981, for example, the 5 percent cut that supposedly took effect October 1 was prorated over the calendar year as a 1.25 percent tax rate reduction for the full year. Calendar year 1982 starting on January 1, not July 1, had a cumulative 10 percent rate cut. On January 1, 1983 and 1984, the cumulative tax rate cuts were 18 percent and 23 percent respectively.[1]

The flaw in this phased-in approach to tax rate cuts was to ignore the role of incentives on individual behavior. Common sense tells us that people don't shop at a store the week before that store has a widely advertised discount sale. Prospects of lower tax rates in future years created incentives for individuals and businesses to reduce their income during 1981 and 1982 when tax rates were high, in order to realize that income in 1983 and 1984 when tax rates would be lower. The economy slowed, unemployment rose, and the deficit swelled. Ironically, the attempt to stave off deficits by delaying tax cuts, in reality, caused those very deficits to soar.

Surely the 1981 and 1982 pronouncements of the Washington, D.C., savants that supply-side economics and, specifically, tax rate cuts were a failure has to be ranked in the highest echelons of disingenuous nonsense. It should hardly come as a surprise to anyone that tax cuts don't work until they take effect.

What appears truly astounding is the rapidity with which the economy responds to incentives. Virtually on January 1, 1983, when the bulk of the tax cuts came on stream, the economy began to recover. The recovery, true to supply-side logic, did not foster the "roaring inflation" so confidently predicted by Walter Heller, but robustly provided jobs, higher capacity utilization, and increased productivity.[2] Even subtle differences in incentives appear to work. The fourth-quarter-1983 slowdown was followed by a first-quarter-1984 rebound in exact conformance with the anticipation and then the realization of the final 5 percent cut in tax rates.

In January 1983, total civilian employment stood at 99,161,000 people, and in January 1989 employment had reached 118,407,000. That is an increase of over 19 percent in five years. The Reagan/supply-side job machine really worked. Real GNP measured in 1982 dollars went from a low of $3166 billion in 1982 to $4024 billion in 1988, a 27 percent increase in real GNP.

With consumer prices rising at an average annual rate of 4.1 percent between 1981 and 1986, inflation was brought under control. By the end of 1986, the price of oil was less than $18 per barrel, and the price of gold was less than $400 per ounce.

Interest rates peaked in the early 1980s and have fallen since. The T-bill rate topped out at 16.30 percent in May 1981 and stood at 7.61 percent in October 1989. Long-term Treasury bond yields reached 14.68 percent in October 1981 before falling to 8.10 percent in October 1989.

With the Jarvis-Steiger-Reagan revolution, the balance of political power has been dramatically changed. Supply-side Republicans were able to effectuate a metamorphosis. They transformed themselves from the tax collectors for the welfare state to the tax cutters for the opportunity society. The political response has been overwhelming. Voters latched on to the tax issue with a vengeance. The new income tax rates that came into effect on January 1, 1988 are extremely conducive to economic growth. The highest federal marginal tax rates on personal and corporate incomes will be 28 percent and 34 percent respectively. The tax structure beginning in 1988 is the most pro-production structure the U.S. has experienced since the Harding and Coolidge administrations reduced the highest marginal tax rate on personal income from 73 percent to 25 percent.

SAVINGS, GOVERNMENT SPENDING, AND DEFICITS

Both the Keynesian and the supply-side approaches predict that a reduction in tax rates will stimulate the economy. However, the source of stimulus is quite different. In the Keynesian framework, the reduction in tax revenues and consequent increase in disposable income lead to higher aggregate consumption, which through the multiplier effect leads to an increase in overall economic activity. In a supply-side framework, the stimulus originates in the reduction of tax rates, which yields higher rates of return to market activity and hence increased output.

A reduction in income tax rates also increases the rate of return to saving, which results in a postponement of current consumption. As a result of higher real after-tax return, aggregate consumption would be expected to decline below where it otherwise would have been. The lower tax rate will result in higher after-tax rates of return of existing and new machines. The reduction in distortions will result in a more efficient economic system, the result being a higher level of output from existing physical and human capital. This higher output will result in an upward revision of existing physical and human capital. The tax rate cuts will result in a rise in private wealth.

The rise in private wealth will increase the permanent consumption level of the economy, and, as a consequence, saving out of current income will decrease. Tax rate increases will have the opposite effect. The experience of the United States during the last two decades indicates a negative relationship between changes in household net worth and the personal savings rate. During the 1970s when inflation-induced bracket creep was pushing the economy into higher tax brackets, wealth was being destroyed. The need to replenish wealth resulted in a higher savings rate. In turn, during the 1980s when wealth was being created, the need to replenish wealth through higher personal savings was being reduced (Figure 7.3).

Figure 7.3
Percent Change in Real Households Domestic Net Worth and Personal Savings as a Percent of GNP, 1971–89

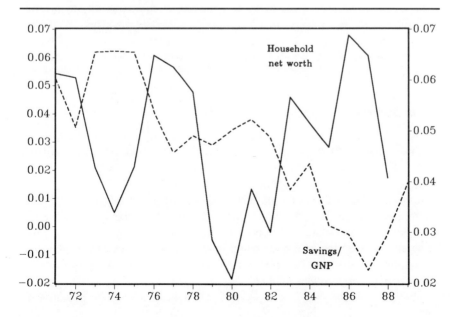

Table 7.1
Components of U.S. Savings as a Share of GNP

	1983–89*	1971–80
Personal	3.35	5.53
Business	1.98	2.43
Total private	5.33	7.96
State and local	1.05	0.87
Federal	-4.11	-1.84
Total private and public	2.27	6.98

Source: *Economic Report of the President, 1989; National Income and Product Accounts*, U.S. Department of Commerce.

* Average of first 2 quarters.

Personal Saving

In our view, the decline in the personal saving rate to 3.35 percent during the 1983–89 period from 5.53 percent during the 1971–88 period is directly attributable to the change in economic policies that arrested the erosion and destruction of wealth caused by inflation-induced bracket creep and restored incentives to the U.S. economy (Table 7.1).

When the economy adjusts to the low tax rate environment the savings rate will, once again, rise to its secular level. In line with our framework, the decline in the personal savings rate appears to have been arrested: During 1989, the personal savings rate rose to 3.97 percent of GNP from 2.96 in 1988 and 2.30 percent in 1987.

Government Dissavings

The only component of the total savings rate that is clearly out of line with the experience of the 1970s is the government dissavings or budget deficit. All else the same, elimination of the budget deficit would increase the economy's total savings rate to a level comparable to that of the 1970s.

A strong argument can be made that the culprit in the decline in the U.S. saving rate has been the federal government. In order to solve the problem, one must determine the source of the government dissavings, a shortfall in revenues or an uncontrolled increase in spending. If the shortfall in revenue is the cause, the solution is a tax increase. In turn, if the cause is runaway spending, spending restraint is the appropriate solution.

Table 7.2

Government Receipts on a National Income and Product Accounts Basis

Fiscal Year	Federal* (Billions)	Percent of GNP	Net State/Local** (Billions)	Percent of GNP	Total % of GNP
1977	$384.1	19.3	$232.6	11.7	31.0
1978	441.4	19.6	253.0	11.2	30.8
1979	505.0	20.1	274.8	11.0	31.1
1980	553.8	20.3	301.3	11.0	31.3
1981	639.5	20.9	337.7	11.1	32.0
1982	635.3	20.1	365.5	11.5	31.6
1983	641.1	19.4	391.9	11.9	31.3
1984	704.7	19.2	430.4	11.8	31.0
1985	788.7	19.6	482.1	12.0	31.6
1986	827.9	19.6	519.5	12.3	31.9
1987	911.4	20.1	553.5	12.2	32.3
1988	972.4	19.9	590.2	12.1	32.0
1989***	1,044.1	20.2	618.9	12.0	32.2

Table 7.3

Government Expenditures on a National Income and Product Accounts Basis

Fiscal Year	Net Federal* (Billions)	Percent of GNP	State/Local (Billions)	Percent of GNP	Total % of GNP
1977	$362.6	18.2	$273.2	13.7	31.9
1978	393.4	17.5	301.3	13.4	30.9
1979	440.6	17.6	327.7	13.1	30.7
1980	526.4	19.3	363.2	13.3	32.6
1981	615.4	20.2	391.4	12.8	33.0
1982	697.3	22.0	414.3	13.1	35.1
1983	733.4	22.2	434.1	13.1	35.3
1984	787.3	21.5	470.7	12.9	34.4
1985	885.9	22.1	516.7	12.9	35.0
1986	928.0	21.9	563.5	13.3	35.2
1987	970.2	21.4	604.8	13.4	34.8
1988	1,006.9	20.6	651.9	13.4	34.0
1989***	1,073.4	20.8	689.6	13.4	34.2

* On and off budget; gross expenditures less grants-in-aid to state and local governments.

** Gross receipts less federal grants-in-aid.
*** Average of first 2 quarters.

Sources: U.S. Department of Commerce, Bureau of Economic Analysis, *Survey of Current Business* and *The National Income and Product Accounts, 1929-82; Statistical Tables.*

A. B. Laffer, V.A. Canto & Associates

A close examination of the data suggests that government receipts as a percent of GNP on a national income and product account basis are higher than they were prior to the Reagan tax rate cuts (Table 7.2). Since 1985, government spending as a percent of GNP has declined. Unfortunately, so is government spending (Table 7.3). The data clearly suggest that government spending is the problem, not revenue. However, the most recent data indicate a slowdown of spending as a percent of GNP, while revenues have held to their recent levels. If the trend continues, the budget deficit, and, hence, government dissavings, will decline in the next few years.

Numbers as those presented in Table 7.2 only partially describe what really happened during the Reagan era. During the 1978–87 period, tax rates were greatly reduced. From January 1, 1983 on, the moment the supply-side agenda was put into place, tax receipts as a percentage of GNP rose. It is very true that in 1983 total government tax receipts as a share of GNP were at 31.3 percent. Federal tax receipts were at 19.4 percent of GNP in 1983, and state and local taxes combined were 11.9 percent of GNP. In the year immediately preceding, the same numbers were 31.6 percent, 20.1 percent, and 11.5 percent, respectively. By 1989, however, federal tax receipts were up to 20.3 percent of GNP and the combined federal, state, and local taxes were at a new all-time high of 32.3 percent of GNP.

The complete tax argument presented here is simple. Tax revenues as a share of GNP initially fell after the tax cuts and then rose because of these same tax rate cuts. Total revenues were double impacted—first as a share of GNP and secondly as a consequence of extraordinary real GNP growth. The decline in inflation and the huge employment growth made the world a win-win situation. Never before have so many gotten so much from so little.

THE BLACK ECONOMY: THE RECORD

In the years following the date when the first tax cut took effect on January 1, 1983, black employment has increased 28.2 percent whereas total employment increased 16.6 percent. Both levels and difference are amazing here. Blacks have scored exceptionally well during the tax cut era.

To put all of these numbers into their proper focus, it should be remembered that the level of black success in the employment arena has been and remains significantly lower than the level of the rest of the population. Also, success has an absolute as well as a relative dimension. Whether blacks improved their lot relative to other Americans or not, there is no doubt that on an absolute scale the results have been exceptionally good. The results of the last seven years have been good for all Americans.

Unemployment and participation rate data add dimension and substance to the story told by the employment numbers. From the 1983 peak in black unemployment to 1989, the black unemployment rate fell by 8.6 percentage points while the unemployment rate for the entire civilian population fell by 4.9 percentage points. From our perspective, this is the proper measure, and it captures this administration's full impact because the tax cuts and the supply-side recovery literally began on January 1, 1983, not January 20, 1981.

However, a reasonable case could be made that the precipitous fall in black unemployment rates relative to the overall population was, in fact, nothing short of an offset to the extraordinary rise in black unemployment rates relative to all Americans from 1980 through 1983: 5.2 percentage points versus 2.5 percentage points. The interpretation of participation rates is far less ambiguous than is the interpretation of unemployment rates. For blacks, participation rates have risen whether viewed in isolation or relative to other Americans.

Where blacks have experienced a noticeable decline relative to other Americans is in the pay they receive (Table 7.4). On an absolute scale, black median weekly earnings have risen by 49 percent over the past nine years. After taking out inflation, however, the gains are virtually nonexistent. This number misstates the true changes because there was a significant reduction in income taxes during this time period and a significant increase in the payroll tax. There has also been substantial regression in the ratio of black median weekly earnings to total median weekly earnings. This means that, on this basis, black median earnings are falling further behind those of the rest of the population.

The numbers, however, when viewed in a vacuum, are misleading. With the enormous relative increase in black employment over the last several years, it seems almost axiomatic that these new job holders would, on balance, be lower income earners and thereby reduce the averages. Given the employment growth, it is surprising that black earnings performed as well as they did.

To attempt a comprehensive measure may be valiant but it misses much of the richness and subtlety of detail. Nonetheless, if the reader will view our attempt with extreme caution, we can combine employment, population, and median earnings into an indicator of total earnings per capita for blacks and the total civilian population. In the table below, the two are compared for the years 1980 through 1989 (Table 7.4).

At best, it is presumptuous to summarize the multiplicity of efforts and factors that go into the performance of black Americans. Nonetheless, putting all of it together, there has been a substantial improvement in the economic performance of blacks during the Reagan era.

This improvement is also quite pronounced when blacks are compared to the overall civilian population. The level of black performance, however, remains considerably below the rest of the population. Since the commencement of the supply-side tax cuts, January 1, 1983, the relative and absolute performance of black America has been much greater. Black real per capita earnings rose by 13.3 percent during this period and went to 73.8 percent of total civilian per capita earnings in 1989 from 69.8 percent in 1982, a gain in relative position of 4 percent. All of this just goes to show that there is no equalizer better than a

Table 7.4
Black Employment and Earnings Relative to Total Civilian Population

	Employment			Population			Median Weekly Earnings			Total Weekly Earnings Per Capita		
	Total Civilian*	Total Black*	Black As % of Total	Total Civilian*	Total Black*	Black As % of Total	Total Civilian	Total Black	Black As % of Total	Civilian	Black	Black As % of Total
1980	99,303	9,311	9.4%	167,745	17,397	10.4%	$266	$218	82.0%	$157	$117	74.1%
1981	100,397	9,355	9.3	170130	17824	10.5	289	238	82.4	171	125	73.2
1982	99,526	9,189	9.2	172271	18219	10.6	309	247	79.9	179	125	69.8
1983	100,834	9,375	9.3	174215	18584	10.7	322	264	82.0	186	133	71.5
1984	105,005	10,119	9.6	176383	18925	10.7	326	269	82.5	194	144	74.1
1985	107,150	10,501	9.8	178206	19348	10.9	343	277	80.8	206	150	72.9
1986	109,597	10,814	9.9	180587	19664	10.9	358	291	81.3	217	160	73.7
1987	112,440	11,309	10.1	182753	19989	10.9	373	301	80.7	229	170	74.2
1988	114,968	11,938	10.4	184613	20842	11.3	385	314	81.6	240	180	75.0
1989**	117,541	12,023	10.2	186329	21012	11.3	398	324	81.4	251	185	73.8

* Thousands, 16 years and over.

** Second quarter

Source: *Employment and Earnings*, U.S. Department of Labor.

healthy, robust economy. When there are fifteen applicants for one job, the employer can and will discriminate. When there are fifteen jobs and only one applicant, the person is hired.

THE POLICY IMPLICATIONS OF THE BUSH ADMINISTRATION

If the past is a guide to the future, the tax rate reductions of 1988 portend continued strong growth over the coming years, a rising stock market, and a corresponding lid on inflation. There are some major initiatives on horizons near and far, that if implemented could make the 1990s exceptional.

The U.S. does not need another visionary; Ronald Reagan did his job. A new era is at hand. What is needed now is good management to change Reagan's revolutionary ideas into the conventional wisdom. A consolidation phase to make the Reagan gains permanent is what is required. President Bush is the right man for the job.

There has been a fundamental shift in personality from Reagan to Bush. Whereas President Reagan was more confrontational, President Bush is more of a consensus builder. His strategy has been to find a position behind the Democratic position which leaves the Democrats two choices: an all-out fight or to fall back to President Bush's position. The minimum wage legislation is an example.

Productivity, savings, and investment are the catchwords of the Bush team's view of economics. Those policies that would increase any or all of those three concepts will be favored policies.

Government Spending

A measure of the government's intrusion in the economy is government spending as a percent of GNP. A reduction in spending implies a reduction in resources under control of the public sector. These resources may now be deployed in the private sector. The reduction in the overall government spending burden will be bullish for the economy. The Bush team will be far more dedicated in reducing government spending than any administration in the last two decades. With the huge deficits during the Reagan era, this area would also seem to be amenable to the reversal Bush proposes. The improvements in the budget deficit may reduce the pressure to raise taxes and to fund pork barrel projects. Budget restraint will exacerbate the political battle as to how resources should be allocated.

The restraint in spending will increase the debate over the relative merit of different programs. The political debate will be healthy for the economy; as priorities are defined, resources will be reallocated among the different programs. The reallocation will have significant impact on the profitability of the sectors most affected by the changes that will take place.

An Overall Tax Increase

The campaign pledge of no tax increases cannot easily be put aside. Until Bush personally negates his pledge, which seems highly unlikely in the near term, there just cannot be a serious tax increase. The Bush team is not a collage of redistributionists and therefore they will shy away from tax rate increases. If their ideal world could be brought to pass, they would love a broad-based consumption tax with savings/investment exemptions, deductions, exclusions, and subsidies.

The remaining question is whether these objectives will be satisfied by lowering the tax rate faced by the favored activities or by raising the tax rates of all other activities. In both cases, the relative attractiveness of the favored programs will increase. In the former option, the overall incentives are increased, while in the latter, the overall economic incentives are reduced. Our belief is that the Bush administration will opt for the option of increasing incentives.

Capital Gains Tax Cut

To the extent the rate cut is on long-term capital gains, the "best" form of investments will be encouraged. Indexation is a critical part of the bill. It will protect capital gains from illusory profits. The increased incentives resulting from capital gains legislation will result in higher output, employment, and asset values. The capital gains bill represents a test of how President Bush will extend and consolidate the revolution started by Ronald Reagan that restored incentives to the private sector. A victory will augur further gains down the road; a setback will give Senate Majority Leader George Mitchell renewed confidence to attempt pushing Democratic programs and ideas previously defeated in Congress and in the general election.

Mandated Benefits

Mandated benefits are the Democrat's alternative to enacting spending cuts and/or tax increases. These mandated benefits increase the cost of doing business in the United States, thereby reducing U.S. competitiveness. If Bush is successful in holding the line on spending, the Democrats will attempt to circumvent the spending and tax limitations through mandated benefits. Mandated benefits will have a negative effect on the economy and the markets. Differential effects across industries are also to be expected.

Accelerated Depreciation, Depletion Allowances, and Investment Tax Credits

As the Bush team matures and settles into its predestined role, watch for the resurgence of depreciation schemes, depletion allowances, and the investment tax credit. These types of proposals have long been the darlings of the business community and are also seen favorably by many economists. They surely aren't harmful if taken by themselves. These types of proposals are sleepers and could materially affect investment returns. To the extent that the economy's marginal tax rate is not increased, no disincentive effects on the rest of the economy will be imposed. The targeted incentives will increase incentives, that is, the rate of return of the industry groups that directly benefit from these policies.

Research and Development, Export, and Educational Tax Credits

As mentioned earlier, all forms of investment are not equal—some are more equal than others. Research and development expenditures, exports, and educational expenditures are truly special. Just as investments in general deserve special treatment, these categories deserve special treatment. The resurrection of these incentives will alter the differential rate of return on industry groups sensitive to the specific programs.

Savings Plans

This administration will turn a friendly face toward Individual Retirement Accounts, Keoghs, and 401Ks. Additional proposals, such as the educational savings account proposed during the campaign, can be expected. Given that many people save the maximum or nothing at all, it is hard to make an argument that these proposals will have an effect on savings. At best, the effect will be marginal. Since no harm is done, however, they are a small plus.

Social Security and Medicare

Michael Boskin has written extensively on the social security system and how it reduces savings and investment. Whether memorialized in writing or not, other key Bush officials believe the same to be true. If social security benefits could be reduced, prospectively or now, or if revenues increased, this would be considered a major victory. Possibilities include extending the age of retirement or taxing retirement benefits. The principle drawback is, once again, politics and campaign promises.

Enterprise Zones

The plight of the inner city is the single most serious and long-lived problem facing Americans today. As a continuing tragedy, it garners far less note than it deserves. The solution is critical to our future.

In order to attract business to the inner city, firms need to anticipate after-tax profits. Firms don't locate their plant facilities as a matter of social conscience.

Given the current absence of profitability in the inner city, a big reduction in tax rates would have little effect on business tax revenues. To the extent that some unemployed found work and some welfare recipients earned more, federal, state, and local spending would fall.

Equally important as locating business in the inner city is the need to assure something other than "absentee businesses"—firms located in the inner city but employing suburbanites. This would require reducing both employer and employee payroll tax rates up to an annual wage rate of $15,000 for firms located in the inner city for hiring an employee whose principal residence is also in the inner city. Such a dramatic reduction in payroll tax rates again would mean little net revenue loss. Every person newly employed would save much more in welfare and unemployment compensation than he would cost in foregone taxes. Higher property values would raise city revenues. Higher income, sales, and other tax receipts would also occur because of more output. Less poverty and despair would ultimately lead to more efficient educational spending and less need for police protection.

The Prospects for Inflation

Although monetary policy is not under the domain of the administration, the economic policies of the Bush administration will have an effect on the U.S.

Figure 7.4
Growth and Inflation in the United States, 1970–89

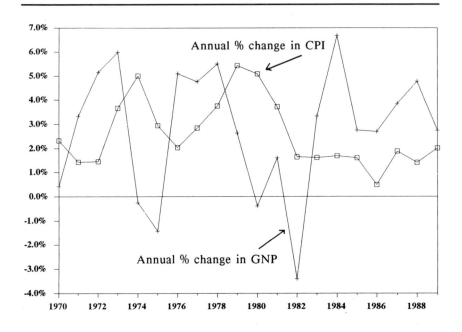

inflation rate. In cliche form, inflation results from too much money chasing too few goods. To assess the prospects for rising inflation, the analysis is divided into the goods market and the money market. The faster the supply of goods expands, the lower will be the rate of inflation. A continuation of Reagan's economic policies will result in higher growth and lower inflation. If output contracts or grows slowly, inflation will be that much higher (Figure 7.4). On the goods side of the inflation equation, the prospects for increased inflation just are not there! In fact, lower inflation would be the direct implication growing out of this analysis of the U.S. goods market.

On the money side of the inflation equation, the case for lower inflation is equally as strong. For some time now, the Federal Reserve has de-emphasized money growth targets in favor of price targets. As a result, interest rates are lower, and commodity prices have become far more stable.[3]

NOTES

1. Charles W. Kadlec and Arthur B. Laffer, "The Ways and Means to an Inadequate Tax Cut," A. B. Laffer Associates, July 23, 1981.

2. Walter Heller, "The Kemp-Roth-Laffer Free Lunch," *Wall Street Journal* (July 12, 1978), p. 20.

3. Arthur B. Laffer and Charles W. Kadlec, "The Monetary Crisis: A Classical Perspective," A. B. Laffer Associates, November 12, 1979.

8

Tax Amnesty:
The Missing Link

Martin G. Laffer and Arthur B. Laffer

"God told me not to file tax returns." "By the time I was required to file, I didn't have the money." "I have not received a payroll check since my first job out of high school." "I was too busy to file and the next time I thought about it, it was too late." "I have not owned a car, real estate, or even registered to vote for the past 10 years." These are but a few of the statements heard by tax practitioners from those who have not filed income tax returns. Many citizens fail to file a single return, often for reasons we are unable to comprehend. The singular act of omission becomes a pattern because of the fear that the one or more omitted tax returns can lead to a prison sentence.

This chapter, by virtue of its existence, exposes a deviant streak in what heretofore had been the unblemished record of a devout supply-sider. This paper is a plea to politicians of all persuasions to raise taxes and raise them now. It is a confession, so to speak, not based on the tax rate/tax revenue dichotomy so appropriately employed over the past decade. It is also not based on sleight-of-hand techniques, by raising taxes on the so-called "sins" or other activities perceived to be harmful to the body politic. Such taxes, whether levied on drug dealers, polluters, or perhaps even lawyers, could well generate revenues all the while making everyone better off.

The tax increase advocated in this paper is a genuine tax increase that could raise anywhere from $40 to $60 billion in its initial years and lesser amounts on an ongoing basis. The rather astounding features of this immodest proposal are twofold:

- The specific payers of this tax will, by their own admission, be better off than they would be if they were not to pay the tax.
- Without arcane doublethink and convoluted chains of economic illogic, output, employment, and production will literally rise as a consequence of the tax increase.

This proposal encompasses a federal tax amnesty program, in cooperation with the individual states, coupled with a massive effort for the government to enter into contractual agreements with taxpayers for the compromising of tax liabilities and collection of tax through installment agreements. Once individuals are assured that they will not be confronted with criminal sanctions and that their homes and other assets will not be seized, they will be willing to step forward and enter the mainstream of the taxpaying population.

THE THEORY

The basic tenet of supply-side economics is that people are attracted to activities they find pleasant and are repelled by activities they find distasteful. In this context, supply-side economics is nothing more nor is it anything less than the pleasure-pain principle which, when put into operational terms, becomes the carrot and the stick. The notion, quite simply, underlying supply-side economics as practiced is that government policies affect change by making activities more or less pleasant to the participants, and as a consequence, the participants alter their behavior.

Taxing an activity or taxing the earnings generated by performing an activity makes that activity less attractive and people will tend to reduce the amount of that activity they perform. Symmetrically, subsidizing an activity will tend to stimulate the now-subsidized activity above its unsubsidized level. Taxes reduce the equilibrium quantity of a commodity while subsidies do quite the opposite. In this context, taxes on work, output, and employment will reduce work output and employment. No matter how technically sophisticated the exposition may be, any answer that contradicts the answer provided above is wrong.

Wrong answers present themselves under a multitude of guises from simple error to ornately adorned fallacy. My favorite example of the latter was provided by Martin Feldstein while chairman of President Reagan's Council of Economic Advisors. He argued that a tax increase on workers and producers would actually increase the number of workers and producers because the tax increase would raise revenues, lower the federal budget deficit, which in turn would reduce "crowding out" and interest rates and thereby increase investment. The higher investment would create more jobs as a consequence of the multiplier effect made famous by Lord Keynes. Feldstein only demonstrates the Irving Kristol dictum that it takes a person with a Ph.D. in economics not to be able to understand the obvious.

Subsidies of nonwork, by the same logic, will increase the amount of nonwork, leisure, and unemployment. The simplicity of this dictum stands foursquare at odds with the practice of stabilizing the economy by increasing transfer payments during a recession and reducing transfer payments during an expansion. While clearly justifiable on humanitarian grounds, the so-called automatic stabilizers are, in truth, automatic destabilizers.

A tax rebate is literally a payment to people based upon the tax liabilities they incurred in the previous year. The tax liabilities of the previous year came as a result of income earned and work effort expended during the previous year. As such, a tax rebate is a payment made to people for the work they performed last year. Quite obviously there is no way people can increase the amount they worked last year. As such, a tax rebate is a payment based upon some characteristic other than current work effort.

The resources used to pay the tax rebate do not come from the "tooth fairy." They come from current workers and current producers. All told, a tax rebate is a transfer payment that detracts from current workers and producers without providing an incentive for increased output and employment. A tax rebate, by its very nature, will reduce output, employment, and production. As far back as George McGovern's demogrant proposal and President Gerald Ford's $50 per capita tax rebate through Jimmy Carter's tax rebate proposal, we have opposed the concept of a tax rebate as being counter productive and inflationary.[1]

But with this framework in mind, a diabolical scheme to increase output would be to increase taxes on last year's income and work effort. If possible, such a tax increase would reduce the burden placed on current workers and producers, and yet there is no way anyone could reduce the number of hours they worked last year. As stated, such a proposal is literally untenable and not within the realm of feasible consideration. There is, however, a way to make the concept of a retroactive tax increase eminently feasible and ultimately practical.

ONE GOAL OF TAX REFORM

One dream of tax reform had always been to reduce the perceived immorality of the tax codes. By lowering individual and business tax rates, so the logic proceeded, the benefits of evading taxes would be reduced and yet the penalties for evading taxes would remain unchanged. Thus, we argued that the calculus of income tax evasion would be sufficiently rearranged that income heretofore churning in the underground economy would resurface as legitimate, aboveground taxable income. How wrong we were.

No one believed that the component of income skulking in the underground economy that was derived from illicit activities would expose itself to the light of federal auditors. But there was a firmly held view that large amounts of underground income resulted exclusively from the straightforward motive to evade tax payments. The government took too much. And, when the government's take diminished, vast amounts of income would be reported: this does not appear to have been the case.

The mistake was to underestimate the enormous power of precedence in conjunction with fear. People who have cheated on their taxes historically find it impossible to confess and pay now even if they never would begin to cheat under the current tax codes. Reporting income for the first time is seen as a sure trigger to receive a federal inquiry. Past tax anomalies under the cold, bright light of the IRS would sooner or later lead to criminal indictment or civil fraud charges and God-knows-what. Better that attention should not be drawn and that unprofitable tax evasion continue. Besides, considering the magnitude of the penalties for being convicted of tax evasion in the first place, the penalties for evading one year more or less appear small in comparison.

While, in theory, lowering tax rates should clearly reduce tax evasion, in practice the effects appear small. The problem simply was that there was no conduit provided to the tax evaders to resurface. They were trapped, unable as they were to allow reality to conform with theory.

The problem was not the magnitude of the underground economy. By all accounts, the underground economy is huge: It has been analyzed to death. It exists, it is enormous, and now is the time to deal with it.

TRADITIONAL ENFORCEMENT

Although the federal government has invested heavily in sophisticated data processing equipment to match income reporting against return filings, it is astounding to learn of the large numbers of those who continue not to file income tax returns. Over the years we have seen physicians who regularly receive medi-care provider payments, contractors who supply equipment to the federal government, and business people with bank accounts and professional licenses who have not filed income tax returns. Then, there are employees who are subject to income tax withholding and are issued W-2 forms, but who do not file tax returns. Many of these W-2 recipients abandon tax refunds by simply not filing returns.

TAX AMNESTY—PURPOSE

Tax amnesty is designed to achieve two goals:

- To raise immediate revenue by collecting tax and interest but not penalties
- To increase the base of tax compliance by bringing into the taxpayer population those who, by various circumstances, are not filing tax returns

OFFER-IN-COMPROMISE

An offer-in-compromise is a contract between the taxpayer and the Internal Revenue Service. It is an agreement between the two parties, whereby the taxpayer agrees to pay a sum certain and the Treasury Department agrees to forgive the balance of taxes, penalties, and interest due. The IRS enters into such a contract only if there is a doubt as to the correctness of the liability or a doubt as to the collectibility of the tax.

Offers-in-compromise are provided for in the Internal Revenue Code and Regulations. However, each district of the IRS has its own procedures and policies for handling "offers." In fact, some districts will not accept offers, while others seek offers as an equitable method of closing collection cases.

OFFERS-IN-COMPROMISE COUPLED
WITH AN AMNESTY PROGRAM

The basis and motivation for entering into offers are very detailed. Factors such as the taxpayer's age, health, education, and future earning capacity are considered. How much to offer is also considered. However, in the context of an amnesty program, the IRS could develop national guidelines, shift experienced tax collectors to this program and, on a large scale, enter into contracts with citizens to compromise the amounts due and/or create payment agreements.

With a large successful effort, outside private collection agencies can then be contracted to act as collection agents for receipt of the installment payments. By bringing in the private sector, the IRS can marshall resources at lower costs and also create additional employment.

TAX AMNESTY—EXPERIENCE

Over the past five years, tax amnesty programs of various sizes and characteristics have become quite popular at the state level. In all, 26 states have utilized a form of tax amnesty. The target taxes varied among the states but included individual income tax, corporate tax, excise tax, and sales tax. The success was limited because the federal government was not a partner in the states' efforts. Nonetheless, the programs were seen by the states themselves as highly successful (Table 8.1).

FEDERAL GOVERNMENT'S NONPARTICIPATION

Each state has a joint treaty with the Internal Revenue Service allowing for a sharing of information regarding the filing of tax returns, amendments to returns, and changes made by taxing authorities in enforcement programs (i.e., audit reports, criminal and civil filings, etc.). It was common knowledge (and, in fact, disseminated with most of the amnesty promotions) that all returns and amendments submitted to the states as part of the states' amnesty would be made available to the federal government. It is believed that the federal government's nonparticipation in the program resulted in diminished success by the individual states.

Table 8.1
A Comparison of State Tax Amnesty Programs

State	Amnesty Period	Major Taxes Covered	Gross Collections ($millions)	Accts. Receivable included
NEW YORK	11/01/85–01/31/86	All/d	401.3	Yes
Alabama	01/20/84–04/01/84	All	3.15	No
Arizona	11/22/82–01/20/83	All	6.0	No
Arkansas	09/01/87–11/30/87	All	1.3	Yes
California	12/10/84–03/15/85	Indiv. income, Sales	146.8	Yes/f
Colorado	09/16/85–11/15/85	All	6.4	No
Florida	01/01/87–06/30/87	Intangibles Tax/a	6.0/b	Yes
Idaho	05/20/83–08/30/83	Indiv. income	0.3	No
Iowa	09/02/86–10/31/86	All	35.1	Yes
Illinois	10/01/84–11/30/84	All	152.4	Yes
Kansas	07/01/84–09/30/84	All	0.6	No
Louisiana	10/01/85–12/31/85	All	1.2	No
Maryland	09/01/87–10/31/87	All	34.0/b	Yes
Massachusetts	10/17/83–01/17/84	All	85.5	Yes
Michigan	05/12/86–06/30/86	All	102.0	Yes
Minnesota	08/01/83–10/31/83	All	12.1	Yes
Missouri	09/01/83–10/31/83	All	0.9	No
New Jersey	09/10/87–12/08/87	All	179.7/b	Yes
New Mexico	08/15/85–11/12/85	All/c	13.9	No

North Dakota	09/01/83-11/30/83	All	0.15	No
Oklahoma	07/01/84-12/31/84	All	13.9	Yes
Rhode Island	10/16/86-01/12/87	Income, Sales	1.9/b	Yes
South Carolina	09/01/85-11/30/85	All	8.8	Yes
Texas	02/01/84-02/29/84	All/e	0.5	No
West Virginia	10/01/86-12/31/86	All	8.0/b	Yes
Wisconsin	09/15/85-11/22/85	All	26.8	Yes

$ 1,248.7

/a   Intangible personal property tax upon individuals, partnerships, associations, and corporations. Florida is requiring a second program from 1/186-6/30/86 for all taxes not included in the first one.

/b   Preliminary figure.

/c   The severance taxes, including tax six oil and gas severance taxes, the resources excise tax, the corporate franchise tax, and the special fuel tax were not subject to Amnesty.

/d   Availability of Amnesty for the corporation tax, the oil company taxes, the transportation and transmission companies tax, the gross receipts oil tax, and the unincorporated business tax restricted to entities with 500 or fewer employees in the United States on the date of application. In addition, a taxpayer principally engaged in aviation, or a utility subject to the supervision of the State Department of Public Service was also ineligible for Amnesty.

/e   Texas does not impose a corporate or individual income tax. In practical effect, the Amnesty was limited to the sales tax and other excises.

/f   Only Personal Income Tax Assessments Receivable.

119

The California "one time only" tax amnesty program lasted for 94 days, between December 10, 1984 and March 15, 1985. The personal income tax collected was approximately $154 million, received from over 147,000 individuals. The cost to generate these results was $5.2 million for personnel and $1.3 million of additional operating expenses. The cost benefit ratio produced by the California Amnesty Program was $24 of collection to each dollar expended.

ESTIMATE OF THE MAGNITUDE

Estimating the potential magnitude of additional tax revenues that would result from a combined federal, state, and local tax amnesty program is an unusually difficult endeavor. Such a program has never been done before in the United States, and, as a consequence, there is no historical precedence on which to base any such estimates. In addition, the size of the underground economy, which is, in essence, the tax base for such collections, is not well ranged. This lack of precision in the estimates is easy to understand given that the purpose of the participants in the underground economy is to avoid detection. Whether understandable or not, however, the plain fact is that any estimate is, perforce the nature of the circumstances, more likened to a guess than it is to a scientific deduction.

Over the past five years, federal personal income tax receipts have totaled $1.992 trillion and federal corporate taxes were $0.397 trillion. In addition, the federal government has collected $0.178 trillion in excise taxes, $1.119 trillion in employment taxes, and $0.034 trillion in gift and estate taxes. The grand total for federal tax collection over the 1983–87 fiscal years is an incredible $3.719 trillion. State and local government revenues are also truly enormous over the past five fiscal years. In total, the numbers are approximately the same size as the gross receipts of the federal government. Individual taxes and corporate taxes are somewhat smaller as a share, with property taxes and sales taxes being larger.

Nonetheless, we are talking about a tax takeover the last five years of over $6 trillion. Assuming that the underground economy disgorges an amount equal to ¾ of one percent additional revenues on a federal, state, and local basis, the total additional revenues would be $40 billion with a one percent yield providing some $60 billion of additional revenues. Our view is that in the first year, a program of tax amnesty coupled with an offer-in-compromise program would yield $50 billion with a lesser sum being generated on in perpetuity.

Although 26 states have had successful programs which resulted in receipt of large amounts of revenue and the expansion of the taxpayer base, their success was limited because the federal government was not a participant. Federal amnesty, coupled with a national program to enter into offers-in-compromise and collect installment agreements, will serve to reduce the federal deficit, increase tax compliance, and, most surprisingly, increase output, employment, and production.

NOTE

1. Charles A. Parker, "A Post-Mortem on the Tax Rebate," *Economic and Investment Observations,* H. C. Wainwright & Co., April 20, 1977; Truman A. Clark, "The Good, the Bad, and the Ugly," *Economy in Perspective,* A. B. Laffer Associates, May 29, 1987.

9

Fifteen Percent Is Fine, but Indexing Is Divine

Victor A. Canto and Harvey B. Hirschhorn

The debate about capital gains taxation has been reopened by President George Bush. During the 1988 presidential campaign Bush stated that the maximum tax rate on capital gains on assets held for over one year should be lowered to 15 percent from the current 28 percent rate. He argued that, over time, the reduction in the capital gains tax rate would raise investment, national income, labor productivity, the capital stock, and the overall standard of living. Bush believes that the proposed tax rate reduction might even increase federal tax revenue. It has been reported that such a two-tiered tax rate reduction would also reduce volatility in the stock market.

Historically, capital gains tax receipts have comprised 5 percent of personal income tax receipts and less than 2 percent of all federal revenue. Moreover, capital gains on stock transactions have accounted for only one-third of total capital gains. Therefore, if viewed from a static framework, the capital gains tax would appear to have minor impact on the economy. If the rate reduction is to have the desired effect on the economy, it must have a profound effect on economic behavior through increased incentives.

THE REVIEW OF THE EVIDENCE

Researchers and policy makers continue to dispute whether a capital gains tax rate reduction would increase or decrease capital gains tax revenues. Accurate tax revenue estimation requires an understanding of the appropriate measurement of the changes in incentives resulting from capital gains tax rate changes as well as the degree of responsiveness to the increase in incentives.

A number of studies have attempted to measure the responsiveness of capital gains tax revenues to capital gains tax rate reductions. An excellent review of the findings and conclusions is reported in a recent Treasury Department study conducted by Treasury Assistant Secretary Michael Darby. Here is an excerpt from Darby's report:

This paper demonstrates that updating the Treasury sample to reflect more recent "actual experience" reverses Minarik's conclusions. When we extend the original Treasury regression specification through 1985, the results imply that the 1978 act produced large and continuing direct revenue gains. Extension of the sample and correction of a flaw in the Treasury report's measurement of inflationary GNP dramatically reduce the estimated losses from the 1981 changes. Finally, substitution of clearly superior regression specifications taken from the 1988 CBO study yields the conclusion that both acts were significantly revenue-enhancing. We further find that the CBO's own conclusion that capital gains preferences would be likely to lose revenue is essentially an artifact of their simulation method, rather than being a straightforward implication of their regressions.[1]

Although somewhat different assumptions were made by the different authors, by and large all the studies used an average marginal tax rate as an explanatory variable. In particular, the Treasury study capital gains tax rate variable used the average rate applicable only to high-income taxpayers. The marginal tax rate estimates were nothing more than the average marginal tax rate on capital gains for taxpayers with more than $200,000 of adjusted gross income (Figure 9.1). The CBO study used a weighted-average capital gains tax rate estimate for six different adjusted gross income groups. Unfortunately, the bases on which these capital gains were calculated were not adjusted for changes in the price level from the time when the asset was purchased. As a result, these measures of effective tax rates substantially underestimate the capital gains tax rate effect on incentives. The use of these tax rates biases downwards the estimated responsiveness (i.e., elasticity estimates) of tax revenue to changes in incentives.

Thus, it is not surprising to find that the study which used the higher effective tax rates found that a capital gains tax rate reduction could expand the revenue base by an amount sufficient to be self-financing. In our opinion, using the higher effective tax rates produces a better measure of incentive effects. The "Laffer curve" is alive and well.

Part of the calculated capital gain is the result of illusory gains resulting from inflation. Adjusting for the changes in the price level would give an estimate of the true economic capital gains. Applying the capital gains tax payments to the true economic capital gains would given an estimate of the true effective capital gains tax rate. This would illustrate the degree to which all of these studies underestimate the disincentives implicit in an unindexed capital gains tax.

The interaction between inflation, the holding period, and the legislated marginal tax rate on capital gains has an additional and significant impact on effec-

Figure 9.1
Capital Gains Tax Rates: Treasury's Estimate of Marginal Tax Rate, 1954–85*

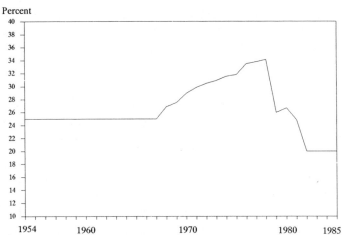

* Marginal tax rate: Average marginal tax rate on a predicted amount of capital gains for taxpayers with more than $200,000 in Adjusted Gross Income in 1982 dollars.

Source: Michael R. Darby, Robert Gillingham, and John S. Greenlees, "The Direct Revenue Effects of Capital Gains Taxation: A Reconsideration of the Time-Series Evidence," *Treasury Bulletin,* U.S. Department of the Treasury, Office of the Assistant Secretary Economic Policy, Spring 1988.

<u>A.B. Laffer Associates</u>

tive marginal tax rates across investments. Consider an asset with an initial value of $100. Assume that at the end of one year the asset increases in value to $120. If sold, the nominal capital gain will be $20 and, under current law, the maximum capital gains tax will be $5.60 (.28 × $20). If during the year inflation accounted for $10 of the gain, then the true economic capital gain would be $10, in which case the effective capital gains tax average rate would be 56 percent, not the 28 percent legislated tax rate. If instead inflation accounted for $20, the nominal value of the asset would then have increased to $130 while the real value would rise only to $110. The nominal capital gain would be $30 and the maximum tax liability would be $8.40 (.28 × $30). Thus, the effective average tax rate rose to 84 percent.

Under current capital gains tax treatment, rising inflation rates increase the effective tax rate on capital gains. This suggests that increases in the inflation rate will at some point result in a tax rate of 100 percent on true capital gains. Table 9.1 reports the combination of inflation and real returns that result in an effective marginal tax rate of 100 percent. In practice, the actual thresholds are lengthened by the numerous provisions in the tax code that allow taxpayers to offset capital losses against capital gains (i.e., the depreciation write-off, the once-in-a-lifetime exclusion of $125,000 gains from sales of owner-occupied houses, roll-over

Table 9.1
**Inflation Rates That Result in an Effective Capital Gains Tax Rate of 100 Percent,
Given Different Combinations of Real Rates of Return and Legislated Capital Gains
Tax Rates**

Real Rate of Return	28 % Capital Gains Tax	20 % Capital Gains Tax	15 % Capital Gains Tax
		Inflation Rate	
1	2.57 %	4 %	5.67 %
2	5.14	8	11.33
3	7.71	12	17.00
4	10.28	16	22.67

A.B. Laffer Associates

provisions). The choice of assets selected may have different depreciation schedules and, hence, different tax shelters. All of these effects may work to reduce some of the negative interactions of inflation and the tax code. The calculations indicate that even a modest increase in the inflation rate will cause a substantial increase in effective tax rates. For example, a capital gains tax rate of 20 percent, real returns of 2 percent per year, and a 1 percent inflation rate will result in an effective capital gains tax rate of 30 percent (Table 9.2). Increases in the inflation rate raise the effective rate dramatically: At an 8 percent inflation rate, the effective rate reaches 100 percent on true capital gains.

EFFECTS OF AN ANTICIPATED INCREASE IN CAPITAL GAINS TAX RATE

Increases in the legislated capital gains tax rate also have a strong and significant impact on the effective tax rate. Assuming a 2 percent real return and a 4 percent inflation rate, an increase in the capital gains tax rate to 28 percent from 20 percent increases the effective marginal tax rate to 84 percent from 60 percent. Thus, an anticipated increase in the capital gains tax rate could induce a sell-off of assets in order to realize capital gains in the present, before the rates take effect. An implication of this analysis is that during the short run, attempts to avoid the statutory increase in tax rates will result in a short-run increase in revenue collection. Over time, investments and hence capital gains will decline. Insofar as the higher tax rates reduce the potential taxable base, revenues will also tend to decline.

The casual, empirical evidence suggests that capital gains tax rate reductions do exert a considerable influence on economic behavior. The 1987 increase in the

Table 9.2
Effective Capital Gains Tax Rate Given Different Inflation, Real Return, and Legislated Capital Gains Tax Rates

Inflation Rate	Real Rate of Return	Effective Tax Rate Under 28 % Legislated Rate	Effective Tax Rate Under 20 % Legislated Rate	Effective Tax Rate Under 15 % Legislated Rate
1	1	56.0 %	40.0 %	30.0 %
1	2	42.0	30.0	22.5
1	3	37.3	26.7	20.0
2	1	84.0	60.0	45.0
2	2	56.0	40.0	30.0
2	3	46.7	33.3	25.0
3	1	112.0	80.0	60.0
3	2	70.0	50.0	37.5
3	3	56.0	40.0	30.0
4	1	140.0	100.0	75.0
4	2	84.0	60.0	45.0
4	3	65.3	46.7	35.0
5	1	168.0	120.0	90.0
5	2	98.0	70.0	52.5
5	3	74.7	53.3	40.0
6	1	196.0	140.0	105.0
6	2	112.0	80.0	60.0
6	3	84.0	60.0	45.0
7	2	126.0	90.0	67.5
7	3	93.3	66.7	50.0
8	2	140.0	100.0	75.0
8	3	102.7	73.3	55.0
9	2	154.0	110.0	82.5
9	3	112.0	80.0	60.0
10	2	168.0	120.0	90.0
10	3	121.3	86.7	65.0
11	2	182.0	130.0	97.5
11	3	130.7	93.3	70.0
12	3	140.0	100.0	75.0
13	3	149.3	106.7	80.0
14	3	158.7	113.3	85.0
15	3	168.0	120.0	90.0
16	3	177.3	126.7	95.0
17	3	186.7	133.3	100.0

A.B. Laffer Associates

top capital gains tax rate to 28 percent from 20 percent provided investors with strong incentives to realize capital gains in 1986. Incentives to realize capital gains also existed for individuals in brackets below the top rate. Supply-side economists, recognizing the power of these incentives, predicted a one-time surge in capital gains tax revenues as taxable investors acted to beat the increases in capital gains tax rates.[2]

A surge in capital gains tax revenues was experienced by the states and by the federal government prior to the higher 28 percent rate becoming effective. Conventional economists failed to foresee this huge increase in capital gains tax receipts in 1987. Then, because they doubted that a one-time opportunity to reduce taxes could have such a pronounced effect, they compounded their original error by assuming that the "surprise" increase in tax collections was a permanent development. This led them to project higher capital gains tax revenues far into the next decade. However, since the special incentives to realize capital gains in 1987 were only temporary, the projected revenues did not materialize. Approximately a dozen states are now facing budgetary pressures because of the unanticipated drop in capital gains tax revenues.[3]

EFFECTS OF A SIMULTANEOUS INCREASE IN CAPITAL GAINS TAX RATE AND INFLATION RATE

An increase in the capital gains tax rate to 28 percent, as articulated in the Tax Reform Act of 1986, combined with the increase in inflationary expectations reflected by the rise in long bonds during the first nine months of 1987, may explain, in part, the decline in equity values experienced before and during October 1987.[4] Furthermore, if correct, our analysis suggests that investors' perception of inflation will have a significant impact on capital gains valuation. Changing expectations of inflation will change market valuation and will be interpreted as an increase in the speculative nature of the market.

It seems reasonable to argue that increasing the capital gains tax rate, combined with a change in monetary policy that moved away from a price rule and toward watching the "real" economy, may have increased the volatility of the expectation of inflation, and as a consequence, the expected effective tax rate on capital gains of the stock market and depressed equity values. The solution to stock market jitters is a policy that induces a reduction in the investor's expected effective tax rate on capital gains. This may be accomplished by a reduction in the capital gains tax rate, indexation of the capital gains tax base, a monetary policy that focuses on a price rule for reducing inflationary expectations, or by a combination of these initiatives.

EFFECTS OF A CAPITAL GAINS TAX RATE REDUCTION

Assuming a 2 percent real return and 5 percent inflation, the results reported in Table 9.2 indicate that a reduction in the capital gains tax rate to 15 percent would reduce the effective tax rate substantially, to 52.5 percent from 98 percent. Assuming a reduction in the inflation rate to 2 percent, the effective capital gains tax rate will further decline to 30 percent. The increase in incentives resulting from the capital gains tax rate and inflation rate reductions would initially reduce capital gains tax revenues. Over time, however, revenues will increase. These implications are consistent with the Treasury Department's recent estimate that the 1978 capital gains tax rate reduction paid for itself. The capital gains tax rate was in the prohibitive range of the Laffer curve. Although the reduction in the capital gains tax rate goes a long way to alleviate the intertemporal bracket creep induced by the interaction of inflation and the tax code, it will not completely eliminate it.

INDEXATION AND REDUCTION IN EFFECTIVE TAX RATES

There are three possible ways to eliminate bracket creep. One is to eliminate the capital gains tax altogether. While this would also eliminate some double taxation of income, it may not be politically viable at this time and will not be considered further. The second way to eliminate bracket creep is to index the capital gains tax base. The third is to adopt a monetary policy that eliminates price inflation. To illustrate the potential impact of indexation, Table 9.3 reports the reduction in the effective tax rate faced by an investor with indexation under 28, 20, and 15 percent capital gains tax rates.

Assuming a 4 percent inflation rate and a 2 percent real rate of return, the effective tax rate is 84 percent under the current capital gains tax structure (Table 9.2). Indexing will reduce the effective tax rate to its legislated level, 28 percent. Thus, indexing will reduce the effective tax rate 56 percentage points (Table 9.3). The impact of indexing on the effective tax rate is dramatic. Out of every dollar of capital gains, investors will, under indexing, be able to keep 72 cents of true capital gains as opposed to 16 percent absent indexing provisions. In this case, indexing will result in a four-fold increase in incentives.

GRH AND CAPITAL GAINS TAX REFORM

Operationally, the constraints imposed by Gramm-Rudman-Hollings (GRH) are such that any budget discussion of the revenue effects of proposed tax rate changes has to be based on "static" revenue analysis. The static revenue losses of a reduction of the capital gains tax rate will be precisely according to the description given at the beginning of this chapter. Recall that the top 1 percent of all equity and the top 1 percent of tax returns account for over 50 percent of all capital gains. Thus, it seems reasonable that at least half of the static revenue losses will decline by the full amount of the tax rate reduction (to 15 percent from 28 percent). Thus, the static revenue losses will decline by at least 25 percent of total capital gains tax receipts. This will result in a reduction of personal income

Table 9.3
Reduction in Effective Capital Gains Tax Rate Due to Indexing

Inflation	Real	Reduction in Effective Tax Rate from 28%	Reduction in Effective Tax Rate from 20%	Reduction in Effective Tax Rate from 15%
1	1	28.0 %	20.0 %	15.0 %
1	2	14.0	10.0	7.5
1	3	9.3	6.7	5.0
2	1	56.0	40.0	30.0
2	2	28.0	20.0	15.0
2	3	18.7	13.3	10.0
3	1	84.0	60.0	45.0
3	2	42.0	30.0	22.5
3	3	28.0	20.0	15.0
4	1	112.0	80.0	60.0
4	2	56.0	40.0	30.0
4	3	37.3	26.7	20.0
5	1	140.0	100.0	75.0
5	2	70.0	50.0	37.5
5	3	46.7	33.3	25.0
6	1	168.0	120.0	90.0
6	2	84.0	60.0	45.0
6	3	56.0	40.0	30.0
7	2	98.0	70.0	52.5
7	3	65.3	46.7	35.0
8	2	112.0	80.0	60.0
8	3	74.7	53.3	40.0
9	2	126.0	90.0	67.5
9	3	84.0	60.0	45.0
10	2	140.0	100.0	75.0
10	3	93.3	66.7	50.0
11	2	154.0	110.0	82.5
11	3	102.7	73.3	55.0
12	3	112.0	80.0	60.0
13	3	121.3	86.7	65.0
14	3	130.7	93.3	70.0
15	3	140.0	100.0	75.0
16	3	149.3	106.7	80.0
17	3	158.7	113.3	85.0

A.B. Laffer Associates

tax receipts of slightly over 1 percent because capital gains tax receipts are some 5 percent of total personal income tax receipts. The loss in revenue from all sources will be on the order of one-half of one percent.

Retroactive indexing of capital gains could result in substantial revenue losses. To illustrate, consider an asset with a $100 capital gain, 10 percent of which was generated by past inflation. Under the current unindexed code, the capital gains tax would be $28. Absent indexing the effective tax rate on the true capital gain would be 31.1 percent ($28/$90). Under retroactive indexing, the taxable base would be decreased 10 percent; hence indexing would result in a $2.80 revenue loss (Table 9.4).

As the percentage gain due to inflation increases to say 80 percent, the revenue losses due to retroactive indexing would be $22.40 on $100 of nominal capital gains (Table 9.4). Furthermore, since the capital gains already realized are based on past behavior and inflation rates, retroactive indexing would not increase incentives to produce. It would amount to a transfer payment based on characteristics other than current or future production incentives. Retroactive indexing would result in revenue losses without increasing marginal incentives to produce. Therefore, from an incentive point of view, retroactive indexing is not recommended.

The static revenue shortfall created by retroactive indexation of the capital gains tax could be substantial and would make retroactive indexation an unrealistic policy change under GRH. However, there is an alternative way to index from this point forward: Adopt a domestic price rule that insures price stability. Under such a price rule, inflation is eliminated. Hence, the impact of inflation on the capital gains tax rate is eliminated from that point forward. Obviously, past investments will still be subject to an effective tax rate in excess of the legislated tax rate. Capital gains from this point forward will not be subjected to the excessive effective rates. Thus, the average capital gains will decline over time for old investment and will approach the legislated rate. For new investment the effective and legislated rates will be identical.

Consider again an asset originally bought for $100 that increases in value to $105. Under an unindexed tax system the capital gain would be $5 and the capital gain tax would be $1.40 ($5 × .28) (Table 9.5). Indexing will increase the

Table 9.4
Impact of Retroactive Indexing on Capital Gains Revenue

Percent of Gain of Value Arising from Inflation	Tax on Indexed Capital Gains	Effective Tax Rate	Revenue Loss Under Indexed System
10 %	28 %	31.10 %	$ 2.80
20	28	35.00	5.60
40	28	46.67	11.20
60	28	70.00	16.80
80	28	140.00	22.40

A.B. Laffer Associates

base from which capital gains are computed by the inflation rate, say 5 percent for the next fiscal year. In which case the asset base will be increased to $105 and the "illusory" gains due to changes in the price level will be eliminated. After adjusting for inflation, there would not be any capital gains. The revenue loss from indexing would be $1.40; 100 percent of the capital gain revenues would be lost to indexation.

In contrast, if the asset increases in value 20 percent (to $120 from $100), under the unindexed tax system the capital gains would be $20 and would generate $5.6 of capital gain tax revenue. Under indexing, the gains amount to $15 and the capital gains tax would be $4.20. In this case, indexing results in a 25 percent reduction in capital gains tax revenue. The estimated revenue losses decline as the share of "illusory" capital gains decreases (Table 9.5). In the limit, as the one-year capital gain approaches 100 percent of the asset value, the reduction in revenue due to indexation approaches the inflation rate (i.e., 5 percent). The indexing alternative need not account for previous changes in the consumer price index, only for changes that take place from the time the legislation is approved. Therefore, the potential revenue losses for the indexing provision are of a similar order of magnitude to those of the reduction in the top rate to 15 percent.

The combinations of inflation and real returns that yield an effective tax rate of 28 percent under a 15 percent unindexed capital gains tax rate are reported in Table 9.6. It thus appears that for reasonable real rates of return (i.e., 5 percent or

Table 9.5

Estimated Revenue Losses from Indexing the CPI under a 5 Percent Inflation Rate Assumption and 28 Percent Capital Gains Tax Rate

Capital Gains	Tax on Indexed Capital Gains	Tax on Unindexed Capital Gains	Revenue Loss as a % of Unindexed Gains
5 %	0.00 %	1.40 %	100.00 %
10	1.40	2.80	50.00
20	4.20	5.60	25.00
30	7.00	8.40	16.67
40	9.80	11.20	12.50
50	12.60	14.00	10.00
60	15.40	16.80	8.33
70	18.20	19.60	7.14
80	21.00	22.40	6.25
90	23.80	25.20	5.46
100	26.60	28.00	5.00

A.B. Laffer Associates

Table 9.6
Combination of Inflation Rate and Real Rates of Return That Yields an Effective 28 Percent Tax Rate under Unindexed 15 Percent Capital Gains Rate

Inflation	Real Rate
0.87 %	1 %
1.74	2
2.61	3
3.48	4
4.35	5

A.B. Laffer Associates

less) and an inflation rate in excess of 4 percent, investors would be better off under indexing.

INFLATION, TAXES, AND HURDLE RATES OF RETURN

One way to investigate the impact of the proposed capital gains tax rate change is to estimate investor's pretax equity returns necessary to generate a 3 percent real after-tax equity rate of return. The pretax equity return to investors is a function of the taxation of dividends and capital gains, the inflation rate, and the required equity return after taxes and after inflation.

In the following analysis, four different situations are considered:

- A top personal income tax rate of 50 percent and a top capital gains tax rate of 20 percent. These were the tax rates that resulted from the Economic Recovery Act of 1981.
- A top personal income tax rate of 28 percent and a top capital gains tax rate of 28 percent. These are the tax rates resulting from the Tax Reform Act of 1986.
- A top personal income tax rate of 28 percent and a top capital gains tax rate of 15 percent. These rates were proposed by President Bush during his campaign.
- A top personal income tax rate of 28 percent and a top capital gains rate of 28 percent, with full indexation of both the personal income and capital gains tax bases. This is our proposal.

The highest marginal tax rate for individuals is used because the top 1 percent of all equity and the top 1 percent of tax returns account for over 50 percent of all capital gains taxes. In order to illustrate the effect of the interaction among the different variables, a 3 percent required equity real return, after taxes and after inflation, is assumed. Historically, equities have been priced to return 2 to 4 percent per annum on this basis. Assuming a 4 percent inflationary expectation, the required after-tax nominal return is 7 percent (Table 9.7). Assuming a 3

Table 9.7
Impact of the Capital Gains Tax Rate on Pretax Rates of Return

	Capital Gains Tax Rate 20%	Capital Gains Tax Rate 28%	Capital Gains Tax Rate 15%	Capital Gains Tax Rate 28% (with indexation)
Required equity return after taxes after infaltion	3.0 %	3.0 %	3.0 %	3.0 %
Inflation expectation	4.0	4.0	4.0	4.0
Required after tax nominal return	7.0	7.0	7.0	7.0
Portion of required after-tax nominal return generated by dividends (3% yield x (1 - income tax rate))	1.5*	2.2	2.2	2.2
Portion of required nominal after-tax return generated by capital gain	5.5	4.8	4.8	4.8
Required pretax return generated by capital gains	6.9	6.7	5.6	5.2
Required pretax nominal return (capital gains plus dividends)	9.9	9.7	8.6	8.1
Required pretax real return	5.9	5.7	4.6	4.1

* When the capital gains tax rate was 20 percent, the individual income tax rate was 50 percent. The Tax Reform Act of 1986 raised the capital gains tax rate to 28 percent as it lowered the top individual income tax rate to 28 percent. In all other cases, a 28 percent top individual income tax rate is assumed.

A.B. Laffer Associates

percent dividend yield and a 72 percent retention rate under the current law, a 2.2 percent nominal after-tax return is generated by dividend payments. This leaves 4.8 percent of the required 7 percent after-tax nominal return to be generated by capital gains, in which case, the required pretax nominal rate of appreciation will be grossed up by the capital gains tax rate. Thus, the pretax nominal appreciation under the current tax system will be 6.7 percent. The combination of the pretax dividend yields and pretax nominal appreciation results in a pretax nominal return of 9.7 percent (Table 9.7, column 2). Under the proposed capital gains tax rate of 15 percent, the required pretax return will decline to 9.7 percent.

In contrast, indexing the current tax rates will cause only the required real appreciation to be subject to capital gains taxes. Thus only 0.8 percent out of the 4.8 percent required equity appreciation will be subject to capital gains taxes (Table 9.7, column 2, row 3). Indexing will eliminate bracket creep and reduce the required pretax nominal return to 8.1 percent from 9.7 percent.

Under the Economic Recovery Act of 1981, with its top personal income tax rate of 50 percent, a 3 percent dividend yield resulted in 1.5 percent of the required pretax return being generated by the dividend policy. This left 5.5 percent of the 7 percent pretax nominal return to be generated by capital gains (Table 9.7, column 1). With a 20 percent marginal tax rate on capital gains, the required pretax equity appreciation was 6.9 percent. This, combined with the pretax dividend, resulted in a pretax nominal return of 9.9 percent.

These calculations can be used to justify a number of positions. For example, one can argue that the Tax Reform Act of 1986, which lowered personal income tax rates to 28 percent from 50 percent while raising the capital gains tax rate to 28 percent from 20 percent, lowered the required pretax nominal return to 9.7 from 9.9. Given our 4 percent inflation assumption, the required real rate of return decreased to 5.7 percent from 5.9 percent. Thus, the recent changes effectively lowered the hurdle rate of return.

Bush's proposal to reduce the maximum marginal tax rate for capital gains to 15 percent from 28 percent would enhance investment prospects. The proposed reform would lower the pretax required real rate of return to 4.6 percent from 5.7 percent, a 24 percent reduction in the required rate of return.

Interestingly, our proposal of indexing the tax code while keeping the 28 percent marginal tax rate would reduce the required pretax real return to 4.1 percent. This is even lower than the 4.6 percent required pretax return under the proposed 15 percent capital gains tax top rate. These calculations suggest that indexing the tax code will have an even larger favorable effect on the hurdle rate of return, and the increased incentives would have an even larger effect on the economy. Either Bush's proposal of reducing the top capital gains tax rate to 15 percent or the indexing of the current rate structure is clearly superior to the present system. Comparing these two alternatives further, it becomes evident that indexing will be the superior alternative.

During the past nine years, U.S. tax policy has been on a steady course toward lower rates. The debate on the Jenkins capital gains bill is much the same as previous debates on tax rate cuts.[5] Proponents of lower and indexed capital gains tax rates focus on the incentive effects of the legislation and argue that the Jenkins plan will result in higher economic growth and higher employment. Opponents focus on the income effects and thus argue that the Jenkins plan is nothing more than a tax cut for the rich that will not improve the overall economy.

Whether capital gains tax reductions actually enhance the performance of the economy or the stock market is an empirical question. In a forward-looking market, stock prices reflect discounted future profits. Since 1969, five major modifications to the capital gains tax rate have taken place. The effective rate was increased in three of those instances: 1969, 1976, and 1986. In the remaining two events, 1978 and 1981, the effective tax rate was reduced. The evidence indicates that the rate of appreciation of the stock market was higher during periods following tax rate reductions and lower during periods when the effective tax rate was increased. The excess return averaged a 6 percent increase for the 12 months following the rate reduction and a 10.5 percent decline for the period following the capital gains tax increase.

The Jenkins plan, through its indexing provision, will reduce the effective tax rate on capital gains.[6] Given the previous experience with capital gains tax rate changes, an above-average stock price return is to be expected in the next 6 to 12 months.

HISTORICAL OVERVIEW OF CAPITAL GAINS LEGISLATION

Since the Revenue Act of 1921, capital gains have been subject to preferentially low rates: from 1942 to 1978 there was a 50 percent exclusion, and from 1979 to 1986 there was a 60 percent exclusion. For much of the period the tax was limited to a maximum of 25 percent.

The Tax Reform Act of 1969 imposed a "minimum" tax on those with very large amounts of capital gains income or those benefitting from preferential provisions. This act also reduced the maximum tax rate on earned income to 50 percent from 70 percent. Additionally, the act phased out over three years an alternative tax which effectively raised the maximum marginal capital gains tax rate to 35 percent in 1972. Taxpayers in the highest tax bracket who were subject to the "minimum" tax faced an effective capital gains rate of 45.5 percent in 1972.

The Tax Reform Act of 1976 effectively raised the capital gains tax rate by increasing the minimum tax rate and reducing allowable deductions from the minimum tax calculation. As a result, taxpayers in the top bracket who were subject to the "minimum" tax had an effective capital gains tax rate of 39.875 percent. If these taxpayers also were subject to the maximum tax calculation, their effective capital gains tax rate would have been 49.125 percent. The 1976 act also increased the holding period for capital gains to be considered long-term from six months to nine months in 1977 and to 12 months in 1978.

The Revenue Act of 1978 (1) eliminated the minimum and maximum tax calculations for capital gains and (2) raised the long-term capital gains exclusion to 60 percent from 30 percent. As a result, the effective maximum capital gains tax rate was lowered to 28 percent. The Economic Recovery Tax Act of 1981 lowered the top rate on ordinary income to 50 percent from 70 percent. The maximum capital gains tax rate was lowered to 20 percent from 28 percent.

The Tax Reform Act of 1986 ended the capital gains exclusion, but it reduced the marginal tax rate for ordinary income for the highest income taxpayers to 38.5 percent for 1987 and to 28 percent in 1988. For 1987, the maximum capital gains tax rate for any taxpayer was 28 percent. However, in 1988, those taxpayers in the 33 percent marginal tax rate bracket also had the 33 percent rate applied to their capital gains.

DO EQUITY VALUES BENEFIT FROM CAPITAL GAINS TAX REDUCTIONS?

One way to estimate the impact of capital gains tax legislation on the stock market is to attempt to determine how the stock market would have performed in the absence of the effective tax rate change. This can be done by looking at the historical performance of the market and using its average growth rate as the expected value. The differential performance between the historical average (expected value) and the actual stock market behavior is attributed to capital gains action.[7] Although not perfect, this technique allows us to estimate the impact of capital gains tax rate changes. If capital gains legislation improves the profitability of domestic industries, then the stock market performance will be above average.

Since there is no definitive procedure for selecting a time period to calculate the cumulative excess returns, two different intervals were chosen within the event period. The first interval begins 12 months before the event month (the month in which the legislation is effective); the second ends 12 months following the event month. The excess return for each month is calculated by subtracting the average mean stock market return for the stock market from the observed stock market performance for the particular month. The cumulative excess returns are calculated by adding the excess returns for each month in the interval period.

The results indicate that for the 12 months following the increase in the effective capital gains tax rate, the stock market declined (Table 9.8). The cumulative decline was 6.59 percent in 1969, 16.40 percent in 1976, and 8.53 percent in 1986. On average, the market declined 10.50 percent. Twelve months after the reduction in the effective capital gains tax rate, the stock market appreciated. The cumulative increase was 6.06 percent for 1978 and 6.44 percent for

Table 9.8
**Combination of Inflation Rate and Real Rates of Return That Yields an Effective 28
Percent Tax Rate under Unindexed 15 Percent Capital Gains Rate**

Inflation	Real Rate
.87 %	1 %
1.74	2
2.61	3
3.48	4
4.35	5

A.B. Laffer Associates

1981. In each instance, within the twelve month period, the effective tax increase
in capital gains resulted in a decline in the stock market, while reductions in the
effective tax rate were associated with increases in the stock market.[8]

CAPITAL GAINS: A PROPOSAL

A Bush administration proposal to reduce the capital gains tax rate has finally
made center stage in the financial press. Some of the key elements include:

• Differential taxation of short-term and long-term capital gains
• A reduction in the tax rate on long-term capital gains to 15 percent from current levels
• A narrowing of the taxable base subject to the 15 percent tax rate: objets d'art, antiques,
  and housing would not be included
• The omission of an indexing provision

Quite clearly, any cut in any capital gains tax rate is, per se, good. But, to
achieve a capital gains tax rate cut in the real world requires an expenditure of a
lot of political capital. As long as the administration is going to pay the price, it
might as well get as much as it can. The administration is erring in not asking for
what is right—a capital gains tax rate cut on all assets (short and long) including
art, antiques, and housing.

We find the administration's proposal on a reduction in capital gains tax
seriously flawed, even though we would reluctantly vote for it if we were members of Congress. Our belief is that:

• There should be no distinction between short-term and long-term capital gains.
• Art, antiques, and housing should be covered fully.
• Every form of investor should be covered.
• Capital gains should be indexed prospectively.

- Excessive depreciation of some assets should constructively be recaptured at ordinary tax rates.

Problems with the Administration's Proposal

The administration proposal, as it stands, will generate at least three undesired effects:

1. *The distinction between short-term and long-term capital gains* effectively introduces a differential tax rate between similar assets that are held for different periods. Whenever differential tax rates are introduced, economic agents have strong incentives to "convert" income normally taxed at higher rates into income taxed at a lower rate. Differential taxation gives rise to tax avoidance and tax sheltering activity that reduces the efficiency of the economy and reduces the revenue collected by the government. Short-term asset holders will be locked in to their investments to the detriment of all. These problems are clearly eliminated by having a uniform tax rate applicable to all maturities.

2. *Excessive depreciation of some assets should constructively be recaptured at ordinary tax rates.* The logic, if such be the case, is that housing has been excessively dynamited as tax shelters, and therefore, to avoid further abuses, these assets were excluded from the capital gains tax cut. Wrong! If excessive depreciation is the problem—and it may well be a problem—then the excessive component of depreciation should be constructively recaptured and taxed at ordinary income tax rates while true capital gains are taxed at the lower rate. The two wrongs are not off-setting although they are off-putting.

3. *The interaction between inflation, the holding period, and the legislated marginal tax rate on capital gains* has an additional and significant impact on effective marginal tax rates across investments.

Consider an asset with an initial value of $100. Assume that at the end of one year, the asset increases in value to $120. If sold, the nominal capital gain will be $20 and, under current law, the maximum capital gains tax will be $5.60 (28 percent of $20). If during the year inflation accounted for $10 of the gain, then the true economic capital gain would be $10, in which case the effective capital gains tax average rate would be 56 percent, not the 28 percent legislated tax rate.[9]

Under current capital gains tax treatment, rising inflation rates increase the effective tax rate on capital gains. The combination of inflation and real returns that yields an effective tax rate of 28 percent under a 15 percent unindexed capital gains tax rate is reported in Table 9.8. It thus appears that for reasonable real rates of return (i.e., 5 percent or less) and an inflation rate in excess of 4 percent, investors would be better off under indexing.

An additional undesired effect of the proposed unindexed tax system is that it "locks in" the asset holder. The current tax system does not accrue the capital gains; therefore, by not cashing in, the asset holder compounds the gains at a pretax rate of return. In turn, if investors realize capital gains, only the after-tax proceeds would be compounded. Similarly, the exclusion of housing from the proposed lower rates will only increase the incentives to hold on to the housing capital gain until homeowners are old enough to qualify for the once-in-a-lifetime exclusion of $125,000. The one-time exclusion is clearly a very crude way the current tax codes have of dealing with the inflation-induced illusory gain.

Indexation, if applied retroactively, might generate substantial revenue loss. Furthermore, correcting for past inflation does not alter future incentives or behavior. Therefore, from a revenue and incentive point of view, the proper solution is prospective, not retrospective, indexation. Prospective indexation will reduce future bracket creep and increase incentives to invest in long-term capital gains.

Indexation does not completely solve the lock-in effect. The only way to deal with lock-in is to accrue capital gains. Politically and practically, however, that may be too controversial. A direct solution (i.e., indexing) will be superior and, as a side benefit, will clearly reduce, although not eliminate, the lock-in effect. The proposal to reduce the top rate will correct some of the past inflation; however, it will not protect the investor against future inflation. Furthermore, prospective indexing would not add anything to the deficit even with relatively small feedback effects, and it would be much fairer for all.[10]

Budgetary Implications

The revenue impact is the most controversial issue. While we believe that the capital gains tax rate should be zero, such a rate is not politically feasible as it would clearly produce a short-term revenue loss. While we believe that, in time, the capital gains tax rate cuts will pay for themselves, under current Gramm-Rudman-Hollings procedures, these revenue losses will have to be made up.

Historically, capital gains tax receipts have comprised 5 percent of personal income tax receipts and less than 2 percent of all federal revenue. Moreover, capital gains on stock transactions have accounted for only one-third of total capital gains. Therefore, if viewed from a static framework, the capital gains tax would appear to have minor impact on the economy. If the rate reduction is to have the desired effect on the economy, it must have a profound effect on economic behavior through increased incentives.

The top 1 percent of all equity and the top 1 percent of tax returns account for over 50 percent of all capital gains. Thus, it seems reasonable that at least half of the static revenue loss will decline by the full amount of the tax rate reduction (to 15 percent from 28 percent). Thus, the static revenue loss will decline by at least 25 percent of total capital gains tax receipts. This will result in a reduction of personal income tax receipts of slightly over 1 percent because capital gains tax receipts are some 5 percent of total personal income tax receipts. The loss in revenue from all sources will be on the order of one-half of one percent.

Consider again an asset originally bought for $100 that increases in value to

$105. Under an unindexed tax system with a 28 percent tax rate, the capital gain would be $5 and the capital gain tax would be $1.40 (Table 9.9). Indexing will increase the base from which capital gains are computed by the inflation rate, say 5 percent for the next fiscal year, in which case the asset base will be increased to $105 and the "illusory" gains due to changes in the price level will be eliminated. After adjusting for inflation, there would not be any capital gains. The revenue loss from indexing would be $1.40; 100 percent of the capital gain revenue would be lost to indexation.

In contrast, if the asset increases in value 20 percent (to $120 from $100), under the unindexed tax system the capital gains would be $20 and would generate $5.60 of capital gain tax revenue. Under indexing the gains amount to $15 and the capital gains tax would be $4.20. In this case, indexing results in a 25 percent reduction in capital gains tax revenue. The estimated revenue loss declines as the share of "illusory" capital gains decreases (Table 9.9). In the limit, as the one year capital gain approaches 100 percent of the asset value, the reduction in revenue due to indexation approaches the inflation rate (i.e., 5 percent). The indexing alternative need not account for previous changes in the consumer price index, only for changes that take place from the time the legislation is approved. Therefore, the potential revenue losses for the indexing provision are of a similar order of magnitude to those of the reduction in the top rate to 15 percent.

To the extent the rate is effectively cut on long-run capital gains, the "best"

Table 9.9
Estimated Revenue Losses from Indexing the CPI under a 5 Percent Inflation Rate Assumption and 28 Percent Capital Gains Tax Rate

Capital Gains	Tax on Indexed Capital Gains	Tax on Unindexed Capital Gains	Revenue Loss as a % of Unindexed Gains
5 %	0.00 %	1.40 %	100.00 %
10	1.40	2.80	50.00
20	4.20	5.60	25.00
30	7.00	8.40	16.67
40	9.80	11.20	12.50
50	12.60	14.00	10.00
60	15.40	16.80	8.33
70	18.20	19.60	7.14
80	21.00	22.40	6.25
90	23.80	25.20	5.46
100	26.60	28.00	5.00

A.B. Laffer Associates

form of investment will be encouraged. We share the administration's view that capital gains tax rate cuts will pay for themselves. However, opponents argue that in the long run the tax rate cuts will be a net revenue loser. Only in the short run, because of the unlocking of past capital gains, will revenue rise. This difference of opinion casts a shadow over any cut in the capital gains tax rate. By the method Gramm-Rudman-Hollings is calculated, a tax cut could lead to a projected deficit. As such, the dynamics of GRH may force the administration to consider other taxes, since additional spending cuts could be required to comply with the law. This makes a cut in the capital gains tax rate a tricky feat to accomplish as a stand-alone. In conjunction with a broader package, however, it is a real likelihood.

One proposal currently being discussed is to trade off the capital gains tax rate cut for an increase in the federal gasoline tax.[11] The gasoline tax is fairly broad-based and attempts to avoid the tax will distort work incentives. An increase in the gas tax will have a differential impact across geographic regions and income groups. It will clearly increase the progressivity of effective tax rates on groups for whom gasoline is a large fraction of their expenditures. Although difficult to assess, the economic effects of the gasoline tax are clearly undesirable. The proposal shifts the tax burden from one group to another. The proposed trade-off will not necessarily increase the efficiency of the economy and is therefore unacceptable. Even when the 5 cent per gallon gas tax was proposed and passed by the Reagan administration, we took our opposition directly to the president. His angry letter of response hangs on our office wall to this day.

A Supply-Side Alternative

There is a simpler way to raise the necessary revenue and to correct some of the disincentive effects of the currently proposed capital gains tax rate reduction. Consider the effects of the Tax Reform Act of 1986. The increase in the top capital gains tax rate to 28 percent from 20 percent provided investors with strong incentives to realize capital gains in 1986. These incentives were greater the longer the investor's planned holding period. Incentives to realize capital gains also existed for individuals in brackets below the top rate. Supply-side econo-mists, recognizing the power of these incentives, predicted a one-time surge in capital gains tax revenue as taxable investors acted to beat the increases in capital gains tax rates.[12]

In state capitols throughout the nation, conventional economists failed to foresee the huge increase in capital gains tax receipts in 1987. Then, because they doubted that a one-time opportunity to reduce taxes could have such a pronounced effect, conventional revenue forecasters compounded their original error. They assumed that the "surprise" increase in tax collection was a perma-nent rather than a temporary development. This led them to project higher capital gains tax revenue far into the next decade. However, since the special incentives to realize capital gains in 1986 no longer existed, the projected revenue did not materialize. In fact, revenues actually declined.

Similar effects can be found at the federal level. The 1986 tax revenue collections increased an unprecedented amount. Revenue more than doubled, increasing to $49.7 billion in 1986 from $24.5 billion in 1985. Approximately 60 percent of the revenue increase is directly attributable to the incentives to realize capital gains induced by the preannounced tax rate increase. The experience with the Tax Reform Act of 1986 may provide evidence of how sensitive the lock-in effect is to preannounced changes in tax rates. It may also provide a way to induce an early revenue gain: temporarily lower the capital gains for one year to a level below the long-run fully-indexed 28 percent rate. Such a move would partially eliminate the previous illusory gains and may also unlock the capital gains and make them available to capital markets. The one-time reduction would generate a short-term revenue windfall not associated with dynamic feedback effects. In fact, opponents of the view that capital gain reductions will be a net revenue loser agree that the short-run effects will be positive because of the unlocking effect.

Our objective was to find a viable solution that solves some of the current perceived budget constraints. Our proposal, designed to capture the unlocking effects as a way to finance capital gain tax rate indexation, is as follows:

• A one-time, one-year reduction to 15 percent. This will ameliorate the lock-in effect and reduce somewhat the inflation-induced illusory capital gains.

A one-year 15 percent capital gains tax rate will create an incentive for asset holders to cash in their already locked-in capital gain. Such a cut in the capital gains tax rate will result in a one-time revenue surge. If past experiences in 1978 and 1986 are a guide, the surge should reduce any GRH budgetary pressure associated with static revenue estimates.[13] In 1986, 60 percent of the surge in capital gains tax revenue ($15 billion) was attributable to incentives for early realization of gains.

However, care must be exercised in the announcement of the rate reduction. For example, if the reduction was to become effective the next January 1, then capital gain realization would diminish between now and year-end. Then a surge in realization would be observed at the beginning of the next year. One way to avoid this problem is to make the lower rate retroactive to the time the legislation is introduced.

• After the year has passed, the capital gains tax rates would go back to their current levels, fully indexed prospectively. Indexation will eliminate bracket creep and will unambiguously increase the incentives to capital formation.

The effect of these actions will be to reduce the hurdle rate of return for new investments, thus setting the stage for increased investment, productivity, and a higher standard of living. In addition, the United States would become more competitive internationally. As both Japan and West Germany have tax codes which generally exempt capital gains from taxation, indexation would bring the United States closer to these countries' codes.

CONCLUSIONS

The proposed reduction in the top capital gains tax rate to 15 percent from 28 percent would have numerous beneficial effects on the economy: It will reduce the hurdle rate of return required by investors leading to higher investment and higher valuation of the current profit (capital gains) stream. This will tend to increase the value of stocks as well as the tax base. In the long run, it will increase capital gains tax revenues. However, under Gramm-Rudman-Hollings, any static revenue losses would have to be made up. Though the move to reduce the capital gains tax will be desirable for the U.S. economy, a potentially superior alternative is available: Indexing the capital gains tax code and adopting a domestic price rule that reduces the inflation rate will have an even stronger beneficial impact on the U.S. economy.

NOTES

1. Michael R. Darby, Robert Gillingham, and John S. Greenlees, "The Direct Revenue Effects of Capital Gains Taxation: A Reconsideration of the Time-Series Evidence," *Treasury Bulletin,* Spring 1988. The two studies cited by Darby are: Joseph Minarik, "Raising Federal Revenues through a Reduction in the Capital Gains Tax," Statement before the Ad Hoc Committee on the Taxation of Capital Gains, February 2, 1988; and Congressional Budget Office, "How Capital Gains Tax Rates Affect Revenues: The Historical Evidence."

2. Truman A. Clark, "When to Realize Capital Gains," A. B. Laffer Associates, September 26, 1986.

3. Dan Walters, "Which One Is Reaching for Taxes in Budget Pinch?" *Wall Street Journal,* June 2, 1988, p. 22.

4. The increase in the legislated capital gains tax rate to 28 percent from 20 percent will increase the effective tax rate to 84 percent. Clearly, this will induce some asset liquidation, but not a massive sell-off. A rise in inflationary expectations will further increase the effective tax rate. At 6 percent expected inflation, an effective marginal tax rate in excess of 100 percent is reached. This suggests that the combination of an increase in the legislated capital gains tax rate and a rise in inflationary expectations could induce a massive sell-off as well as a massive correction in equity values.

5. Arthur B. Laffer, "Reagan's Economic Proposals within a Supply-Side Framework," A. B. Laffer Associates, March 13, 1981; Arthur B. Laffer, "Economic and Investment Observations: Capital Gains Tax Rate Reduction," in Arthur B. Laffer and Jan Seymour, eds., *The Economics of the Tax Revolt* (New York: Harcourt, Brace, Jovanovich, 1979), pp. 95–105.

6. See Chapter 10; Victor A. Canto and Arthur B. Laffer, "Capital Gains," A. B. Laffer Associates, May 4, 1989.

Table 9.10
Inflation Rates That Result in an Effective Capital Gains Tax Rate of 100 Percent, Given Different Combinations of Real Rates of Return and Legislated Capital Gains Tax Rates

Real Rate of Return	28% Capital Gains Tax	15% Capital Gains Tax
	Inflation Rate	
1	2.57 %	5.67 %
2	5.14	11.33
3	7.71	17.00
4	10.28	22.67

A.B. Laffer Associates

7. For a more detailed description of the methodology, see Victor A. Canto, J. Kimball Dietrich, Adish Jain, and Vishwa Mudaliar, "Protectionism and the Stock Market: The Determinants and Consequences of Trade Restrictions on the U.S. Economy," A. B. Laffer Associates, March 20, 1985.

8. The only remaining issue is the statistical significance of the estimates. In most cases, the estimated t-statistic is below the usual significance level (i.e., a value of 2). However, this result is not totally unexpected. Given that the variance increases around the event month, it is likely that we have overestimated the standard error in calculating the t-statistic.

9. Increases in the inflation rate will at some point result in a tax rate of 100 percent on true capital gains. Table 9.10 reports the combination of inflation and real returns that results in an effective marginal tax rate of 100 percent. The calculations indicate that even a modest increase in the inflation rate will cause a substantial increase in effective tax rates. In practice, the actual thresholds are lengthened by the numerous provisions in the tax code that allow taxpayers to offset capital losses against capital gains (i.e., the depreciation write-off, roll-over provisions, the once-in-a-lifetime exclusion of $125,000 gains from sales of owner-occupied houses, etc.). The choice of assets selected may have different depreciation schedules and, hence, different tax shelters. All of these effects may work to reduce some of the negative interactions of inflation and the tax code.

10. Alan Murray and Michael McQueen, "Bush to Unveil Big Package of Proposals on Taxes Next Week, Including Capital-Gains Levy Cut to 15 Percent," *Wall Street Journal*, January 30, 1989, p. A3; David Wessel, "Bush Sees $5 Billion Revenue Gain from Cut in Tax on Capital Gains," *Wall Street Journal*, February 8, 1989, p. A3.

11. In a recent article in the *Wall Street Journal*, Alan Murray and Jeffrey H. Birnbaum attributed to one of us the willingness to trade a gas tax increase for the Bush proposal. The statement is not correct. We do not favor such a trade-off. See Alan Murray and Jeffrey H. Birnbaum, "Opposition Stirs to Possible Boost in Gasoline Tax," *Wall Street Journal*, May 2, 1989, p. A2.

12. Truman A. Clark, "When to Realize Capital Gains: Update," A. B. Laffer Associates, September 26, 1986.

13. Arthur B. Laffer, "Capital Gains Tax Rate Reduction," H. C. Wainwright & Co., August 1, 1978; Michael R. Darby, Robert Gillingham, and John S. Greenlees, "The Direct Revenue Effects of Capital Gains Taxation: A Reconsideration of the Time-Series Evidence," *Treasury Bulletin,* June 1988.

10

Stylized Facts and Fallacies of Capital Gains Tax Rate Reductions and Indexation

Victor A. Canto and Arthur B. Laffer

A capital gains tax rate cut from the current 28 percent to 15 percent without indexing should be preferred over pure indexing if the real return on the investment exceeded the rate of inflation. With inflation higher than the real return, the preference would be for indexing. At a 20 percent capital gains tax rate, the breakpoint occurs when inflation is 40 percent the size of the real yield.

This explains why people who are after "the big kill" prefer almost any rate reduction over indexing. But we should never let the best become the enemy of the good. Our view is that, on balance, we'll get more of a capital gains tax reduction with indexing than we could ever realistically get with a rate reduction. Future congresses would be far more likely to raise rates back up again than they would be to remove indexing. As a final point, it also seems likely to us that an indexing proposal would have broader coverage than would rate reduction.[1]

Whatever happens, be it rate reduction, indexing, or some combination, we all will be a lot better off. The logic underpinning any tax whatsoever on capital gains is flawed to the core. In spite of Herb Stein's exalted forum on the editorial page of the *Wall Street Journal,* his analogy between a basketball player earning a cool million and an entrepreneur's capital gain of a million is wrong.[2] They are not equivalent events. Capital gains is not income nor is the value of an asset income. Treating changes in the value of an asset as income is sparkle-headed. If income is to be taxed, then capital gains should not be taxed. A government can choose to tax either the value of an asset or its yield, but it should not tax both! That is double taxation.

Capital gains is literally the appreciation in the value of an existing asset. And, as such, any appreciation merely reflects an increase in the after-tax rate of return on that asset. The taxes implicit in the asset's future after-tax earnings are already fully reflected in that asset's price or change in price. A 50 percent income tax on the earnings of an asset will reduce the pretax capital gain on any asset by 50 percent. Any additional tax is strictly double taxation and thereby totally inappropriate.

The correct stance having been enunciated, any reduction in the effective tax rate on capital gains is for the better. The anticipation and eventual realization of a capital gains tax reduction has added, and could still add considerably, to the stock market and economic growth.

At least three different proposals are currently being discussed in the press.[3]

1. *The Bush Plan* would lower the capital gains tax rate to 15 percent on long-term assets without indexing. This proposal excludes real estate, timber, and collectibles.

2. *The Jenkins Plan* would cut the rate on assets held more than one year to 19.6 percent if sold before the end of 1991. It would then boost the top rate back up to 28 percent with indexing. This proposal includes real estate and timber but still excludes collectibles.[4]

3. *The Rostenkowski Plan* would index assets purchased after July 31, 1989. There would be no indexing at all for assets purchased prior to July 31, 1989. For assets held more than five years and also purchased after July 31, 1989, the seller has the option of indexing or paying tax on 75 percent of the sales price regardless of actual gains. After 10 years, the seller may use indexing or opt to pay tax on 50 percent of the sales value. This plan excludes preferred stocks, bonds, stocks in foreign corporations, and intangibles, but includes real estate, corporate stock, and timber.

STYLIZED FACTS

Passage of capital gains tax legislation will significantly affect effective tax rates and the cost of capital to companies. Capital gains taxes, under current tax laws, are levied on nominal capital gains. Therefore, capital gains are not adjusted for changes in the price level. As a result, statutory tax rates substantially underestimate the capital gains tax effect on incentives.

Part of any calculated capital gain is illusory, resulting from inflation. Adjusting for changes in the price level would give an estimate of real capital gains. Applying all capital gains tax payments to the real capital gains would give an estimate of the effective capital gains tax rate.

To illustrate the degree to which all of the legislated tax rates underestimate the disincentives implicit in an unindexed capital gains tax, consider an asset with an initial value of $100. Assume that at the end of one year the asset increases in value to $120. If sold, the nominal capital gain will be $20 and, under current law, the maximum capital gains tax will be $5.60 (.28 × $20). If during the year inflation accounted for $10 of the gain, then the real capital gain would be $10, in which case the effective capital gains tax rate would be 56 percent, not the 28 percent rate legislated. If instead, the asset appreciated to $130 and inflation accounted for $20, then the real value would still have risen to $110. The nominal capital gain, however, would be $30 and the maximum tax liability would be $8.40 (.28 × $30). Thus, the effective average tax rate would have risen to 84 percent.

Whenever the inflation rate equals the real yield, the effective rate on capital gains will be twice as large as the nominal rate. Likewise, when the inflation rate is twice the real yield, the effective tax rate will be three times the statutory rate or 84 percent, and so on. The combinations of inflation, real yields, and the corresponding effective tax rates are shown in Table 10.1. The table reports the same effects for a capital gains tax rate of 15 percent, as has been proposed by President Bush.

Effects of a Capital Gains Tax Rate Reduction

Under all circumstances, a cut in the capital gains tax rate from 28 percent to 15 percent will increase effective yields by 46.4 percent. However, whenever real yields are 28 percent of total yields, that is, inflation is 72 percent of the total yield, then a reduction of the capital gains tax rate to 15 percent from 28 percent will reduce the effective tax rate from 98 percent to 52.5 percent. Examples of this include a situation where inflation is 5 percent and the real yield is 2 percent, or when inflation is 2.5 percent and the real yield is 1 percent.

Alternatively, when inflation is relatively lower, say 50 percent of the total yield, then a reduction in the capital gains tax rate from 28 percent to 15 percent will reduce the effective tax rate from 56 percent to 30 percent. Obviously, if there were no inflation, the effective tax rate would fall from 28 percent to 15 percent.

Indexing for inflation, on the other hand, drops all effective tax rates to the statutory rate. Therefore, indexing drops the effective 98 percent rate (see earlier example) to 28 percent, while lowering the tax rate to 15 percent only brings the 98 percent rate to 52.5 percent. At the other end of the scale, where there is no inflation, indexing has no effect.

Everyone who expects real yields to exceed 53.6 percent (slightly over half) of total yields will prefer a rate reduction from 28 percent to 15 percent to a simple indexing at 28 percent. When real yields are expected to be less than 53.6 percent of total yield, then indexing is preferred. If real yields are more than 70 percent of the total yield, then people would prefer the 19.6 percent capital gains tax rate of the first two years of the Jenkins proposal to the current 28 percent plus indexing.

The Rostenkowski Option

The Rostenkowski alternative tax options are rather unusual, to say the least. However, the Rostenkowski alternatives may deserve some scrutiny. From our perspective, the biggest problem is whether Congress will allow these options to

Table 10.1

Effective Tax Rates on Capital Gains Resulting from the Interaction of Inflation and Capital Gains Tax Rate (Bold 28 percent, Small 15 percent)

Isoimpact scaling factors: 1.17* 1.25* 1.33* 1.5* 2* 3* 4* 5*

Real Yield	Rate	Inflation Rate 2	4	6	8	10	12	14	16	18	20	22	24
24	28	30.3	32.7	35.0	37.3	39.7	42.0	44.3	46.7	49.0	51.3	53.7	56.0
24	15	16.3	17.5	18.8	20.0	21.3	22.5	23.8	25.0	26.3	27.5	28.8	30.0
22	28	30.5	33.1	35.6	38.2	40.7	43.3	45.8	48.4	50.9	53.5	56.0	58.5
22	15	16.4	17.7	19.1	20.5	21.8	23.2	24.5	25.9	27.3	28.6	30.0	31.4
20	28	30.8	33.6	36.4	39.2	42.0	44.8	47.6	50.4	53.2	56.0	58.8	61.6
20	15	16.5	18.0	19.5	21.0	22.5	24.0	25.5	27.0	28.5	30.0	31.5	33.0
18	28	31.1	34.2	37.3	40.4	43.6	46.7	49.8	52.9	56.0	59.1	62.2	65.3
18	15	16.7	18.3	20.0	21.7	23.3	25.0	26.7	28.3	30.0	31.7	33.3	35.0
16	28	31.5	35.0	38.5	42.0	45.5	49.0	52.5	56.0	59.5	63.0	66.5	70.0
16	15	16.9	18.8	20.6	22.5	24.4	26.3	28.1	30.0	31.9	33.8	35.6	37.5
14	28	32.0	36.0	40.0	44.0	48.0	52.0	56.0	60.0	64.0	68.0	72.0	76.0
14	15	17.1	19.3	21.4	23.6	25.7	27.9	30.0	32.1	34.3	36.4	38.6	40.7
12	28	32.7	37.3	42.0	46.7	51.3	56.0	60.7	65.3	70.0	74.7	79.3	84.0
12	15	17.5	20.0	22.5	25.0	27.5	30.0	32.5	35.0	37.5	40.0	42.5	45.0
10	28	33.6	39.2	44.8	50.4	56.0	61.6	67.2	72.8	78.4	84.0	89.6	95.2
10	15	18.0	21.0	24.0	27.0	30.0	33.0	36.0	39.0	42.0	45.0	48.0	51.0
8	28	35.0	42.0	49.0	56.0	63.0	70.0	77.0	84.0	91.0	98.0	105.0	112.0
8	15	18.8	22.5	26.3	30.0	33.8	37.5	41.3	45.0	48.8	52.5	56.3	60.0
6	28	37.3	46.7	56.0	65.3	74.7	84.0	93.3	102.7	112.0	121.3	130.7	140.0
6	15	20.0	25.0	30.0	35.0	40.0	45.0	50.0	55.0	60.0	65.0	70.0	75.0
4	28	42.0	56.0	70.0	84.0	98.0	112.0	126.0	140.0	154.0	168.0	182.0	196.0
4	15	22.5	30.0	37.5	45.0	52.5	60.0	67.5	75.0	82.5	90.0	97.5	105.0
2	28	56.0	84.0	112.0	140.0	168.0	196.0	224.0	252.0	280.0	308.0	336.0	364.0
2	15	30.0	45.0	60.0	75.0	90.0	105.0	120.0	135.0	150.0	165.0	180.0	195.0

Inflation Rate

* Isoimpact scaling factor. The isoimpact rays describe the combination of real yields and inflation rates that have the same impact on the effective rate.

The scaling factor multiplied by the nominal rate yields the effective capital gains tax rate.

A.B. Laffer, V.A. Canto & Associates

last into the late 1990s. Anyone vaguely familiar with the quixotic nature of politics knows that continuity is a lot to expect from Congress. Why Rostenkowski would propose such fanciful options is intriguing.

Like the Jenkins proposal, the Rostenkowski proposal allows the asset holder to choose between a 28 percent rate on capital gains indexed for inflation or an ordinary income tax rate on 75 percent of the value (principal plus gain) of the asset if held for five years. After 10 years, the amount excluded rises to 50 percent.

If an asset is bought for $100, and over 5 years it appreciates another $100, the asset holder could choose indexing the gains for tax purposes or paying the tax on 75 percent of the asset value. Under both options, the tax rate stops at 28 percent. Under the second alternative, the tax liability would be $42 (.75 × 200 × .28). If the price level remained unchanged during the 5 years, the real capital gain would be $100 and the associated tax liability would be $28. The taxpayer, even with no inflation, would not choose Rostenkowski's option. If inflation occurred, the gain and the tax liability would be reduced in proportion to the increase in the price level. In this example, the exclusion option still would not be selected and the asset holder would choose to pay the capital gains taxes.

Assuming no inflation and the five year option, the asset holder would choose the five year option over indexing if, and only if, the value of the asset appreciated by over 300 percent or 32 percent per year. Then, and only then, would 28 percent of three fourths of the asset's value be less than 28 percent of the asset's value less $100. With inflation, the numbers become even more extreme (Table 10.2).

After ten years, the Rostenkowski option would be to pay full tax on half the asset's value or index and pay full tax on the real capital gains. Again, if there were no inflation, to prefer the option, the real yield would have to be 7.18 percent per year (see Table 10.2). Clearly, as inflation rises, real yields have to rise as well. The combinations are shown in Table 10.2. The Rostenkowski

Table 10.2
Asset's Nominal Annual Yield for Break Even Point for Rostenkowski's Proposal: Alternative Capital Gains Tax versus Indexing

Inflation	5 Year Option of 3/4 of Asset's Value	10 Year Option of 1/2 of Asset's Value
0 %	31.96 % P.A.	7.18 % P.A.
1	33.28	8.25
2	34.60	9.32
3	35.92	10.39
4	37.24	11.46
5	38.56	12.54
6	39.88	13.61
7	41.20	14.68
8	42.52	15.75
9	43.84	16.82
10	45.16	17.89

A.B. Laffer, V.A. Canto & Associates

option will benefit people whose investments have exceptionally high rates of return.

Indexing Problems

The way all of those proposals approach the concept of indexing is flat-out wrong-headed. They all take the percentage change in the overall Consumer Price Index over the period of the investment and multiply that number times the initial investment. That product becomes the adjusted base. God forbid that a person should have a real return as well, because this method of calculation would then *not fully* index for inflation.

In the first, second, third, fourth, and subsequent years, there is an increasing interaction effect between the prior years' real return and the current year's inflation. That effect is not indexed. If a $100 asset in its first year has a 30 percent real return and 10 percent inflation, the asset's nominal yield will be 43 percent ($1.1 \times 1.3 - 1.0$) or $43 where the 3 percent ($3) is this interaction term. From the standpoint of indexing, the inflation-adjusted base would be $110 and taxes would be levied on both the $30 of real return and the $3 for the interaction term.

A second year example should make the point clearer. If the following year

Table 10.3
Effective Tax Rates under Current Indexing Proposals

Real Yield	Inflation	Effective Tax Rate Under Current Indexing Proposals
1 %	1 %	28.70 %
2	2	29.39
5	5	31.40
10	10	34.55
50	50	49.48
100	100	54.30
1	3	30.32
10	30	50.98
100	300	108.50
2	1	28.64
20	10	33.47
200	100	41.83

A.B. Laffer, V.A. Canto & Associates

there were no real yield but only 10 percent inflation, the asset would be worth $157.30 at the end of the second year (1.1 × 143). Each indexing proposal would give only an additional $11 for inflation for year two (110 × 1.10 − 110). In fact, your asset would have had an inflation gain of $14.30. The difference of $3.30 is an illusory capital gain, pure and simple, and is subject to taxation.

What is clear is that the longer an asset is held and the greater the real yield and the greater inflation, the greater will be the illusory gain subject to the capital gains tax. These effects may well be significant. In Table 10.3 we take a five year horizon à la Rostenkowski to illustrate the magnitude of this effect using the mistaken formulae of Jenkins, Rostenkowski, et al.

THE STOCK MARKET AND CAPITAL GAINS

Any cut in the capital gains tax should, in and of itself, raise the real value of existing assets and thus the stock market. Two questions arise. First, what would the magnitude of the rise be under the different proposals? Second, how much of the expected rise is already in the market? With regard to the second question, our belief is that we've experienced about half of the effect to date.

To range the magnitude, we must make several assumptions. If we can assume a stable price earnings ratio in after-tax terms to the shareholder, our problems are substantially lessened. With inflation assumed at 4 percent and investors requiring a 3 percent real yield after *all* taxes, then the after-all-tax yield to shareholders has to be 7 percent.

For corporations, a dividend yield of 3 percent paid by corporations would, after the 28 percent personal income tax, be equivalent to 2.2 percent yield to the shareholders. This leaves 4.8 percent to be generated by after-all-tax nominal capital gains. With a capital gains tax of 28 percent, the pretax capital gains would have to be 6.7 percent to yield a 4.8 percent after-all-tax return to the shareholders.

Putting it all together, a corporation would have to pay shareholders 3 percent in dividends and 6.7 percent in capital gains for a total 9.7 percent pretax (to the shareholders) for the shareholders to receive 7 percent after all taxes. With the corporate tax at 34 percent, then the pre-corporate pre-personal tax yield on the assets would have to be 14.7 percent.

The Bush proposal anticipates lowering the capital gains tax rate for individuals only from 28 percent to 15 percent for long-term capital gains. Short-term gains would still be taxed at the 28 percent rate, and even for long term gains, the cut would not apply to all assets. Nonetheless, if all capital gains tax rates were cut from 28 percent to 15 percent—clearly a big exaggeration of the Bush proposal—we could calculate the overall effects rather easily.

By our assumptions, shareholders would still get dividends of 2.2 percent after-all-taxes (3 percent after corporate taxes but pre–personal income taxes) and 4.8 percent after-all-tax capital gains (Table 10.4). With a 15 percent capital gains tax instead of 28 percent, the pretax yield would be 5.6 percent instead of

Table 10.4
Impact of the Capital Gains Tax Rate on Pretax Rates of Return

	Capital Gains Tax Rate 28 %	Capital Gains Tax Rate 15 %	Capital Gains Tax Rate 28 % (with indexation)
Required equity return after taxes after inflation	3 %	3 %	3 %
Inflation expectation	4	4	4
Required after tax nominal return	7	7	7
Portion of required after-tax nominal return generated by dividends (3% yield x (1-income tax rate))	2.2	2.2	2.2
Portion of required nominal after-tax return generated by capital gain	4.8	4.8	4.8
Required pre-personal income tax return generated by capital gain	6.7	5.6	5.2
Required pre-personal income tax nominal return (capital gains plus dividends)	9.7	8.6	8.1
Required pre-personal income and corporate income tax nominal return (capital gain plus dividend)	14.7	13.0	12.3

A.B. Laffer, V.A. Canto & Associates

6.7 percent. Therefore, the after-corporate-tax yield would be 8.6 percent instead of the 9.7 percent to give an after-all-tax yield of 7 percent to shareholders.

Pre-corporate tax yields would have to be 13.0 percent instead of the 14.7 percent required with a 28 percent tax rate. Assuming nothing else changed save asset valuations, then there would be a 13 percent appreciation in all asset values $[(14.7) \div (13.0)] - 1$. In terms of the Dow Jones Industrial Average, that would come out to about 250 points. If we recognize the exaggeration effect of our assumptions, somewhere between 100 points and 150 points seems reasonable for the Bush proposal.

Doing all the same calculations for indexing—mindless, boring, and dull as they are—would give a pre-corporate tax yield of 12.3 percent instead of the 14.7 percent without indexing. Assuming nothing changed save asset valuation, there would be an initial appreciation of asset values by some 19.5 percent $[(14.7) \div (12.3)] - 1$ or, in DJIA equivalents, around 500 points. The exaggeration effect for indexing is not nearly as large as it is for cutting the tax rates à la Bush. Best guess on indexing would be a 300 to 400 point effect on the DJIA.

WEIRDOS, DEVIANTS, AND SPARKLE-HEADS

Fortunately for those of us who need breaks from the stress of daily activities, the debate surrounding capital gains has provided some real fun. Exaggeration and overstatement have taken on new meaning when expounded by Harvard's Larry Summers. Imagine his flush as he described the Bush proposal as "probably the worst tax proposal in the history of the Republic."[5] Summers is responsible for another great one-liner: "If you accommodate inflation, you eliminate the political pressures that would be brought to bear to mitigate inflation."[6] This is sort of the greater-pain version of political economy. But the humor comes from what is not said and yet totally devastates Summers's comment. With indexing, the government wouldn't benefit from inflation. How on earth would removing that huge carrot "encourage inflation"?

Ron Goodgame of *Time* magazine attributes the following to some of "the experts": "Target new investments, not old ones, by cutting capital-gains taxes only on assets bought after, say, January 1, 1990."[7] Now might not this just cause some quick sale/resale transactions to become eligible? But Goodgame continues, undaunted by logic or consistency, to suggest further: "Impose a securities transaction tax on each sale of stock or bond to further encourage longer-term investment over churning."[8]

Perhaps the best of all was written by Alan Reynolds in a paper entitled "Indexing Isn't Enough":

Just as people have to sell their old house before buying a new one, they likewise often have to sell stock in a fading company in order to channel equity into a new winner. Besides, a capital-gains tax is a penalty on selling assets, not on buying.[9]

The silliness is best seen by realizing that for every seller of an existing asset, there is a precisely identical buyer. One person may sell a house to buy another, but all people cannot, on balance, sell one house to buy another. For every buyer there has to be an equal and opposite seller. Markets don't sell one type of asset to move into another. All that markets can do is alter the relative prices of existing assets.

Just as consistently silly is the notion that any tax is on either the buyer or seller exclusively. All taxes are wedges which impact both the price paid (the buyer's price) and the price received (the seller's price). Every tax is on buyers and sellers, even capital gains taxes.

NOTES

1. See Chapter 9.

2. Herbert Stein, "Common Sense on Capital Gains," *Wall Street Journal,* August 23, 1989, p. A11.

3. David Wessel, "Competing Capital Gains Plans in Congress Pit High-Rolling Investors against Cautious Crowd," *Wall Street Journal,* August 9, 1989, p. A12.

4. The Jenkins proposal is very similar to our earlier proposal for implementation of a capital gains tax reduction. See Victor A. Canto and Arthur B. Laffer, "Capital Gains," A. B. Laffer Associates, May 4, 1989.

5. Don Goodgame, "Losing Big in Capital Gains," *Time,* August 14, 1989, p. 53.

6. Wessel, "Competing Capital Gains Plans in Congress."

7. Goodgame, "Losing Big in Capital Gains."

8. Ibid.

9. Alan Reynold, "Indexing Is Not Enough" (Morristown, N.J.: Polyconomics, Inc., August 4, 1989).

11

Friday the 13th: Triple Witching Hour for the Government

VICTOR A. CANTO AND ARTHUR B. LAFFER

Visions of translucent spirits, eerie hollow sounds, slippery slimy sensations, and musky fetid stenches have been enjoined in a journalistic witches' brew as news account after news account relates what happened to the U.S. stock market on Friday, October 13, 1987. The truth, unfortunately, is not so dramatic. But the events of that Friday do expose the culprits and the dastardly deed perpetrated.

Senate Majority Leader George Mitchell single-handedly cost working Americans 7 percent of their accumulated pension benefits and precipitated a market retreat that encircled the earth. If allowed to be carried through, his actions will also cost jobs—lots of jobs—in the months and years ahead and will, his protestations notwithstanding, lead to larger deficits.

On Friday, the thirteenth of October, the Senate killed the capital gains tax cut. The fact that it was Friday the 13th had nothing to do with the fall in the stock market. George Mitchell deserves full credit for that. The decline in the stock market was due to the fact that, in a forward-looking market, events alter investors' perceptions and thereby equity valuations. In our own analysis, we estimated that passage of the capital gains legislation would add between 400 to 500 points to the market.[1] We also estimated that approximately half of the gain was already incorporated in the market. Thus, if capital gains legislation did not materialize, the market would have to decline 200 to 250 points (Figure 11.1).

Financial markets recently have corroborated our view. Earlier during the week, when it became likely that Senator Mitchell, through procedural moves, could block the capital gains amendment, the markets started declining. The

Figure 11.1
Dow Jones Industrial Average

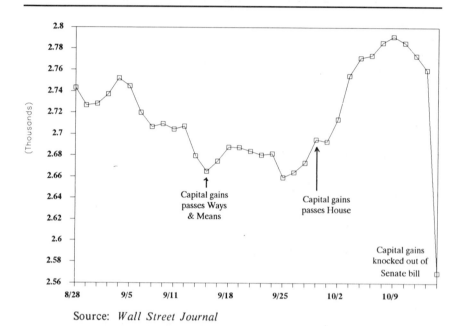

Source: *Wall Street Journal*

cumulative decline, inclusive of Friday, was 214 points—well within the 200–250 points projected by our analysis in the event that capital gains would fail. We personally do not feel there was much more to that week's events than this unanticipated suffocation of a truly good policy.

Those who now gloat over their success at denying Bush and the American people what they so anxiously wanted will not gloat for long. Democratic fundraising has been irreparably damaged. The liberal rich-bashing rhetoric of the last month does not sit well anymore. Senator Mitchell and his coconspirators' ability to wreak short-run damage to the U.S. economy by denying the capital gains tax cut will impose a heavy reciprocal cost on them for years to come. The dream in America today is not to make the rich poor but, instead, to make the poor rich.

The most common explanation for Friday's market fall is the failed attempt to obtain financing for the United Airlines takeover. However, careful examination of the high yield market indicates that the deterioration of the high yield market started several months earlier (Figure 11.2). In fact, the decline in yield paralleled the thrift bail-out legislation.[2] The restrictions on the lending and holding of high yield bonds by financial institutions had the effect of eliminating a large demander from the market. It should not be surprising that in order to increasingly attract other holders, the yield of these bonds had to rise. The deterio-

Figure 11.2
Fidelity High Income Fund versus 30-Year Treasury Bond (Percent Yield)

Percent

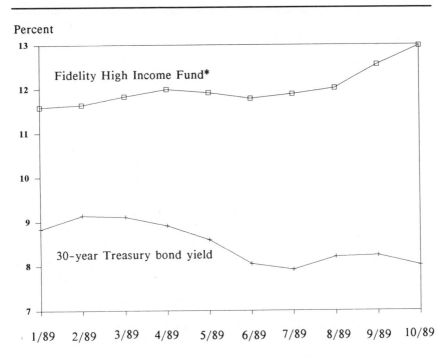

1/89   2/89   3/89   4/89   5/89   6/89   7/89   8/89   9/89   10/89

* Inverse of net asset value

Sources: *Wall Street Journal*; *U.S. Federal Reserve Statistical Release.*

ration of the high yield bond market happened to be a coincident event and not a major cause of the correction.

During the first nine months of 1989, the Dow Jones Industrial Average rose 604 points to a high of 2773 from 2169—a 27.5 percent increase. This type of climb does provide a serious cushion for the market as did the enormous stock market rise in 1987 that preceded the October crash of that year. In retrospect, 1987 turned out to be a slight up year for the stock market in spite of the "crash." The crash of 1987 also was not followed by a recession, depression, or any other such untoward event. The market events of October 1989 were not any different in this regard either.

The precipitous actions of 1987 that led to the October crash were somewhat different than they are today but were nonetheless variations on a common theme—bad politics. In 1987, we had a foundation set by the 1986 Tax Reform Act. The negative effects of that increase in the capital gains tax rate to 28 percent from 20 percent were compounded by a series of policy changes. First and foremost was the rise of inflationary expectations as reflected by the rise in yield of long bonds that took place during the first nine months of 1987. The combination of rising inflationary expectations and higher nominal tax rates on capital gains had a devastating effect on effective tax rates (Table 11.1).[3]

To illustrate, under a 20 percent capital gains tax rate, a 2 percent real return and a 4 percent inflation rate will result in an effective tax rate on real gains of 60 percent. An increase in the capital gains tax rate to 28 percent will lead to an increase in the effective tax rate to 84 percent from 60 percent. If, in addition to a rise in the tax rate there is also a rise in inflationary expectations to 6 percent from 4 percent, this will lead to an effective tax rate of 112 percent. This simple calculation suggests that the rise in capital gains tax rates and the rise in inflationary expectations could have a catastrophic effect on equity values.

In contrast to 1987, during 1989 inflationary expectations, as reflected by the long bonds, declined. Symmetric information on the dollar in the foreign exchanges reinforced this inflationary expectations view. During 1987, the dollar had been falling while it rose during 1989.

In October 1987, a significant disagreement was reported in the press between the United States and its trading partners. Treasury Secretary Baker was reported to have threatened our trading partners to lower the foreign exchange value of the dollar through U.S. action if they did not cooperate and help improve the U.S. trade position. The Fed supported, or at the very least did not disagree with, the dollar-bashing view that prevailed in the administration. Today, the press has reported on a major disagreement between administration officials and Fed members on the appropriate course for the dollar. Fed members have been quoted in the press as arguing that monetary policy should focus on domestic price stability and let the dollar seek its own level.

In the past year we have been critical of the Fed's rhetoric on the appropriate way to conduct monetary policy. However, the Fed's actions have been much different from its rhetoric, and the performance of the inflation indicators, such as interest rates, gold prices, and the foreign exchange value of the dollar, have been excellent. High marks must be given for the conduct of monetary policy in 1989.

The removal of the fear of rising inflation dampens the negative impact of the failure to include capital gains legislation in the recent bill approved by the Senate, making the outlook less bleak. It is also reassuring to know that right after the 1987 crash, the Fed acted responsibly, bringing reserves into the system providing enough liquidity to accommodate the flight to quality that resulted as an aftermath of the crash. We have no reason to believe the Fed will not act in the same manner this time around.

Perhaps the single event that triggered the 1987 crash was proposed legislation in the House Ways and Means Committee headed by Congressman Dan Rostenkowski. What Rostenkowski had proposed was a scarcely veiled tax increase and an antitakeover set of policies. The market unabashedly let Rostenkowski know how it felt about his brainchild. In 1987, the Democrats were attempting to

Table 11.1
Effective Capital Gains Tax Rate Given Different Inflation, Real Return, and Legislated Capital Gains Tax Rates

Inflation Rate	Real Rate of Return	Effective Tax Rate Under 28 % Legislated Rate	Effective Tax Rate Under 20 % Legislated Rate
1	1	56.0 %	40.0 %
1	2	42.0	30.0
1	3	37.3	26.7
2	1	84.0	60.0
2	2	56.0	40.0
2	3	46.7	33.3
3	1	112.0	80.0
3	2	70.0	50.0
3	3	56.0	40.0
4	1	140.0	100.0
4	2	84.0	60.0
4	3	65.3	46.7
5	1	168.0	120.0
5	2	98.0	70.0
5	3	74.7	53.3
6	1	196.0	140.0
6	2	112.0	80.0
6	3	84.0	60.0
7	2	126.0	90.0
7	3	93.3	66.7
8	2	140.0	100.0
8	3	102.7	73.3
9	2	154.0	110.0
9	3	112.0	80.0
10	2	168.0	120.0
10	3	121.3	86.7
11	2	182.0	130.0
11	3	130.7	93.3
12	3	140.0	100.0
13	3	149.3	106.7
14	3	158.7	113.3
15	3	168.0	120.0
16	3	177.3	126.7
17	3	186.7	133.3

A.B. Laffer, V.A. Canto & Associates

Table 11.2

Performance of Investor's Daily Industry Indices, September 28 to October 9 and October 9 to October 13

				10/9/89 10/13/89	9/28/89 10/9/89
Auto/Truck Replacement Parts	LC	FI	T	-5.815	3.843
Banks - Money Center	LC	FI	N	-10.473	2.921
Beverages - Soft Drinks	HC	FI	N	-6.555	2.310
Bldg - Resident/Commercial	HC	FI	N	-4.750	2.864
Broadcasting - Radio/TV	HC	FI	N	-4.227	3.738
Chemicals - Fibers	HC	FI	T	3.081	3.679
Computer Mini/Micro	HC	RI	T	-5.949	7.078
Containers - Metal	HC	FI	T	-3.043	3.772
Containers - Paper/Plastic	LC	FI	N	-4.134	2.896
Cosmetics and Toiletries	HC	FI	N	-3.659	3.336
Drugs	HC	FI	T	-5.952	3.656
Elect Comp-Semiconductors	HC	RI	T	-4.991	3.087
Finance - Consumer Loans	HC	FI	N	-8.485	5.854
Finance - Investment Mgmt	HC	RI	T	-4.718	4.452
Food - Canned	HC	FI	T	-8.355	5.014
Food - Confectionary	HC	FI	T	-4.322	3.470
Food - Sugar & Refining	LC	RI	T	-7.561	9.050
Glass Products	LC	RI	N	-6.760	2.387
Health Maintenance Orgs	HC	FI	N	-7.122	13.009
Hospitals	HC	RI	N	-6.291	4.912
Insurance - Life	HC	FI	N	-3.154	2.991
Insurance - Multi-Line	HC	FI	N	-4.354	3.981
Leisure & Recreation Services	HC	FI	N	-5.535	3.120
Machinery - Electric Utility	LC	RI	N	-6.278	2.809
Machinery - Electrical	HC	RI	T	-5.691	2.757
Machinery - Farm	LC	RI	T	-9.258	3.895
Medical Products	HC	FI	T	-4.856	4.381
Medical/Dental Supplies	HC	FI	T	-5.088	2.742
Metal Ores - Miscellaneous	LC	RI	T	-6.392	4.116
Metals Non Ferrous	LC	RI	T	-7.668	6.392
Motion Picture & Services	HC	FI	N	-6.526	3.647
Oil & Gas - Field Services	LC	RI	N	-4.732	2.989
Oil & Gas - Intl Integrated	LC	RI	T	-6.172	7.727
Oil & Gas - U.S. Integrated	LC	RI	T	-7.325	5.020
Pollution Control Equip & Svcs	HC	RI	T	-4.381	3.437
Publishing - Newspapers	HC	FI	N	-5.246	3.030
Publishing - Periodicals	HC	FI	N	-7.787	2.611
Retail - Supermarkets	HC	FI	N	-4.828	3.092
Rubber - Tires	LC	FI	T	-5.408	4.248
Soap & Cleaning Preparations	HC	FI	T	-6.122	6.357
Telecommunication Equipment	LC	FI	N	-5.678	5.091
Telecommunication Services	LC	FI	N	-5.529	5.191
Tobacco	HC	FI	T	-6.811	4.867
Tools - Hand Held	LC	FI	T	-3.574	3.707
Transport - Air Freight	LC	FI	T	-6.390	6.475
Transportation - Airline	LC	FI	T	-7.056	6.685
Utility - Telephone	HC	FI	N	-5.161	4.588

U.S. Stock Markets

Investor's Daily Stock Index	-6.375	2.869
S&P 500	-7.330	3.267
Dow Jones Industrial Average	-7.925	3.540

raise tax rates on the economy. This time, their efforts are limited to preventing tax rate reductions. Therefore, the impact on the economy will be less negative.

WINNERS AND LOSERS

One way to determine the groups that are mostly affected by the policy changes currently under consideration is to calculate the performance of the Investor's Daily industry groups during the following two periods:

1. From the date when the capital gains legislation was passed by the House of Representatives to the market peak of October
2. The time period from the market peak to the Friday, October 13th drop

Comparing the list of those industry groups during the two time periods helps identify those that are most sensitive to the capital gains legislation. Our analysis predicts that the groups most likely to benefit from lower capital gains tax rates are High-CATS, non-traded, falling interest rate.

Therefore, we expect those groups favored by the economic environment to outperform the market during the up period. Although likely to, it does not follow that those groups need to underperform during the October 1989 correction. Although capital gains was removed from the legislation, other economic indicators (i.e., declining interest rates and a stable dollar) may favor some of the industry groups. Table 11.2 reports the industry groups most likely to benefit from the passage of a capital gains bill.

NOTES

1. See Chapter 10; Victor A. Canto and Harvey B. Hirschhorn, "Capital Gains and the Stock Market," A. B. Laffer, V. A. Canto & Associates, October 10, 1989.
2. The Fidelity High Income Fund is used as a proxy for the high yield bond market. The yield is calculated as one over the net asset value.
3. See Chapter 9.

12

Debt and Taxes Are the Only Certainty

ARTHUR GRAY, JR., AND ARTHUR B. LAFFER

Taxes can have some of the darndest consequences. While there is not yet a Guinness book of the world's most unusual tax developments, seemingly un-called-for events surely warrant a cursory tax analysis. To pervert an overused cliche, the ramifications of taxes range from the sublime to the meticulous. The surge of births in late December—just in time for the wee duffer to be a tax deduction—appears to have some nontrivial element of tax planning. The record recovery of the Reagan revolution, too, claims inspiration from an alteration of the tax codes.

But some tax effects are far from obvious to the layman and analyst alike. For years, the effects of state taxation were literally ignored as a factor determining state growth, employment, and output. Even today, we find an analytic vacuum when it comes to research on the returns of stock by location of fixed factors and state tax policies. If minuscule variations in the earth's environment can lead to dramatic evolutionary changes in the genetic structure of species, then surely tax changes can lead to profound variations in the organization of finances among American businesses. Incentives do matter and matter a lot.

IMPACT OF TAX RATES ON THE CHOICE OF DEBT VERSUS EQUITY FINANCING

In 1980, the year before Reagan took office, the maximum tax rate was 46 percent on corporate income and 70 percent on personal income. Interest expense was tax deductible to the corporation, but was taxable as unearned income to the individual. In that year, as is still true to this day, dividends were not deductible to the corporation (i.e., dividends bore the full brunt of corporate taxation) and yet were taxed again at the unearned income rate for individuals.

To illustrate the consequences of the rather odd tax dichotomy between interest and dividends that existed in 1980, imagine a corporation, its shareholders, and its bondholders all to be in the highest income tax bracket. If the corporation earned one additional dollar of income and the full impact of that dollar was directed toward dividends, then the corporation was required to pay 46 cents additional corporate tax. This left the corporation 54 cents to distribute to its shareholders in the form of dividends. The tax liability of the shareholders rose by some 37.8 cents (70 percent of 54 cents), leaving them with a net gain of 16.2 cents. Therefore, the after-tax incentive for the corporation to earn one additional dollar in profits in order for the shareholders to earn additional dividends was 16.2 cents.

If, however, the corporation earned one additional dollar in profits to pay the bondholders as much additional interest as was possible, then there was no additional corporate tax liability. Corporate interest payments were fully deductible against corporate income in 1980, as they are today. Therefore, the additional dollar of income was matched by one additional dollar of interest paid to the bondholders. The net effect on corporate taxable income was naught. Bondholders, meanwhile, received one full dollar of pretax income, whereas shareholders received only 54 cents. Because the bondholders are presumed to have been in the highest tax bracket, their additional personal income tax liability was 70 cents, leaving them with 30 cents.

In 1980, there was a 14 cent incentive to convert a dollar of corporate income devoted into dividend income to a dollar of corporate income devoted to interest income (16 cents versus 30 cents). There was an enormous advantage in biasing the corporate capital structure toward debt and away from equity.

Quite clearly, given the ridiculous height of tax rates in 1980, the corporation had numerous alternatives besides sole payments of dividends or interest. Tax shelters, corporate featherbedding, and other nonproductive tax diversions proliferated. Investments in tax shelters flourished and taxable corporate investments did not fare very well. But that's all well documented.

EFFECTS OF THE REAGAN TAX RATE CUTS

With the Reagan tax revolution of the 1980s, corporate and personal tax rates were altered dramatically. Inadvertently, so was the relative advantage of corporate debt versus corporate equity. The reduction in top personal income tax rates to 28 percent in 1988 from 70 percent in 1980 increased the after-tax return on interest income to 72 cents from 30 cents on the dollar (Table 12.1, row 6). Table 12.1 also reports the total corporate and personal tax rates payable on an additional dollar of income directed toward dividends and toward interest from 1980

Table 12.1
The Effect of Personal and Corporate Income Tax Rates on After-Tax Dividends and Corporate Interest Income

	1980	1981	1982	1983	1984	1985	1986	1987	1988
Maximum corporate income tax rate	46.0%	46.0%	46.0%	46.0%	46.0%	46.0%	40.0%	34.0%	34.0%
Maximum personal income tax rate	70.0	69.125	50.0	50.0	50.0	50.0	50.0	38.5	28.0
Total tax on dividends	83.8	83.33	73.0	73.0	73.0	73.0	73.0	63.1	52.5
Total tax on interest	70.0	69.125	50.0	50.0	50.0	50.0	50.0	38.5	28.0
Net (retention rate) receipt dividends	16.2	16.6725	27.0	27.0	27.0	27.0	27.0	36.9	47.5
Net (retention rate) receipt interest	30.0	30.875	50.0	50.0	50.0	50.0	50.0	61.5	72.0
Net (retention rate) receipt interest over dividends advantage cents per dollar of corporate income	13.8	14.2	23.0	23.0	23.0	23.0	23.0	24.6	24.6

Source: Joseph Pechman, Federal Tax Policy, Fifth Edition, Brookings Institute.

through 1988. The final row of Table 12.1 shows the advantage corporate debt has over dividends in percent of pretax corporate income plus interest.

Dividend income is subject to both corporate and individual income taxes. In 1988, a dollar of dividend income would be subject to 34 percent corporate tax, leaving the individual investor with 66 cents of dividend income subject to a 28 percent income tax. When all is said and done, the dollar of dividend income results in 47.5 cents of after-tax income. In contrast, a dollar of dividend income in 1980 resulted in only 16.2 cents of after-tax personal income (Table 12.1, row 5).

The reduction in across-the-board corporate and personal income tax rates during the Reagan administration increased the after-tax dividend income to 47.5 cents per dollar of pretax corporate income in 1988 from 16.2 cents in 1980. This resulted in a 31.3 cent increase per dollar of pretax corporate profits. Similarly, the tax rate reduction increased the after-tax return of interest income to 72 cents on the dollar in 1988 from 30 cents on the dollar in 1980. The tax rate reduction resulted in a 42 cent increase per dollar of interest income.

While it is fairly clear that the Reagan tax rate reduction increased the after-tax return of both corporate shareholders and corporate bondholders, the tax rate cuts differentially favored the after-tax return to bondholders: 42 cents versus 31.3 cents per dollar of pretax corporate income. In fact, the tax rate cuts increased the after-tax return advantages of interest income over corporate dividends to 24.5 cents per dollar in 1988 from 13.8 cents per dollar in 1980. The differential is calculated by subtracting the after-tax return of corporate dividends from the after-tax return of interest income.

The tax rate reduction resulted in an expansion of the economy. The stock market, and private and public debt increased substantially during the Reagan years. The rise in the stock market is directly related to increased incentives from the lower tax rates. The increase in public debt was largely the result of the budget deficit. In turn, the increase in corporate debt was largely a shift in financing away from equity issues and into corporate issues (Figure 12.1 and 12.2). The surge in bond financing and the decline in equity financing occurred once the Reagan tax rate cuts were fully in place in 1984.

The incentive to shift from equity to debt financing from the differential tax treatment increased to 24 cents on the dollar in 1988 from 14 cents on the dollar in 1980. It should come as no surprise that the markets saw this and reacted to the change in incentives. Corporate takeovers provided the mechanism through which the returns created by this increased incentive were realized. At the margin, investors were willing to pay 24 cents to convert dividend income into interest income. All that they required were the takeovers to perform the tax arbitrage function for them.

CORPORATE TAKEOVERS AS TAX ARBITRAGE

Tax arbitrage is feasible when corporations are carrying assets at historical cost. Given a positive inflation rate and carried at the historical cost, these assets

Figure 12.1
Nonfinancial Corporate Borrowing as a Percent of Total Market Value of Equities

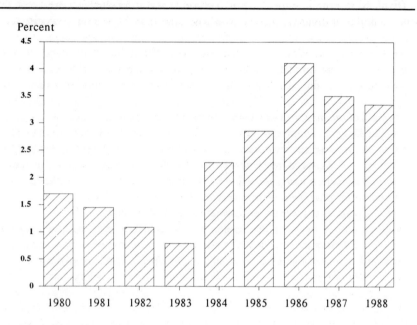

Figure 12.2
Net Share Issues as a Percent of Market Value Equities

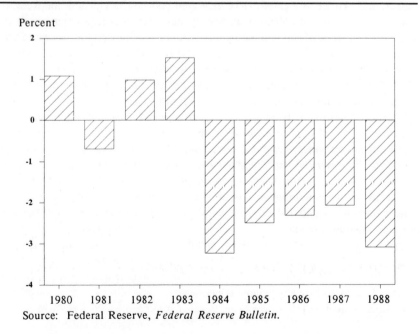

Source: Federal Reserve, *Federal Reserve Bulletin*.

are highly underdepreciated, implying that their replacement value is much higher. With undervalued assets it can be seen that in some cases the actual sum of the parts of the company is greater than the whole (i.e., the current market value). The corporate raider recognizes this disparity and raises the money necessary to take over the company.

This larger amount paid for the company more realistically values the corporation's capital. The takeover agent then sells off components of the company at their actual value and realizes a substantial capital gain. A substantial one-time capital gains tax (a lower rate than the corporate tax rate) is levied on this capital gains realization and the company is now free to use all of its cash flow to service the debt. The previous earnings stream that was once tapped for dividends is freed to pay interest. To the corporation, the increased interest payments are tax-free; the previously paid dividends were not. The effective tax rate on the company has been substantially reduced. The shareholder who now has sold his stock at an increased price also walks away smiling.

The differential tax treatment that has allowed this tax arbitrage to occur can very efficiently be rectified. An implication of this analysis is that the proposed reduction in the top capital gains tax rate to 15 percent, while increasing incentives to invest in new ventures, will also reduce the cost of takeovers.

POSSIBLE SOLUTIONS TO THE CORPORATE "DEBT PROBLEM"

Congressional worries with present levels of debt will likely lead to measures making debt capital less attractive and equity capital more attractive. The measures will be largely a matter of tax treatment between stocks and bonds.

In general, it is difficult to determine whether markets have overreacted or underreacted to the significant shift in incentives toward debt versus equity. If linguistics be true, then debt is being damaged less than equity, and additionally, the damage done to debt has declined by more than the damage done to equity. We do know that debt is not being subsidized. Anyone who argues that debt is being subsidized does so from the dark side, for to balance the ledger exclusively by further inhibiting debt is to pull down capital formation and production. Balancing down has never been the answer.

We personally prefer to balance the ledger up by conferring on dividends the tax deductible status now afforded corporate interest payments. This option, no matter how correct it may be, faces seemingly insurmountable political opposition from those who are phobic with regards to static tax revenue losses. We believe that if dividend deductibility, implemented as a stand-alone, did lead to a revenue shortfall it would be far less than the static thinkers think. In addition to overestimating the revenue shortfall, indulgence in static thinking constrains these people from seeing the further blooming of the Reagan revolution—with prosperity attaining heights not seen in generations and the additional fulfillment of dreams across all levels of American society.

A REVENUE-NEUTRAL PROPOSAL

The static thinkers, in spite of the last six-plus years, appear to occupy center stage today. The best we can hope for is to avoid balancing down, even if balancing up is now not an option. Balancing even is an option. We propose the following revenue-neutral plan to eliminate the tax differences between debt and equity without any static tax revenue consequences: A reduction of taxation on what is now called corporate income balanced with a rise in the taxation at the corporate level of corporate interest disbursements. The correct balance would be struck when the tax structure on corporate income was identical to the tax structure on interest disbursements (e.g., when corporate income plus corporate interest disbursements could be aggregated fully and taxed as an entity).

The logic behind any taxation of corporate interest payments is not well founded. To see why interest should always be tax deductible, imagine a company that borrows $100 million at 10 percent per annum and lends that same $100 million at 10 percent interest. By so doing, the company has defined itself purely as a conduit and should not be liable for taxation. There has been no economic function provided. If interest income is taxable, then interest expense must be deductible against income for tax purposes.

If that company, on the other hand, borrows the $100 million at 10 percent interest and then turns around and lends the funds at 15 percent interest, clearly the profits should be taxable. The company has added value. Therefore, interest income should always be taxable and interest expense should likewise be deductible. There are no exceptions in theory and there should be none in practice, either.

The only reason we recommend such a practice is because the proposal inextricably ties the lowering of taxation on corporate income to the rise in taxation of corporate interest payments—an even greater good offsetting the evil. From the standpoint of economics, there should be no taxation of either corporate income or corporate interest payments. The ideal solution would be to constructively impute the income a corporation earns to its shareholders and have them liable for any and all taxation.

Although any attempt by Congress to restrict allowances for corporate interest payments will be met with resistance, a measure to equate equity and debt financing is possible. Keeping revenue-neutrality paramount in our minds, a simple tax incidence shift to corporate interest payments from corporate earnings (dividend flow) results in a more equitable tax structure. Many countries have attempted to integrate, to some degree, the corporate and individual income tax structure to produce a more equitable environment. We propose not only a more equitable tax structure, but a shift in tax burden that is revenue neutral. The tax structure built on these principles would expand the corporate tax base to include corporate interest payments (Table 12.2, row 5) in addition to corporate profits (Table 12.2, row 2).

In order to maintain revenue-neutrality, the now larger base of corporate

Table 12.2
Estimates of the Revenue-Neutral Tax Rate on Corporate Interest Payment and Profits

	1980	1981	1982	1983	1984	1985	1986	1987
Profit tax liability	84.8	81.1	60.7	77.2	95.4	96.4	106.6	133.8
Corporate profits	177.2	188.0	150.0	213.7	266.9	282.3	298.9	310.4
Average corporate tax rate	47.9	43.1	42.1	36.1	35.2	34.1	35.7	43.1
Maximum corporate tax rate	46.0	46.0	46.0	46.0	46.0	46.0	40.0	34.0
Total corporate interest paid	344.6	477.0	515.0	476.1	535.8	568.6	NA	NA
Total corporate interest + income	579.2	698.1	680.5	683.7	775.7	792.8	NA	NA
Implied average tax rate	14.64	11.62	8.92	11.29	12.30	12.16	NA	NA
Implied maximum tax rate	18.6	14.6	11.2	14.0	14.2	13.0	NA	NA

Source: Joseph Pechman, Federal Tax Policy, Fifth Edition, Brookings Institution; Internal Revenue Service, Statistics of Income; Department of Commerce, Survey of Current Business; Economic Report of the President.

A.B. Laffer Associates

profits plus interest payments (Table 12.2, row 6) must generate the same amount of revenue as the corporate income tax (Table 12.2, row 1). Estimates of the average tax rate applicable to the larger tax base that would have resulted in the same revenue collection range from a low of 8.92 percent in 1982 to a high of 14.64 percent in 1980 (Table 12.2, row 7).

In order to estimate the highest marginal tax rate and to preserve the progressivity of the corporate tax rate, the average tax rate on combined profits and interest payments is multiplied by the ratio of the maximum corporate tax rate (Table 12.2, row 4) to the average corporate tax rate (Table 12.2, row 5).[1] The maximum tax rates applicable to corporate profits and interest payment range from a high of 18.6 percent in 1980 to a low of 11.2 in 1982 (Table 12.2, row 8). The calculation suggests that a tax rate of 15 percent will, on a static revenue basis, generate slightly higher revenue than the current structure.

CONCLUSIONS

The new tax will be neutral with respect to financing choice (i.e., debt versus equity). Therefore, when considering new investment projects, corporate America will now focus on the merits of the project and not on the relative tax consequences. Choice of financing, debt versus equity, will now be irrelevant and will not determine the investment decision.

The proposal we are forwarding in this paper is literally a second-best solution and does entail the elimination of interest expense deductibility. In this case, the old adage that the best should never be the enemy of the good holds. Our proposal is not the *optimum optimorum,* but it is a lot better than what is being practiced today. Given the fiscal politics of Washington, D.C., our proposal may just be attainable.

NOTE

1. In a few years the estimated average rate exceeds the highest marginal tax rates. This arises from the fact that NIPA calculations of corporate profits include corporations showing losses during a particular year. NIPA profits tax liability figures, on the other hand, are calculated based only on those companies with positive profits. In this way, the tax base is underestimated and the average tax is thus overstated.

13

Borrowed Prosperity: The Astrology of Consumer Debt

JOHN E. SILVIA

In 1956, total outstanding consumer debt was, by modern standards, a paltry 9.5 percent of personal disposable income. And yet, back in the age of mellow Ike, such indebtedness was viewed with alarm. One would-be vizier shouted aloud the warning chant, "The enormous gain included 'borrowed prosperity' supported by an accumulation of consumer credit that could not be maintained. A rise in consumer's credit so out of proportion to the rise in national product must eventually overburden the consumer's budgets with required payments."[1]

Our friendly forecaster's predictions in 1956 appear to have ended up somewhat wide of the mark. Since that time, the ratio of consumer debt to personal income has increased (Figure 13.1). Today, consumer debt is inching up to 19 percent of personal disposable income, and as of yet, the world has not come to an end. But forecasters, as they have done for the past 32 years, still warn that the "end is nigh."

To simply denigrate a prediction made so many years ago misses the kernel of truth contained in the admittedly inaccurate forecast. Fear of excessive debt in relation to the ability to service that debt is not an economist's version of astrology. Debt does have its limits, if only the tautological limit that debt cannot be so great that the cost of servicing it exceeds total income.

DEBT: VICE OR VIRTUE?

Everyone hates their liabilities and loves their assets. Designated as a liability, consumer debt surely is to be hated. Future interest and principal payments

Figure 13.1
Consumer Installment Debt Outstanding as a Percent of Personal Disposable Income

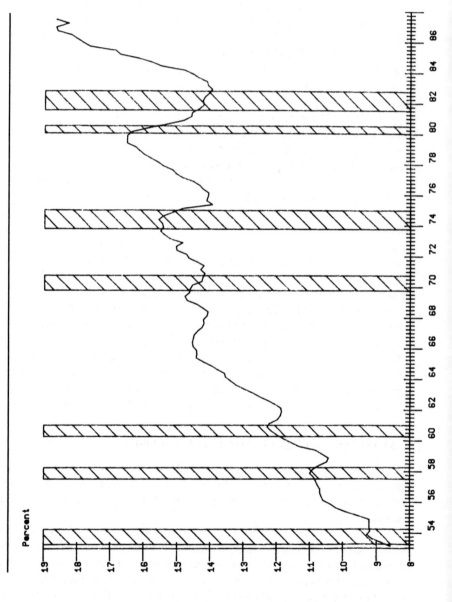

detract directly from the debtor's income stream. In the extreme, debt and the payments that debt mandates have the ability to impoverish. Chapter VII and Chapter XI cases abound, from the John Connallys to the Mexicos of this world.

Debt can also be a useful tool, allowing individuals, businesses, and nations to acquire assets they otherwise could not have obtained and to consume outside the constraints of their current income. If one has the ability to borrow at 10 percent and can relend those funds without risk at 20 percent, there is no limit to the amount that person should borrow. However, to the compulsive shopper caught in a frenzy of buying, the ability to obtain consumer debt is a disaster.

Debt, *per se,* is neither good nor bad. In order to evaluate debt, we have to know the purpose to which the funds were used and the ability of the borrower to repay the debt. The maximum amount of debt that a consumer can incur without going bankrupt is limited by the discounted present value of his future income plus current net worth. Changes in his income or in his current asset values will clearly affect the consumer's debt capacity.

A consumer's debt capacity is also determined, in part, by market conditions. Lenders, in the presence of adverse changes in interest rates and expectations about their future income, will alter their lending limits in order to reduce consumer bankruptcy risks. These changes will tend to bring the economy's debt ratio in line with the new market conditions. In principle, the adjustment could lead to a disruption in the financial market that would, in turn, bring about a retrenchment in the economy. This suggests that changes in consumer debt could be used to forecast the future path of the economy.

The debt to current income ratio focuses on the absolute level of current income in the belief that consumption follows current income during our lifetime. But households do tend to pursue a consumption pattern that is quite different from current income alone. We consume more than our income when we are young and setting up households, and in our mature years we save to repay earlier debt and provide for retirement. The relevant income constraint is not current income but the present value of the income stream over our lifetime.

A REFORMULATION OF DEBT AND INCOME

Households attempt to maintain a smooth consumption pattern even though their income streams vary over the business cycle. That is, the trend of consumption is proportional to long-run income. The proportion depends upon real interest rates.

Declining real interest rates or a rise in expected future income raises the present value of household wealth. Permanent consumption and the current value of assets would rise despite no change in measured current income. Therefore, the change in wealth resulting from expectations about the future will increase the debt to income ratio. Therefore, at any given level of income, a rise in real assets that leads to higher consumption must also decrease savings since consumption plus savings must equal the given level of income.

Increased real wealth reduces the need to save and thereby lowers the household savings rate. This analysis suggests that changes in aggregate asset values in conjunction with the debt to income ratio provide a much clearer picture of the conditions under which a change in debt is a vice or a virtue.

Inflation and interest rates have fallen in the current recovery. This resulted in a tremendous increase in the real value of bonds and a five-year bull market in equities. The increase in wealth has offset the rise in consumer debt so that household net worth has continued to provide a positive impetus to consumption. Lower interest rates also reduced the interest burden of debt. This allowed households to increase their consumption and debt relative to measured income. The much cursed decline in the personal savings rate is really the result of prosperity, not the precursor of poverty.

An increase in the debt to current income ratio is a misleading tool for forecasting consumption. The thirty year downward trend in the ratio of household financial assets to liabilities was reversed in 1982. While consumer debt has risen during the current economic recovery, consumer assets have risen even faster.

Higher household net worth due to declining interest rates precedes gains in both consumption and installment debt. Changes in household net worth lead households to alter their expected permanent income which, in turn, leads to changes in consumption. Installment debt, which accompanies changes in consumption, also lags household net worth.

In its simplest state, debt is a stock concept that appears on a balance sheet while income is a flow concept contained in an income statement. Debt is not a component of an income statement nor is income an item to be found on the balance sheet. Two items being compared should be dimensionally alike. Debt should be compared to other items on the balance sheet such as net worth or wealth, while income would be more appropriately compared with debt service or total interest payments. When the current ratio of household financial assets to total liabilities is calculated, a much different picture emerges (Figure 13.2).

THE LIMITS OF CONSUMER BORROWING

A good deal was written in the 1950s about consumer debt growing out of control. Curiously enough, the rapid growth of consumer debt in the mid-1980s parallels the growth spurt of the 1950s. Consumers began both periods with low debt levels. Prior to both periods, government regulation depressed consumer credit usage. Credit controls during the period of the Korean War artificially limited consumers' ability to borrow. With the removal of restrictions after the war, the growth rate of consumer credit soared.

The early 1980s saw the growth in consumer credit limited by credit controls and usury laws. High nominal interest rates bumped into old nominal interest rate ceilings. But with economic recovery, deregulation, and the end of formal controls, consumer debt experienced rapid growth.

To those who perceive excessive debt as dangerous, the danger level is the

Figure 13.2
Current Ratio of Household Financial Assets to Total Liabilities

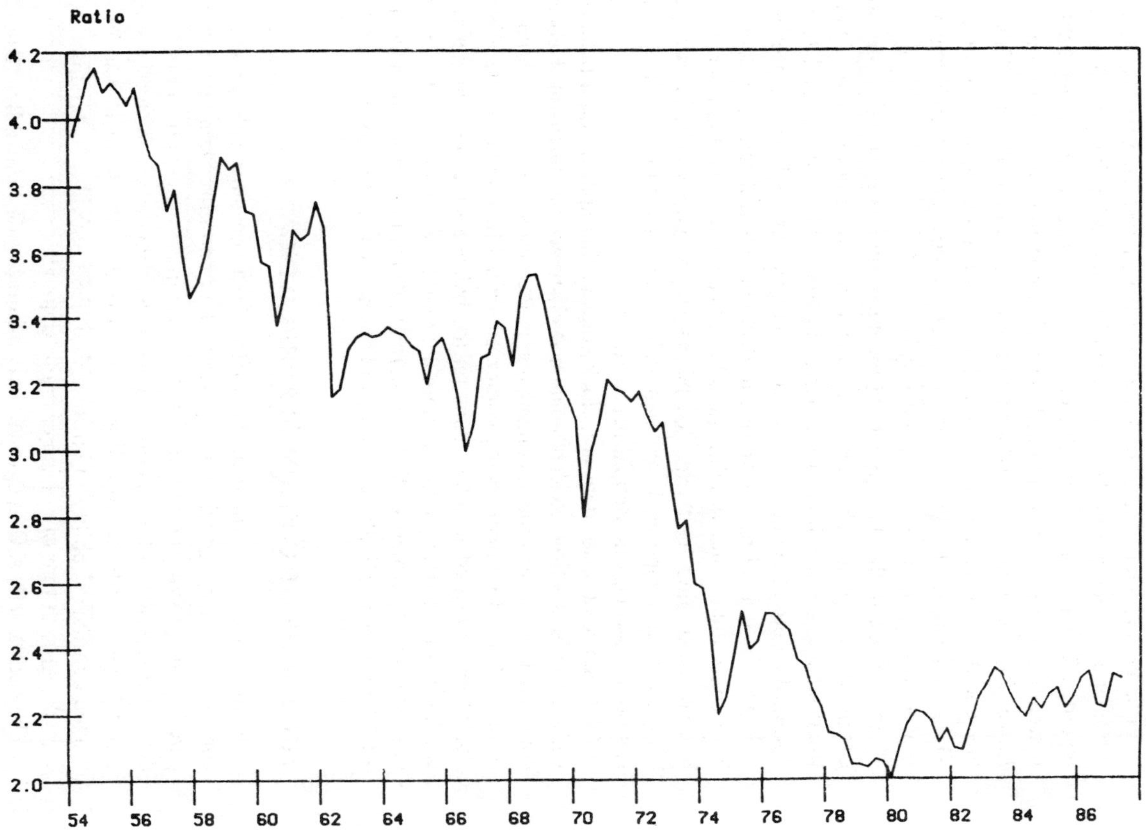

Figure 13.3
The Debt-to-Income Ratio: Enthoven's Limit versus Actuals

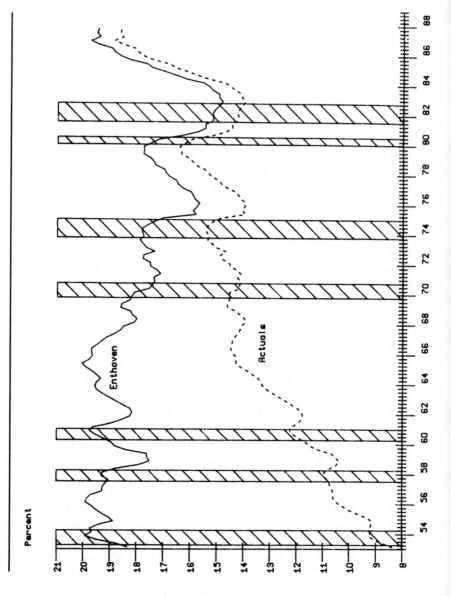

point where consumer debt hits a high level with respect to consumer income. As consumer debt approaches debt capacity, the odds favoring a quick downturn in consumer spending are expected to rise. When debt goes beyond the danger level, consumer spending will retrench. The high level of installment debt is thought to be, by itself, the catalyst of a reduction in consumer spending.

Rapid growth in consumer debt in the 1950s was analyzed by Alain Enthoven in 1957. Taking a multi-year, dynamic approach to life cycle consumption, personal income is projected to grow at its long run rate, r, each year. In this paper, the annualized growth of income is defined as a simple linear combination of personal income the same year and prior years.[2]

New consumer borrowing each year is proportional to income that year. Repayments are a linear combination of new borrowing in prior years. Since the increase in consumer debt equals the difference between new borrowing and repayments and since repayments themselves are a linear combination of income of prior years, then the increase (sensitivity) in debt each year is a function of income in prior years. Therefore, the theoretical limit of the increase in debt each year is a linear combination of incomes in the same year and prior years. As income grows, the theoretical limit of debt grows.

Comparing the actual debt-to-income ratio against the theoretical limit, the actual ratio does approach the theoretical limit asymptotically (Figure 13.3). However, this ratio is sensitive to the business cycle. It is driven by a measure of consumers' willingness to take on debt in relationship to their income. Therefore, the theoretical debt limit is not fixed.

But some caution is advised. The current spread between the theoretical and estimated debt ratio limit is not large. Debt service payments as a percent of income are also very high. Under these conditions the structure of consumer debt could lead to economic weakness if shocked by a sudden, sharp rise in interest rates or a decline in real disposable income. The lesson derived from the study of consumer debt is that debt itself is not the issue, but it can become the issue. Debt could create a constraint on economic flexibility when high debt levels are combined with sudden and unexpected shocks (such as a stock market crash).

The recognition that there exists a moving limit is especially useful when looking at the peaks of the business cycle. The peaks of the debt limit correspond well to the peaks of the business cycle. The sensitivity of borrowing reflects the willingness of households to take on debt, over the course of the business cycle, as proxied by the rate of growth of debt. It appears that this willingness to take on debt is endogenous to the business cycle itself. That is, the growth of consumer debt itself is a reflection of the state of the business cycle and may not be the independent factor affecting consumer spending that some analysts claim.

THE SUBSTITUTION OF MORTGAGE DEBT FOR CONSUMER DEBT

The usefulness of the commonly reported debt-to-income ratio is diminished by the Tax Reform Act of 1986. Home equity loans are a new factor affecting the interpretation of all measures of consumer debt since tax reform eliminated the interest cost deduction for consumer installment debt but retained it for home mortgage loan interest. To measure total consumer indebtedness, home equity loans must be removed from mortgage debt outstanding and added back into the consumer installment debt series.

The impact of tax reform is to alter the after-tax cost of borrowing for those consumers with the choice of credit sources. This change in the cost of borrowing only applies to those home equity loans that are taken out for tax-deductible purposes, but money is fungible. Both the demand for and supply of home-equity credit are expected to rise. Households will tap this new line of credit for two reasons: First, households will seek to take advantage of the tax deduction provisions. Second, the interest rate on home equity loans is lower than straight installment credit. On the supply side, lenders will have an increased willingness to make "home equity backed" loans, because the collateral on the loan is a secure asset. Since the home that serves as collateral backing the loan is also a long-term asset, lenders offer longer maturities than they would typically with consumer credit. The net result is a lower monthly interest payment with a corresponding rise in consumer debt.

In terms of monthly payments, changing the form of debt from installment to home equity loans results in a lower debt service burden. In addition, consumers benefit from a lower after-tax interest rate than the traditional installment loan. This will also tend to lower the monthly interest payment on a home equity loan compared to an installment loan of a similar size.

Theory suggests that consumers will substitute home equity debt for installment debt. This substitution effect emphasizes the point that the consumer installment debt to personal income ratio is simply too narrow a measure for the influence of credit conditions on consumer behavior.

To test the substitution effect, two models were developed. The first model estimated the change in home mortgage debt as a function of the change in home values and lagged mortgage rates. The second model estimated the change in consumer installment debt as a function of the change in consumer spending and consumer credit interest rates. If the introduction of home equity loans has the expected substitution effect, then actual mortgage debt should rise more than the model forecast while actual consumer credit should be less than its model forecast. The rise in mortgages in excess of home values reflects, in part, the influence of home equity loans.

The model results confirm our expectations (Table 13.1). Beginning in the fourth quarter of 1986, consumer debt (installment credit) fell sharply below its predicted level. At the same time, mortgage debt rose sharply above its predicted level. Notice the character of the forecast errors. Until the fourth quarter of 1986, the forecast errors for both equations tended to move in the same direction—reflecting the influence of common factors, such as consumer confidence, that influence both equations in the same way (Figure 13.4). But note how the errors are significantly different beginning in 1986. This reflects the substitution effect of home equity loans on the consumer's choice of the form of credit financing.

Table 13.1
The Influence of Home Equity Loans ($ Billion)

Period	Mortgage Debt			Installment Credit		
	Forecast	Actual	Difference	Forecast	Actual	Difference
1986:4	38.6	55.6	17.0	13.5	6.5	-7.0
1987:1	37.4	51.4	14.0	15.0	2.1	-12.9
1987:2	29.5	56.2	26.7	16.4	7.9	-8.5

The standard errors of the regressions are $5.0B (Mortgages) and $2.9B (Installment Credit) whereas the out-of-sample mean errors are $15.9B (Mortgages and -$9.5 (Installment Credit). These results again emphasize the offsetting nature of the errors and the large difference between in-sample and out-of-sample errors.

FORECASTING THE ECONOMY WITH CONSUMER DEBT

Rising consumer debt does not necessarily indicate economic evil. When consumer spending is moving the economy forward, consumer debt will increase. This is a positive indicator of economic expansion. Consumer debt is an economic good enabling consumers to take advantage of rising expected income for the purchase of consumer durables.

The consumer confidence expressed in the decision to take on debt is a positive indicator by itself, but when backed up with a multiplier, it is a "substantial" driving force of economic growth. Consumer installment debt enters the Commerce Department leading indicator index as a positive indicator, suggesting that increases in consumer debt are associated with an increase in economic growth. Net monthly changes in the stock of consumer installment credit outstanding as a percent of personal disposable income lead to turning points in the economy (Table 13.2).

The hypothesis that consumer debt acts as a signal of future consumer retrenchment can be restated simply as the proposition that consumer debt has some forecasting value regarding future consumption. To test the validity of this hypothesis, a series of regressions were computed. The regression analysis included lagged values of both consumption and consumer debt, as well as other consumer financial measures as explanatory variables of the behavior of present consumption. If these financial measures have some forecasting value, then lagged values of these same measures will have a statistically significant impact on the behavior of economic activity when lagged values of economic activity are also included in the regression.

The results in general do not support the argument that consumer debt can be used to forecast future consumer spending (Table 13.3). The predictive variable

Figure 13.4
Comparing Forecast Errors: Mortgage Debt versus Consumer Debt

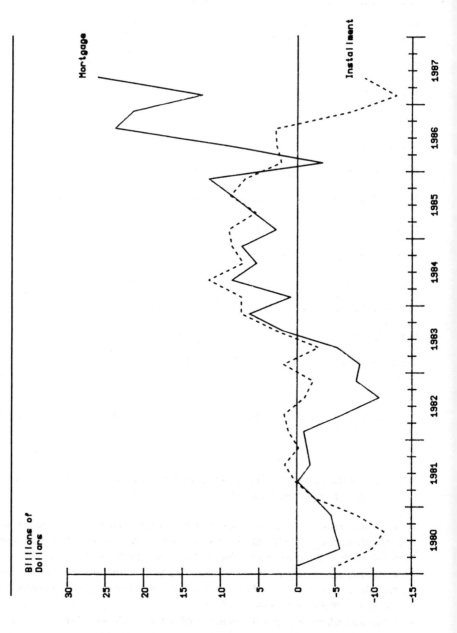

Table 13.2
Debt as an Indicator

Trough Credit	Business Cycle	Lead (months)	Peak	Trough
Peak Oct. '59	Apr.' 60	6	6	
Trough Apr. '61	Feb. '61	-2		-2
Peak June '65		-	-	
Trough May '67	-	-		-
Peak Feb. '69	Dec. 69	10	10	
Trough May '70	Nov. '70	6		6
Peak Mar. '73	Nov. '73	8	8	
Trough Jan. '75	Mar. '75	2		2
Peak June '78	Jan. '80	19	19	
Trough July '80	July '80	0		0
Peak May '81	July '81	2	2	
Trough Dec. '81	Nov. '82	11		11
Average			9	4

The table shows how many months the accelerated debt-to-income series leads the business cycle.

in the estimated pairwise relation is reported in each cell. Four possible relationships are identified in Table 13.3:

1. A one-way causal relationship going from the financial variables to the measure of aggregate economic activity. For example, according to the Granger test, lagged values of net worth help predict future values of real consumption (column 1, row 5).
2. A one-way relationship going from economic activity to the financial variable. For example, lagged values of real consumption help predict future values of changes in debt to income ratios (column 1, row 2).
3. A two-way relationship in which both variables cause each other. For example, real consumption is useful in forecasting traditional debt to income ratios, and vice versa (column 2, row 1).

Table 13.3
Causality Testing for Financial Activity Measures and Economic Activity

	Real Consumption (Granger Test)	Real Consumption (Modified Sims Test)	Real GNP (Granger Test)	Real GNP (Modified Sims Test)
Traditional Debt to Income	None	Bi-directional	None	Credit
Change in Debt/ Income	Consumption	Consumption	None	Credit
Debt Service/ Income	None	Consumption	GNP	Bi-directional
Assets/Liabilities (A/L)	A/L	A/L	A/L	A/L
Net Worth	Net Worth	None	Net Worth	Net Worth
Stock Market (S&P)	None	S&P	S&P	S&P

The predictive variable in the estimated pairwise relation is reported in each cell. All the data series have been detrended prior to the analysis. For definitions of the Granger and Sims tests, see Footnotes 3 and 4.

4. A lack of causal relationship, in which case only a contemporaneous relationship would be observed. For example, lagged values of traditional debt to income ratios do not help forecast future real consumption, and vice versa (column 1, row 1).

The first row shows the comparison between the traditional installment debt to personal disposable income measure and real consumption and real GNP respectively. For real consumption, the Granger test shows no relationship.[3] The Modified Sims test suggests a bi-directional (two-way) relationship between the debt ratio and consumption (Table 13.3).[4] For real GNP, however, it appears that there is a one-way relationship between the traditional debt ratio and GNP, that is, the debt ratio can be used to forecast real GNP without distortion of a feedback relationship from GNP to the debt ratio (Table 13.3).

For the second financial measure, the change in debt to income ratio, it appears that, unfortunately, consumption can actually be used to predict the debt ratio. This debt ratio appears better suited to predict GNP. In general, these two debt ratios do not appear useful in forecasting consumption but are useful in forecasting real GNP. It is reassuring to us that our result is consistent with the standard practice of using a credit aggregate in the Department of Commerce's leading indicators of real GNP. It also supports the usefulness of the change in debt to income ratio measure in forecasting turns in GNP that was examined earlier in this paper.

The broader household financial measures, such as the financial assets/ lia-bilities, net worth, and the stock market appear as clear, useful measures to forecast future consumption spending as well as future GNP. They do not suffer from any feedback effect and the results are consistent for both informativeness tests. In summary, the broader measures of consumer finance appear well suited to forecasting consumption. Both consumer debt measures and the as-sets/liabilities and stock market measure appear useful in forecasting future GNP.

SUMMARY

Different views are expressed regarding the relationship of consumer debt to economic activity. Everyone hates their liabilities and loves their assets. Desig-nated as a liability, consumer debt surely is to be hated. Future interest and principal payments detract directly from the debtor's income stream. In the extreme, debt and the payments that debt mandates have the ability to im-poverish. But debt also allows individuals and companies to acquire assets they otherwise could not have obtained and to consume outside the constraints of their current income. In order to evaluate debt, we have to know the purpose to which the proceeds were used and the ability of the borrower to service the debt.

The maximum amount of debt that a consumer could incur without going bankrupt is limited by the discounted present value of his future income plus current net worth. Changes in the income path, interest rates, and current asset values will clearly affect the consumer's debt capacity.

A consumer's debt capacity is determined, in part, by market conditions. Lenders, in the presence of adverse changes in interest rates and market expecta-tions about their future income, will alter their lending limits in order to reduce consumer bankruptcy risks. These changes will tend to bring the economy's debt ratio in line with the new market conditions. In principle, the adjustment could lead to a disruption in the financial market that would, in turn, bring about a retrenchment in the economy. This suggests that changes in consumer debt could be used to forecast the future path of the economy.

Increased real wealth reduces the need to save and thereby lowers the house-hold savings rate. This analysis suggests that changes in aggregate asset values in conjunction with the debt to income ratio provide a much clearer picture of the conditions under which a change in debt is a vice or a virtue.

NOTES

1. *Economics of Eisenhower: Symposium Review of Economics and Statistics,* vol. 38, November 1956.

2. Long-run income growth, r, is calculated from:

$$YFX_t = YPX_o (1 + r)_t$$

Next, the sensitivity of debt, a, to the business cycle (as proxied by personal income) is given by:

$$DX_t = a(l + r)/r(YPX_o ((l + r)^t - 1)) + DX_o$$

Finally, the theoretical debt limit is given by:

$$DX_t/YPX_t = a(l + r)/r$$

See John E. Silvia and Barry Whall, "Consumer Debt as an Indicator of the Business Cycle," paper presented at the National Association of Business Economists Meeting, September, 1987.

3. The Granger test estimates the relationship between current values of a measure of economic activity, say real GNP, and past values of consumer debt as well as past values of consumption. If, given the lagged variables of real GNP, the coefficients for the lagged consumer debt variable indicate a statistically significant relationship, then the consumer debt has some forecasting value. In which case, consumer debt is said to cause real GNP. Symmetrically, if past values of consumption help explain the consumer debt, then real GNP is said to cause consumer debt. C. Granger, "Investigating Causal Relations by Econometric Models and Cross Spectral Methods," *Econometrica*, July 1969, pp. 424–38.

4. The Sims test estimates the relationship between current values of a measure of economic activity, say real GNP, and future values of consumer debt as well as future values of real GNP. If the set of future coefficients for consumer debt are different from zero, then real GNP causes consumer debt. C. A. Sims, "Money, Income and Causality," *American Economic Review*, September 1972, pp. 540–52.

14

The Savings Monster

Victor A. Canto and Arthur B. Laffer

Teratology, if we are to translate the ancient Greek literally, is the study of monsters. In practice, it is more concerned with biological deformities than with any real or imagined monsters. Teratology focuses on an individual in a species with some bodily part missing or some extra part, or a part greatly mutated. Atavistic genetic alterations often seem to be the source of the mutation. The contribution of teratology has been to show how minuscule deviations in chromosomal genetic timing can really have profound implications on the adult life form that results.

A similar phenomenon exists in economics. Archaic concepts long submerged get resurrected time and again only to flourish in the minds of academic scribblers until they fall into the hands of tradesmen. The resultant failure condemns the concept to a nether world until memories, once again sufficiently dimmed, allow its resurgence. Natural selection at its best.

John Maynard Keynes, along with other top academics of his time, faced an incredible intellectual dilemma. How on earth could society create the conditions of seemingly interminable unemployment on a global scale? The Great Depression had been to mainstream academic thought what Steve Garvey is to planned parenthood. A new view just had to be found.

Fortunately for Keynes, there existed an underconsumption theory that fit his needs precisely—an antiquated, discredited view of the world that stressed secular unemployment. The theory of underconsumption had long kicked around in the backwash of mainstream economics and had never flourished before Keynes took its cause ʋʋ heart. Werner Sombart, Hla Mynt, Paulo Sylos Labini, and Thorstein Veblen were its largely unsuccessful champions. And then, along came Keynes.

For Keynes, the attraction to the theory of underconsumption was two-fold. First, the theory did provide for an equilibrium level of unemployment. And, second, it was central casting perfect for a massive media blitz unparalleled in its day. The world of the Great Depression—distraught by the ravages of poverty and unemployment—was fertile ground for a "new view," especially one proffered by such an eminent scholar as John Maynard Keynes.

What Keynes postulated was an elegantly simple model whereby total demand would fall short of full employment supply and have no tendency to rise. The price level could fall sharply and still there would be no move from this unemployment equilibrium. Say's Law, so beloved by the classical economists, was shattered. All the while, Say's common sense feedback loop was maintained.[1]

What Keynes did was simply to alter the marginal propensity to spend out of income. Say's Law, and virtually all economists of that day and age, would have set the marginal propensity to spend at one, if the notion ever crossed their minds. Supply created its own demand and the world always moved toward full employment. Keynes set the marginal propensity to spend at something less than one and he called it consumption, not just spending. If other spending, such as net exports, investment, and government spending, plus consumption were less than full employment income so be it. Unemployment would exist and have no tendency to diminish.

What was not consumed out of income was called savings. On the margin as well, what wasn't consumed was saved, and therefore one minus the marginal propensity to consume was called the marginal propensity to save. Keynes' theory was as much a theory of oversavings as it was a theory of underconsumption. Both savings and consumption were nothing but different aspects of the economic whole. The rest of this story is now history.

KEYNESIAN VIEW OF SAVINGS

Postulated at the time as a sidebar comment to the critical discourse of Keynes' general theory, some crucial elements were almost accidentally introduced into economic thought. While introduced by Keynes, these concepts quite quickly spread and prospered in the minds and papers of academic writers who were by no means advocates of Keynes' general theory. It wasn't really until Richard Nixon and his immediate successors tested Keynes' theories in the real world that they were rejected.[2] But Keynes' concepts remained.

At least one peculiar concept of Keynes, his notion of savings, has spread almost as if it were a virus of some sort. Keynes' specific concept of savings and the importance subsequent economists have attached to savings does countless damage to this very day. Keynes and the early Keynesians were clearly antisavings as no one is today. Greater savings, to the early Keynesians, meant more unemployment and poverty. The early Keynesians were virtually phobic when it came to savings. And, while few today worry about underconsumption and excessive savings, the passion for savings survives.

The world at large totally accepts Keynes' definition of savings as well as the central role Keynes assigned savings. While it was the concept of savings Keynesians felt so strongly about, ultimately it was the definition of savings that provided the standard of measure. The Keynes definition of savings, so appropriate for the use to which he put it, has been totally misappropriated for today's purpose of capital accumulation.[3]

To Keynes, savings is the absence of consumption. Savings, along with taxation and imports, is a leakage from the circular income stream. That portion of disposable income not consumed therefore is, by definition, saved. In an economy, expenditure leakages must be replenished by expenditure injections to maintain balance. Savings, taxes, and imports must all be countered by investment, government spending, and exports. Because of the extraordinary benefits Keynes attached to consumption, any increase in savings was considered an additional drain on the circular income/expenditure stream. The result would be a recession, or worse.

In the vernacular of the Keynesian, businesses and government too have savings. In the case of government, however, savings correspond to budget surpluses. Surpluses were few and far between even back then. Thus, deficits became government dissavings—a net injection into the income stream.

In a closed economy, using these standardized concepts, total savings had to equal total investment per force an accounting identity. When the economy was opened to international trade, total savings still had to equal total investment, but now total investment included net foreign investment. Where economics replaced accounting was at the point of equilibrium. Equilibrium was defined as that level of income where desired savings equaled desired investment.

To a Keynesian of old, an increase in savings was exactly the same as a reduction in consumption and therefore total demand.[4] With lower aggregate demand, a slowdown was sure to follow. They didn't even discuss inflation back then. Therefore, to keep the economy as recession-proof as possible, the idea was to keep consumption as high as possible and savings as low as possible. Keynesian policies developed into a set of distinctly antisavings actions that we all know and hate so well today.

A Counterrevolution

Today's mainstream economists are as rabid in their anti-Keynesian focus as the Keynesians of old were pro-Keynes. The depth of the anger of the jilted lover was only matched by the earlier intensity of the love. Both Keynesians and anti-Keynesians live in a world where savings and consumption reign supreme. One group hates savings and loves consumption while the other loves savings and hates consumption. We of the classical persuasion observe their frenetic machinations in alternating states of amusement and terror.

The Keynesians and the anti-Keynesians raise issues in their controversies that range from the sublime to the ridiculous. The danger they represent, however, doesn't result from their malevolent motivations or their perverse morality. The real and present danger is akin to a blind javelin-thrower in a crowded auditorium or a bunch of cowboys shooting real bullets into the air. Every now and then their actions kill or maim someone.

Classical or supply-side economics treats savings as a normal byproduct of the choice between labor and leisure and leisure and future versus current consumption. No great importance is attached to savings per se from the perspective of public policy. If people work to consume, that's fine. If people work to save, that's fine, too. To a classical economist, the focus is on work and not on savings or consumption. If people are motivated to work to acquire wealth for their grandchildren, so be it. If, instead, they are energized by visions of Las Vegas vacations and fancy cars, that's OK, too. To classical thought, the primary objective is to make work as attractive as possible.

To Keynesians and their anti-Keynesian mirror images, people will not make the correct choices for the global good in an unfettered environment. They must be helped along to choose what is best for all. To the new anti-Keynesians, the share of income saved must be increased above what it otherwise would have been. With income growth a direct result of savings and the level of income determined by the existing capital stock, anything that can be done to discourage consumption and encourage savings is worthwhile.

To recapitulate, the ancien regime believed investment was a given and therefore the lower the savings rate, the greater the output. Classical economists believe that personal incentives determine output which may alternatively be prosavings or proconsumption. The new wave anti-Keynesians believe current output is fixed and future output is directly a consequence of higher current savings. A more contentious mixture is hard to imagine.

The Bush administration has a number of influential advisors who are gurus of the new view on savings. In fact, these advisors dominate discussions of the Bush agenda. Here, now, is their story.

The Anti-Keynesian View

The way the Bush team views economic growth is by postulating that a country's total production of goods and services ultimately depends upon the quality and quantity of its labor force and capital stock and the technology in existence for combining that labor and capital into its final product. This so-called technology, of course, is what the normal world calls productivity.

In the eyes of the Bush team, productivity is primarily brought to fruition by being embodied in the capital stock. Obviously, they do understand that better-trained workers also improve productivity, but nonetheless, they feel that these skills are less amenable to economic policy than are capital improvements. For the long haul, labor is critical, and as a consequence, President Bush firmly sees himself as the education president. He personally sees an educated labor force as the key to the future of the U.S. economy, just as it was the key to his future.

Simply stated, the total production of goods and services measured as total real output per unit time (real GNP per year) depends on the total capital stock available for production and the average technology embedded in that capital stock. The average technology embedded in the capital stock is, in the traditional literature, referred to as the output/capital ratio. Thus, output (Y) equals the output/capital ratio (σ) times the available productive capital stock (K). The relevant capital stock measure is net of all true depreciation whatever the accounting standards may be.
Algebraically:

$$Y_t = \sigma_t K_t$$

where

Y_t = current real output;

σ_t = current output/capital ratio (i.e., the productivity of capital);

K_t = current net capital stock.

Quite clearly, the growth in output is constrained by the growth in the capital stock. The Bush team, as well as many many others, believe that all spending categories are not of equal benefit to the future of the U.S. economy. Investment is special. The growth in the economy directly depends upon the growth of America's net capital stock and that is net investment:

$$\Delta Y_t = \sigma_t \Delta K_t$$

where

Δ = the time change in a variable in absolute terms.

Investment, therefore:

$$\Delta K_t = \frac{\Delta Y_t}{\sigma_t}$$

This is a simplified abstraction of the views held, but it does capture the essence of the Bush administration's thought process. They really love investment, but they don't love all investments equally. Just as they prefer investment over consumption, so too, they prefer venture capital investment, research and development investment, and basic research investment over inventories, housing, and corporate limousines. Thus, they are focusing on reducing the capital gains tax rate on long-term capital gains as opposed to all capital gains. Their love for investment often gets blurred and emerges as an active dislike for consumption. While many advocates of these views do not hail from puritanical roots, their rhetoric could fool a person.

To complete the picture, demand siders of all ilks shift their attention to the aggregate net savings "quid" from the investment "pro quo." In a closed economy, and using their bizarre economic concepts, investment must equal savings. For equilibrium, *ex ante* savings must be the same as *ex ante* investment. That is, balance will result when the amount people want to save is the same as the amount people wish to invest.

In the surge of "full employment," investment can always be manipulated by changes in the real rate of interest so that ex post it will equal savings. The higher the real rate of interest, the lower investment will be. The key to the Bush team's view of maintaining full employment is to have sufficient investment to provide the requisite capital to employ the labor force gainfully. Controversy, needless to say, hovers around such concepts as the sustainable growth potential for the U.S. economy. The estimates range from an Alan Greenspan low of about 2.5 percent per year to a Michael Boskin high of something over 3.0 percent per year. Putting it all together, investment must equal savings:

$$S_t = \Delta K_t = \frac{\Delta Y_k}{\sigma_t}$$

where

$$S_t = \text{total savings per time period.}$$

The demand-side view of savings is also quite straightforward. Savings is that part of income not consumed. Keynes, in *The General Theory of Income Employment and Prices* described consumption in this way:

When employment increases, aggregate real income is increased. The psychology of the community is such that when aggregate real income is increased aggregate consumption is increased, but not by so much as income. . . . It follows, therefore, that, given what we shall call the community's propensity to consume, the equilibrium level of employment, i.e., the level at which there is no inducement to employers as a whole either to expand or to contract employment, will depend on the amount of current investment.[5]

Therefore, savings, too, depends on income. The higher the income, the higher the savings. If (s) is the marginal propensity to save out of income then total savings (S_t) is:

$$S_t = sY_t$$

With savings equal to investment as described before:

$$S_t = s_t Y_t = \frac{\Delta Y_t}{\sigma_t} = \Delta K_t$$

or

$$\frac{\Delta Y_t}{Y_t} = s_t \sigma_t$$

This last relationship, while highly simplified, does describe the essence of the Bush team's view of the U.S. economy: real economic growth is defined by the nation's savings rate and the productivity of capital. The more people save and the more productive the capital stock, the faster the economy will grow. How to encourage savings, investment, and productivity is the central question for the Bush team.

The Anti-Keynesian Building Blocks. The low U.S. savings rate is a legacy of misguided Keynesian policies directly linked or related to tax policies, government deficits, and social insurance. These policies have resulted in excessive consumption and a low savings rate.

Countries with Higher Savings Grow Faster. In order to illustrate their point of view, the new anti-Keynesians relate the net savings rate to productivity growth. The international comparison reported in Figure 14.1 tells an apparently compelling story:

1. Countries with high savings rates experience high productivity growth.
2. Policies directed toward increasing the savings rate will result, it would seem, in higher productivity growth, higher real GNP growth, and a higher standard of living for the country. Therefore, the challenge to the administration is to increase the savings rate in the United States.

The Components of U.S. Savings. The U.S. savings rate has declined over the last 17 years. Careful examination of the components of U.S. savings provides information as to the sources of the decline in the U.S. savings rate (Table 14.1). The business savings rate declined slightly from the 1971–79 period compared to the 1983–87 period. During that time, the state and local savings rate actually increased. The two sources of decline in the savings rate are the significant declines in personal savings and the federal budget deficit (euphemistically monikered government dissavings).

In terms of the anti-Keynesian model, the decline in personal and federal savings is directly attributable to the Reagan tax rate cuts. It was, in fact, a similar policy undertaken during the Kennedy administration that had been proffered as a stimulant to consumption. In their view, the tax cuts caused two things: (1) huge budget deficits, (e.g., government dissavings) and (2) a consumption binge on the part of consumers. A reversal of these negative effects would clearly lead to an increase in the savings rate.

Figure 14.1
International Savings Rates and Productivity, 1971–85

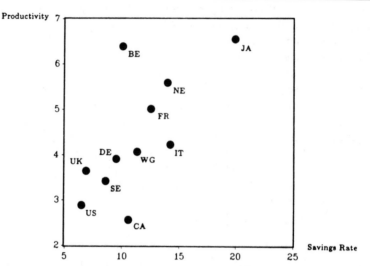

Productivity is the average annual percent change in output per hour for the period. Savings rate is savings as a percent of GNP.

Sources: Bureau of Labor Statistics, *Handbook of Labor Statistics*, June 1985; *Statistical Abstract of the United States, 1988*; OECD, *National Accounts, 1960-86*; *International Financial Statistics*.

A.B. Laffer Associates

Table 14.1
Components of U.S. Savings as a Share of GNP

	1983-87	1971-80
Personal	3.30	5.53
Business	2.24	2.43
Total Private	5.54	7.96
State and Local	1.47	0.87
Federal	-4.58	-1.84
Total Private and Public	2.42	6.98

Source: *Economic Report of the President, 1989.*

A.B. Laffer Associates

The anti-Keynesians argue that some of the declines in the savings rate will reverse themselves. They point out that the federal budget deficit is now less than 3 percent of GNP and improving. In their view, the flexible freeze and other spending restraints will go a long way toward eliminating the public sector's dissaving. Every dollar not spent will reduce government dissavings by one dollar. This leaves personal consumption/private savings as the major source of the decline in savings.

The desired objective, according to their view, is to reduce government dissavings and to increase private savings. They would devise a consumption tax that optimally would not affect, in a detrimental way, private savings.

In order to develop a solution, we must examine the composition of savings among different groups. This can be done by studying assets held by different groups. The implications derived from the data are that most Americans do very little financial saving (Tables 14.2 and 14.3). In fact, the data suggest that older and higher income individuals account for the bulk of personal asset holdings. In the context of the anti-Keynesian model, the data on household financial savings yield the following policy implications:

1. Care must be exercised in initiating a tax or revenue increase so as not to distort or reduce the savings currently taking place. Thus, any tax should fall disproportionately on those sectors of the economy that save little. A tax on families who have no savings would reduce consumption dollar for dollar while a tax on families with savings could well result in reduced savings. A consumption tax or other specific excise taxes, such as a gasoline tax, would fit that criterion.

2. Steps must be taken to induce Americans to increase their financial savings. According to this view, the tax exemptions curtailing IRAs in the Tax Reform Act of 1986 reduced the savings rate. A possible cost-effective way to reduce this effect is through the introduction of nondeductible, but tax-free accounts. Similarly, special incentives for inducements to buy common stocks should be considered (for instance, the reduction in capital gains tax rates for long-term investments).

Additional Effects on the U.S. Economy. Until 1982, the United States invested more abroad than foreigners invested in the United States. Since 1983, foreigners have invested more in the United States than Americans have invested abroad: Foreign investment increased to 2.68 percent of GNP in the 1983–87 period from −0.25 percent of GNP in the 1971–80 period (Table 14.4). The implication derived from the anti-Keynesian view is that the low savings rate makes the United States more dependent on the inflow of foreign capital. Policies that increase the domestic savings rate will have the added benefit of reducing foreign dependency.

A SUPPLY-SIDE INTERPRETATION OF SAVINGS

In order to explain the decline in the savings rate, a theoretical framework is needed. Our view is that the economy is forward-looking and economic agents

Table 14.2
Household Net Worth: Ownership Rates, 1984

Characteristic	Number of Households (1,000)	Interest Earning Assets	Other Interest Earning Assets	Regular Checking Accounts	Mutual Fund Shares	Business or Profession	Motor Vehicles	Own Home	Rental Property	Other Real Estate	U.S. Savings Bonds	IRA or KEOGH Accounts
Total	86,790	71.8	8.5	53.9	20.0	12.9	85.8	64.3	9.8	10.0	15.0	19.5
Age of householder:												
Less then 35 yrs	25,730	64.5	4.8	50.6	13.1	10.3	87.5	40.3	3.8	5.2	13.0	10.3
35 to 44 yrs	17,393	72.4	7.9	59.0	22.9	18.3	91.7	69.3	10.0	10.4	17.8	21.6
45 to 54 yrs	12,596	72.9	9.1	60.0	23.1	19.7	91.6	77.7	14.3	15.4	17.5	31.4
55 to 64 yrs	12,920	76.0	11.5	55.4	25.5	15.1	89.1	80.2	15.4	15.9	18.3	38.9
65 yrs and over	18,151	77.5	11.6	48.5	21.1	5.1	71.4	73.0	10.8	8.4	11.3	8.5

Source: Statistical Abstract of the United States, 1988. Original data reported in Current Population Reports, Bureau of the Census.

A.B. Laffer Associates

Table 14.3
Household Net Worth: Median Value of Holdings, 1984

Characteristic	Net Worth	Interest Earning Deposits	Other Interest Earning Assets	Regular Checking Accounts	Stock and Mutual Fund Shares	Equity in Own Home	IRA and KEOGH Accounts
Total	32,667	3,066	9,471	449	3,892	40,597	4,805
Age of householder:							
Less than 35 yrs	5,764	901	2,318	327	1,218	17,586	2,484
35 to 44 yrs	35,581	1,894	5,260	410	3,197	37,268	4,438
45 to 54 yrs	56,791	3,387	7,766	538	4,048	48,172	5,351
55 to 64 yrs	73,664	7,340	13,559	568	5,662	54,059	6,390
65 yrs and over	60,266	13,255	18,144	651	6,882	46,192	6,369

Source: Statistical Abstract of the United States, 1988. Original data reported in Current Population Reports, Bureau of Census.

A.B. Laffer Associates

Table 14.4
Components of U.S. Investment as a Share of GNP

	1983–87	1971–80
Real net private domestic investment	5.02	7.15
Real net foreign investment	2.68	-0.25

Source: *Economic Report of the President, 1989.*

<u>A.B. Laffer Associates</u>

save to provide a sustainable level of consumption yielded by the return on wealth. Absent borrowing or lending, individual consumption would be limited to the income earned at a particular point in time. Thus, borrowing and lending afford a greater degree of flexibility that increases the individual's welfare. The savings behavior is determined by the desire of the household to smooth out their consumption stream over the life cycle. The ability to borrow and save allows the individual to separate the timing of consumption (i.e., consumption path) from the timing of earning (i.e., income path).

The higher rate of return will provide incentives for individuals to save and invest for future consumption. However, that is not all. Expectations about the future and changes in asset values also affect current savings rates. If income growth is expected to be high in the future, it is only natural that individuals will enjoy a consumption level that exceeds current income. The borrowings will be paid in future years when the income growth materializes.

This analysis suggests that over the life cycle, young people are likely to be net borrowers and will not accumulate financial assets. As they mature and their earnings grow, the early years' borrowing will be repaid and assets will be accumulated to provide for retirement years.

This life cycle view of the world yields a very simple implication: young people will be borrowers and older people will be savers. Savings behavior is the direct result of a lifetime maximization process. Therefore, the financial asset accumulation only identifies the life cycle stage of individuals, not their frugality or other inherent characteristics. At some point in their life, everyone will reach that stage.

The level of savings and the timing of savings will be influenced by the real rate of interest and the level of wealth. If interest rates increase, then incentives to save and to provide for the future will unambiguously increase. Therefore, a policy that increases the after-tax rate of return will be clearly desirable since it will increase incentives to work, save, and invest.

Increases in wealth will result in higher consumption from all levels through-out a lifetime. If wealth increases faster than income, the increase in consumption will be greater than the increase in income, hence the savings rate will decline. However, this is not cause for alarm; the higher wealth reflects a net increase in the society's resources.

The Reagan Tax Rate Cuts

Reducing marginal personal income tax rates has three effects on saving.

Income Effects. First, at any given level of national income, less tax revenue is raised at the reduced income tax rates. This is the effect emphasized by demand-side analyses and, to a large extent, by the anti-Keynesians. As a result, unless government spending is also reduced, government saving (the surplus) falls by the amount of the tax cut while personal disposable (after-tax) income rises by the amount of the tax cut. If the tax cut is permanent, households can consume more from any given national income than they could before the tax cut. Histor-ically, U.S. households have consumed more than 90 percent of any permanent increase in disposable income. Focusing solely on this effect, it follows that at any given national income, private saving generally rises by less than 10 percent of a tax cut. Within this framework, reducing personal tax rates lowers total national saving (private plus government saving) because private saving in-creases by less than the government's borrowing requirement, thus leaving fewer resources available to finance capital formation.

Substitution Effects. The second effect, generally ignored by demand-side analyses, is the incentive effect of the tax cut. A reduction in marginal personal income tax rates raises the real after-tax return to saving, thereby raising the saving rate—the amount that households wish to save from any given disposable income. Saving tends to rise because a higher real after-tax return to saving makes all of the things for which households save—their retirements, rainy days, their children's educations—more attractive.[6]

Consider, for example, a person who earns a nominal before-tax return of 15 percent on investments and who wishes to save for retirement 30 years hence. Suppose this person has sufficient income to be in the 70 percent bracket. The nominal after-tax return would be 4.5 percent [15 × (1 − .70]. If inflation is expected to average 10 percent a year for the next 30 years, the real after-tax return to savings is −5.5 percent (4.5 − 10). A reduction in this household's marginal tax rate to 28 percent would raise its real after-tax return to 0.8 percent. Without the tax cut, assets lose 5.5 percent of their value each year, so that sacrificing one unit of current consumption yields $(1 0.055)^{30}$, or .18 units of retirement consumption 30 years from now. But with the tax cut, the same sacrifice would yield $(1.008)^{30}$, or 1.27 units of retirement consumption. The tradeoff between current consumption and retirement consumption improves nearly seven-fold, roughly twice the magnitude as an increase in the price of crude oil from $10 to $30 per barrel. Just as an oil price increase of this magnitude caused dramatic changes in the pattern of energy consumption, a similar change in the price of current consumption in terms of foregone future consumption could be expected to result in a substantial reduction in current consumption and a corresponding increase in savings.[7] The effect just described would be smaller, though still appreciable, for all but those in the lowest tax brackets. The allegation that tax rate cuts would do nothing for saving is simply not credible.

Inflation could potentially eliminate any real after-tax rate of return, thereby reducing the before-tax interest sensitivity of savings. Indexing could change the real after-tax return from a negative to a positive number. The policy implication of the analysis is quite clear. Indexing the tax code will significantly reduce the disincentive effects generated by bracket creep and will increase the incentives to save.

Wealth Effects. The third effect is the wealth or macroeconomic effect. Both the Keynesian and the supply-side approaches predict that a reduction in tax rates will stimulate the economy. However, the source of stimulus is quite different. In the Keynesian framework, the reduction in tax revenues and the consequent increase in disposable income lead to higher aggregate consumption, which through the multiplier effect leads to an increase in overall economic activity. In a supply-side framework, the stimulus originates in the reduction of tax rates, which yields higher rates of return to market activity and hence increased output.

A reduction in income tax rates also increases the rate of return to saving, which results in a postponement of current consumption. As a result of higher real after-tax return, aggregate consumption would be expected to decline below where it otherwise would have been. The lower tax rate will result in higher after-tax rates of return of existing and new machines. The reduction in distortions will result in a more efficient economic system, the result being a higher level of output from existing physical and human capital. This higher output will result in an upward revision of existing physical and human capital. The tax rate cuts will result in a rise in private wealth.

The rise in private wealth will increase the permanent consumption level of the economy, and, as a consequence, saving out of current income will decrease. Tax rate increases will have the opposite effect. The experience of the United States during the last two decades indicates a negative relation between changes in household net worth and the personal savings rate. During the 1970s when inflation-induced bracket creep was pushing the economy into higher tax brackets, wealth was being destroyed. The need to replenish wealth resulted in a higher savings rate. In turn, during the 1980s when wealth was being created, the need to replenish wealth through higher personal savings was being reduced (Figure 14.2).

Personal Saving. In our view, the decline in the personal saving rate to 3.30 percent during the 1983–87 period from 5.53 percent during the 1971–80 period is directly attributable to the change in economic policies that arrested the erosion and destruction of wealth caused by inflation-induced bracket creep and restored

Figure 14.2
Percent Change in Real Households Domestic Net Worth and Personal Savings as a
Percent of GNP, 1971–88

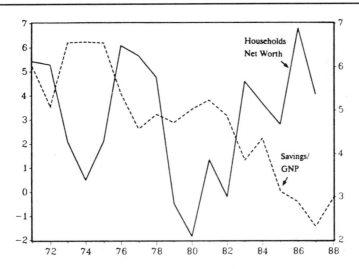

Sources: *Economic Report of the President, 1989*; Federal Reserve System, *Balance Sheets for the U.S. Economy, 1948-87*; Bureau of Economic Analysis, *Survey of Current Business*.

A.B. Laffer Associates

incentives to the U.S. economy. When the economy adjusts to the low tax rate environment, the savings rate will, once again, rise to its secular level. In line with our framework, the decline in the personal savings rate appears to have been arrested: During 1988, the personal savings rate rose to 2.97 percent of GNP from 2.30 percent in 1987.

Attempts to increase the savings rate by reducing the double taxation of income implicit in the income tax code (e.g., capital gains tax rate reductions and full restoration of tax exemptions to IRA programs) will increase the overall economy's incentives to save, invest, and produce. As such, they are welcomed policy recommendations.

Savings Rates and the Life Cycle. Care must be exercised that the incentives are not targeted to specific income or age groups. While it is a fact that a small fraction of Americans account for a large fraction of financial savings, their holdings are easily explained in terms of a life cycle. Prime-age workers repay the debt incurred during their starting years and save to provide for their retirement years.

Using tax increases to single out and penalize young taxpayers or lower income taxpayers or both because they don't save enough will be a policy mistake. The tax on younger workers will reduce their after-tax income and, as such, will reduce their incentives to accumulate and invest in human capital. This will reduce their lifetime earnings, although their life cycle saving profile and saving rate will not change because they will save the most during their prime years. The levels of saving will decline as a consequence of the lower income earned because they have invested less in human capital.

Government Dissavings. The only component of the total savings rate that is clearly out of line with the experience of the 1970s is the government dissavings or budget deficit. All else the same, elimination of the budget deficit would increase the economy's total savings rate to a level comparable to that of the 1970s.

A strong argument can be made that the culprit in the decline in the U.S. saving rate has been the federal government. In order to solve the problem, one must determine the source of the government dissavings—a shortfall in revenues or an uncontrolled increase in spending. If the shortfall in revenue is the cause, the solution is a tax increase. In turn, if the cause is runaway spending, spending restraint is the appropriate solution.

A close examination of the data suggests that government receipts on a national income and product account basis as a percent of GNP are higher than they were prior to the Reagan tax rate cuts (Table 14.5). Unfortunately, so is government spending (Table 14.6). The data clearly suggest that government spending is the problem, not revenue. The most recent data indicate a slowdown of

Table 14.5
Government Expenditures on a National Income and Product Accounts Basis

Fiscal Year	Net Federal* (Billions)	Percent of GNP	State/Local (Billions)	Percent of GNP	Total % of GNP
1977	$362.6	18.2	$273.2	13.7	28.9
1978	393.4	17.5	301.3	13.4	30.9
1979	440.6	17.6	327.7	13.1	30.6
1980	526.4	19.3	363.2	13.3	32.6
1981	615.4	20.2	391.4	12.8	33.0
1982	697.3	22.0	414.3	13.1	35.1
1983	749.7	22.0	440.2	12.9	34.9
1984	802.0	21.3	475.9	12.6	33.9
1985	884.9	22.1	516.5	12.9	34.9
1986	925.1	21.8	561.9	13.3	35.1
1987	971.5	21.5	602.8	13.3	35.0
1988	1,006.1	20.7	647.9	13.3	34.0

* On and off budget; gross expenditures less grants-in-aid to state and local governments.

Sources: U.S. Department of Commerce, Bureau of Economic Analysis, *Survey of Current Business* and *The National Income and Product Accounts, 1929-82; Statistical Tables.*

A. B. Laffer Associates

Table 14.6
Government Receipts on a National Income and Product Accounts Basis

Fiscal Year	Federal* (Billions)	Percent of GNP	Net State/Local** (Billions)	Percent of GNP	Total % of GNP
1977	$384.1	19.3	$232.6	11.7	31.0
1978	441.4	19.6	253.0	11.2	30.9
1979	505.0	20.1	274.8	11.0	31.1
1980	553.8	20.3	301.3	11.0	31.3
1981	639.5	20.9	337.7	11.1	32.0
1982	635.3	20.1	365.5	11.5	31.6
1983	659.9	19.4	401.5	11.8	31.2
1984	726.0	19.2	446.9	11.8	31.1
1985	788.6	19.7	479.9	12.0	31.6
1986	827.4	19.5	511.9	12.1	31.6
1987	916.5	20.2	553.0	12.2	32.5
1988	975.2	20.0	591.5	12.2	32.2

* On and off budget.

** Gross receipts less federal grants-in-aid.

Sources: U.S. Department of Commerce, Bureau of Economic Analysis, *Survey of Current Business* and *The National Income and Product Accounts, 1929-82: Statistical Tables*

A. B. Laffer Associates

spending as a percent of GNP, while revenues have held to their recent levels. If the trend continues, the budget deficit, and, hence, government dissavings, will decline in the next few years.

Savings and Economic Growth

The anti-Keynesians argue that real economic growth is defined by the nation's savings rate and productivity of capital. The more people save and the more productive the capital stock, the faster the economy grows. A direct test of the anti-Keynesian proposition is to examine the relationship between savings rate and economic growth. The results reported in Figure 14.3 find a weak positive relationship between the two variables. The empirical evidence deals a devastating blow to the anti-Keynesian view of the world.

From a supply sider's viewpoint, the lack of strong direct correlation is not difficult to explain. To make the point extreme, consider the case of a city block. There is no reason to expect that the savings of residents of the block will match their investment in the city block. More than likely, their investments will be somewhere else. The location of the investments will depend on the rate of return earned elsewhere vis-à-vis the city block. However, as the dimension of the area is expanded to include a state or a nation, the likelihood of investment being in

Figure 14.3
International Savings Rates and Growth in Real Gross National Product, 1971–85

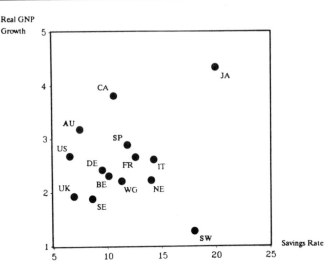

Real GNP growth is average annual percent change in real GNP or GDP for the period. Savings is net savings as a percent of GNP. Countries shown are Australia, Belgium, Canada, Denmark, France, Italy, Japan, Netherlands, Spain, Sweden, Switzerland, United Kingdom, United States, and West Germany.

Sources: OECD, *National Accounts, 1960-86; International Financial Statistics.*

<u>A.B. Laffer Associates</u>

the same jurisdiction as the area where the savings takes place will unambiguously increase. In the extreme, for the world as a whole (i.e., a closed economy), savings will equal investment. Therefore, the use of savings as a proxy for investment and possible source of growth is a misguided analysis.

That is not to say that savings and investment are unimportant. Quite the contrary. Nevertheless, a different interpretation is provided by supply siders. Higher investment rates will result in higher growth rates. The increased capital accumulation will result in an increase in output per worker (e.g., higher productivity). The higher income and prospects for continued growth and higher rate of return will increase incentives to save. Therefore, a positive correlation between savings and productivity will be observed that is a direct result of the economic policies that fostered higher rates of return. A far more complete approach would increase the total value of human capital which is rarely paid lip service. The implications of including human capital are truly fundamental—not merely a refinement.

In addition, focusing on productivity alone, or on new capital (i.e., investment) misses a major source of growth stressed by supply-side economics. The low tax rate environment increases incentives to use old and new machinery alike. Similarly, it increases the incentive to work for young and old people alike without discriminating by age of individual or machinery. Focusing on new machinery ignores the increase in output from existing productive capacity that is used more effectively under the new tax system.

NOTES

1. Jean Baptiste Say (1769–1832) early in the nineteenth century expounded the principle that has come to be known as Say's Law: supply creates its own demand. Production creates demand sufficient to purchase all goods produced.

2. Arthur B. Laffer, "The Ellipse," A. B. Laffer Associates, July 28, 1980.

3. Robert J. Barro, "The Ricardian Approach to Budget Deficits," *Journal of Economic Perspectives* 3, no. 2 (Spring 1989), pp. 37–54.

4. The discussions that surrounded savings were not unlike those today about taxes. Savings rates were to be sharply differentiated from total savings just as today we distinguish tax rates from total revenues.

5. John Maynard Keynes, *The General Theory of Employment, Interest, and Money*, (New York: Harcourt, Brace, Jovanovich, 1964), p. 27.

6. The saving rate might increase for yet another reason. Suppose that the reduction in tax rates lowers tax receipts, that the government does not reduce spending, and that the resulting deficit is financed by issuing more government debt. This debt issue obligates the government to make future principal and interest payments whose present value is equal to the amount of the debt issue. In addition, private disposable income increases by the amount of the debt issue, that is, by the amount of the reduction in current tax payments. Some economists argue that rational individuals will realize that this increase in the present value of their future tax payments (implied by the government's future principal and interest payments) is exactly equal to the increase in their current disposable income. Therefore, individuals will save all of the tax cut (the increase in current disposable income) in order to meet these higher future tax payments. If so, private saving will increase by the full amount of the debt issue (the reduction in government saving), leaving unaffected total national saving and the resources available for capital formation. Since the entire debt-induced increase in disposable income is saved, the economy's average saving rate increases. This effect is thus empirically indistinguishable from an increase in the saving rate brought about by the incentive effect, as discussed in the text. See Robert J. Barro, "Are Government Bonds Net Wealth?" *Journal of Political Economy* 84 (April 1976), pp. 343–49.

7. Gerald W. Bollman, Victor A. Canto, and Kevin A. Melich, "Oil Decontrol: The Power of Incentives Could Reduce OPEC's Power to Boost Oil Prices," *Oil and Gas Journal* 80, no. 2 (January 11, 1982), pp. 92–101.

15

Are We Climbing the Wall of Resistance toward National Health Insurance?

JAMES BALOG

The issues surrounding health care policy are extremely important to the future of our country, not only on social grounds but on economic grounds as well. We must deal with the problem of health care spending in order to maintain our competitive standing in the world. The United States is now spending a larger proportion of its GNP on health care than any other country. American business is now devoting 50 percent of its corporate operating profit to health care for its employees and retirees. Estimates of these hidden liabilities range from $169 billion to $2 trillion and could equal all other liabilities on the balance sheets of American corporations. The Financial Accounting Standards Board wants the hidden liability of corporate health care expenditures brought into the open. The current proposal calls for accrual accounting on the profit and loss statement by 1992 and the recording of a "minimum" liability on balance sheets by 1997. Health benefit costs may be as important to American business as the economic integration of Europe in 1992 or the Chinese takeover of Hong Kong in 1997. How did the problem get so big and how might it be resolved?

HISTORY

The idea of government sponsored health care, retirement systems, and other social programs began in 1883 in Bismarck's Germany. The entry age was established at 65, a sufficiently high level since life expectancy was then under 50 years. Not many people were expected to be able to take advantage of the national health insurance program. Since then, life expectancy has risen to 70–75 years of age in most of the developed world, and medical technology has made possible more ways to treat and sustain life longer for more people. All of this, though, is at an ever-increasing cost.

By now most countries have some form of national health insurance, universal health coverage, or comprehensive medical care. The United Kingdom began its plan in 1948; Canada's policy evolved over 20 years to a complete plan by 1971. A national health insurance plan was first proposed for the United States by President Truman in 1948. Instead we adopted the Medicare program in 1965, choosing to care only for those persons reaching the Bismarckian age standard.

In all countries of the world, the specter of crushing cost burdens haunts policymakers. Faced with overwhelming demand for services, public and private health care administrators are feverishly attempting to control costs while still providing decent and affordable care. A common denominator of universal plans is pay-as-you-go financing through general revenues derived from broad-based taxes on wages. Cost control attempts include provisions such as:

- Copayments: For all or most services the patient pays something
- Deductibles: Plan coverage begins only after the patient has incurred some minimum of personal cost each year
- Spending Caps: Governments pay only a certain amount per patient in each time period
- Regulated Provider Fees: Hospital and physician fees are preset and increases regulated
- Queuing: Usually as a consequence of other cost control techniques (but perhaps by design), medical services are rationed by assigning priorities for type of procedure, patient's age, or other criteria

COMPARATIVE STATISTICS

A comparison of health care spending in five major developed countries reveals that the United States has the highest spending as a percentage of GNP and per capita. But the most startling fact is that the United States is unique in having such a small percentage funded by the government (Table 15.1).

There are big differences among countries in the level of satisfaction with the system. A recent survey asked approximately 1,000 to 1,250 consumers in each of three countries how satisfied they were with the medical care system (Table 15.2). In spite of the high per capita cost and the high percentage of GNP devoted to health care, Americans are the least happy with the system, though there is a significant degree of unhappiness in the United Kingdom and Canada. Canadians seem to like their health care system the best, but that may merely be a function of the fact that they have had their system about half as long as the British. It may be that any system breeds dissatisfaction because of the inevitable need to constrain spending and ration services.

Canada has begun its system without copayments or deductibles, both of which can contribute to excessive spending. Instead, Canada has relied upon

Table 15.1
Summary of Health Care Expenditures

	Percent of Gross National Product	Per Capita Expenditures*	Percent Government Funded
United Kingdom	6.5	$ 715	90 %
West Germany	8.0	1,031	80
France	9.5	1,039	80
Sweden	9.0	1,195	90
United States	11.0	1,926	40

* Adjusted for purchasing power parity with the U.S. dollar.

capping total costs and rationing services. In all probability, dissatisfaction will rise with time. Yet there seems to be an attraction for Americans with the idea of a Canadian system—universal coverage funded by general taxation. Sixty-one percent of Americans would prefer the Canadian system, whereas only 3 percent of Canadians and only 12 percent of the British would want the American system.

In many other ways there are significant differences in health care patterns among countries. The average French citizen gets 28 prescriptions per year; the average English citizen and American get 7 prescriptions per year. In Germany, prescription drugs take up 15 percent of health care spending, twice that of most other nations. This is generally attributed to the fact that the German drug industry is very powerful and able to maintain prices on its home turf. American costs are significantly impacted by malpractice claims, probably 10 times the incidence in Canada. In Canada, verdicts are not by jury but by judges only, and the losing plaintiff pays legal costs if the doctor or hospital is found innocent.

Administrative costs differ among countries. In France the administration of the health care system employs 250,000 people and devours 8 percent of total

Table 15.2
Level of Satisfaction with Health Care Delivery Systems

	System Needs Fundamental Change	Satisfaction With Doctor Visit
United States	89 %	54 %
United Kingdom	69	63
Canada	42	73

health care spending compared with about 3 percent for the U.S. Medicare system and 3 percent for the Canadian system.

THE U.S. EXPERIENCE

In the United States the Medicare Act was passed in 1965 as part of President Johnson's Great Society program. Seemingly in every year since 1965, political leaders from across the political spectrum have been advocating a full national health insurance program to extend coverage to all persons. In fact, the bulk of government expenditures have taken place for the Medicare population, persons aged 65 or above, and some extension of coverage has been made for the disabled and poor.

In 1965, health care spending in the United States was $52 billion or 5.9 percent of GNP. By 1987, health care spending rose to $550 billion or 11.1 percent of GNP. The rate of increase has not slowed and in fact, may be accelerating. The 1986–87 period was particularly unnerving for many corporate plans, with increases of 30 percent quite common. One reason for this major increase is that Medicare's Diagnosis Related Group (DRG) system has limited hospital payments and has shifted costs to private plans. Over the past 20 years there has been a continual and significant shift in health care spending (Table 15.3).

Table 15.3
Percent Change in Spending on Health Care Delivery Systems

Payor	1967	1987
Patient	43 %	30 %
Private Plans	22	30
Government	34	40

THE MEDICARE DILEMMA

The Medicare plan was adopted over the objections of organized medicine and fiscal experts—one group fearing socialized medicine and the other runaway costs. To a greater or lesser degree, both have been right. The Medicare system was based on "fee for service" so that doctors would feel little change in their relationships with a patient and could charge their normal and customary fee. They would remain the gatekeeper for access to the hospital. Hospitals were made the primary point for delivery of medical care. Why? Policymakers were fearful that if medical services were delivered in an outpatient or home setting, control of usage would be very difficult and costs would climb out of control. With a doctor as the gatekeeper and the hospital as the venue, it was felt that costs could be limited. The result of these two concerns—a " non-socialized" system and a hospital-based delivery system—is an expensive system. For care to be covered, it must be delivered in a hospital setting. Hospitals are not "care" facilities; they are "cure" facilities. Many of the elderly need care not cure, yet the system keeps them in expensive hospitals even though outpatient treatment might be more cost effective and medically sound. Overall, few changes were made in the delivery system—Medicare pumped more demand into a cost-plus fee for service system.

Part A of Medicare covers hospital stays. It is totally financed by payroll taxes assessed on the working population to pay for those 65 and older, regardless of whether or not the beneficiaries are working and regardless of whether or not they are medically indigent. Usage is controlled by deductibles and copayments. Most notably, the first day's hospital stay is paid for by the patient.

Part B of Medicare covers doctor bills. It was originally designed for 50-50 payment, half by general revenues and half by beneficiaries. As costs escalated, it became politically undesirable to raise the Part B premiums. The beneficiary proportion dropped to 25 percent and general revenues picked up about three-quarters. In the Reagan years, an unsuccessful attempt was made to restore the 50-50 split. The primary method for cost control is the use of copayments. Basically, the patient pays 20 percent of the normal and customary doctor's fee set by Medicare. Significantly, doctors' fees set by Medicare have been limited to an economic index since 1972, and rates of increase for some years were frozen entirely. As a result, the patient often pays much more than 20 percent of the doctor's bill since the doctors are billing more than the Medicare allowable.

The next step in Medicare coverage, the Medicare Catastrophic Coverage Act of 1988, had an entirely different basis. The most fundamental difference is that catastrophic coverage is an insurance program paid for entirely by the covered population and does not involve any outside funding from payroll taxes or general revenue. Moreover, it is a mandatory insurance program—every participant in Medicare must belong to the insurance program. Another significant departure is that not all members of the insurance program pay the same amount. All participants pay $4 per month, per person. But there is an income tax surcharge of 15 percent levied on those who pay taxes and therefore have income. The cap is $800 per person, per year. Thus, those who have more pay more—a vastly different concept than is true in the rest of the Medicare program. But, even with this income tax surcharge, there is still an overall subsidy of some $700 per year across all parts of Medicare even for those persons who pay the maximum surcharge.

Another feature of the Catastrophic Coverage Act is that it will for the first time pay for drugs, beginning in 1992. There is a very high deductible of $800 above which the catastrophic coverage will pay for drugs. In Medicare Parts A and B, drugs are not covered, except those given in a hospital stay, a legacy of the fear of runaway costs.

The catastrophic plan is still new and it may not live to an old age; already there are disputes over whether or not the funding is excessive, too low, or unfair. The political heat has gotten very high because of the income tax surcharge. Yet there are others whose calculations purport to show that the drug component of catastrophic coverage is headed for bankruptcy even before it starts. President Bush recently indicated he would not advocate a change in the terms of the bill to reduce premiums; the Chairman of the House Ways and Means Committee has endorsed that position. This is probably a wise course of action since estimates of health care spending have been notoriously off the mark. For instance, when the bill was passed, Medicare expenditures in 1990 were expected to be $10 billion. The current estimate for 1990 is $110 billion.

The Medicare system has two major flaws. First, it does not take care of those who are unable to make required payments, either copayments or deductibles. In order to provide a safety net for poor persons, the Medicaid program operates at the state level. Medicaid costs in America now run at $46 billion, but Medicaid suffers from highly variable coverage from state to state and requires spenddown. Spenddown means that in order to take advantage of the Medicaid safety net, one must have assets no greater than $2,000 per person and $3,000 per couple. Many older people are reluctant to become financially destitute in order to pay for needed health care services. The system also encourages asset shifting by the elderly to their dependents in order to meet spenddown requirements.

The second major flaw is that the current system is not designed for long-term care. The "Medicure" system has inadequate mechanisms for providing the type of care required by many elderly people, especially those over 75. Moreover, the lack of "care" facilities means that costly cure facilities are overburdened with persons who can be cared for more economically in facilities other than hospitals.

THE LONG-TERM CARE ISSUE

Long-term care was not included in the Catastrophic Coverage Act largely because the costs were unknown but believed to be astronomical. There has been limited actuarial experience by private insurance carriers for the concept of long-term care. In addition, there was a feeling that Medicaid provided a safety net for those in need of long-term care, albeit with the onus of the spenddown provision. But the push is on for long-term care coverage, and one of the principal mandated objectives of the Bipartisan Commission is to make recommendations to Congress for long-term care coverage. The estimated cost for long-term care in the first year is $45 billion (compared with 1988 spending for Medicare of $78.9 billion). This $45 billion is not all incremental health care spending; it is estimated that long-term care provided by private plans, Medicaid, and private spending now consumes about $11 billion. Nonetheless, long-term care is a major economic commitment.

COMPREHENSIVE HEALTH CARE

Another major issue for the future is to cover some 37 million people who are not now covered by Medicare or by private plans. The frequently quoted figures

Table 15.4
Age Distribution of Population without Health Insurance, 1987

Age	Percent
Under 18	27
18–24	20
25–34	23
35–64	29
65 and over	1
Total	100

are in the 31–37 million range though there are some statistical problems. For one, about one-fifth of the total represents people who are "not covered" because they chose to be covered under a spousal plan. For another, about 10 percent of "employed but not covered" have not yet completed eligibility requirements. Typically, Americans are reasonably well off, medically speaking, if they are 65 or older or are employed by a major corporation. Virtually 100 percent of all firms with 500 or more employees provide coverage, but only 46 percent of those with 1–9 employees and 78 percent with 10–24 employees do so. Younger people who are unemployed or self-employed and people employed by small business have the greatest problem accessing medical care for economic reasons (Table 15.4).

A strong drive is being made currently to do something about this problem. Complicating the solution and the cost estimates is the fact that most AIDS patients fall into this category. The health care cost for an AIDS patient is about $100,000 per year, and a typical AIDS patient is treated for approximately 18 months to 24 months. This represents around $15–$20 billion to treat all current AIDS victims. The current therapies for AIDS merely prolong life—and medical costs—for varying amounts of time but the disease remains fatal. In major cities such as New York, the AIDS problem is already paralyzing the health care delivery system. The utilization of health care resources is one problem, and the other is that there is no adequate way for the hospitals and doctors to be compensated for services. The likelihood is for additional major cost shifting to private plans.

THE UNFUNDED LIABILITY PROBLEM

As if the sheer size of the overall health care problem and its rapid growth were not enough for American business, the accounting profession is now considering instituting a further burden: reserves for unfunded liabilities. That is, a corporation has an obligation, stated or implied, to provide health care coverage for its employees and its retired employees. Good accounting standards require companies to recognize this future cost by charging it to the profit and loss statement each year and building up an adequate reserve to pay for it. The effect on American business would be devastating. The required reserve for current retirees of American business is about $200 billion. Including the liability for employees currently working brings the estimate to $2 trillion. These liabilities for health benefits will exceed all the liabilities on the balance sheet of American business—a gigantic economic problem.

HOW DID WE GET INTO THIS MESS?

The U.S. health care system now finds itself in the financial intensive care unit because it did not follow the standards of that other great employee benefit, the pension system. The private pension system:

- Assumes a defined liability, a certain contribution, or a specified dollar amount of benefit
- Is based on actuarial assumptions of life span
- Covers the employee and often the spouse, not other family members
- Does not carry the inflation risk; the beneficiary does

In addition, reserves were established and contributions to the fund are tax deductible when made.

Health benefits are largely *undefined*. Because the cost of the benefit was not expected to be large, most companies did it on a pay-as-you-go basis without a reserve build-up. Contributions to the pension fund are deductible in the year in which the contribution is made—contributions to a health care trust fund are not tax deductible, so most companies do not have a trust fund for future liabilities of retirees. And, finally, the specter of inflation is aggravating the problem because costs for medical care are going up at 2 to 3 times the inflation rate. The employer most often assumes the burden of health care at any cost.

FORECASTS

Forecasts are hazardous in any field but especially so in health care policy. The progress of policy is heavily intertwined with social and economic trends. Our country is now running huge fiscal deficits and there is no general revenue to share without more general taxes. Until the Tax Act of 1984 we had a silent, politically easy way to raise taxes: bracket creep. As inflation drove nominal wages higher and higher, tax rates went into higher and higher brackets. The government collected more taxes without having to legislate a tax increase. Wage earners saw their after-tax purchasing power decline. Bracket creep was eliminated when income tax brackets were indexed to inflation. Any increases to pay for the cost of government now require politically risky tax increases.

Congress has discovered a substitute for bracket creep: mandated benefits. This is the simple expedient of having Congress pass laws to require corporations and insurers to provide certain benefits which they then must put into their cost and price structure. This, of course, has economic implications for U.S. competitiveness that will manifest themselves only in the longer run. The short run is more relevant. My guess is that Congress will attempt to mandate that long-term care benefits be incorporated into private plans. This will add to unfunded liabilities and force a solution to the unfunded liability problem. Then what?

THE GLOBAL SOLUTION

I have observed over the years of watching public policy being made that one must look for a confluence of events which ultimately pushes policy over the wall of resistance. The weakening of resistance combines with continued pressure for change. Here is how the constituencies are lining up on the universal health insurance debate:

- Many Americans are dissatisfied with their public or private health care plan (or their lack of one) and want something better.
- Business is faced with a humongous unfunded liability problem and it will welcome a global solution. Certainly small business would be reluctant to pick up a share of the 31–37 million uncovered persons.
- Hospitals are going bankrupt at an alarming rate (about one per week in this decade) and are ready for a different funding mechanism.
- The doctors are feeling the hobnails of the bureaucratic boot and are getting more and more frustrated with how to deliver the quality care their education trains them for while dealing with fiscal restraints. The National Medical Association has already endorsed a national health insurance program. It is a long way from the NMA to the AMA, but the frustration level is rising, even among doctors. In an editorial in July 1986, the *New England Journal of Medicine* noted, "Perhaps even the medical profession, disenchanted with the private corporations and the competitive market will some day be leading the campaign for a publicly financed alternative."
- The bureaucracy is ready.

CONCLUSIONS

It remains to be seen how much of a dent the United States Bipartisan Commission on Comprehensive Health Care will make in solving this massive problem. Perhaps, more correctly, this issue is not a dent in solving the problem but rather the extent to which the commission will make a *beginning* toward a comprehensive solution of a comprehensive problem. It may give rise to some long-term care initiative—another expansion of Medicare. For the longer term, will the larger solution continue to involve the private sector or will it become a national health insurance program? If we do not solve the problem with a major new private sector involvement, I predict that by the year 2000 all the constituencies will unite to climb the wall to a comprehensive health care program funded from general taxation.

PART THREE

INTERNATIONAL ECONOMIC ISSUES

16

Tax Rate Reductions and Foreign Exchange Rates

VICTOR A. CANTO

A subtle but important distinction is being neglected in current discussions of the foreign exchange value of the U.S. dollar. It is true that monetary disturbances, such as a deliberate devaluation of a country's currency, will lead to roughly offsetting inflation. It also is true that under a regime of floating exchange rates, differential inflation rates resulting from monetary disturbances will lead to a roughly offsetting change in exchange rates. These relationships reflect what is commonly referred to as purchasing power parity.

The long-run relevance of purchasing power parity is exceptionally strong. A close correspondence exists between the movement of foreign price levels (converted to dollars) and the movements of prices in the United States. However, saying that monetary disturbances result in differential inflation rates and offsetting exchange rate changes does not preclude other factors from also affecting exchange rates. Under a domestic price rule with floating exchange rates, real disturbances, such as fiscal policy changes or shifts in the terms of trade, can cause dramatic changes in exchange rates without the slightest pressure for offsetting inflation. Under fixed exchange rates, real disturbances can also result in differential inflation rates that do not exert any pressure on the foreign exchange markets. In such cases, purchasing power parity will not hold.

The concept of purchasing power parity maintains that the equilibrium exchange rate between the currencies of two countries equals the ratio of their price levels. This, in turn, implies that differences between the inflation rates of two countries will correspond to proportionate changes in the exchange rate. From

1950 through 1970, devaluations were rare and purchasing power parity was not thought to be terribly relevant. With exchange rates fixed, all differential inflation patterns have to reflect deviations from purchasing power parity. With strict adherence to purchasing power parity, therefore, a truly fixed exchange rate means that each and every country will have the same rate of inflation. The implication that results from purchasing power parity is that inflation is a global phenomenon, not one resulting from domestic policies.

Under a fixed exchange rate system, shifts in the terms of trade become the major source of differential inflation across countries. Differences in the composition of countries' price indices can also result in seeming deviations in purchasing power parity. In the 1830s, the price of tobacco rose in both the United States and Britain. As tobacco was an important component of U.S. output and inconsequential to U.K. output, the price level in the United States rose relative to the price level in Britain. In this instance, differences in the composition of the American and British price indices accounted for a failure of purchasing power parity. While such dramatic examples are undoubtedly the exception, different weights in price indices can account for differences in observed inflation patterns.

In the late 1960s and 1970s, the United States and the rest of the developed world embarked upon an ill-advised experiment in unhinging the world's paper currencies. Initially, the experiment was simply a sequence of currency devaluations and restrictions on capital flows.[1] Later, as the experiment progressed, the Bretton-Woods system of fixed exchange rates and gold convertibility was completely disassembled. The gold pool countries no longer stabilized the gold value of the U.S. dollar, and, as a final departure, interest rates were no longer stabilized. A quantity rule of money and flexible exchange rates supplanted a fixed price of gold and fixed exchange rates.[2]

Under floating exchange rates, purchasing power parity became an incredibly important analytic tool for predicting the consequences of monetary disturbances. However, policymakers were slow to recognize this development. The sheer force of events required even the most doctrinaire of traditionalists to concede the predictive capacity of purchasing power parity. Acceptance eventually became so complete that, for some, the belief in purchasing power parity meant the rejection of everything else. This rejection of everything other than purchasing power parity is a logical trap. Just as inflation rates can differ under fixed exchange rates, so too can changes in exchange rates be unrepresentative of relative inflation patterns. Over the past eight years, purchasing power parity has done little to explain exchange rate movements or differential rates of inflation.

During the 1980s, the Reagan administration has moved the world back toward domestic price and interest rate stability. As a consequence, purchasing power parity has again faded as the dominant force underlying differential inflation rates and exchange rate movements. Under a domestic price rule, the changes in exchange rates reflect changes in the terms of trade.

THE U.S. EXPERIENCE, 1980–86

A major political structural change has been taking place in the United States since 1978. The logical underpinnings of demand-side economic theory were discarded and supplanted by the basic precepts of supply-side economics. In 1978, the Jarvis-Gann property tax cuts swept California and were followed by similar initiatives in other states.[3] The Steiger-Hansen capital gains tax cut became law. By 1981, monetary reform was well on its way, and the President's across-the-board income tax cuts passed Congress. All in all, marginal tax rates were drastically reduced, oil prices were decontrolled, and inflation and interest rates tumbled.[4] A new era was at hand.

For a world conditioned to demand-side economic policies, tax cuts, monetary reform, and oil decontrol were an elixir for economic growth. The Economic Recovery Act of 1981 substantially reduced income tax rates for individuals. The maximum marginal tax rate on income was reduced to 50 percent from 70 percent effective January 1, 1982. Individual marginal tax rates were reduced across-the-board by 23 percent. The reduction was phased-in as follows: 1.25 percent for calendar year 1981, 10 percent for calendar year 1982, 19 percent for calendar year 1983, and 23 percent for calendar year 1984 and subsequent years.

The scheduled reduction induced income substitutions from 1981 into all future years, from 1982 to all future years, and from 1983 into all future years. These income deferral effects implied that the economy would be weakest in 1982 with increasing strength in economic activity beginning in 1984. The economy's performance during this time was consistent with this view. In 1982, real GNP declined 2.6 percent. In 1983, it increased by 3.5 percent, and in 1984 real GNP grew at a 6.5 percent rate.

In the international arena, the implications were equally as clear. The demand for U.S.-located assets increased with the rise in after-tax-returns on U.S. assets. Lower taxes, decontrolled oil, and monetary reform made the United States a far more attractive place to invest. Consequently, foreigners increased their investments in the United States, and Americans reduced their investments abroad. This resulted in an increase in the trade balance deficit.

The deferral effect on the overall level of aggregate demand was partially offset by the prospect of higher income in the future. Current goods became relatively scarcer. The excess demand for current goods was satisfied by both an increase in net imports and an increase in the price of current consumption relative to future consumption. The real interest rate increased initially, then gradually declined to 3.9 percent in 1985 from 6.6 percent in 1982.[5]

The trade balance can be viewed as the means by which the aggregate economy can adjust its temporal patterns of consumption and investment, on the one hand, and production and savings, on the other hand. Furthermore, as the tax rate reductions took effect, the U.S. growth rate relative to the rest of the world accelerated, and the trade balance deteriorated further. The merchandise trade deficit as a percent of GNP rose to 3.0 percent in 1984 from 1.2 percent in 1982.

AN EXPLANATION FOR THE RISE AND FALL IN THE U.S. DOLLAR, 1980–86

The terms of trade effect induced by the first Reagan tax rate cut go a long way toward explaining the behavior of the foreign exchange value of the dollar. The reduction in the top personal income tax rate in the United States to 50 percent from 70 percent resulted in an increase in after-tax take home pay in the United States to 50 cents from 30 cents, a 20 cent increase in take home pay for every dollar earned by those in the top bracket. In other words, the after-tax rate of return in the United States increased 66 percent.

If the United States and its trading partners were truly on a price rule, exchange rate changes would reflect a fluctuation in the terms of trade. Absent tax rate reductions by our trading partners, the foreign exchange value of the U.S. dollar was expected to increase 66 percent. On a GNP weighted basis, the foreign exchange value of the dollar increased 60.7 percent from 1980 through the end of 1984 (Figure 16.1). The magnitude of the increase was consistent with the tax-induced terms of trade effect.

During 1980–84, the appreciation of the foreign exchange value of the dollar was a gradual one. An explanation for the partial adjustments is that the tax rate reductions were phased-in. In addition, if adjustments in the reallocation of resources of the economy are costly, the increased after-tax returns generated by the tax rate reductions would not be eliminated instantaneously. The tax rate reduction generated a gradual capital inflow which, in the long run, arbitraged the international differences in after-tax rates of return.[6]

An implication of this analysis is that the initial dollar appreciation would be reversed by the capital flows. The process would be completed when the dollar returned to its pretax levels. The experiences of the U.S. dollar are consistent with our analysis. The dollar appreciation peaked during the first quarter of 1985, when it started a sustained decline lasting more than two years. In December 1987, the foreign exchange value was 6.5 percent below its 1980 value (Figure 16.1).

Theoretically, foreign tax reform could have offset the effects of U.S. tax reform. However, during the 1980–84 period, there was little or no tax rate action among our trading partners (Table 16.1). The only exception was the United Kingdom which lowered its top rate to 60 percent from 98 percent. However, the apparent rate reduction was, in fact, a net tax rate increase. The United Kingdom lowered the rates on taxes that no one paid and raised the tax rates that no one could avoid (e.g., the Value Added Tax).[7]

The decline in the U.S. dollar during the 1985–87 period could be attributable, in part, to excess domestic money creation. The fraction of the dollar fluctuation due to monetary policy is estimated by netting out the terms of trade effect from the fluctuation in the nominal foreign exchange value of the dollar. The data suggest that very little of the fluctuation, approximately 5 percent in the foreign exchange value of the dollar, is attributable to monetary policy (Figure

Figure 16.1
Nominal and Real Foreign Exchange Value of the Dollar, 1980–87

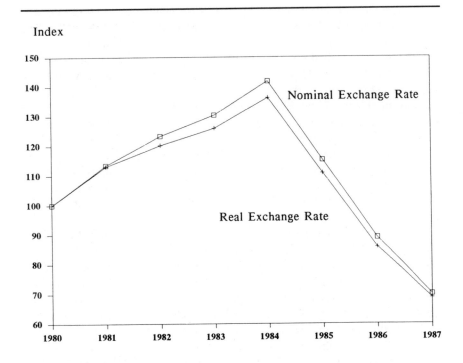

Table 16.1
Highest Personal Income Tax Rates, 1979–90

	1979	1984	1985	1986	1987	1988	1989	1990
Australia	61.5	60.0	60.0	55.0	49.0	49.0	49.0	49.0
Canada	61.9	51.0	52.0	55.0	53.0	45.0	45.0	45.0
Denmark	73.0	73.0	73.0	73.0	68.0	68.0	68.0	68.0
France	60.0	65.0	65.0	58.0	57.0	57.0	57.0	57.0
Germany	56.0	56.0	56.0	56.0	56.0	56.0	56.0	53.0
Italy	72.0	65.0	62.0	62.0	62.0	60.0	60.0	60.0
Japan	88.0	88.0	88.0	88.0	88.0	76.0	76.0	76.0
Netherlands	72.0	72.0	72.0	72.0	72.0	70.0	70.0	70.0
Sweden	86.5	82.0	80.0	80.0	77.0	75.0	75.0	75.0
United Kingdom	98.0	60.0	60.0	60.0	60.0	60.0	40.0	40.0
United States	70.0	50.0	50.0	50.0	38.5	28.0	28.0	28.0

Source: *World Tax Reform: A Progress Report*, Edited by Joseph A. Pechman, Brookings Dialogues on Public Policy, The Brookings Institution, Washington, D.C., 1988.

16.1). As predicted by our analysis, the 1985–87 decline offset the 1980–84 surge in the value of the dollar. Therefore, the decline in the foreign exchange value of the dollar during the 1985–87 period is the result of the arbitrage process that equilibrated the after-tax rate of return in the United States relative to our trading partners.

The performance of the U.S. stock market vis-à-vis its trading partners can also be explained by the Reagan tax rate reductions. In the simplest of terms, the after-tax rates of return on existing assets in the United States rose sharply—both absolutely and relative to those of the rest of the world. Market forces worked to utilize both U.S. labor and U.S. capital more fully, as well as to combine them more efficiently. Unemployment fell while employment, average hours, capacity utilization, and productivity rose. The aggregate stock market index outperformed its European counterpart during the 1981–84 period (Table 16.2) when U.S. tax rates were declining.

During 1985 and 1986, the differential performance was reversed. The resurgence of the European stock market relative to the U.S. market can be attributed, in part, to the decline in the foreign exchange value of the dollar. Another reason for the relative surge in the European stock markets is also attributable, in part, to the adoption of supply-side tax rate reduction policies (Table 16.1). Lower tax rates are the lasting supply-side mark that Ronald Reagan will leave the world, and as a result of Reagan's economic policies, supply-side ideas are being imported by our trading partners.[8]

The differential performance across industry sectors can also be explained in terms of the Reagan tax rate cuts. During the 1981–85 period, the nontraded sector industry groups outperformed the internationally traded industry groups (Table 16.3). In 1985, the dollar started a sustained decline. As predicted by our framework and consistent with our earlier research, the decline in the foreign exchange value of the dollar had a lagged response that resulted in a reversal in the differential performance of the two groups.[9] During 1986 and 1987, the internationally traded sector groups outperformed the nontraded sector groups (Table 16.3).

Table 16.2.
U.S. and European Stock Price Performance, 1981–87

	1981	1982	1983	1984	1985	1986	1987
U.S. (S&P500)	-9.73	14.76	17.27	1.40	26.33	14.62	2.03
Europe	-15.77	0.00	17.33	-2.78	73.30	40.29	1.43

Source: Standard and Poor's; *Capital International Perspective*, Capital International, 1987.

Table 16.3
Stock Price Performance of International Traded and Nontraded Sectors, 1981–87

	1981	1982	1983	1984	1985	1986	1987
Non-traded	0.79	31.66	18.04	-0.76	26.68	12.67	-7.46
Traded	-5.71	20.82	17.85	-6.23	20.81	15.65	10.05
S&P 500	-9.73	14.76	17.27	1.40	26.33	14.62	2.03

Source: Standard and Poor's.

THE TAX REFORM ACT OF 1986

Since the enactment of the Tax Reform Act of 1986, the United States has undergone the second round of tax rate reductions this decade. Our framework would predict a performance similar to that of the first Reagan tax rate reduction. Yet in spite of the similarities, differences remain. The negative effects of the phase-in were not as pronounced for the Tax Reform Act of 1986 as they were for the Tax Reform Act of 1981. Three reasons account for these differences. First, the phase-in period was shorter so that the negative impact on the front end was smaller. Second, the increase in incentives from the Tax Reform Act of 1986 was smaller than that of the Tax Reform Act of 1981.[10] Hence, the induced substitution effects would be smaller. Finally, it is possible that in 1982 effective marginal tax rates increased as a result of bracket creep and increases in payroll taxes. By contrast, tax rates were lower in 1987 than in 1986 for most individuals.[11]

THE FOREIGN EXCHANGE VALUE OF THE DOLLAR IN 1988

The slide in the dollar has been averted during 1988. The Tax Reform Act of 1986 goes a long way to explain the surge in the dollar. Tax reform resulted in a reduction of the top marginal personal income tax rate to 28 percent in 1988 from 50 percent two years go. The increase in after-tax rate of return took place over a two year period. During 1987, the after-tax rate of return increased 23 percent; with the second installment, the cumulative effect will be 44 percent. The total tax rate reduction increases the after-tax income to 72 cents on the dollar from 50 cents on the dollar. Everything else the same, the U.S. dollar is expected to increase 23 percent reaching a peak of 44 percent, at which point the dollar could be expected to decline to its long-run terms of trade equilibrium.

However, everything else is not the same. During 1988, our trading partners

Table 16.4

Increase in After-Tax Rate of Return Resulting from Foreign Tax Rate Reductions

1984	1985	1986	1987	1988	1989	1990
4.58	5.11	7.23	9.08	46.21	50.79	51.92

A.B. Laffer Associates

have enacted tax rate reductions that will increase the after-tax rate of return in the rest of the world by approximately the same amount as the United States (Table 16.4). Therefore, only the 1987 installment of the tax rate reduction was not matched by our trading partners.

The implications of this analysis are that the appreciation of the dollar will peak at approximately 23 percent and will subsequently decline. This may be difficult to test because our major trading partners are altering their tax rates or influencing their exchange rate through monetary policy or both. Switzerland and Germany have not enacted major legislated tax rate changes; furthermore, their monetary policy is widely accepted as being a price rule. Hence, fluctuations in the dollar/Swiss franc and dollar/German mark exchange rate will reflect disturbances in the U.S. monetary and fiscal policies. Consistent with our analysis, since December 1987, the dollar has risen to 1.61 from 1.31 against the Swiss franc, a 22.9 percent appreciation. Similarly, the dollar has risen to 1.90 from 1.57 against the West German mark, a 21.0 percent increase. These numbers suggest that the dollar is close to its peak, and if, in fact, the appreciation was the result of a U.S. tax rate reduction, the dollar will decline during the next few months. The dollar has appreciated by a lesser amount against the currencies of countries that have enacted their own tax rate reductions. Since December 1987, the dollar has appreciated a modest 8 percent against the Australian dollar and by only 5 percent against the Canadian dollar.

In addition to the terms of trade effects, monetary policy also influences the foreign exchange value of the dollar. Given the assumption that our trading partners are pursuing a price rule, the only undershooting or overshooting of the dollar appreciation may be attributable to U.S. monetary policy. Therefore, if monetary policy is expansionary, the dollar appreciation will fall short of the 23 percent appreciation implied by the terms of trade effect. Yet this will not affect the subsequent 23 percent decline in the dollar as the world economy approaches its long-run terms of trade equilibrium. If monetary policy has been excessive, the U.S. inflation rate and long-term interest rates will increase in the face of a rising dollar.

THE OUTLOOK

Tax reductions abroad increase the after-tax rate of return of foreign-located assets. The effect of foreign tax reform on the foreign exchange value of the dollar is opposite to that observed during the 1981–85 period. The increase in incentives from a tax rate reduction depends positively on the magnitude of the reduction, as well as the initial tax rate. Consider the case of a hypothetical reduction to 70 percent from 90 percent. The take-home pay will rise to 30 cents on the dollar from 10 cents on the dollar: a 300 percent increase in incentives. In contrast, a reduction in tax rates to 10 percent from 20 percent will increase the take-home pay to 90 cents from 80 cents, a 12.50 percent increase in incentives. Although our trading partners are lowering their tax rates by a smaller amount, they are starting from a higher tax rate.

Using the reduction in personal income tax rates of our trading partners (Table 16.1), the average increase in incentives from foreign tax reform can be calculated. Foreign tax rate reductions have slowly increased the after-tax rate of return of foreign-located assets during the 1980–87 period (Table 16.4). However, the tax rate reductions in 1988 and 1989 have resulted in a substantial increase in after-tax rates of return abroad. In 1988, the increase in incentives resulting from foreign tax actions more than offset the increase in incentives resulting from the Tax Reform Act of 1986. Only the increase in incentives through 1987 will have a net effect on the U.S. terms of trade and exchange rates. Taken at face value, the assumption of a costly adjustment suggests that the real exchange value of the dollar should increase by approximately 23 percent in 1988 and decline thereafter.

Further reduction of foreign tax rates will create downward pressures on the dollar. To illustrate this, consider the reform currently being implemented in England. The top income tax rate went to 40 percent from 60 percent. After-tax income will rise to 60 cents on the dollar from 40 cents on the dollar, a 50 percent increase in incentives. Since the foreign tax rate reduction will overtake the second Reagan tax rate cuts, the terms of trade effect will lead to a decline of the dollar vis-à-vis the pound in excess of 23 percent in 1989–90. Thus, the British pound will tend to appreciate as a result of the change in the terms of trade induced by the tax rate reduction. Attempts to prevent the rise in the foreign exchange value of the pound through monetary policy will result in a rise in the British inflation rate. These effects are already evident in the British economy. According to *The Economist,* the British inflation rate is running at a 10 percent annual rate.[12]

A first order approximation is that Germany, Japan, and Switzerland will continue a prudent monetary policy. This leaves only U.S. domestic monetary policy as a possible source of disturbances to the foreign exchange market value of the dollar against those currencies. The shift in emphasis from a price rule to fine-tuning the economy based on a Phillips-Curve relationship suggests that the Fed will slow the growth rate of the monetary base during periods of robust economic growth. Conversely, the Fed will increase the rate of growth of the monetary base during periods of slow growth. This suggests that the new operating policies will be deflationary during periods of rapid growth and inflationary during periods of slow growth. In addition, if the Fed is reacting to the real economy and information on the economy is collected with a lag, the monetary response will also occur with a lag. Thus, the outlook is for an increased variability of interest rates.[13]

There is one additional variable to consider in the outlook for monetary policy. If our analysis is correct, the terms of trade effect will produce downward pressure on the U.S. dollar during 1989, just as it did during 1985–87. The decline in the dollar in 1989 need not be inflationary. Insofar as the Fed gets worried about the decline in the dollar, the response will be to slow the rate of growth of the monetary base in order to stabilize the dollar's value. This could be extremely bullish for bonds, and 1989 could well be a good year for the bond market.

SUMMARY IMPLICATIONS: IMPACT OF TAX RATE CHANGES ON THE INTERNATIONAL SECTOR

Tax rate cuts result in higher after-tax rates of return for domestically located assets. The higher after-tax return will result in a net capital inflow. Ultimately the capital inflow will reduce the after-tax return to its long-run equilibrium. Under a floating exchange rate system, the balance of payments must always be zero. Hence, the capital inflow will mirror the trade balance. Therefore, our framework predicts that:

- A tax rate reduction will lead to the gradual appreciation of domestic currency. However, the surge in the foreign exchange value of the currency will ultimately be reversed.
- The tax rate reduction and capital inflow will generate a corresponding deterioration of the trade balance.
- Initially, the domestic stock market will surge relative to the rest of the world.
- A sectorial effect will also become evident. During the appreciation phase, the non-traded sector industries will outperform the traded sector industries while during the depreciation phase, the relative performance will be reversed.

The U.S. experience during the 1980s is entirely consistent with our framework. Since they are lowering their personal income tax rate from 60 percent to 40 percent, our analysis suggests that during the next several years, the British economy will experience many of the symptoms experienced by the United States during the 1980s.

NOTES

1. For an analysis of the policies of this period see: Arthur B. Laffer, "Balance of Payments and Exchange Rate Systems," *Financial Analysts Journal*, August 1974; "Monetary Policy and the Balance of Payments," *Journal of Money, Credit and Banking*, February 1972; "The United States Balance of Payments—A Financial Center View," *Journal of Law and Contemporary Problems*, August 1969; "The Economic Consequences of Devaluation of Reserve Currency Country," *World Monetary Disorder*, ed. Patrick Boarman and David Tuerck (New York: Praeger, 1976); "Two Arguments for

Fixed Rates," in *Economics of Common Currencies,* ed. Harry G. Johnson and Alexander Swoboda (London: George Allen and Unwin, 1973); "International Financial Intermediation: Interpretation and Empirical Analysis," in *International Mobility and Movement of Capital,* ed. National Bureau of Economic Research (New York: Columbia University Press, 1972), pp. 661–75.

2. The merits of a price rule are discussed in: Charles W. Kadlec and Arthur B. Laffer, "Has the Fed Already Put Itself on a Price Rule?" *Wall Street Journal,* October 28, 1982. For a discussion on the quantity targeting experience, see Arthur B. Laffer and Charles W. Kadlec, "Monetary Crisis: A Classical Perspective," in *Financial Analysts Guide to Monetary Policy* (New York: Praeger, 1986), pp. 1–18.

3. Charles W. Kadlec and Arthur B. Laffer, "The Jarvis-Gann Tax Cut Proposal: An Application of the Laffer Curve," in *The Economics of the Tax Revolt,* ed. Arthur B. Laffer and Jan P. Seymour (New York: Harcourt, Brace, Jovanovich, 1979).

4. An analysis of the implications of these policies is presented in the following papers: Victor A. Canto and Charles W. Kadlec, "The Shape of Energy Markets to Come," *Public Utilities Fortnightly* 117, no. 1 (January 9, 1986), pp. 21–28; Charles W. Kadlec and Arthur B. Laffer, "The Oil Price Decline in Perspective," *Economy in Perspective,* A. B. Laffer Associates, February 16, 1983; Gerald W. Bollman, Victor A. Canto, and Kevin A. Melich, "Oil Decontrol: The Power of Incentives Could Reduce OPEC's Power to Boost Oil Prices," *Oil and Gas Journal* 80, no. 2 (January 11, 1982), pp. 92–101; Arthur B. Laffer, "The Laffer Curve," *Political Economy,* A. B. Laffer Associates, April 17, 1984; Victor A. Canto, "Fuel-Use Patterns in the U.S. Outlook for the 1980s," *Oil and Gas Journal,* August 23, 1982; Victor A. Canto and Douglas H. Joines, "Budget Deficits: Reaganomics Is not the Problem," *Economic Study,* A. B. Laffer Associates, February 24, 1986.

5. The real rate is calculated as the difference between the average three-month Treasury bill rate and the CPI inflation rate.

6. Arthur B. Laffer, "Minding Our Ps and Qs: Exchange Rates and Foreign Trade," *Economic Study,* A. B. Laffer Associates, June 14, 1986; Victor A. Canto, "Exchange Rates and the Stock Market: Ps and Qs Meets the CATS," *Economic Study,* A. B. Laffer Associates, November 14, 1986.

7. Arthur B. Laffer, "Margaret Thatcher's Tax Increase," *Wall Street Journal,* August 20, 1979, p. 10; Arthur B. Laffer, "Britain's Economic Tragedy: A Lesson for America," *Economic Study,"* A. B. Laffer Associates, October 24, 1980.

8. Alan Murray, "Lower U.S. Tax Rates Go International," *Wall Street Journal,* April 4, 1988, p. 1; Robert Bartley, Whither Voodoo Economics?" *Wall Street Journal,* August 18, 1988, p. 22.

9. Victor A. Canto, "Exchange Rates and the Stock Market: Ps and Qs Meets the CATS," *Economic Study,* A. B. Laffer Associates, November 14, 1986.

10. The Economic Recovery Tax Act lowered the maximum tax rate to 50 percent from 70 percent. As a result, a person in the highest bracket could keep 50 cents of a marginal dollar of income instead of 30 cents. That was a 66 percent increase in incentives. The Tax Reform Act of 1986 lowered the top rate to 28 percent from 50 percent. This is only a 44 percent increase in incentives.

11. Truman A. Clark, "Just Wait 'Til '88," *Economy in Perspective,* A. B. Laffer Associates, August 26, 1986.

12. *The Economist,* August 20, 1988, p. 83.

13. Paul Evans, "What Monetarism Has Done to Us," *Economic Study,* A. B. Laffer Associates, February 3, 1984.

17

The Trade Balance: Don't Worry, Be Happy

Arthur B. Laffer

> "The only label I willingly wear is 'made in America'."
> Michael Dukakis, Democratic Candidate
> for President.

> "We simply cannot allow this huge trade deficit to persist."
> Clayton Yeutter, Special Trade Representative,
> Reagan administration.

At a time shortly after international trade accounting had its genesis, one distinguished between an "international balance of payments" and an "international balance of receipts." But, as time evolved, such an objective depiction of what was crumbled before the more emotive dichotomy of a "balance of payments deficit" and a "balance of payments surplus." At roughly an equivalent time, the words "debit" and "credit" were eclipsed by the words "worsen" and "improve." Who honestly could prefer worsening over improvement? With such linguistic devolution it is easy to comprehend the metastasis of bad theory and ultimately the proliferation of noxious policy.

The mercantilists of old quite deservedly were labeled as intellectually flawed by the likes of Adam Smith and other enlightened trade experts. However, the influence of accounting was far from crushed. Misnamed trade designations were quickly resurrected to replace simple truth with complex error. Neomercantilists dominate both thought and policy to this very day. If anything, the dominance of the current mindset exercised by neomercantilism borders on complete.

The basic premise that trade deficits are a symptom of misguided policies is simply not correct. The fact that this premise alone is false is more than sufficient to negate the entire panoply of policy analysis and prescriptions being proffered today. Views expressed so eloquently by neomercantilists are granted total credence even to the point where alternative interpretations are provided scarcely any exposure. When put to the test, neomercantilists' ideas fail.

A current account or merchandise trade deficit is not bad per se, in spite of the fact that to have a trade deficit requires a "worsening" of the trade balance. If domestic loans from foreigners and capital acquisitions by foreigners are not guaranteed by taxpayers, then the existence of a trade deficit is a matter of private concern. Such transactions should be subjected to public "benign neglect." There is no difference between a Pennsylvania firm borrowing from a Sensei from Stockton, California and that same Pennsylvania firm borrowing from an ethnic Japanese from Hokkaido. In either case, the successful or nonsuccessful performance of that loan is an issue solely between the lender and the borrower. Public policy should not be concerned.

There is also good reason to expect and even welcome trade deficits when an economy experiences a renaissance of performance as has been the case for the United States during the last six years. The accounting counterpart of the current account deficit is the capital account surplus. Growth companies borrow money, so do growth countries.

To see the supply-side perspective of the debate, one need only ask whether it would be preferable to have capital lined up on a country's borders trying to get out of that country or lined up on a country's borders trying to get in to that country. Clearly, a country's capital surplus is a sign of economic health, not malaise. The only way investors can generate a dollar cash flow in order to invest in the United States is for the United States to run a current account deficit.

A primary lemma of supply-side economics postulates that if there are two locations, A and B, and if taxes are lowered in B and not in A, then producers and manufacturers will attempt to move from A to B. With the inflation and interest rate successes of Paul Volcker, and the tax successes of Howard Jarvis, Bill Steiger, and Ronald Reagan, the United States has become the Bermuda of the developed world, a veritable magnet for foreign capital. Capital quite naturally goes to where the action is.

As a consequence of the rejuvenation of the American economy, foreigners have more than willingly provided the United States with the real resources to increase our output, employment, and productivity. Far from being a problem, the U.S. trade deficit was a solution. Both the foreign lenders and the American borrowers were better off with the deficit than they would have been had trade been balanced or in a U.S. surplus position. Since the commencement of our trade deficit, the first quarter of 1983 when the Reagan tax rate cuts became effective, the United States has created over fifteen million jobs. Our foreign deficit has not cost jobs, but instead has provided the resources to facilitate our labor force's surge toward full employment (Figure 17.1).

There are any number of ways to define, and define precisely, a trade balance, deficit or surplus. Each precise definition, which is interchangeable with all others, does direct thought in a perilously specific fashion. The trade balance, for example, is literally the difference between the value of exports and the value of imports during some period of time. When defined as such, it is only natural that an understanding of the trade balance would entail an understanding of a country's exports and its imports. Truth, it would seem, is to be found by understanding why people buy goods from abroad and sell goods to foreigners. Taking the logical choice one step further, it seems obvious that prices and availability are key elements of any "make or buy" decision. Thus, quotas, tariffs, and exchange rates, as well as differential productivity rates, have to be the essential ingredients determining a country's trade balance.

But yet another definition of the trade balance, precisely equivalent to and equally as valid as exports less imports, is the difference between what a country saves and what it invests. With this definition in mind, tariffs, quotas, and

Figure 17.1
Trade Balance as a Percent of GNP versus Total Civilian Employment, Quarterly, First Quarter 1980 through Second Quarter 1988

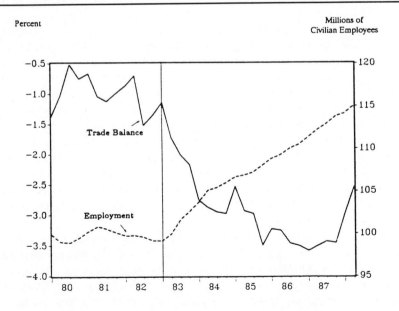

Sources: Department of Commerce, *National Income and Product Accounts*; Bureau of Labor Statistics, *Revised Seasonally Adjusted Labor Force Statistics, 1978-87*; Bureau of Labor Statistics. *Employment and Earnings*.

exchange rates appear particularly irrelevant to the comprehension of a country's excess savings (or deficient investment). Taxation, research and development expenditures, subsidies, budget deficits, and the like come to the fore as fruitful avenues leading to understanding.

The international trade balance is also identically equal to the international capital balance. As such, interest rate differences, taxation of capital gains, and relative business climate would emerge as relevant considerations. The trade surplus is exactly equal to the capital deficit and vice versa. The international trade balance is also identical to the difference between a country's income and its expenditures. This definition, once again, leads one's thoughts in different directions.

In spite of the divergent alternatives, dogmatic incantation predominates. We have become, as Keynes so elegantly described, enslaved by defunct economists and academic scribblers.[1] The hoax is that *he* now has us enslaved even though he has been dead for many years. If one can only write the rules and the definitions, one's adversaries will wither.

This chapter is not the appropriate forum for a detailed evaluation of the scientific literature. Suffice it to say that the fact that West Germany and Japan were the two countries with the largest trade deficits in the period 1946 through 1960 is a reasonable, albeit extreme, parallel with the United States of the Reagan era.

The trade deficits of third world countries are not at all comparable to the current U.S. trade deficit. Third world trade deficits are more a consequence of government interventions subverting free market forces than of private mis-calculations. Countries that increase their growth rates, as a natural course of events, attract foreign investors and thereby experience trade deterioration.

The recent sharp deterioration of the British trade accounts following the 1982 and subsequent tax rate reductions is similar to what happened in the United States (Figure 17.2). The argument that somehow indulgent fiscal policy is the root cause of these deficits is surely not the case for Britain—their budget is in surplus. The received doctrine in Britain, as it is here, is that trade deficits must be stopped. Convoluted error has replaced simple truth. The problem is not the red ink splashed on the trade ledgers; it is with faulty analysis. If believed, the faulty analysis will result in real solutions being imposed on nonproblems.

The United States, from the mid–17th century until the 1870s, ran huge trade deficits by the prevailing standards of the time. These trade deficits lasted for over two centuries. Ultimately, those U.S. trade deficits provided America the wherewithal to create the preeminent economic force in the world.

The neomercantilist analysis of late despairs over the observation that the United States has become a net debtor nation of incredible and increasing magnitude (Figure 17.3). International assets are, however, book value data and most likely unrelated to market values. In 1987, the United States had a surplus of investment income which would seem to imply that U.S. assets abroad are sufficiently undervalued relative to foreign assets in the United States and that the

Figure 17.2
Percent Change in Real U.K. Gross Domestic Product (GDP) versus Merchandise Trade Balance as a Percent of GDP, 1979–87

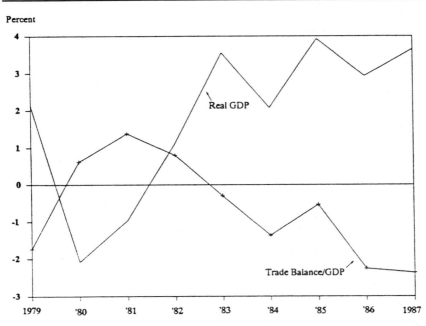

Source: International Monetary Fund, *International Financial Statistics.*

United States is, in reality, not a net debtor nation in market value terms (Figure 17.4).

Whether the United States is or is not a net debtor nation is beside the point. The relevant point is whether the United States is better off as a consequence of its debt position. Reliance on the number zero is no defense against the market's assessment of what should be. The essence of international trade as a discipline is that trade in goods and assets improves welfare.

The trade balance is the consequence of individual actions of market participants and not some *deus ex machina* imposed. When an economy experiences an increase in demand for goods resulting from an overt change in the attractiveness of goods, then equilibrium can be restored several ways. One way is for the price of goods to rise thus making them less attractive and offsetting the initial force leading to their heightened attractiveness.

Yet another way is for the quantity of goods supplied to increase to meet the heightened demand. These increased supplies could emanate from both domestic and foreign sources. Save for pathological cases, all three paths to the restoration of equilibrium will be employed simultaneously. In the field of chemistry, this same concept is named Le Chatellier's principle. The importation of goods is a

Figure 17.3
Net Investment Position of the United States

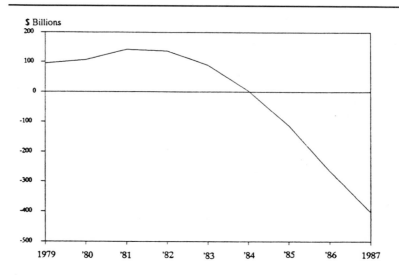

Sources: Department of Commerce, *Survey of Current Business*; *Economic Report of the President*; *Federal Reserve Bulletin*.

Figure 17.4
Net Investment Income and Other Services

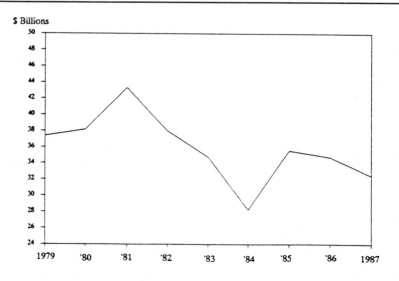

Sources: Department of Commerce, *Survey of Current Business*; *Economic Report of the President*.

trade deficit while the augmentation of domestically supplied goods is none other than our beloved economic growth. The faster an economy grows, the greater will be the degree to which its trade deficit worsens. The use of the word "worsen" happens to be one of the glaring examples of linguistic gobbledegook where words were deliberately chosen to obfuscate an essential first principle, all of which leads to the detriment of humans.

To worry that foreigners are somehow like a herd of deer in a meadow waiting anxiously to bolt at the slightest sign of danger is clearly way off base. Japanese investors over the past three years have suffered large annual yen losses and yet remain active participants in the U.S. capital markets.

Just imagine how precarious U.S. investors would perceive the situation if, instead of foreign investments in the United States, the concern were U.S. investments abroad. Here, the Japanese and businessmen from many other countries are committing huge amounts of capital to the U.S. economy. They have no vote in U.S. elections and are subjected to a substantial amount of abuse in the political arena. All it would take to destroy vast amounts of their wealth is one bill squeaking through Congress and then signed into law. The only recourse they would have would be in the host nation, surely not an enticing attribute of U.S.-located assets above and beyond normal market movements.

It wasn't long ago when the United States was the source of foreign concern. Europeans were aghast at the Americanization of Europe. Several years ago, Canada's Trudeau parlayed anti-Americanism into a political posturing. Canada's Liberal party leader Joe Turner is doing the same thing today. Surely, foreign investors today cannot be oblivious to the risks they incur by investing in the United States.

Why Japanese or other foreign investors' criteria would differ from their American counterparts' is not self-evident. If economic policies were to change such that the long-term investment horizon of the United States were to worsen, then foreigners might well wish to take some of their capital back out of the United States. This would precipitate a sequence of unpleasant events.

American investors, however, would also want their capital out of the United States, and if foreigners did not beat them to the punch, they would precipitate the ominous consequences. It is unreasonable to assume that somehow foreigners are any different from Americans. In matters of the pocketbook, nationality does not count for much. Therefore, whether foreigners have a large or small involvement in the U.S. economy is really of little importance. Bad economic policies will cause capital flight for both domestic and foreign capital.

No policy that I can think of is more generically disruptive to investors than is a tax increase. Given the current political milieu, tax increases show a total inability of governments to control their spending, and in addition, they illustrate a failure of the body politic to control government. The tax side of a proposal to eliminate the budget deficit is, in my view, the sine qua non of the debacle neomercantilists so earnestly wish to avoid.

NOTE

1. The precise quote is "But apart from this contemporary mood, the ideas of economists and political philosophers, both when they are right and when they are wrong, are more powerful than is commonly understood. Indeed the world is ruled by little else. Practical men, who believe themselves to be quite exempt from any intellectual influences, are usually the slaves of some defunct economist. Madmen in authority, who hear voices in the air, are distilling their frenzy from some academic scribbler of a few years back." John Maynard Keynes, *The General Theory of Employment, Interest, and Money.*

18

National Paedomorphosis:
U.K. Progenesis, U.S. Neoteny

Arthur B. Laffer

The United Kingdom's version of the supply-side revolution is "in a pickle" to say the least. High interest rates and high inflation seem in the eyes of British voters to have more than offset the euphoria of lower taxes. Margaret Thatcher, now serving her fourth term as Prime Minister, can still pull it out, but, to date, she doesn't seem to have any intention of doing so.

The most recent data for the United Kingdom show just how serious is the plight for Thatcher. British gilts have a yield a smidgeon below 10 percent as compared to long-term Treasury bond yields in the United States of a little less than 8 percent. Short-term Treasury securities in the United Kingdom are yielding about 14 percent whereas their U.S. counterparts have a yield less than 8 percent. Individual consumer loans in the United Kingdom cost as much as 22 percent annually. The British pound has been soft against the U.S. dollar of late and has been holding its own against other European currencies. U.K. inflation is high and rising.

The Labour party has been bolstered by the virtual demise of all third parties. These third parties had siphoned votes away from Labour in early elections. In addition, Labour, under the stewardship of Neil Kinnock, appears and probably is somewhat less radical than it has been heretofore. No longer does the articulate Fabian socialist Wedgwood Benn hold sway. And Michael Foote is also out of the picture. Labour, while still far to the left, does not appear nearly so dogmatic to the average U.K. voter.

Lastly, and probably illogically, people are simply tired of the sameness and almost would like change for change's sake: Margaret Thatcher has been in office a long, long time. Her dominant personality has afforded no opportunity for a successor to be groomed. Flowers rarely grow in trampled fields.

THE EFFECTS OF TAX RATE CUTS

The basic economic problem is rather intuitive. Taxes are a cost of doing business and marginal taxes are a marginal cost. If one country cuts its taxes while a neighboring country does not, it only stands to reason that production and manufacturing will tend to migrate to the country that had lowered taxes. Production goes where that action is.

If all goods and services were costless to transport, everything would quickly end up in the country with the lower taxes. Whether by artificial barriers such as tariffs, quotas, and red tape, or by natural barriers such as transportation costs, goods and services clearly are not costless to transport across national boundaries. In fact, some goods are a lot easier to transport than are others. These more easily transported goods simply have lower costs of transportation. Over the whole spectrum of goods and services, there is likewise a whole spectrum of transportation costs.

If one country cuts its taxes and the other doesn't, the rate of return on assets in the tax-cutting country will increase as a consequence of now lower costs.[1] The "bottom line" will be the initial beneficiary of lower taxes. Goods and services for which the transport costs are not prohibitive will begin to move to the lower taxed country from the higher taxed country. The lower taxed country will experience a trade deficit, for example, goods and services flowing into it. A trade deficit is the accounting counterpart to a capital surplus simply because the sum of the trade accounts and capital accounts must equal zero.[2] Such is the way of double-entry bookkeeping. Trade deficits are a direct consequence of tax cuts. And, if there were no transport costs, that would be the end of it. But there are!

To offset the added advantages of lower taxes, goods and services will keep flowing into the lower taxed country until the added transport cost more than offsets the improved tax treatment. Rates of return, in real terms, between the two countries will come back into balance. But to do so, prices will have to rise in the lower taxed country relative to prices in its neighbor. Thus, there has to be a change in the terms of trade.[3]

There is also a microeconomic counterpart to the trade deficit found in the terms of trade. If foreign goods weren't relatively cheaper, why would people choose to buy more of them and foreigners fewer domestic goods? Higher prices in the lower-taxed country are the sine qua non of a deteriorating trade balance.

The magnitude of the changes in the terms of trade depends upon (1) the size of the tax cut and thereby the corresponding increase in profitability, and (2) the overall spectrum of transport costs for goods and services. The bigger the tax cut and the greater transport costs, the greater will be the terms of trade effect.[4] There is a direct trade-off between the terms of trade effect and the deterioration of the trade balance. For any given tax cuts, the greater the terms of trade effect, the less will be the trade balance deterioration and vice versa.

Now comes the crux of the British question. So far all is fine and dandy. A tax cut will, for the tax-cutting country, lead to a trade balance deterioration and an increase in the terms of trade. That increase in the terms of trade, however, can be accommodated by exchange rate changes and relative inflation. If the currency of the tax-cutting nation appreciates, then it will experience less inflation. If, on the other hand, the currencies don't change in value, then the entire change in the terms of trade will materialize via relative rates of inflation with the tax-cutting country having the higher inflation.

THE U.S. EXPERIMENT

The United States during the 1980s illustrated the above principle, as the Brits themselves might say, "to a tea." In 1980, with Ronald Reagan, the tax-cutter, winning primary after primary and then the general election, an era of supply-side tax cuts was at hand.[5]

The tax bill passed in 1981, but the tax cuts actually began on January 1, 1983 and continued unabated through to this very day. The results were picture perfect. United States economic growth began in the first quarter of 1983 when the real tax cut took effect. Using fourth quarter over fourth quarter growth rates in real GNP, the results are striking. For 1980, 1981, and 1982, real growth was −0.77 percent, 1.94 percent, and −1.75 percent respectively, while the next six years were, seriatim: 6.31 percent, 4.51 percent, 2.85 percent, 3.03 percent, 5.27 percent, and 3.34 percent. So much for the idea that low tax rates don't cause economic growth.

Likewise, it was the first quarter of 1983 when the U.S. trade balance tumbled in the red ink. In 1980, 1981, and 1982, the trade balance's share of GNP moved to around −1 percent. In 1983, that number fell to almost −2 percent and in 1984 it fell further to about −3 percent. It continued that trend until 1987 when the number troughed at −3.48 percent.

Starting in late 1980, the dollar skyrocketed in value against other currencies, peaking in early 1985 just as theory would suggest (Figure 18.1). Tax cuts were accompanied by trade deficits, rapid economic growth, and the precipitous rise in the terms of trade. In fact, it was the equally precipitous rise in the dollar on the foreign exchanges that permitted a change in the terms of trade without a resurgence in U.S. inflation (Figure 18.1). Inflation fell to a reasonably low level and stayed there (Figure 18.2).

THE U.K. EXPERIMENT

On May 1, 1979, the Conservative Party led by Margaret Thatcher swept to a 43-seat Commons majority in Parliament. The Conservatives acquired 339 seats to Labour's 268, with 28 seats going to the Liberals, Nationalists, and others.

Figure 18.1
British Pound, U.S. Dollar Exchange Rate

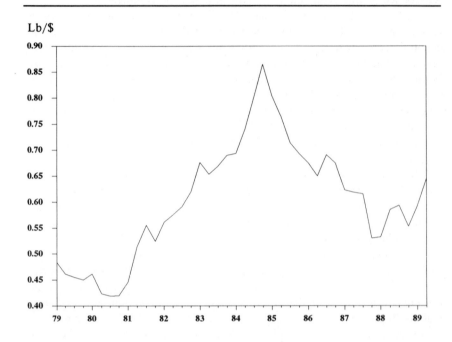

Lb/$

Figure 18.2
U.S. Inflation

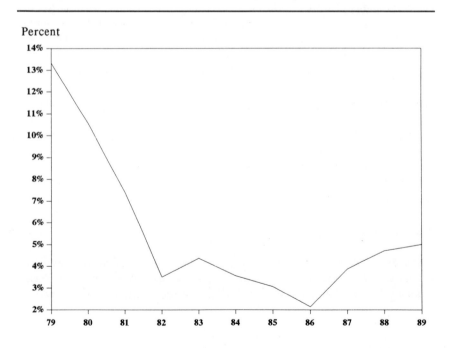

Percent

The Conservatives ousted the well-entrenched Labour Party by promising to reintroduce private economic incentives into the United Kingdom.

Of Margaret Thatcher's mandate, *The Economist* said, "She will need no reminding of her first priority. She has shouted it from every husting in the country: reduce taxation and with it the scale and pervasiveness of the public sector."[6] The headlines of the *Financial Times* read, "Election Euphoria Lifts Equities to New High Levels."[7] The British economy was poised and ready to reverse thirty years of relative decline. Since that watershed day in 1979, major political structural change has been taking place in the United Kingdom. The logical underpinnings of demand-side economic theory have been discarded and supplanted by the precepts of supply-side economics. But the road has not been easy, the route not direct.

When the Conservatives took office, the rate of inflation was 10.3 percent, and real GDP growth was 2.3 percent. From June 12, 1979, the day Sir Geoffrey Howe introduced the prime minister's first budget, the British economy got worse, not better. The malaise continued for three years. Howe's first, second, and third budgets imposed substantially higher taxes on the British economy. In his first budget, for example, reductions in Britain's personal income tax rates were more than offset by increases in the value-added tax.[8] A lower deficit, it was argued, was a necessary precondition to restoring health to the British economy. During these first three years of the Thatcher government, tax revenues rose to 30 percent of Gross Domestic Product (GDP) from 25.3 percent.

However, Britain's budget deficit, known in the United Kingdom as the Public Sector Borrowing Requirement (PSBR), increased 43 percent to 13.2 billion pounds. Relative to the size of the British economy, that was equivalent to a $202 billion U.S. budget deficit. The reason for this "unexpected" flood of red ink was that the British economy fell into its worst recession since the Great Depression. Output declined by 2.1 percent in 1980 and 1.0 percent in 1981, double the rate of decline posted during the 1974–75 recession. Inflation more than doubled, peaking at 17.9 percent in 1979 compared to 8.2 percent in 1978.

Unemployment, too, reached record proportions. After hitting a low of 5.2 percent in the second quarter of 1979, the last quarter before the Thatcher tax increases took effect, the unemployment rate rose to an average of 8.3 percent in the fourth quarter of 1981. Interest rates also shot up, with long-term government bond yields rising from 12.1 percent in the second quarter of 1979 to 15.7 percent in the fourth quarter of 1981.

London equity values plunged. The Financial Times Industrial Index, which had peaked at 558.6 on May 4, 1979, the day after Thatcher's first election, hit a low of 406.9 on January 3 of the following year. At the end of 1981, it was still below its May 1979 peak in spite of a 43 percent increase in the price level.

Quite simply, the policies put into place by Margaret Thatcher and the Conservative Party were not oriented toward free markets. Taxation definitely was increased and the preponderance of the policies enacted by the government reflected further drift from the basic precepts of private incentives and free markets. The changes that were made were more traditional in the context of European politics; they represented a shift from a prolabor statist government to a probusiness statist government. The Conservatives implemented fiscal policies which had the effect of lowering statutory tax rates at the upper end of the income brackets and on the returns from capital, while raising tax rates on the lower and middle income ranges. The Conservative Party's policies could have been characterized as lowering tax rates where effective tax rates were relatively low and raising tax rates where they were effectively higher. In addition to this shift in the incidence of taxation, the Conservative government's June 1979 budget raised the overall rate of taxation. Inflation, in conjunction with progressive tax rates, raised effective marginal rates of taxation even when the tax codes themselves were not altered. Even if the static analysis had shown no tax increase whatsoever, effective tax rates still increased dramatically.

Other policies were advanced by the Conservatives. A number of international credit and exchange controls were terminated, and full exchange flexibility for the pound was permitted. In conjunction with pledges to reduce government spending, attempts were made to reduce subsidies to failing enterprises and to extricate the government from state-controlled enterprises. Though aspirations far exceeded accomplishments, there is little doubt that the Conservatives made headway. Substantial advances were made in removing government from the wage bargaining process.

In 1982, the British economy began its move to the supply side. The inflection point was the change in economic policy manifested in the Thatcher government's first budget following its reelection. The new budget, presented by Chancellor of the Exchequer Nigel Lawson, eschewed the austerity policies that entrapped the first Thatcher government in the snare of higher tax rates.[9]

One of the cornerstones of the supply-side revolution was the 1984 reduction in corporate tax rates. This allowed a major shift in economic policy away from targeted incentives and investment tax credits and toward lower tax rates and higher incentives to produce and invest. The shift toward the supply side culminated with the reform of the social security system. These reforms, first proposed in 1985, took effect in 1988 and reduced the effective marginal tax rates for people facing the poverty trap. Because benefits are now related to income exclusive of tax payments rather than income inclusive of tax payments, marginal tax rates in excess of 100 percent for the disenfranchised have disappeared.

The British corporate tax system had consisted of a high corporation tax rate combined with a high initial allowance for some, but not all, investments. In 1984, the United Kingdom eliminated the expensing provision and used these changes to lower corporate tax rates. Britain then led the world in eliminating tax preferences and reducing corporate tax rates (Table 18.1).

The United States also reduced the stamp duty by one percentage-point, and there was a one percentage-point reduction in the National Insurance Surcharge and an increase in the threshold at which the lowest personal income tax rate of 30 percent took effect. Moreover, the personal income tax system was fully

Table 18.1
Highest Corporate Income Tax Rates, 1984–90[a] (Percent)

	1984	1985	1986	1987	1988	1989[b]	1990[b]
Sweden	52	52	52	52	52	52	52
Denmark	40	50	50	50	50	50	50
France	50	50	45	45	42	42	42
Netherlands	43	43	43	42	42	42	42
United Kingdom	45	40	35	35	35	35	35
Germany[c]	56	56	56	56	56	56	50
Italy[d]	36	46	46	46	46	46	46
Canada[e,f]	51	52	53	52	48	44	44
Australia	46	46	46	49	49	49	49
United States[d]	51	51	51	45	39	39	39
Japan[c,d]	53	53	53	52	52	52	52

a. Combined national and local tax rates.
b. Assumes no unscheduled changes in current tax provisions unless otherwise indicated.
c. Tax on undistributed profits only; tax of 36.0 percent on distributed profits in Germany and 33.3 percent in Japan.
d. Takes into account the deductibility of local tax from national tax.
e. Rate for a non-manufacturing corporation; tax for a manufacturing corporation will be lower.
f. Assumes a provincial tax rate of 15.5 percent.

Source: *World Tax Reform: A Progress Report*, Edited by Joseph A. Pechman, Brookings Dialogues on Public Policy, The Brookings Institution, Washington, D.C., 1988.

A. B. Laffer, V.A. Canto & Associates

indexed, so there was no hidden tax increase offsetting these significant reductions in marginal rates. Similarly, the immediate reductions in the "small business" corporate income tax, the stamp tax, the capital transfer tax, and the exemption of stock options from the personal income tax all augmented incentives to dramatically increase production.

The promise of an individual income tax rate reduction in fiscal 1986 did not fully materialize. Lawson said changes in personal tax rates or a simplification of Britain's tax system, both of which had been expected, needed long public debate. He stated that these rate reductions would not be enacted until 1987 or later. Lawson believed that, "A substantial reduction in [government borrowing] must take precedence over tax cuts."[10] This illustrates the static revenue approach of the British government when analyzing the effect of tax rate cuts. The transformation of British economic policy away from demand management and static revenue analysis toward a supply-side fiscal policy focused on incentives was arduous and was resisted every step of the way.[11]

Given the static revenue mentality of British officials, the tax rate cuts could not be implemented unless some revenue source to finance the tax rate reductions was developed. Viewed in this context, the privatization efforts of the British government played a major and important role in making possible the British move to the supply side. In addition to the usual benefits of letting market forces dictate the functioning of the newly-privatized companies, their sale generated revenues that could be used to finance the tax rate reductions.[12]

In spite of the reticence to enact tax rate reductions, the British stock and bond markets reacted favorably to reductions in the tax rate announced for the fiscal year ending March 1987. The Financial Times Industrial shares rose 14.9 percent to 1389.5, and the price of long-term British bonds surged as much as 2.5 points.[13] The pressure to pay more attention to tax rates was being increased by tax rate reductions in the United States.[14] The U.S. Tax Reform Act of 1986 was a major catalyst pushing Great Britain to the supply side. During this time, the United States was contemplating another round of tax rate cuts that would leave the top personal income tax rate at 28 percent. The maximum U.S. tax rate would then be approximately the same as the British lowest tax rate. The Prime Minister herself discussed the potential problem for Britain's economy if high tax rates remained in effect relative to the low tax rates in the United States.

Tax rate competition from the United States shifted the British focus away from reductions in only their "basic rate." Without touching the punitive top rates, the progressivity of the British tax system increased.[15] It is only by cutting the top tax rate that incentives, and hence revenues, begin to increase.[16]

In his 1988 budget message, Lawson unveiled a tax rate reduction package for the United Kingdom. The reform consisted of a cut in the base income tax rate to 25 percent from 27 percent, and he pledged the Conservative government to a goal of 20 percent. He also slashed the top tax rate to 40 percent from 60 percent. These rate reductions were largely in response to the U.S. Tax Reform Act of 1986. Among the reasons stated for the reform, the Chancellor said, "Excessive rates of income tax destroy enterprise and drive talent to more hospitable shores overseas."[17]

Evidence of the supply-side response is growing. We have argued that the 1979 reduction in the top rate to 60 percent from 83 percent, combined with the imposition of a value-added tax, amounted to an increase in the effective tax rate of the British economy. It is possible, however, that for upper-income individuals the effective marginal tax rates may have been reduced. Not surprisingly, in Great Britain as in the United States, reductions in the top income tax rate have been accompanied by an increase in the share of income paid by top income taxpayers. For example, in the United Kingdom during 1978–79, 24 percent of the income tax was paid by the top 5 percent of taxpayers. By 1986–87, that figure had risen to 28 percent. In the United States, the top 1 percent income earners saw their share of the tax burden increase to 26.1 percent in 1986 from 18.1 percent in 1981. The higher increase in share in the United States is attributable to the fact that overall effective marginal tax rates declined more for U.S. taxpayers than for British taxpayers.

The tax rate reductions announced by the Thatcher government in March 1988 took effect on April 5, 1988. The reform lowered the top personal tax rates to 40 percent from 60 percent, increasing the take-home pay to 60 pence from 40 pence. This represents a 60 percent increase in after-tax rate of return. In addition, the social security reform announced in 1985 became effective in 1988.[18] Because benefits are now related to income after taxes and after national insurance contributions, marginal tax rates in excess of 100 percent have disappeared. These reforms have lowered the effective tax rates on the lower strata of British society. The effective tax rates implicit in the means tests of the social programs have been reduced. The end result will be higher employment levels for the groups directly affected by the poverty trap.

An inevitable result of this expansion was a deterioration in Britain's trade balance.[19] As the country's growth rate accelerated relative to the rest of the world, its expenditures rose faster than production. Purchases of new plant and equipment, for example, were not matched with a commensurate increase in production. As a result, the British purchased more of their own output, leaving less for export, and increased their imports.

With the tax rate reductions, incentives to invest in Britain, for the Briton and foreigner alike, increased under a system of floating exchange rates. The only way to export capital to the country is to sell more goods and services in Britain than are purchased there.[20] Thus, the current account in Britain moved into deficit in order to accommodate the capital inflow attracted by that country's improved economic climate.

Britain, once described as an "undeveloping country," quickly became an economy to be reckoned with. The tax increase splurge ended in 1982. With lower tax rates and higher incentives to produce came economic growth, lower inflation, lower interest rates, higher equity values, and a lower deficit. Since 1983, the British economy has grown in real terms: The 1983 real GDP growth of 3.79 percent was the best performance under a Thatcher government until 1987 when it grew at 4.21 percent. During the transition period, Britain's top marginal corporate income tax rate went from among the highest to among the lowest of the major industrial countries (Table 18.2). As a result, production that would have been located elsewhere in the world found its way to the United Kingdom, and production that would have otherwise left the United Kingdom remained.

The London market responded unfavorably to early Conservative policies and favorably to recent fiscal and monetary changes enacted by the Thatcher government. The stock market, as measured by the Financial Times Industrial Index, declined 12.07 percent in 1979. In real terms the drop was even more pronounced: a 25.56 percent decline in 1979. During the austerity years, a real decline in stock prices was gradually reduced to 3.37 percent in 1980, and there was almost no decline in 1981. It was not until the supply-side reforms were announced that the market showed positive real growth. In 1982, the Industrial index increased 3.93 percent, and in 1983 the real gain of the London stock market amounted to 25.40 percent. Although the real gains continued in subsequent years, they declined to 0.5 percent in 1987.

Table 18.2
Highest Personal Income Tax Rates, 1979–80

	1979	1984	1985	1986	1987	1988	1989	1990
Australia	61.5	60.0	60.0	55.0	49.0	49.0	49.0	49.0
Canada	61.9	51.0	52.0	55.0	53.0	45.0	45.0	45.0
Denmark	73.0	73.0	73.0	73.0	68.0	68.0	68.0	68.0
France	60.0	65.0	65.0	58.0	57.0	57.0	57.0	57.0
Germany	56.0	56.0	56.0	56.0	56.0	56.0	56.0	53.0
Italy	72.0	65.0	62.0	62.0	62.0	60.0	60.0	60.0
Japan	88.0	88.0	88.0	88.0	88.0	76.0	76.0	76.0
Netherlands	72.0	72.0	72.0	72.0	72.0	70.0	70.0	70.0
Sweden	86.5	82.0	80.0	80.0	77.0	75.0	75.0	75.0
United Kingdom	83.0	60.0	60.0	60.0	60.0	40.0	40.0	40.0
United States	70.0	50.0	50.0	50.0	38.5	28.0	28.0	28.0

Source: *World Tax Reform: A Progress Report*, Edited by Joseph A. Pechman, Brookings Dialogues on Public Policy, The Brookings Institution, Washington, D.C., 1988.

A. B. Laffer, V.A. Canto & Associates

In line with our analysis, the phase-in of the corporate tax rate reduction slowed the British real GDP growth rate to 1.76 percent in 1984 from 3.79 percent in 1983. However, the economy bounced back with a 3.64 percent real growth rate in 1985, 3.40 percent in 1986, 4.21 percent in 1987, and 2.59 during 1988.

The deterioration of the trade balance from a surplus to a deficit position coincided with the 1983 expansion. In 1982, when Great Britain's real GDP grew at 1.1 percent, the trade balance showed a surplus of .8 percent of GDP. In 1983, as the rate of growth of GDP increased to 3.54 percent, the trade balance account turned from a surplus position in 1982 into a deficit position of .29 percent of GDP (Figure 18.3). The deterioration of the trade balance continued with the economic expansion, with the trade deficit peaking in 1988 at 4.52 percent of GDP.

PROGENESIS VERSUS NEOTENY

The tax rate reduction in the United Kingdom resulted in a deterioration of the trade balance. The reason for this is clear: the demand for British-located assets will increase with the rise in after-tax rates of return on British assets. Consequently, foreigners will increase their investments in the United Kingdom, and the British will reduce their investments abroad. Under a floating exchange rate system, the balance of payments must always add up to zero. Therefore, capital flow into Britain will be matched by a trade balance deterioration.

Figure 18.3
Percent Change in U.K. GDP versus Merchandise Trade Balance as a Percent of GDP

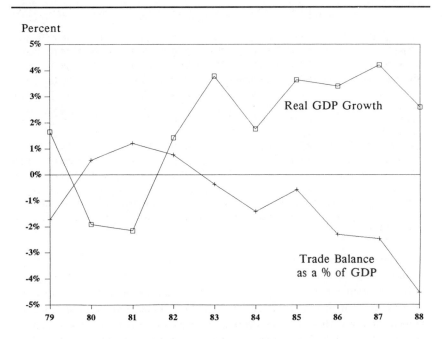

The impact of the tax rate reduction is similar to that experienced by the United States in the early 1980s when the first Reagan tax rate cuts were being implemented. As in the United States, the British economy's expansion was being described as a consumer-led expansion. The British trade balance deteriorated and interest rates have remained high. All of this has taken place in the presence of a budget surplus.[21]

The similarities between the response of the U.S. and the U.K. economies suggest that in both cases their expansion was fueled by the increase in incentives resulting from tax rate reductions. Given the surplus, the British expansion cannot be attributed to deficit spending. Likewise, the deterioration in the British trade balance and the rise in interest rates cannot be attributed to a nonexistent budget deficit. The explanation lies in the increase in incentives resulting from the tax rate reductions of the last few years.

Attempts to prevent the rise in the foreign exchange value of the pound through monetary policy will result in a rise in the British inflation rate. These effects are already evident in the British economy. The monetary objective of the British government during the supply-side tax rate reduction period appears to have been a policy of stabilizing the foreign exchange value of the pound, a position supported by most supply-side economists.[22] Our analysis suggests that

British tax reform would have created an appreciation of the pound vis-à-vis other currencies. Thus, a policy of exchange rate stability would have resulted in an excessive monetary expansion in order to prevent the rise in the pound. The tendency for the pound to rise will present a policy dilemma for British monetary authorities. They will have to choose between exchange rate or interest/inflation rate stability.[23]

Britain has been headed in the wrong direction recently. The British pound over the past year, on a trade-weighted basis, has depreciated by about 4 percent while the dollar rose by almost 3 percent. Figure 18.1 shows the entire history of the relationship between the dollar and the pound sterling during the era of the supply-side revolution. The inflationary consequences should not have been surprising.

What is more, government officials in the United Kingdom look embarrassed whenever they discuss tax cuts. While they may recognize the enormous political and even macroeconomic appeal of tax cuts, they just don't feel good talking about lower tax rates. They feel guilty as though somehow the years and years of imprinted liberal ideology make them ashamed of what they are saying. Selfish, unfeeling, and just plain bad are the emotions attached to those who advocate tax cuts. They can't help it, they were raised that way. To them, the Kennedy ideas that the best form of welfare is a good, high-paying job, or the concept of the rising tide, are simply not part of the British psyche. It's foreign to them. In the long run, Britain will have a very hard time living with low taxes.

NOTES

1. See Chapter 22.
2. See Chapter 17.
3. Arthur B. Laffer, "Minding Our Ps and Qs: Exchange Rates and Foreign Trade," A. B. Laffer Associates, April 14, 1986.
4. See Chapter 16.
5. Arthur B. Laffer, assisted by James C. Turney and Valerie J. Paul, "Reagan's Economic Proposals with a Supply-Side Framework," Testimony before the House Ways and Means Committee (March 4, 1981).
6. "Mistress of Downing Street," *The Economist,* May 5, 1979, p. 13.
7. "Election Euphoria Lifts Equities to New High Levels with 30-Share Index Closing 8.7 up at Peak of 553.3," *Financial Times,* May 4, 1979.
8. Arthur B. Laffer, "Britain's Economic Tragedy: A Lesson for America," A. B. Laffer Associates, October 24, 1980.
9. For a detailed analysis of this period see Charles W. Kadlec, "Adam Smith Invades the Land of Lord Keynes," A. B. Laffer Associates, July 13, 1984.
10. George Anders and Peter Truell, "Britain Drops Plans for Big Tax Cuts, Outlines Tight Budget for Fiscal 1986," *Wall Street Journal,* March 20, 1985.
11. David Howell, "Will Thatcher Shrink from Growth Opening?" *Wall Street Journal,* February 19, 1986, p. 29.
12. Peter Norman, "UK Sees Revenue Near Doubling from Sales of State Companies," *Wall Street Journal,* November 13, 1985.

13. Matthew Winkler and Peter Norman, "Interest Rates Fall, Markets Rally in Response to Britain's Budget," *Wall Street Journal*, March 20, 1986.

14. William McGuin, "British Show Little Interest in Dropping Tax Rates," *Wall Street Journal*, March 26, 1986, p. 31; "Hope in Britain," Editorial, *Wall Street Journal*, May 13, 1986.

15. "Britain's New Deal," *Wall Street Journal*, November 11, 1986.

16. To illustrate the incentive power of tax rate reductions, consider the effect of the Tax Reform Act of 1986. The income tax rate for the highest tax bracket was 50 percent in 1986 and 69.125 percent in 1981. Thus, for every extra dollar earned in the top bracket, taxpayers kept 50 cents in 1986 as opposed to 30.875 cents in 1981. That is nearly a 62 percent increase in the after-tax retention rate. In the lowest income tax bracket, the tax rate declined to 11 percent from 13.825 percent. The increases in the take-home pay from an extra dollar of income were only 3.3 percent. Clearly, since tax rate reductions increased the incentives more for those in the highest income bracket, it is not surprising to see a larger response by those in the top bracket.

17. "The Budget: The Chancellor's Speech," *Financial Times*, 1984.

18. British Department of Health and Social Services, *Reform of Social Security*, vol. 1, (London: HMSO, 1985).

19. Victor A. Canto, Arthur B. Laffer, and James C. Turney, "Trade Policy and the U.S. Economy," *Financial Analysts Journal* 38, no. 5 (1982), pp. 27–46.

20. Leif H. Olson, "No Money Inflows, No Money Outflows," *Wall Street Journal*, April 10, 1984.

21. "Lawson's Lesson," Editorial, *Wall Street Journal*, May 26, 1988.

22. "Lawson's Lesson," 1988.

23. Lindley Clark, "The Outlook: A New Monetarism Reigns in UK and US," *Wall Street Journal*, June 22, 1988, p. 1.

PART FOUR

PORTFOLIO STRATEGIES

19

Part I: The Legend

Victor A. Canto and Arthur B. Laffer

Theory and common experience postulate that general economic factors impact stock prices in the aggregate. These same factors can also have substantially different effects depending upon the industry group being considered. The across-the-board reduction in tax rates of the 1980s, for example, was exceptionally good for the overall stock market, sending the S&P 500 from a low of 112.8 in 1981 to a high of 336.8 in 1987. But the equities of some industry groups were benefited far more than others. Table 19.1 illustrates the variability among selected industry returns over the 1981–87 time period when the overall stock market went from trough to peak.[1]

According to street lore, changes in oil prices, exchange rates, interest rates, inflation, and trade restrictions also have significantly different effects across industry lines. Few would doubt that these economic shocks have an overall impact on market aggregates. During the past decade, oil prices, exchange rates, interest rates, and inflation have covered an extraordinarily wide range of values. It would seem only natural that such a wide range of values would elicit equivalently dramatic responses from equities. In other words, in addition to an overall stock market effect, there would exist the potential, at least, for great differences in stock returns among the various industry groups as well. The grouping of equities by industry classifications is a fruitful avenue for extending in-depth analysis.

The finance literature of the past several decades has taken a different tack, however. Industry performances have been relegated to a minor role in modern

Table 19.1
Selected Industry Returns, September 1981–August 1987*

Ten Best Performers		Ten Worst Performers	
Industry	% Apprec.	Industry	% Apprec.
Broadcasting	544.49 %	Offshore Drilling	-56.06 %
Pollution Control	481.66	Oil Well Equip. & Serv.	-30.34
Containers/Paper	473.23	Coal	-3.88
Foods	448.98	Steel	2.20
Beverages/Brewers	446.60	Regional Banks	10.77
Textile/Apparel Mfg.	428.91	Machine Tools	25.07
General Merchandise	401.13	Metals/Miscellaneous	28.28
Containers/Metal & Glass	390.52	Machinery	35.39
Department Stores	387.65	Bond Funds	44.64
Electric/Major Companies	372.85	Investment Companies	49.62

S&P 500   168.58

* Selected out of 79 industry groupings for which data were readily available.

finance.[2] The detailed institutional research of former times has been unable to secure a niche in the highly theoretical and automated world of modern finance.[3] Just as specific industry analysis has been overshadowed, so has analysis of specific events.

Having been participants in the dramatic emergence of modern finance, we have a perspective on how it all came to be. In our opinion, modern finance research has been incredibly productive. The developments have been rich in empirical implications, and simultaneously the tools were fashioned to exploit the vast reservoirs of data. Modern finance has changed for the better: the entire field of finance—from theory to practice. In the interests of progress, however, a great deal was discarded that we believe should now be resurrected. What follows is our edition of the legend: the loves, the hates, the excesses, and the shortcomings. As participants, our perspective is personal as well as professional.

MODERN FINANCE: THE LEGEND

Although the location and the date of the conception remain shrouded in long lost historical annals, the deliverance of modern finance was at the University of Chicago's south side campus in the late 1960s.[4] High speed data processing and irrepressible enthusiasms were both in attendance at this, the most significant of times. Faster than even the horror of its detractors could imagine, modern finance grew and spread. This strapping young concept clambered up the ladder of success, the rungs of which had been tightly wrapped with the reputations of those who preceded.

Armed as they were with reams of computer output, an arcane new language, and supported by single-minded battalions indoctrinated in the litany, the conquest by intimidation was swift and ruthless. All the research that had come before, save an aberrant fistful, was consigned to the ever expanding tomes of intellectual refuse. This was a theory without a past, revealed to a select few there, and then: an observed genesis in our time.

To the cognoscenti, random walks, martingales, and efficient markets supplanted experience, knowledge, and most tragically, economic theory. Hand-over-mouth giggles were willfully extended to each and every nonbeliever while knowing glances and faintly visible nods were freely exchanged among cabal participants.

And so it was back then. Gothic edifices of established universities were the cathedrals to the high priests of academe. It was in these hallowed institutions that flocks of students were irretrievably imprinted by repetitive incantations. As incredible as it may seem, strict discipline and literal adherence to dogma were rigidly maintained merely by the threat of disapproval—and the threat of withdrawal of perceived sanctions. The similarities with religious cults are extraordinary. Within this environment, the theory of random walks and efficient markets were the coin of the realm.

RATIONAL EXPECTATIONS AND MARKET EFFICIENCY

In its basic form, the theory of market efficiency postulates that available information will be exploited to the point where it has no profit potential.[5] Stock prices, therefore, must follow a random walk. If they did not follow a random walk, then the pattern to be found in their past price behavior could be exploited to earn exceptional returns. If the statistical series themselves could be presumed to be well behaved, then the consequences of efficient markets are simply that a location and a dispersion parameter were all that was needed to describe a data series.

In its semi-strong form, the random walk notion was extended beyond the pattern of past prices to any and all publicly available information. Monkeys throwing darts at the financial page of the *Wall Street Journal,* so it was told, would, on balance, perform as well as money managers.[6] Knowing money managers as we all do, such an appeal is hard to resist. In fact, there is considerable comfort to be found in a view of the world where experts are no better than novices and where hard work and perseverance yield no benefits. Is this not the ingenue's dream?

Term paper after term paper and dissertation upon dissertation were produced to show why, in this or that specific instance, what had been deemed an accurate filter rule, in truth, was a scam. Failures to document fraud were seen as either meaningless oddities or abject incompetence on the part of the researcher.[7] Inability to find a specific filter rule that enhanced the odds of being profitable was erroneously seen as confirmation of the efficient market theory. Failure to reject the null hypothesis was taken as an acceptance of the null hypothesis. Academic incentives were structured in such a way that researchers knew full well what they were to find, and the consequences if they did not.

More than rejection of prior research, however, was needed to construct an entire theory of finance. Something constructive had to be found upon which to build. Fortunately, the work of Tobin and Markowitz was at hand.[8] People, it was asserted, dislike risk and, therefore, require a premium to bear risk. The greater the risk, the higher the expected return must be. Even in a world where people are not risk-averse, the chance of a loss must be accompanied by higher returns when the project is successful. The higher returns when the project is successful are needed to offset the probability of loss and the magnitude when loss occurs. But what modern finance theory asserts is something more. Modern finance asserts that the sum total of the returns, including both losses and profits, will have to increase with risk.

As mentioned earlier, random walks and well-behaved functions permit the description of an asset's value series with only two parameters: location (mean return) and dispersion (volatility of return). In the case of a normal distribution, the mean is the arithmetic mean and dispersion is well described by the variance of the series. It was with a leap of extreme expediency that the scientists of modern finance equated the concept of risk with a measure of volatility. The stage is set.

One subtle, but delightful, implication of risk aversion and efficient markets is the distinction between a portfolio's or asset's absolute variance and its covariance with the market. Some assets with a great deal of return volatility may, in fact, be far less "risky" than other assets with demonstrably less volatility. Such a seeming paradox becomes readily understandable only if another asset is found that moves in exactly the opposite pattern to the first asset. By combining the high volatility assets that move in opposite directions into a common portfolio, that common portfolio will have markedly less volatility than any of its separate asset components had when standing alone. Thus emerges the distinction between diversifiable risk and nondiversifiable risk or, stated statistically, the differences between an asset's variance and its covariance with the market.

Without belaboring the story unnecessarily, the only risk that cannot be diversified is the risk of the market itself. Therefore, an asset's only risk worthy of a market premium is the degree to which that asset moves with the market. All else can be removed through diversification. In measured form, risk is the covariance any asset has with the market—colloquially known as its Beta. While true Betas are intrinsically unmeasurable because they relate to how an asset will behave in the future, approximations based upon past values are easily obtained. Thus, the transition from the theory of modern finance to its practical application is an algorithm of extraordinary simplicity based upon past data.

A MEASURE IN SEARCH OF A THEORY

As a point of departure, we consider ourselves to be extreme advocates of the virtues of simplicity. There is also absolutely nothing wrong with using the past to predict the future. In fact, in some deep sense, there can be no alternative. But, the procedures actually pursued by modern finance result in numbers devoid of theory.

As a consequence of methodological differences, the researchers of modern finance missed an extraordinarily rich opportunity to press outward the frontiers of knowledge much further. A sequence of questions relating to the essential features of modern finance have arisen over the past several years but none is more in keeping with intellectual pursuits than to question why a given asset has a specific Beta. Quite simply, it is not sufficient to respond with an empirical answer? Betas are not what they are because they are what they are. If such a theory is to contain kernels of truth, as we believe this theory does, it is because far deeper and more basic principles are at work.

Just how an asset acquires a specific value for its Beta depends upon production technologies, resource availability, governmental policies, and human tastes. To proffer, as we do, additional considerations is not to damn all research by asserting unattainable standards but merely to reiterate what in other fields is common knowledge. Economics has advanced considerably in the theories of both individuals and firms and how these, in turn, mesh to form a general equilibrium framework. To ignore all of this does not make sense and is tantamount to an inefficient intellectual market.

AN EXAMPLE OF MISGUIDED TECHNIQUE

To illustrate the need for basic economics, let us take a retrospective look at the airline industry. Had you exclusively used modern finance as your guide in 1982, airlines would have been classified as very high Beta stocks. The ensuing years of an incredibly robust bull market, had it been foreseen, should have meant even greater returns for the airline stocks. The greater returns, however, were simply not destined to be. Airline stocks performed quite poorly in light of the bull market and their high Betas. The explanation, we believe, is quite simple (Table 19.2).

Prior to 1980, the airline industry in the United States was tightly regulated. Fares, route structures, and the like were totally under the control of federal agencies. Thus, when the economy performed well and as a consequence people traveled more, airlines increased their profitability in exaggerated proportion to the state of the economy. Nothing was priced or produced on a marginal basis. The airline industry was highly levered to the U.S. economy and thereby the stock market. A high Beta seems somewhat intuitive. But then came deregulation.

Table 19.2
Annual Returns for the Airlines as Related to the S&P 500, 1981–87

	1981	1982	1983	1984	1985	1986	1987
Airlines	-6.74	86.06	9.53	-6.55	9.46	15.64	-12.68
S&P 500	-9.73	14.76	17.27	1.40	26.33	14.62	2.03

With deregulation, competition forced marginal cost pricing and intense route competition. No longer were airline services inelastically supplied to the market place. The appearance of minuscule excess profits invited fierce competition from new and old carriers. When it comes to profits, not even the Reagan bull market, or the fall in interest rates and oil prices can supplant one good regulatory commission. The supply curve of airline services had moved from inelastic to elastic and thus threw out of the window the analysis of the historically determined Beta (Table 19.2). A little basic economics could have taken modern finance a long way.[9]

While at the extreme, the example of the airlines industry does bring the point home, the application of economics is more far-reaching than just one extreme example. If a bull market results from tax cuts, there is no reason why we should presume the same Betas as would occur when the bull market results from a fall in oil prices or deregulation or disbanding trade barriers. Numbers devoid of theory leave a great deal to be desired.

CONTRIBUTIONS OF MODERN FINANCE

Modern finance, in spite of its shortcomings, has contributed richly to our understanding of the world in which we live. Among the contributions are the concept of a rigorous test and the pricing implications of profit maximization.

Scientific rigor requires an ability to discriminate among alternatives. Modern finance, with its statistical sophistication, in conjunction with high-speed computers, demonstrably increased our abilities to discriminate. All the while, the theory of profit maximization carried forward as it was in the finance field, did much to alter the way we all view the world. The straightforward question of "if you can see it, why doesn't everybody else see it?" was carried to a new realm of importance. A number of the earlier filter rules were quite rightly relegated to the domain of discarded thought, seen for what they were, ill-conceived notions impeding intellectual progress.

TOWARD A NEW THEORY: THE CATS APPROACH

The marriage of classical economics with modern finance surely must have been conceived in heaven. The considerable assets of modern finance have extended the frontiers of our knowledge uncommonly far. Recognized experts in the field of finance, as recently as one quarter of a century ago, would be totally lost in the field today. The classical economic theory of how markets adjust to external shocks, sometimes called after the French word *tatonnement,* is the contribution that fills the void in the field of finance.

Without drifting too far afield, markets are nothing more than conceptual locations where demanders meet suppliers. Prices are the ratios of commodities in the actual act of exchange. When markets clear, demanders have acquired all they want and suppliers have supplied all they want. The clearance of a market is associated with a specific price and quantity and is referred to as equilibrium.

A given shock to a market is a term used to describe a shift in either demanders' or suppliers' preferences. If such a shock occurs, the previous equilibrium price and quantity will no longer be apropos of this market. The new equilibrium clearance conditions will be satisfied by price and quantity adjustments. Just how and to what degree a specific market adjusts is key to that market's industries' profitability. Therefore, how a market adjusts to shocks will determine that industry's future profitability and, as a consequence, its equity values.

The Capital Assets Tax Sensitivity (CATS) approach redresses several of modern finance's more serious shortcomings. It proceeds directly from the theory of the firm and the household to establish the principle as to how any market returns to equilibrium following a macroeconomic shock. It principle, equilibrium is restored by some combination of price and quantity adjustment. Whether the alteration in the market operates through the industry's demand schedule or supply schedule, price and quantity will be the rebalancers. Quite clearly, from the standpoint of any specific firm within an industry, the greater the impact of macroeconomic shocks and the greater the role played by price in the adjustment process, the greater will be the sensitivity of that industry's profits and stock value. Different shocks could well result in widely different industry responses. As a consequence, the CATS research has broadened the scope of measuring the impact of macroeconomic shocks on the various segments of the stock market.

While rooted in economic theory, both the conception and the measurement of equity responses to macroeconomic events are straightforward. Pillaging data from the more recent past has allowed us to establish links between macroeconomic events and the returns of equities by industry. In the past, tax policies have changed a number of times, as have the course of inflation, interest rates, exchange rates, and protectionist activities. All the while immersed in deep silence, markets have reassessed the equity values of the various industry categories. From all we are able to uncover, the market's reassessment of equity values is far from haphazard. There are distinct patterns that emerge. Some are focused with great resolution while others are only dimly visible through the vast array of numbers.

The CATS strategy overlies the vector of more traditional macroeconomic events on the matrix of asset relatives. If data patterns recumbent in our past observances can be presumed to extend into the future, then knowledge of what is to be for the economy can readily be translated into what is to be for stock returns. As a guide for asset managers such linkages may prove quite valuable. Asset managers are one group with the curse to be always fully committed. Whether in or out of the market, their performance is continuously at risk. They have no choice.

INCIDENCE VERSUS BURDEN

Where the ultimate burden of any given macroeconomic shock finally comes to rest depends on the industry's demand and supply elasticities and, of course, on the nature of the specific shock itself.[10] Where the supply of products is price elastic, industries will satisfy fluctuations in demand primarily by altering production levels without significant changes in profitability (Figure 19.1). The meaning of an elastic supply curve is definitionally that the appearance of incipient excess profits calls forth more product and thereby costs and lower product prices up to the point where the excess profits vanish. As a consequence, the price of that industry's stock will be relatively stable.

Industries are not able to alter production plans easily where supply is inelastic and therefore these industries will ration fluctuations in demand by changing prices (Figure 19.2). For these industries, profitability and stock prices will reflect fluctuations in demand. Analogous effects pertain to supply shocks as they do to demand shocks. Industries facing elastic demand will not be able to alter their product's prices when supply conditions change. Therefore, any macroeconomic shock impacting production costs will have a direct impact on an industry's profitability and thereby its stock price (Figure 19.3).

Industries faced with inelastic demand should be able to pass on any cost

Figure 19.1
Elastic Industry: Quantity
Changes in Response to a Shift in
Demand

Figure 19.2
Inelastic Industry: Price Changes
in Response to a Shift in Demand

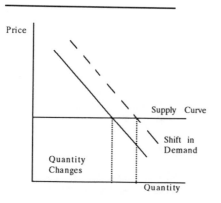

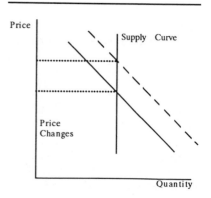

Figure 19.3
Elastic Industry: Quantity
Changes in Response to a Shift in
Supply

Figure 19.4
Inelastic Industry: Price Changes
in Response to a Shift in Supply

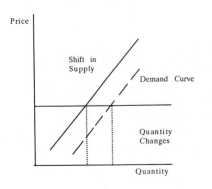

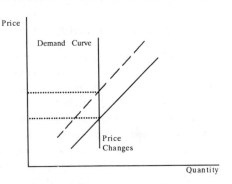

increase by way of higher prices (Figure 19.4). Because of the inelasticity of demand and the competitive conditions within the industry itself, any reduction in cost will not be captured by the industry but instead passed on to the consumers.

Knowledge of the relevant supply and demand elasticities for each and every type of macroeconomic shock on an industry by industry basis would be ideal to allow us to gauge the precise impact of any macroeconomic event. However, direct measurement of the relevant supply and demand elasticities for even one industry is so arcane a task as to render such an endeavor futile. To imagine the extension to all industries is to imagine the squaring of our ignorance. Far more tractable would be an equivalent approach to measure the impact of various shocks directly on the industries' stock prices.

APPENDIX

Table 19A.1
Industry Returns Ranked by 1981–87 Performance

	1981–87	1981	1982	1983	1984	1985	1986	1987
Broadcasting	520.79	21.09	47.01	10.51	13.64	67.33	22.06	35.97
Beverages/Brewers	441.05	22.91	59.53	11.30	1.80	58.45	23.71	24.24
Foods	359.61	15.11	33.07	21.46	15.60	58.97	30.59	2.94
Containers/Metal & Glass	348.41	6.19	0.02	40.04	33.06	37.56	54.62	6.51
Containers/Paper	345.39	10.56	13.73	77.21	-10.90	21.19	49.97	23.43
Pollution Control	331.71	-4.80	44.89	-0.11	-3.59	59.63	58.28	28.63
Textile/Products	331.86	20.06	40.78	30.97	-14.81	40.26	31.50	18.41

Table 19A.1 (*continued*)

	1981–87	1981	1982	1983	1984	1985	1986	1987
Restaurants	271.17	25.85	46.34	22.37	14.58	40.07	6.14	-3.32
Beverages/Soft Drinks	256.23	15.13	27.13	10.27	13.99	43.52	24.42	8.43
Tires	249.35	13.48	72.06	-5.30	-15.52	26.37	34.26	31.81
Department Stores	248.08	15.01	72.87	22.82	-1.75	38.89	25.17	-16.55
Food Chains	248.08	1.77	55.58	12.98	10.19	32.63	17.99	12.84
General Merchandise	245.77	1.23	82.09	31.23	-9.10	24.66	24.28	1.50
Publishing	241.57	10.61	45.62	21.77	0.84	33.98	17.88	9.34
Retail/Composite	234.33	6.40	72.41	25.86	-3.87	30.95	22.85	-6.37
Newspapers	231.79	13.46	55.76	13.43	6.45	27.74	20.22	1.24
Tobacco	217.23	6.76	18.93	18.72	15.17	11.22	53.65	6.93
Computer Services	216.64	-25.47	46.32	21.16	20.74	52.50	21.29	7.31
Truckers	215.37	19.16	40.79	38.40	-12.08	35.98	25.98	-9.82
Soaps	212.35	13.86	42.61	1.08	1.85	32.53	25.97	11.94
Retail/Drug	209.76	16.66	51.72	26.03	-1.50	14.07	18.93	3.92
Consumer Goods	193.72	4.48	38.12	14.31	2.84	34.95	23.50	3.89
Textile/Apparel Mfg.	178.99	-17.09	50.77	26.55	-17.70	87.43	43.91	-20.56
Household Furnish/App.	178.85	15.67	63.54	32.92	-20.60	16.90	38.82	-13.93
Drugs	170.11	-2.03	15.95	4.22	11.29	38.01	36.37	8.93
Leisure Time	167.94	26.66	0.12	53.74	6.42	16.38	27.69	-13.11
Automobiles	167.01	-15.60	81.62	29.28	5.39	2.94	15.30	7.71
Life Insurance Companies	163.92	4.78	49.36	26.76	25.41	22.97	4.12	-17.15
Entertainment	154.52	11.39	-3.09	-1.24	-3.65	83.71	12.68	19.69
Hotels & Motels	141.68	-5.55	23.88	29.53	-5.31	34.44	22.42	2.32
Hospital Supplies	136.89	3.96	40.00	-7.11	-17.50	51.03	34.51	4.55
Auto Parts/Aftermarket	133.02	4.46	46.41	5.03	-2.23	16.34	18.66	7.47
Chemicals	130.60	-9.44	2.66	31.49	-16.58	43.02	38.59	14.10
Paper	130.18	-8.35	10.64	36.02	1.15	21.32	27.11	6.98
Shoes	123.81	8.57	63.42	4.78	-0.76	27.27	5.47	-9.63
Chemicals/Diversified	121.81	-15.08	4.65	40.93	0.05	22.78	33.02	8.38
Insurance/Property & Casu.	119.16	10.02	17.94	7.32	9.26	37.30	6.74	-1.71
Building Materials	111.55	-8.28	21.67	14.18	-3.54	38.15	40.35	-11.23
Auto Parts/Original Equip	111.08	2.64	16.85	32.69	-8.75	15.83	11.95	12.10
Personal Loans	106.60	-8.00	41.42	31.76	5.07	33.08	15.73	-25.53
Electric Equipment	96.49	7.27	28.91	2.77	-1.42	23.37	7.09	6.16
Airlines	96.32	-6.74	86.06	9.53	-6.55	9.46	15.64	-12.68
Electronics/Instruments	91.73	-11.09	63.89	11.07	-18.93	7.04	7.00	27.59
Insurance/Multi-Line	91.60	18.07	4.20	6.95	7.24	49.46	2.84	-11.66
Utility/Electric Power	82.82	8.24	22.97	3.45	11.65	15.45	20.82	-14.75
S&P 500	82.00	-9.73	14.76	17.27	1.40	26.33	14.62	2.03
Manufactured Housing	79.89	26.84	116.11	5.16	-13.05	-4.84	3.07	-26.82
Computer/Business Equip.	73.91	-19.43	49.82	24.61	-2.25	20.48	-8.69	7.52
Semiconductors	70.26	-27.98	52.52	55.58	-21.56	0.26	-9.06	39.31
Cosmetics	66.57	-15.68	9.93	-4.68	0.20	35.86	31.10	5.63

Table 19A.1 (*continued*)

	1981-87	1981	1982	1983	1984	1985	1986	1987
Capital Goods	66.51	-16.01	15.00	23.35	-4.15	24.81	5.35	10.89
Brokerage Firms	61.57	27.39	58.17	6.69	-11.79	24.35	10.17	-37.80
Gaming Companies	60.08	-6.48	-8.60	22.03	-5.54	40.52	11.63	3.59
New York City Banks	60.03	7.41	20.44	1.85	10.17	34.55	15.65	-29.15
International Integrated Oil	57.54	-25.23	-8.31	23.10	12.11	16.36	34.46	6.44
REIT	54.91	17.41	31.94	6.63	7.30	-0.25	24.75	-29.76
Savings & Loans	54.67	-24.59	81.31	3.49	-22.36	46.08	33.32	-27.70
Conglomerates	53.33	-13.20	-6.13	39.11	-7.53	25.42	17.54	-0.77
Auto & Truck Parts	43.39	3.56	27.82	51.00	-17.36	0.61	-7.15	-7.06
Metals/Miscellaneous	40.77	3.68	-4.40	22.93	-25.00	-9.50	-1.90	73.49
Aluminum	39.23	-26.48	20.25	39.79	-22.29	4.88	-6.73	48.21
Railroads	38.71	-17.20	-2.91	32.89	-8.82	34.40	-2.88	9.09
Forest Products	35.26	-15.47	26.05	-3.14	-11.21	7.34	32.93	3.44
Bond Funds	27.27	-3.99	21.52	-0.94	0.83	16.43	8.53	-13.56
Air Freight	25.60	8.90	11.95	24.60	-24.63	51.51	6.76	-32.18
Aerospace	21.41	-36.15	35.36	31.50	5.98	16.18	9.13	-20.50
Natural Gas Prod. & Devel.	18.18	-19.62	-12.60	27.37	3.08	32:40	3.36	-6.37
Gold Mining	13.06	-26.61	41.32	-5.90	-29.38	5.91	-0.50	55.68
Hospital Management	12.81	-3.71	64.65	-12.46	4.82	1.18	-22.42	-1.22
Domestic Integrated Oil	5.90	-23.93	-18.93	24.11	12.48	13.47	0.65	7.69
Machinery	3.49	-13.64	-25.09	19.43	-12.92	14.16	-0.21	35.03
Toys	-8.99	-17.63	26.32	-20.95	42.80	30.88	-7.59	-35.93
Steel	-10.50	-5.22	-25.91	42.41	-26.93	-5.01	-17.87	56.99
Investment/Composite	-23.29	-15.84	19.22	2.82	-17.89	10.97	11.03	-26.50
Machine Tools	-24.17	-17.38	11.68	35.67	-32.25	-6.06	-5.40	0.61
Home Building	-28.24	-43.78	70.52	-0.97	-10.26	-5.06	22.97	-27.85
Regional Banks	-29.40	-8.59	-7.18	10.53	-15.49	11.94	1.87	-21.89
Coal	-33.41	-9.19	-30.43	15.09	-8.73	8.93	7.30	-14.15
Oil Well Equip & Leasing	-64.43	-29.76	-29.05	8.64	-25.87	-5.16	-6.09	-0.48
Offshore Drilling	-83.17	-6.50	-44.31	11.23	-22.57	-27.30	-52.87	26.98

Source: Standard & Poors' 500.

NOTES

1. The data used in the study were obtained through Data Resources (DRI). Table 19A.1 reports the stock price performance of the industries for which data were available from January 1981 to December 1987. Seventy-nine industry groups are reported in the appendix. In addition to the overall period performance, the annual performance is also reported.

2. Benjamin F. King, "Market and Industry Factors in Stock Price Behavior," *Journal of Business* 39 (January 1966), pp. 139–90.

3. There exists no modern-day equivalent to the company reports produced by my old firm, H. C. Wainwright & Co.

4. Eugene F. Fama, "The Behavior of Stock Market Prices," *Journal of Business,* January 1965, pp. 34–105; Eugene F. Fama, "Efficient Capital Markets: A Review of Theory and Empirical Work," *Journal of Finance* (May 1970), pp. 383–417.

5. A sequence of developments referred to as rational expectations was evolving at the same time at the same universities as efficient markets. While the focus of the two was slightly different, on a conceptual level they were virtually identical. See, for example, J. F. Muth, "Rational Expectations and the Theory of Price Movements," *Econometrica* 29 (July 1961), pp. 315–35; R. E. Lucas, "An Equilibrium Model of the Business Cycle," *Journal of Political Economy* 83, no. 6, pp. 1113–44; R. E. Lucas, "Expectations and Neutrality of Money," *Journal of Economic Theory* 4 (April 1972), pp. 103–24; T. J. Sargent, "Rational Expectations, the Real Rate of Interest and the Natural Rate of Unemployment," *Brookings Paper of Economic Activity* 2 (1973); R. J. Barro, "Rational Expectations and the Role of Monetary Policy," *Journal of Monetary Economics* 2 (January 1976), pp. 1–32.

6. On its face, a counter example sufficient to reject such a notion is readily at hand. If a high-tax bracket person's monkey randomly hit taxable bonds while the low-tax bracket person's monkey hit tax exempt bonds, they both obviously could be made better off by switching assets.

7. There is one subset of research where the existence and acceptance of a filter rule actually were employed to reinforce the theory of efficient markets. In Fischer Black and Myron Scholes, "The Pricing of Options and Corporate Liabilities," *Journal of Political Economy* 81 (May–June 1973), pp. 637–54, stock options were at times convincingly found to be inefficiently priced. Such a finding was seen as proof positive of the intellectual superiority of the researchers even over the active market. All the more in keeping, once demonstrated and provided to the world at large, the inefficiencies quickly disappeared.

8. James Tobin, "Liquidity Preference as Behavior towards Risks," *Review of Economic Studies* 25 (February 1958), pp. 65–86; Harry Markowitz," Portfolio Selection," *Journal of Finance* 7 (March 1952), pp. 77–91.

9. Victor A. Canto and Wayne Steele Sharp, "Holding Patterns: The Outlook for Air Transportation Industries under Partial Deregulation," *Investment Observation,* A. B. Laffer Associates, September 18, 1987.

10. In a less complicated time, we could envision these shocks as having both price and income effects on any given industry. The elasticities above referenced would be the percentage change in demand or supply resulting from a given percentage change in price or income. For the world in which we live, relevant considerations may also include cross elasticities, income distribution, and factor augmentation effects.

20

Part II: Macroeconomic Shocks and Stock Prices

Victor A. Canto and Arthur B. Laffer

Over the past decade, research at A. B. Laffer Associates has focused on measuring the effects of macroeconomic shocks on specific industry stock returns. Our CATS (Capital Assets Tax Sensitivity) strategy predicts the relative performances of individual industry stocks in the aftermath of these economic shocks.[1]

The CATS strategy classifies industry groups into High-CATS and Low-CATS categories. This classification is based primarily on how stocks performed following tax rate reductions in the 1960s.[2] Stocks which performed best when tax rates were low and falling are designated as High-CATS. In contrast, Low-CATS industry groups are those which performed poorly, on a relative basis, when tax rates were low and falling. It follows that Low-CATS stocks tend to outperform High-CATS stocks (and the market) during periods when tax rates and other production disincentives are increased.

CLASSIFICATION TECHNIQUE

The specific criterion used for the High-CATS/Low-CATS border was whether the industry's stock return outperformed the S&P 500 index during the base period 1962–66. These five years were selected because they encompass the trough to the peak of the bull market which followed the Kennedy income tax rate reductions.[3] Depending upon the individual industry's stock performance during 1962–66, the industry received a CATS classification of either High-

CATS (HC) or Low-CATS (LC). Based on this classification, an index was constructed for the High-CATS and Low-CATS groups.

Within each CATS category there are varying degrees of homogeneity. For some High-CATS industries, equity values almost precisely match the overall High-CATS index with little residual variation. For these industries, the High-CATS effect dominates movements in stock prices. Conversely, other industries display a great deal of residual variation in spite of the fact that their stock prices are positively correlated with the High-CATS index. This second group appears to be influenced by the High-CATS effect, but other factors also cause synchronous movements in industry stock prices.

In order to discriminate between those High-CATS stocks with and without the influence of other factors, correlations were computed between the return of one individual High-CATS industry and the High-CATS composite stock index. Those industry stocks with an R2 (coefficient of determination) greater than 50 percent were classified as High-CATS 1 (HCI). Industries with an R2 less than 50 percent were designated High-CATS II (HCII).

Low-CATS industry stocks were bifurcated using the same criteria. Industries which proved to have a higher correlation with the Low-CATS index were designated as Low-CATS II (LCII), while those industries which displayed a lower correlation with the index were designated as Low-CATS I (LCI). In all, 59 industries were categorized as HC. Of those 32 were HCI and 27 were HCII. A total of 38 industries were classified as LC industries; 23 were LCI and 15 were LCII.

The criteria for categorizing an individual industry are quite arbitrary. Postulating a precise demarcation of the industries into two CATS categories is simply due to our choice of analyzing the industry stocks in terms of discrete groups of CATS characteristics rather than along a continuum. The selection of discrete groupings allows the research to be manageable and at the same time allows the topic to be well ranged. For example, the HCII industry with the highest correlation to the HC index is very similar to the HCI industry with the lowest correlation. In the same vein, the lowest HC industry is very similar to the highest LC industry, and so forth. In spite of the arbitrary nature of the definitions used, the importance of the characteristics themselves should also be clear.

The dominant characteristic of High-CATS stocks is that these industries outperform the market during periods of tax rate cuts. As such, the High-CATS effect is well defined. The remaining universe of industries was classified as Low-CATS. By the very nature of the classification technique, all that we now know for certain about the Low-CATS are their lack of correlation with the High-CATS index.

Patterns of synchronous stock price movements may exist that relate to factors other than tax cuts; for instance, precipitous changes in interest rates or in the rate of inflation may well be associated with systematic patterns in equity markets. Changes in exchange rates or changes in the price of oil also appear to be reasonable candidates for inducing similar patterns in the stock market.

INTEREST RATES AND CATS PERFORMANCE

Interest rates and inflation rates move closely together, as do the LC index and the price of oil. Further work on inflation and the price of oil as macroeconomic shocks is subsumed under interest rates and LC respectively. Eliminating the price of oil from the analysis is ironic: one of the earliest papers using the CATS analysis was "Oil Decontrol: The Power of Incentives."[4] In that paper, stock price sensitivity to oil price changes was estimated using industry performance during the 1973 oil embargo. The losers during the 1973 shock were projected to be winners during the expected decline in oil prices in the early 1980s.

In one of the original papers documenting the CATS strategy, Kevin Melich and Marc Reinganum used a 20-month period, February 1972 through September 1973, to isolate an interest rate effect.[5] In later work, these patterns were checked for consistency using data from the last several decades.[6] Stocks were categorized into two groups. One group benefited from falling interest rates, while the other group benefited from rising interest rates.

Further refinements of the Melich-Reinganum paper appeared to add little to our understanding of the interest rate effect. Estimates of interest rate sensitivity were reported in "Geronimo: The Case for a 400 Basis Point Rise in Interest Rates." In that paper, whether stocks were impacted by the level of interest rates or the change in interest rates remained unanswered.[7] In response to comments by Gerald Bollman and A. Richard Markson, the ambiguity was resolved: rising and falling (changes) interest rate categories were the factors impacting stock prices rather than high and low (level) interest rate categories.[8]

With respect to both general and specific stock performance, a decline in interest rates has effects somewhat similar to those of an income tax rate reduction. Both macroeconomic events are bullish for the overall stock market. In addition, the category that benefits the most from tax rate cuts, HC, contains a disproportionately large number of stocks that benefit from falling interest rates. Of the 59 HC industries, 47 benefit from falling interest rates. Of the 38 LC industries, 22 benefit from rising interest rates.

In spite of the similarities, the impact on industry stock prices resulting from a decline in interest rates is far from identical to an income tax rate reduction. Not all HC industries benefit from falling interest rates nor, when they do, do they benefit to the same degree. Understanding the subtle differences in behavior between the CATS classification and interest rate sensitivity has added substantially to our knowledge about the behavior of equity returns.

TRADABILITY AS A CATS FACTOR

The final factor that currently plays a role in our CATS strategy is the degree to which an industry's products are traded internationally. Sensitivity to both exchange rate movements and trade restrictions appears to have a substantial as well as independent impact on the returns to individual equities.[9]

Table 20.1
Industries' CATS Classification, Interest Rate Sensitivity, and Tradability

High-CATS

Industry			Industry		
Aerospace	RI	N	Retail/Composite	FI	N
Bond funds	FI	N	Retail/Food Chains	FI	N
Brewers	FI	T	Retail/Specialty	FI	N
Brokerage Firms	RI	N	S&L Assn. Holding Cos.	FI	T
Capital Goods	FI	T	Shoes	FI	T
Cement	RI	T	Soap	FI	T
Chemicals	FI	T	Soft Drinks	FI	N
Chemicals – Diversified	FI	T	Telephone Companies	FI	N
Computer Services	RI	N	Textiles – Products	FI	T
Computer & Business	RI	T	Textiles – Apparel mfg.	FI	T
Conglomerates	RI	N	Tobacco	FI	T
Cosmetics	FI	N	Toy Manufacturers	RI	T
Consumer Goods	FI	T			
Department Stores	FI	N	**Low-CATS**		
Distillers	FI	T	Air Freight	FI	T
Drug Stores	FI	N	Airlines	FI	T
Drugs	FI	T	Aluminum	RI	T
Electric Equipment	RI	T	Auto Parts/Aftermarket	FI	T
Electric – Major Companies	FI	T	Auto parts/Original Equipment	FI	T
Electric Power	FI	N	Auto Trucks & Parts	FI	T
Electronics/Defense	FI	N	Automobiles	FI	T
Electronics/Instruments	RI	T	Banks/NYC	FI	T
Electronics/semiconductors	RI	T	Banks/Outside NYC	FI	N
Entertainment	FI	N	Building Materials	FI	N
Foods	FI	T	Coal/Bituminious	RI	T
			Communication Equipment	FI	N

Industry	Interest	Dollar
Gaming Companies	FI	N
Gen. Merchandise Chains	FI	N
Health Composite	FI	N
Health/Diversified	FI	N
Health/Miscellaneous	FI	T
Homebuilding	FI	N
Hospital Management	RI	N
Hospital Supplies	FI	T
Hotels	FI	N
House Furnish/Appl.	FI	N
Insurance/Life	FI	N
Insur/Multi-Line	FI	N
Insurance/Prop/Casualty	FI	N
Investment Cos.	RI	T
Leisure	RI	N
Mfg. Housing	FI	N
Metal/Glass Containers	FI	T
Mobile Homes	FI	T
Newspapers	FI	N
Personal Loans	FI	N
Pollution Control	RI	T
Publishing	FI	N
Radio/TV Broadcasters	FI	N
Restaurants	FI	N
Goods	FI	T
FI	N	

Industry	Interest	Dollar
Containers/Paper	FI	N
Copper	RI	T
Fertilizer	RI	T
Forest Products	FI	T
Gold Mining	RI	T
Hardware	FI	N
Home Furnishings	RI	T
Machine Tools	RI	T
Machinery/Const.	RI	T
Machinery/Farm	RI	T
Machinery/Indust./Spec	RI	N
Metals/Misc.	RI	T
Nat. Gas Distrib/Pipe	RI	T
Oil/Can.Gas Explor.	RI	T
Oil/Crude Producer	RI	T
Oil/Domestic Integrated	RI	N
Oil/Integrated Intern.	RI	T
Oil/Offshore Drilling	RI	T
Oilwell Equip./Serv.	RI	T
Paper	FI	N
Railroads	RI	T
REIT	RI	N
Steel	RI	N
Sugar Refiners	RI	N
Tires & Rubber	RI	T
Truckers	RI	T

RI = Benefits from rising interest rates
FI = Benefits from falling interest rates

T = Benefits from a falling dollar
N = Benefits from a rising dollar

Traded goods are, just as the name would suggest, items that are traded in international markets.[10] We define traded goods industries as those industries which either import or export more than a trivial amount of their product. Measurement of the volume of trade on an industry-by-industry basis was based on the Department of Commerce's *National Income and Product Accounts* (NIPA). Unfortunately, the NIPA industrial categories do not exactly match the trial classifications that exist for stock prices. The correspondence of industrial classifications of stock prices with the NIPA groups is not identical.

Of the 59 HC industry groups, 36 were classified as nontraded goods industries, while 23 were classified as traded goods industries. Of the LC industry groups, 11 were nontraded and 27 were traded. The fact there was such an even distribution of traded and nontraded industries in each of the CATS categories suggests that a division of the CATS portfolios into traded and nontraded categories provides new information. Table 20.1 contains a listing of the various industry groups, their CATS classification, their interest rate sensitivity, and their tradability.

PORTFOLIO STRATEGY BASED ON MARKET FUNDAMENTALS

The overall economic environment helps determine the choice of stocks (Table 20.2). Depending on the outlook for tax rates, interest rates, and exchange rates, the portfolios are further refined to take advantage of changing trends in their macroeconomic factors. For example, if tax rates are expected to fall, the dollar

Table 20.2
Relationship between Market Fundamentals and Industry Group Selection, September 1981 to August 1987

Market Fundamentals	Outlook (Forecast)	Actual Performance	Recommendations
Tax rates	lower	personal income tax rate declined to 24%	HC
Oil prices	lower	-62.80%	HC
Dollar	stronger	-14 %	N
Interest rates	lower	-542 basis points	FI

Overall Recommendation HCNFI

A.B. Laffer Associates

is expected to appreciate, and interest rates are expected to decline, the industry group most favored would be the High-CATS non-traded portfolio that benefits from falling interest rates (HCNFI)(HC=High-CATS; N=non-traded; FI=falling interest rates). Similarly, the portfolio least favored in this environment would be the Low-CATS traded portfolio that benefits from rising interest rate (LCTRI).[11]

Identification of how macroeconomic shocks impact industry relative performance is a necessary condition but not a sufficient condition to ensure superior portfolio performance. One must also forecast the economic environment. A superior portfolio strategy is the joint result of the quality of the macroeconomic forecast and the validity of the incidence models.[12]

CATS AND REAGANOMICS

The CATS strategy has evolved over the last ten years. In fact, development of the CATS strategy came as a direct consequence of California's Proposition 13, the Steiger-Hansen capital gains tax rate reduction, the 1981 Reagan tax cuts, and the Tax Reform Act of 1986. It was our view then, as it is now, that such a radical change in economic policy will have widely divergent effects by industry. It is a natural extension of our supply-side perspective to address the issue of relative asset yields.

As we wrote in 1980:

The call for a 30 percent across-the-board reduction in personal income tax rates embodied in Presidential Nominee Ronald Reagan's acceptance speech makes certain that fiscal policy will be at the center of the economic debate. President Jimmy Carter's insistence that tax rate reductions now would be irresponsible assures that the debate will be an important element in the Presidential contest. Thus, the stage is set for a public referendum on the otherwise arcane distinctions between classical and Keynesian economic policies. Ironically, Reagan's policy prescriptions are akin to those espoused by "liberal" President John Kennedy and implemented between 1961 and 1965, and virtually opposite of the fiscal policies instituted under "conservative" President Richard Nixon and President Carter.[13]

In 1981, our outlook for the Reagan years was:

The era of income and capital gains tax cuts is here and now. On both empirical and theoretical grounds, tax rate cuts are associated with increased economic growth, increased savings, and increased equity values, lower rates of inflation, smaller budget deficits, and improved conditions for the poor. Arguments for increasing taxes on consumption and cutting taxes on business or investment to stimulate savings are fallacious. Savings is future consumption. Thus a "consumption tax" reduces savings. If growthist economic policy initiatives prevail, the highest marginal tax rate on any form of income will be 36 percent by the end of 1984; in an historical perspective, the 1980s will be viewed in the same light as the roaring '20s and early '60s.[14]

The Reagan bull market has been primarily fueled by the reduction in personal and business income tax rates, and the decontrol of energy prices. During the 1981–87 period, the real price of oil declined 62.80 percent. The foreign exchange value of the dollar rose to an index level of 134 in December 1984 from 92.41 in 1981, and then declined to 79.12 in 1987. On balance, during this period, the dollar has declined 14 percent. During 1981–87, the three-month T-bill yield has declined 542 basis points and the 10-year T-bond has declined 515 basis points. These policies provided an economic environment that strongly favored the High-CATS industries. The success of the Reagan-Volcker monetary policies also resulted in lower inflation.

Since the cornerstone of the Reagan economic policies was a tax rate reduction, the CATS classification was a primary screen in the development of a portfolio strategy. These results are consistent with the forecasts that we have made since 1980. These forecasts of the fundamentals imply that (Table 20.3):

1. High-CATS (HC) will outperform the market during the Reagan years. The Low-CATS (LC) will underperform the market during the Reagan years.

2. The industry groups that benefit from falling interest rates (FI) would outperform the industry groups that benefit from rising interest rates (RI).

3. The nontraded sector (N) industries will outperform the traded sector (T) industries.

4. Within the High-CATS groups, those industries that benefit from falling interest rates (HCFI) and a stronger dollar (HCN) should do even better than the entire HC category. The best performing group should be industries classified as High-CATS nontraded that benefit from falling interest rates (HCNFI).

5. Within the Low-CATS groups, those industries that benefit from rising interest rates (LCRI) and a weaker dollar (LCT) should underperform the market. The worst performing group should be Low-CATS industries that benefit from rising interest rates and a falling dollar (LCTRI).

In order to capture as closely as possible the Reagan bull market from trough to peak, the performance of the different portfolios has been calculated from

Table 20.3
Stock Price Index Performance, Percentage Change, September 1981 to August 1987

S&P 500	168.58 %
HC	237.72
LC	94.95
RI	59.37
FI	235.72
T	162.04
N	193.72

A.B. Laffer Associates

January 1981 to August 1987. Though the results clearly indicate a wide variation in the behavior of the various portfolios, these performance differentials
were as we predicted. This is evidence that, on average, the CATS strategy has
been able to identify the incidence of the different macroeconomic shocks.

HIGH-CATS VERSUS LOW-CATS INDUSTRY GROUPS

The High-CATS (HC) portfolio appreciated 237.72 percent during the 1981–
87 period (Table 20.3). In contrast, the S&P 500 appreciated 168.58 percent, and
the Low-CATS (LC) portfolio increased only 94.95 percent. As predicted by the
CATS strategy, the High-CATS portfolio outperformed the Low-CATS portfolio
and the overall stock market during this period.

RISING INTEREST RATES VERSUS FALLING INTEREST
RATES INDUSTRY GROUPS

Our forecast called for the industries benefiting from falling interest rates (FI)
to outperform those that benefited from rising interest rates (RI). During the
September 1981 to August 1987 period, industries benefiting from falling interest rates (FI) appreciated 235.72 percent versus 89.37 for the industry groups
benefiting from rising interest rates (RI).

TRADED VERSUS NON-TRADED INDUSTRY GROUPS

Our economic forecast also called for a stronger dollar. Since nontraded goods
industries benefit from a stronger dollar while traded goods industries are helped
by a weak dollar, our analysis predicted that the nontraded sector industries (N)
would outperform the traded sector industries (T).[15] That was, in fact, the case;
the nontraded sector (N) portfolio appreciated 193.72 percent versus 162.04
percent for the traded sector (T) industry portfolio (Table 20.3). The behavior of
the dollar explains why the performance differential is not as dramatic as for
other factors: The dollar rose during the early years of the Reagan administration,
but during the last two years the rise in the dollar was more than offset.

A MORE REFINED STRATEGY

Our outlook for lower tax rates and lower oil prices during the Reagan years
led us to favor the High-CATS (HC). Similarly, our outlook for lower interest
rates favored the falling interest rate (FI) group. Finally, our outlook for a higher
dollar led us to favor the nontraded sector industry group (N). A combination of
the three screens led to an overall recommendation of the HCNFI. The same
logic prompted us to select the LCTRI as the worst performing group during the
Reagan years.

The actual performance of our three-screen portfolios during the Reagan years
closely matched our predictions. Our selection for the period, the High-CATS

nontraded falling interest rates (HCNFI) portfolio, was the second best performer with a 240.68 percent appreciation. The best performing group was the High-CATS traded sector falling interest rates (HCTFI) which appreciated 270.07 percent (Figure 20.1). As expected, within High-CATS the worst performing portfolio was the industry group that benefited from a weaker dollar and rising interest rates (HCTRI); it appreciated only 171.81 percent. Another portfolio that underperformed the market was composed of industry groups that benefit from a rising dollar and rising interest rates (HCNRI). This portfolio appreciated only 179.06 percent.

The traded and nontraded screens did not appear materially to affect the differential performance. This is explained by the rise and fall of the dollar during the Reagan administration. This behavior of the dollar is consistent with our view that tax-induced terms of trade changes will have no lasting effect on the exchange rate. In contrast, monetary policy during Paul Volcker's tenure as Federal Reserve Chairman moved the United States in the direction of price stability and a concomitant decline in interest rates. It is not surprising to find interest rates to be a significant screen. The superior performance of the HCNFI and HCTFI, and the under performance of the HCNRI and HCTRI portfolio, indicates that the interest rate sensitivity screen greatly enhanced the refined CATS portfolios.

The Low-CATS, as predicted, underperformed the market. Low-CATS (LC) appreciated only 94.95 percent (Figure 20.1). The tradability and interest rate sensitivity screens identified further underperformers. The worst performer was the Low-CATS traded portfolio that benefits from rising interest rates, (LCTRI) portfolios, which declined 36.45 percent. The second worst performer was the Low-CATS nontraded portfolio that benefits from rising interest rates (LCNRI), which declined 50.02 percent.

Within the Low-CATS, the best performer was the traded sector portfolio that benefits from falling interest rates. The LCTFI group appreciated 191.72 percent, followed by the nontraded sector falling interest rate portfolio (LCNFI), which appreciated 157.77 percent. Once again, the result indicates that the interest rate sensitivity screen greatly enhances the refined CATS portfolio.

Interestingly, two of the most sophisticated Low-CATS portfolios, LCTFI and LCNFI, either outperformed the market or nearly equaled the performance of the S&P 500. These portfolios included the Low-CATS industries that benefit from falling interest rates. In contrast, two of the most sophisticated High-CATS portfolios that underperformed the market, HCNRI and HCTRI, were groups that benefit from rising interest rates.

The results show the importance of correctly identifying the economic environment. For HCNRI and HCTRI, the HC component captured the effect of the tax rate reductions which fueled part of the Reagan bull market, but the RI component excluded from the portfolio stocks that benefited from falling inflation and interest rates. Lower inflation and falling interest rates were the result of a monetary policy focused on price and interest rate stability. In turn, for the LCTFI and LCNFI portfolios, the LC component missed the tax rate effect while

Figure 20.1
CATS Performance, September 1981 to August 1987

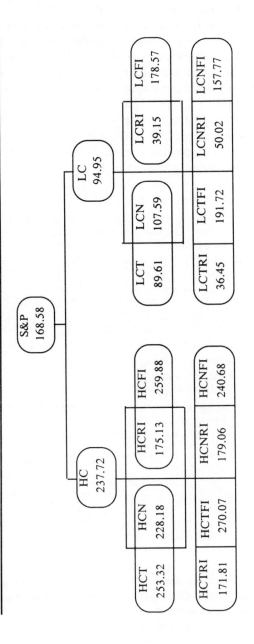

the FI component captured the monetary policy effect. Not surprisingly, the performance of these groups closely approximates the overall market return.

The evidence clearly suggests that proper identification of the overall economic environment (e.g., the tax rate and monetary policy effects) would result in the selection of the top performing portfolios (HCNFI and HCTFI) as well as the avoidance of the worst performing portfolios (LCTRI and LCNFI). In turn, incorrect identification of the overall economic environment would lead to the selection of the portfolios whose performance was not much different from that of the market (LCTFI, LCNFI, HCTRI, and HCNRI).

The fact that the best performing portfolios were HCNFI and HCTRI supports our view that the driving force behind the Reagan bull market was a tax rate reduction and the adoption of a monetary policy that moved the U.S. back to price and interest rate stability.

NOTES

1. Victor A. Canto, "The CAT'S Meow: A Portfolio Strategy for the Modified Flat Tax," *Financial Analysts Journal* 42, no. 1 (January/February 1986), pp. 26–29; Victor A. Canto, "The CAT'S Meow and the Stock Market," *Investment Study*, A. B. Laffer Associates, November 14, 1985; Victor A. Canto, "The Fat CAT'S Strategy for Portfolio Selection," *Financial Analysts Journal*, January/February 1987, pp. 43, 44–51; Victor A. Canto, "Fine-Tuning the CAT'S Meow," *Financial Analysts Journal*, November/December 1987, pp. 56–66; Victor A. Canto, "The CATS: Large and Small," *Investment Observation*, A. B. Laffer Associates, August 24, 1987; "Industry Classification Update," *Investment Observation*, A. B. Laffer Associates, September 25, 1987; "Redefining the CATS: Individual Stock Classification," *Investment Observation*, A. B. Laffer Associates, May 6, 1988.

2. Victor A. Canto, "The CAT'S Meow: A Portfolio Strategy for the Modified Flat Tax." The technique for selection and classification of stocks arose from numerous discussions among Charles Kadlec and ourselves.

3. Douglas H. Joines, "The Kennedy Tax Cuts," *Economic Study*, A. B. Laffer Associates, September 25, 1980.

4. Gerald Bollman, Victor Canto, and Kevin Melich, "Oil Decontrol: The Power of Incentives Could Reduce OPEC's Power to Boost Oil Prices," *Oil and Gas Journal* 80, no. 2 (January 11, 1982), pp. 92–101. Although not listed as authors, Charles Kadlec and Tom Nugent contributed greatly to the paper and should have been listed as authors.

5. Kevin Melich and Marc Reinganum, "A Historical Guide to the Bull Market of the Eighties," *Portfolio Strategies*, A. B. Laffer Associates, April 8, 1983.

6. Victor A. Canto, "The CAT'S Meow: A Portfolio Strategy for the Modified Flat Tax."

7. The interest rate sensitivity was initially reported in David F. England and Arthur B. Laffer, "Geronimo! The Case for a 400 Basis Point Plunge in Interest Rates," *Economic Study*, A. B. Laffer Associates, February 28, 1987.

8. Victor A. Canto and Truman A. Clark," Geronimo and the Stock Market," *Investment Observations*, A. B. Laffer Associates, May 14, 1987.

9. Numerous individual studies have been published documenting the effects of trade restrictions on individual industries: Victor A. Canto, Richard V. Eastin, and Arthur B.

Laffer, "The Failure of Protectionism: A Study of the Steel Industry, *Columbia Journal of World Business* 17, no. 4 (Winter 1982), pp. 43–57; Victor A. Canto and Arthur B. Laffer, "The Trade Weapon," A. B. Laffer Associates, October 4, 1983; Victor A. Canto, Richard V. Eastin, Charles W. Kadlec, and Arthur B. Laffer, "A High Road for the American Automobile Industry," *The World Economy* 8, no. 3 (September 1985), pp. 267–86; Gerald Bollman, Victor A. Canto and Kevin Melich, "Oil Decontrol the Power of Incentives"; Victor A. Canto and Charles W. Kadlec, "The Shape of Energy Markets to Come," *Public Utilities Fortnightly* 117, no. 1 (January 9, 1986), pp. 21–28. A summary of the effects of trade restrictions can be found in Victor A. Canto, J. Kimball Dietrich, Adish Jain, and Vishwa Mudaliar, "Protectionism and the Stock Market: The Determinants and Consequences of Trade Restrictions on the U.S. Economy," *Financial Analysts Journal* 42, no. 5 (September/October 1986), pp. 32–42.

10. The impact of real exchange rates on the economy is discussed in Arthur B. Laffer, "Minding Our Ps and Qs: Exchange Rates and Foreign Trade," *International Trade Journal* 1, no. 1 (Fall 1986), pp. 1–26; it was extended to industry performance in Victor A. Canto, "Exchange Rates and the Stock Market: Ps and Qs Meets the CATS," *Economic Study,* A. B. Laffer Associates, November 14, 1986.

11. For the purposes of this paper, the differences between HCI and HCII or LCI and LCII are not pertinent.

12. To the extent that there are lags in the relationships between economic events and equity performances, the incidence models by themselves could have value.

13. Arthur B. Laffer, "The 'Ellipse': An Explication of the Laffer Curve in a Two Factor Model," *Economic Study,* A. B. Laffer Associates, July 28, 1980.

14. Arthur B. Laffer, "Reagan's Economic Proposals Within a Supply-Side Framework, Testimony before the House Ways and Means Committee March 4, 1981," A. B. Laffer Associates, March 13, 1981.

15. Victor A. Canto, "Exchange Rate Changes and the Stock Market: The Ps and Qs Meets the CATS."

21

The Small-Cap and State Competitive Environment: 1989–90 Update

VICTOR A. CANTO AND ARTHUR B. LAFFER

People tend to move to where they can improve their standard of living. This supply-side tenet has long been ingrained when it comes to East European immigration to the West or Mexican immigration to the United States. But, when this concept combines with the "one man (*sic*) one vote" principle, the effects are explosive.

Population changes over the past decade projected onto the 1990 census suggest that the three biggest winners will be California, Texas, and Florida. Georgia and Arizona may also pick up as many as two congressional seats each. New York leads the list of losers followed closely by Pennsylvania, Illinois, Ohio, and Michigan.

States where taxes are high and/or increasing relative to the national norm tend to experience relative population declines. Likewise, in states where taxes are low or falling, population growth is often above average. Congressional seats are allocated to states according to population as measured by decadal census data. It therefore follows that state economic policies, in due course, help to determine political power. Some states are so small that even large changes in their relative tax burdens are not sufficient to warrant a change in their congressional delegations. Likewise, some states are so close to the national norm in tax policies that they, too, experience little change. And finally, while tax policies are important, other factors also play a significant role.

In spite of the myriad of qualifications inherent in this type of research, the results are promising. The state tax burden (i.e., state and local revenue collected per $100 of state personal income), as crude as that measure is, is used to gauge the level and changes in state tax policies relative to the nation. States with high and increasing tax burdens during the 1978–87 period—Wisconsin, Iowa, Minnesota, Ohio, Michigan, West Virginia, Kentucky and Illinois—are likely to lose congressional districts (Table 21.1). In contrast, states with low tax burdens— Texas, Florida, Georgia, and Virginia—are gaining congressional seats.

In the remaining states, the level and change in tax burden have opposing effects on the state competitive environment. For example, in California, taxes have fallen with a vengeance since 1978. In 1978, California ranked as the fourth highest tax rate state in the nation. Then along came Proposition 13 and the accompanying tax cuts. By 1987, California had fallen to the 16th highest tax

Table 21.1
State Competitive Environment and Reapportionment

State	Ranking of State and Local Tax Revenue per Hundred Dollars of Personal Income		Number of Congressional Seats
	FY 1978	FY 1987	
Wisconsin	7	7	- 1
Minnesota	8	5	- 1
Iowa	33	22	- 1
Ohio	49	29	- 2
Michigan	15	11	- 2
West Virginia	28	18	- 1
Kentucky	36	31	- 1
Illinois	34	32	- 2
Texas	43	43	+ 4 or 5
Florida	47	47	+ 3 or 4
Virginia	38	38	+ 1
Georgia	39	36	+ 1 or 2
California	4	16	+ 5 or 6
Arizona	6	12	+ 1 or 2
North Carolina	40	25	+ 1
New York	1	3	- 3 or 4
Massachusetts	5	13	- 1
Montana	11	21	- 1
Kansas	30	37	- 1
Pennsylvania	26	28	- 2 or 3

Sources: Bernadette A. Budde, "Decisions 1989, Census 1990: Politics 1992 and Beyond," A.B. Laffer, V.A. Canto & Associates (November 2, 1989; *Interstate Tax Comparisons and How They Have Changed Over Time*, Legislative Finance Paper #66, National Conference of State Legislatures, February 1989.

rate state. California could pick up as many as 6 congressional seats. With the possibility of a Republican governor and a centrist supreme court, California may well get rid of its outrageous gerrymandering. All told, California could increase the number of its Republican delegation by as many as ten people. Arizona, while less exaggerated, went from the 6th highest tax state in 1978 to the 12th highest in 1987. Arizona could pick up as many as 2 seats.

New York was number one in the tax "star search" for 1978. It was edged out in 1987 by Wyoming and Alaska and will lose three or four congressional seats resulting from the next census. With its recent politics, New York is obviously pleased with its record and determined to maintain its dubious distinction as the tax hero. Massachusetts is less clear-cut, having improved its relative position from 1978 to 1987 and yet still losing one seat. But with what we know as the Dukakis legacy, the voters foresee clearly what simple numbers partially obfuscate.

Pennsylvania appears the only true exception. It really isn't that bad on taxes as states go and yet it'll probably lose two seats. Maybe W. C. Fields' comments were more prophetic than anyone had heretofore thought. When taxes combine with democracy, Adam Smith merges with Charles Darwin. Not only do the anachronistic high tax states wither away in political influence, but progressive low tax states flourish. It boils down to only a matter of time.

THE FRAMEWORK

From a competitive point of view, changes in relative tax burdens among states are what matter. States lowering their relative burdens can be expected to experience accelerated economic growth, while those increasing their relative tax burdens should exhibit a slower pace of economic expansion.[1] Due to the connection between state and local tax policy and economic performance, the values of assets located in states that alter their tax policies will fluctuate in predictable directions. Assets will tend to become more valuable in states that are cutting tax rates while tax-rate increases will tend to depress asset values.

Every state that raises its tax burden above the national average will find it difficult to retain existing facilities and to attract new businesses. Mobile capital and labor will emigrate to seek higher after-tax returns in other states, and immobile factors of production will be left behind to bear the burden of the state and local taxes. Corporations with many plants or outlets in states that are increasing their relative tax burdens will fare poorly compared to companies with facilities concentrated in states that are reducing their relative tax burdens.

Consider two identical steel mills that are located forty miles apart: One mill is located in Kentucky, the other in Ohio. Since both steel mills sell virtually identical products in the U.S. market, competition will force them to sell their products at approximately the same price. Because the two steel facilities are only forty miles apart, they both have to pay the same after-tax wages to their employees and the same prices to their suppliers.

Given this situation, consider what would happen if Ohio doubled its income tax rate while Kentucky lowered its income tax rate. Because the steel market is highly competitive, the Ohio company would not be able to pass the tax hike on to its customers in the form of higher prices. Likewise, the Ohio company would not be able to pass the tax hike backward to its suppliers or employees. Initially, at least, the Ohio steel mill would have to absorb the tax increase through lower after-tax profits. This drop in profits would be reflected by a fall in the Ohio mill's stock price. Clearly, the mill in Kentucky would benefit in the short run.

To summarize, changes in tax rates have different effects depending on the mobility of factors of production:

- The quantities and pretax prices of mobile factors within a state will change so that their after-tax rates of return are unchanged.
- The quantities and pretax rates of return of factors that cannot leave a state will have their after-tax rates of return altered.

The investment implications of these observations are straightforward: Buy the stocks of companies located in states that are lowering tax rates and sell the stocks of companies in states that are raising tax rates. As simple as this strategy is, it is difficult to apply in practice because most major corporations operate in many states and, perhaps, in several countries. Thus, the impact of a particular state's tax changes on the values of the stocks of multistate corporations may be relatively minor.

An investment strategy based on changes in the state competitive environment may be even more rewarding if it is applied to small companies. The operations of small companies are more likely to be concentrated in one or a few states, and small companies typically are less able to pass tax-rate changes forward to consumers or backward to suppliers. Thus, changes in states' relative tax burdens may have more pronounced effects on the after-tax returns and stock market performances of small corporations. The negative relationship between relative tax burden and economic growth combined with knowledge of enacted and proposed tax legislation can be used to forecast the states most likely to gain or lose competitiveness.[2]

PORTFOLIO STRATEGY

Changes in state and local taxes can be used to develop a portfolio strategy. This strategy requires the identification of changes in state tax policies and the identification of producers who are unable to pass state and local taxes forward or backward. Under ideal circumstances, the strategy would be applied to companies having all their production facilities located in one state. Few companies with publicly traded securities satisfy this requirement. As an alternative, the strategy can be applied to the stocks of small-capitalization companies. Small-cap corporations are more likely to have their operations concentrated in one or a few states. It also is likely that small companies are less able to pass tax-rate changes forward or backward. Thus, state taxes may be relatively more important for small-cap stocks than for large-cap stocks.

Estimates of the changes in states' relative tax burden for 1988 (FY 1989) are reported in Table 21.2.[3] The changes in tax burden have been used to forecast the relative performance of the various states. The stocks examined are those of companies in the lowest market-value decile of the New York and American stock exchanges. For each of these small-cap companies, an attempt was made to locate the corporate headquarters.[4] The procedure identified 261 companies.

Table 21.2
Relative Change in FY 1989 Tax as a Percent of 1987 State and Local Tax Revenue

Top 25 States			Bottom 25 States		
State	Increase in State Taxes*	Increase in State Taxes Relative to the U.S. Average**	State	Increase in State Taxes*	Increase in State Taxes Relative to the U.S. Average**
South Dakota	-4.25	-4.63	Wyoming	0	-0.38
Utah	-2.93	-3.31	California	0	-0.38
Kansas	-1.50	-1.88	Ohio	0	-0.38
Vermont[1]	-1.45	-1.84	Michigan	0	-0.38
Delaware	-0.97	-1.36	Arkansas	0	-0.38
Wisconsin	-0.64	-1.02	New Hampshire	0.07	-0.31
Connecticut[1]	-0.62	-1.00	Illinois	0.09	-0.29
Hawaii	-0.24	-0.62	Missouri	0.17	-0.21
Florida	-0.17	-0.55	Tennessee	0.50	0.12
Oklahoma	-0.15	-0.53	Washington	0.55	0.16
North Carolina	-0.11	-0.49	Maine	0.57	0.19
Maryland	-0.05	-0.43	New Jersey	0.62	0.24
Virginia	-0.04	-0.42	Indiana	0.64	0.26
Alaska	0	-0.38	Kentucky	0.89	0.51
Mississippi	0	-0.38	Massachusetts	0.93	0.55
Georgia[1]	0	-0.38	Oregon	1.05	0.67
New York	0	-0.38	Idaho	1.11	0.72
Alabama	0	-0.38	Iowa	1.36	0.98
Colorado	0	-0.38	North Dakota	1.40	1.02
Montana	0	-0.38	Texas	2.25	1.87
South Carolina	0	-0.38	New Mexico	2.29	1.91
Nebraska	0	-0.38	Minnesota	2.56	2.18
Rhode Island	0	-0.38	West Virginia	3.17	2.79
Nevada	0	-0.38	Arizona	3.52	3.14
Pennsylvania	0	-0.38	Louisiana	5.85	5.47

* Fiscal year 1989 tax increases as a percent of 1988 state and local tax revenue.
** The U.S. average tax increase for FY 1989 is .38 percent.

Source: "State Budget Actions in 1988", Legislative Finance Paper #59, National Conference of State Legislatures, Denver, Colorado, September 1988.

[1] Although at the time of publication these states were not planning to raise their taxes during the fiscal year, they did.

A.B. Laffer, V.A. Canto & Associates

Small-cap companies headquartered in the states with declining relative tax burdens are in the "buy" portfolio and companies based in states with rising relative tax burdens are in the "sell" portfolio. The 1988 results are consistent with earlier results.[5]

One possible screen to be used in the selection process is the change in absolute tax burden. This will reflect directly on the absolute profitability of the companies located within the states. Thus, the screen would tend to identify the companies that would have an absolute appreciation in their stock prices. Unfortunately, only 31 stocks were located in the category located in states for which the tax burden was declining in absolute terms, making the sample too small to provide a reliable estimate.

Another possible screen to be used in the selection process and reported in the study is the change in relative tax burden. This screen identifies companies that would have an above-average appreciation in stock performance. However, if, on average, stock prices decline, this would not ensure positive stock returns; it would only provide above market-average returns. The relative performance of the stocks is consistent with our framework. As of November 7, 1989, the stock of the 261 companies in the sample declined 8.73 percent (Table 21.3). One hundred seventy stocks were located in states with declining relative tax burdens; this portfolio decreased an average of 7.55 percent (Table 21.3). In contrast, the portfolio of 91 stocks located in states with a rising relative tax burden declined 10.93 percent. The differential performance is clearly discernible. The small companies located in states with declining relative tax burdens outperformed the portfolio of companies located in states with rising relative tax burdens by 3.38 percent. The only puzzling result is that, as a whole, the portfolio declined in value 8.73 percent. Although small caps have underperformed larger caps, smaller cap indexes such as NASDAQ have increased during the year. One

Table 21.3
Stock Performance Using Relative Tax Burden Screens, December 1, 1988 to November 7, 1989

	Price Appreciation	Number of Stocks
Small capitalization stocks in states with declining relative tax burdens	-7.55	170
Small capitalization stocks in states with rising relative and absolute tax burdens	-10.93	91
Small capitalization stocks combined	-8.73	261

possible explanation is that the stock considered are the smallest capitalization stocks and those are most sensitive to the deterioration of the high yield bond market and the failure of capital gains tax rate legislation to pass.

STATE TAX CHANGES IN 1989 (FOR FY 1990)

The effects of the rounds of tax rate reductions are still being felt at the state level.[6] These effects are two-faced. First, in forty states, the federal tax rate reduction has resulted in stronger economic growth than anticipated by state economic forecasts. As a result, revenue collections in 1989 were larger than projected. In 10 states—Connecticut, Florida, Massachusetts, New Hampshire, New Jersey, New York, Rhode Island, Tennessee, West Virginia, and Wyoming—revenue collections were lower than projected. Eight of these states had been identified as states in which the tax burden was not declining.[7] Second, the larger than anticipated revenue collection will have a magnified effect on the states' ending balances inclusive of rainy day funds.

The surge in revenues in the majority of the states may further affect future revenue projections. Forecasting mistakes could easily be made if substitution effects that we have emphasized are not taken into account. Many states experienced a revenue windfall as a result of the 1986 tax reform act. The 1987 increase in the top capital gains tax rate to 28 percent from 20 percent provided investors with strong incentives to realize capital gains in 1986. Incentives to realize capital gains also existed for individuals in brackets below the top rate. Recognizing the power of these incentives, we predicted a one-time surge in capital gains tax revenues as taxable investors acted to beat the increases in capital gains tax rates.[8]

A surge in capital gains tax revenues was experienced by the states and by the federal government prior to the higher 28 percent rate becoming effective. Other economists failed to foresee this huge increase in capital gains tax receipts in 1987. Doubting that a one-time opportunity to reduce taxes could have such a pronounced effect, they compounded their original error by assuming that the "surprise" increase in tax collections was a permanent development. This led them to project higher capital gains tax revenues far into the next decade. Since the special incentives to realize capital gains in 1986 and thereby pay the taxes in 1987 were only temporary, the projected revenues did not materialize. As a result, a number of states were projecting revenue shortfalls and/or precarious ending balances in their rainy day funds. California is a prime example. In 1988, the state had a large shortfall in personal income tax revenues because of forecasting errors.[9] This led to a small deficit, and the state forecasted the possibility of another deficit in 1989. Similar stories were told in the Northeast, in particular, in Massachusetts.

The policy options available to states to correct their projected fiscal budget problems include a reduction in spending below the level originally appropriated, or an increase in state taxes. Tax actions will alter the states' competitive environment. Unlike the northeastern states, California considered but did not increase tax rates. In the interim, the rate reduction to a top federal personal income tax rate of 28 percent became fully effective. The overall economy grew more than expected, and, as a consequence, so did California's revenue collection. In contrast, the Northeastern states increased their effective tax rates, and their relative performance declined. For the first time since the beginning of the recovery, the Northeast did not lead the nation in real economic growth.

The root of the Northeast problem can be traced to their lack of understanding of the incentive effects. The federal tax rate reduction resulted in an overall U.S. expansion and in unexpected revenue collection. However, the states failed to realize that, once the tax rate reductions were in place, the pace of economic growth would settle to a sustainable steady growth. The states' forecast neglected this fact and the overly optimistic growth estimates resulted in equally optimistic revenue projections. The lack of understanding of the impact of relative tax burden on the state competitive environment has led the state policy makers to compound their mistakes. In response to the slower than projected growth in state economic activity and tax revenues, the Northeast states have reacted by raising tax rates. These increases in state tax burden will result in further deterioration of their state economic performance.

The experiences of California, Massachusetts, Connecticut, and New Jersey illustrate the rapidity with which a state's economic fortunes and outlook can change. It also illustrates how traditional analysis that ignores incentive effects and the state competitive environment may lead to policy recommendations, such as tax rate increases, that will further impair the states' economic performance.

The California experience also illustrates the effect of spending limitations on state fiscal policy. During the FY 1989 projected shortfall, California considered raising taxes. However, a number of factors quickly led to the abandonment of the idea. One factor was the possible backlash from the voters and another was the Gann spending limitation. If slower growth materialized, even if revenues were collected, there was the possibility that the Gann spending limitation would become binding. Therefore, spending controls became the only viable option. The whole issue became moot as revenues exceeded projections.

The incident illustrates how the spending limitation weakened the case for an unnecessary tax increase. The issue has not been lost to California politicians, who have attempted to modify the spending limitations. In each instance, the voters have turned down the initiatives. It appears that the political tide may be changing in California. Largely as a result of the San Francisco earthquake, California has enacted a temporary sales tax increase and there is talk of removing some public expenditures from the Gann limits.

Overall, 1989 was an lively year for state actions. The static revenue effects of the tax changes enacted in 1989 are estimated to be $4.7 billion. The only other years in this decade where there were similar increases were 1983 and 1987. However, the economic conditions were vastly different. Both 1983 and 1987 were transition years for implementation of the Reagan tax rate cuts of 1981 and 1986. Once these rate reductions became effective, the national economy grew at a rate faster than predicted by conventional economic models that ignored the substitution effects induced by the phaseins. Not surprisingly to a supply-sider, once the tax rates became effective, economic activity and state revenue collection were larger than projected. In 1989, forty states had larger than projected revenue collections. Collectively, these states have the dubious distinction of reversing the previous economic policies that resulted in a reduction in effective tax rates relative to the rest of the United States. The effect of the new economic policies at the state level will be to raise the relative tax burden and, as a consequence, lower the Northeast's competitive environment.

The bulk of state actions in 1983 and 1987 was, in part, to offset the static revenue effects of federal tax reform. However, the situation is much different in 1989. No federal tax rate changes are contemplated; therefore, state actions will represent a net change in state competitive environment. The overall increase represents an increase in the cost of doing business in the United States and a reduction in the overall competitiveness of the U.S. economy. Since the actions differ across states, the competitive environment and relative economic performance will also be affected.

Eight states had serious problems at the end of fiscal 1989. Alabama, Arkansas, Kentucky, Louisiana, Massachusetts, New York, North Carolina, and Wyoming ended the fiscal year with balances below 1 percent of spending. For 1990, Wyoming is projecting a deficit. In addition, Alabama, Arkansas, Iowa, Kentucky, Louisiana, Massachusetts, Missouri, New York, North Carolina, South Dakota, Texas, Virginia, and West Virginia are anticipating balances below 1 percent of spending.

Many states have balanced budget provisions that limit their fiscal policy options. These provisions force states either to alter their expenditures or tax rates whenever a shortfall in revenue is anticipated. Currently, 38 states maintain "rainy day" funds or revenue stabilization funds or reserves. Restrictions are placed on the use of rainy day funds, but the funds offer some potential for "smoothing" changes in state tax rates. The twelve states without rainy day funds are Arizona, Arkansas, Hawaii, Illinois, Kansas, Louisiana, Montana, Nevada, North Carolina, Oregon, South Dakota, and West Virginia.

Several states have spent down their rainy day funds in fiscal 1989 because of budget problems: Connecticut, Florida, Massachusetts, Minnesota, and Wyoming exhausted large portions of their funds. Of the eighteen states that have tax expenditure limitations currently in force, Oregon, Tennessee, and Texas were affected by them in 1989.

Personal Income Taxes

Connecticut, Illinois, Massachusetts, Montana, North Dakota, and Vermont broadly increased their state personal income taxes. The tax increases were temporary. In one state, Vermont, the increase was the result of a lapse in a temporary tax rate decrease. Five states reduced income taxes—Hawaii, Kansas, Maine, Nebraska and South Carolina. There is some question as to whether New York will follow Massachusetts with the last installment of its tax rate cut. Iowa increased the capital gains tax and enacted an earned income tax credit. Although the effect is estimated to be revenue neutral, the changes will result in an increase in the effective marginal tax rate in Iowa. As a result of the Supreme Court decision *Davis v. Michigan,* eleven states changed the treatment of state and federal programs—Arizona, Colorado, Iowa, Missouri, North Dakota, Oklahoma, Oregon, South Carolina, Virginia, West Virginia, and Wisconsin.

Corporate Income Taxes

Connecticut, Illinois, Missouri, Montana, and Rhode Island increased corporate income taxes.

Sales Taxes

Five states increased sales taxes, but only in Louisiana and West Virginia were the increases significant. Massachusetts and Arizona broadened their tax base. Three states enacted minor reductions in the sales tax—South Dakota, Kansas, and Minnesota. Illinois imposed a tax on photo finishing.

Motor Fuels Taxes

Nine states increased motor fuel taxes—Arizona, Idaho, Indiana, Iowa, Kentucky, Maine, Minnesota, South Dakota, and Tennessee. Four states implemented previously enacted increases—Connecticut, New Jersey, Nevada, and Oregon. Four states increased their tax rates according to a formula—Nebraska, New Mexico, Ohio, and Wisconsin. Only in one state, North Carolina, did the formula result in a reduction in motor fuel taxes.

THE COMPETITIVE ENVIRONMENT FOR FY 1990

Changes in the state competitive environment are predicted based upon the change in each state's tax burden relative to the average of all states. Changes in tax burdens reflect the effects of federal tax reform as well as state tax rate changes. Based on tax changes enacted for FY 1990, states can be classified into one of two groups:

1. *States Gaining Competitiveness:* Gains in relative economic performance are expected in states with declining relative tax burdens in FY 1990. Recent tax changes point to Hawaii, Maine, Maryland, Texas, and Wisconsin as the states most likely to gain in competitiveness this year (Table 21.4).

Table 21.4

Relative Change in FY 1990 Tax as a Percent of 1987 State and Local Tax Revenue*

| | Top 25 States | | | Bottom 25 States | |
State	Increase in State Taxes**	Increase in State Taxes Relative to the U.S. Average***	State	Increase in State Taxes**	Increase in State Taxes Relative to the U.S. Average***
Hawaii	-0.26 %	-0.41 %	New Hampshire	0.06 %	-0.09%
Wisconsin	-0.25	-0.41	Washington	0.07	-0.08
Texas	-0.11	-0.26	New Mexico	0.08	-0.08
Utah	-0.09	-0.24	Oregon	0.09	-0.07
Maine	-0.06	-0.21	Colorado	0.11	-0.04
Maryland	-0.04	-0.19	Missouri	0.12	-0.04
Iowa	-0.02	-0.17	Wyoming	0.12	-0.03
Michigan	0.00	-0.16	California	0.14	-0.01
Alabama	0.00	-0.16	Ohio	0.16	0.00
Virginia	0.00	-0.16	New York	0.16	0.01
Idaho	0.00	-0.16	Tennessee	0.18	0.02
Indiana	0.00	-0.16	Montana	0.18	0.02
Delaware	0.00	-0.16	Arizona	0.18	0.03
Kentucky	0.00	-0.16	Nevada	0.26	0.10
South Dakota	0.00	-0.16	Vermont	0.32	0.16
Louisiana	0.00	-0.16	Pennsylvania	0.32	0.16
Oklahoma	0.00	-0.16	Rhode Island	0.34	0.18
South Carolina	0.00	-0.15	North Carolina	0.37	0.22
Nebraska	0.01	-0.14	Massachusetts	0.41	0.26
Arkansas	0.02	-0.14	Illinois	0.48	0.32
Florida	0.03	-0.12	Georgia	0.68	0.52
Minnesota	0.04	-0.12	North Dakota	0.77	0.62
Mississippi	0.05	-0.10	Connecticut	1.01	0.86
New Jersey	0.06	-0.10	West Virginia	1.42	1.27
Kansas	0.06	-0.10	Alaska	1.69	1.53

* The burden is calculated as the static revenue change generated by the tax action divided by the state personal income first quarter of 1989 at an annual rate.

*** The U.S. average tax burden for FY 1990 is .13 percent.

Source: *Survey of Current Business*, U.S. Department of Commerce, Bureau of Economic Analysis.

A.B. Laffer, V.A. Canto & Associates

2. *States Losing Competitiveness:* A state that has raised its tax burden above the national average will find it more difficult to retain existing facilities and to attract new businesses. Recent tax changes point to Alaska, Connecticut, Georgia, Illinois, Massachusetts, North Carolina, North Dakota, Rhode Island, and West Virginia as the states most likely to become less competitive (Table 21.4).

INVESTMENT IMPLICATIONS

The investment implications of this analysis are straightforward: buy the stocks of companies located in states experiencing a decline in their absolute and relative tax burdens and sell the stocks of companies in states expecting an

Table 21.5
States with Declining Absolute and Relative Tax Burdens

State

Hawaii
Maine
Maryland
Texas
Utah
Wisconsin

A.B. Laffer, V.A. Canto & Associates

Table 21.6
Small Cap Companies with Headquarters Located in States with Declining Absolute and Relative Tax Burdens

Ticker Symbol	Company Name	Ticker Symbol	Company Name
AE	Adams Res & Energy Inc	KEC	Kent Electronics Corp
ACT	American Centy Corp	KMW	KMW Systems Corp
A	American Med Bldgs Inc	LHC	L & N Hsg Corp
AHI	Amern Healthcare Mgmt Inc	LQP	La Quinta Mtr Inns Ltd
BMI	Badger Meter Inc	LAN	Lancer Corp Tex
BTX	Banctexas Group Inc	LFC	Lomas Financial Corp
BFO	Baruch Foster Corp	M	Mcorp
BSN	BSN Corp	NHR	National Heritage
BFX	Buffton Corp	NRM	NRM Energy Co L P
CND	Caspen Oil	OMD	Ormand Inds Inc
CXV	Cavalier Homes Inc	PSD	Penobscot Shoe Co
CDC	Compudyne Corp	PNL	Penril Corp
LLB	Computrac Inc	PTG	Portage Inds Corp Del
CEP	Convest Energy Prnrs Ltd	RGL	Regal Intl Inc
DRL	DI Inds Inc	RMI	Residential Mtg Invts Inc
DNA	Diana Corp	SMN	Seamans Corp
EM	Entertainment Mkting Inc	SEI	Seitel Inc
ESI	ESI Inds Inc	QSM	Southmark Corp
FFP	FFP Partners	SWL	Southwest Rlty Ltd
FRD	Friedman Inds Inc	SEC	Sterling Electrs Corp
JIT	Frozen Food Express Inds Inc	SBN	Sunbelt Nursery Group
GHO	General Homes Corp	TMI	Team Inc
GWA	Greater Washington Invs Inc	TEL	Telecom Corp
HII	Healthcare Intl Inc	THR	Thor Energy Resources Inc
HNW	Hein Werner Corp	TWP	Two Pesos Inc
RTH	Houston Oil Rty Tr	UPK	United Park Mining
ITG	Integra-A Hotel & Restaurant	WBC	Westbridge Cap Corp
PWR	International Pwr Machs Corp	HBW	Wolf Howard B Inc

Table 21.7
States with Unchanged Absolute Burden and Declining Relative Tax Burden

State

Alabama
Delaware
Idaho
Indiana
Iowa
Kentucky
Louisiana
Michigan
Oklahoma
South Carolina
South Dakota
Virginia

A.B. Laffer, V.A. Canto & Associates

increase in absolute and relative tax burdens. This strategy should be applied to small-cap companies because they are likely to have operations concentrated in one or a few states. The performance of a state-based portfolio strategy may be enhanced by taking into consideration the January effect.[10]

Companies located in states with declining absolute and relative tax burdens are expected to experience an above-average absolute price appreciation. A list of states with declining absolute and relative tax burdens is reported in Table

Table 21.8
Small Cap Companies with Headquarters Located in States with Unchanged Absolute Burden and Declining Relative Tax Burden

Ticker Symbol	Company Name	Ticker Symbol	Company Name
BOF	Bank San Francisco Hldg Del	LSB	LSB Inds Inc
CHR	Champion Enterprises	NEI	National Enterprises Inc Ind
CMX	CMI Corporation	NSD	National Std Co
CDM	Crowley Milner & Co	NEW	Newcor Inc
FFS	First Federal Bancorp Inc Del	PPD	Pre Paid Legal Svcs Inc
FRL	Forum Retirement Prtnrs L P	ROW	Rowe Furniture Corp
HX	Halifax Engr Inc	SDV	Sandy Corp
HMF	Hastings Mfg Co	SST	Shelter Components Corp
HNF	Hinderliter Inds	SKN	Skolniks Inc
HOW	Howell Inds Inc	URT	USP Real Estate Invt Tr
IVT	Iverson Technology Corp	VSR	Versar Inc
KIN	Kinark Corp	WAC	Wells Amern Corp
HYU	Lilly Eli & Co	UPB	Wiener Enterprises Inc

Table 21.9
States with Rising Absolute and Relative Tax Burdens

State

Alaska
Arizona
Connecticut
Georgia
Illinois
Massachusetts
Montana
Nevada
New York
North Carolina
North Dakota
Ohio
Pennsylvania
Rhode Island
Tennessee
Vermont
West Virginia

A.B. Laffer Associates

21.5. A list of small-cap companies with headquarters located in those states is reported in Table 21.6.

Companies located in states with unchanged absolute tax burdens are not expected to be significantly affected by the state's fiscal policy. To the extent that the state's relative tax burden is declining, the stock price performance of companies located in those states will experience above-average price appreciation. However, the price appreciation will be lower than that of companies located in states with declining absolute and relative tax burdens. Table 21.7 lists the states with unchanged absolute and declining relative tax burdens. Table 21.8 lists the small-cap companies with headquarters located in those states.

Companies located in states with rising absolute and relative tax burdens are likely to underperform. Table 21.9 lists the states with rising absolute and relative tax burdens, while Table 21.10 lists the small-cap companies with headquarters located in those states.

Table 21.10
Small Cap Companies with Headquarters Located in States with Rising Absolute and Relative Tax Burdens

Ticker Symbol	Company Name	Ticker Symbol	Company Name
ACU	Acme Utd Corp	CHP	Charter Por Sys Inc
ACI	Action Inds Inc	CVR	Chicago Rivet & Mach Co
ATN	Action Corp	CLG	Clabir Corp
AEE	Aileen Inc	CGN	Cognitronics Corp
AIM	Aim Tels Inc	CFK	Comfed Bancorp
AXO	Alamco Inc	CPT	Compumat Inc
AWS	Alba Haldensian Inc	CIS	Concord Fabrics Inc
AFN	Alfin Frangrances Inc	CON	Connelly Containers Inc
AG	Allegheny Intl Inc	KCS	Conston Corp
AHA	Alpha Inds Inc	CNY	Continental Information Sys
ABL	American Biltrite Inc	CUO	Continental Matls Corp
AZE	American Maize Prods Co	DEP	Damson Energy Co LP
ASE	American Science & Engr Inc	DXR	Daxor Corp
AHR	American Hotels & Rlty Corp	DSG	Designatronics Inc
AHH	Amerihealth Inc Del	DJI	Designcraft Inds Inc
AMK	Amer Tech Ceramic Corp	DVH	Divi Hotels NV
AIS	Ampal Amern Israel Corp	DSR	Dresher Inc
ADL	Andal Corp	EAC	EAC Inds Inc
AND	Andrea Radio Corp	EAG	Eagle Finl Corp
AZB	Arizona Comm Bk Tuscon	EML	Eastern Co
AZL	Arizona Land Income Corp	EB	Ehrlich Bober Finl Corp
RK	Ark Restaurants Corp	ESG	Electrosound Group Inc
ART	Armatron Intl Inc	ELS	Elsinore Corp
AI	Arrow Automotive Inds Inc	EHP	Emerald Homes LP
ASI	Astrex Inc	EOA	Empire of Amer Fed Svgs Bk NY
AIX	Astrotech Intl Corp New	EGX	Engex Inc
AVA	Audio Video Affiliates Inc	ESP	Espey Mfg & Electrs Cjorp
VOX	Audiovox Corp	EE	Esquire Radio & Electrs Inc
BAL	Baldwin Secs Corp	FNF	Fidelity Natl Finl Corp
BPI	Bamberger Polymers Inc	FCO	First Conn Small Business In
BIS	Barrister Information Sys Cp	FCR	Firstcorp Inc
BAS	Basix Corp	FIS	Fischbach Corp
BAY	Bay Finl Corp	FPI	Fountain Pwr Boat Inds Inc
BBE	Belden & Blake Energy Co	FPO	FPA Corp
BLV	Belvedere Corp	FKL	Franklin Hldg Corp
BKY	Berkey Inc	FRV	Fur Vault Inc
BET	Bethlehem Corp	GRR	GRI Corp
BPH	Biopharmaceutics Inc	JOB	General Employment Enterprise
BNP	Boddie Noell Restaurant Ppty	GWH	General Housewares Corp
BOM	Bowmar Instr Corp	GMW	General Microwave Corp
BUE	Buell Inds Inc	GFB	GF Corp
CCX	CCX Inc	GHM	Graham Corp
CGL	Cagles Inc	GFI	Graham Field Health Prods
CD	Canandaigua Wine Inc	HWG	Hallwood Group Inc
CGE	Carriage Industries Inc	HDG	Halsey Drug Inc
CGR	Chariot Group Inc	HU	Hampton Utilities Tr

Table 21.10 (*continued*)

HRA	Harvey Group Inc	PLR	Plymouth Rubr Inc
HMI	Health Mor Inc	PNU	Pneumatic Scale Corp
HCH	Health-Chem Corp	POR	Portec Inc
H	Helm Res Inc	PDL	Presidential Rlty Corp New
HIP	Hipotronics Inc	PFP	Prime Finl Partners LP
HOF	Hofmann Inds Inc	PCE	Professional Care Inc
HFS	Home Owners Svgs Bk FSB	PUL	Publicker Inds Inc
HS	Hopper Soliday Corp	RBW	RB & W Corp
HZN	Horizon Corp	RAY	Raytech Corp
HGC	Hudson Gen Corp	RRF	Realty Refund Tr
IRE	Integrated Res Inc	RSI	Realty South Invs Inc
INP	Intelligent Sys Masters LP	RCE	Reece Corp
IBL	Iroquois Brands Ltd	BRX	Response Technologies Inc
ISI	ISS Intl Svc Sys Inc	RDI	River Oaks Inc
JLN	Jaclyn Inc	RMS	RMS Intl Inc
JET	Jetronic Inds Inc	RMK	Robert Mark Inc
JPC	Johnson Prods Inc Del	RR	Rodman & Renshaw Cap Group
KWN	Kenwin Shops Inc	RYR	Rymer Foods Inc
KCH	Ketchum & Co Inc	SBS	Salem Corp
KVU	Kleer Vu Inds Inc	SLS	Selas Corp Amer
LSA	Landmark Svgs Assn Pittsburg	SRC	Service Res Corp
LKI	Lazare Kaplan Intl Inc	SVT	Servotronics Inc
LPO	Linpro Specified Pptys	SFM	SFM Corp
LRC	Lori Corp	SHD	Sherwood Group Inc
LVI	LVI Group Inc	SIA	Signal Apparel Inc
MNH	Manufactured Homes Inc	SRG	Sorg Inc
MXC	Matec Corp	SBM	Speed O Print Business Mach
MW	Matthews & Wright Group Inc	SPR	Sterling Cap Corp
MRI	McRae Inds Inc	SUW	Struthers Wells Corp
MCH	Med-Chem Prods Inc	TOC	Tech Ops Sevcon Inc
MGP	Merchants Group Inc	TCC	Teleconcepts Corp
MBC	Mickelberry Corp	TDD	Three D Depts Inc
PMR	Micron Prods Inc	TI	TII Inds Inc
MMD	Moore Med Corp	TNZ	Tranzonic Companies
MR	Morgans Foods Inc	TRSG	Triangle Corp
MSM	Motts Hldgs Inc	THP	Triangle Home Prods Inc
MSR	MSR Expl Ltd	TDX	Tridex Corp
MYR	Myers L E Co Group	UFD	United Foods Inc
NAN	Nantucket Inds Inc	UMM	United Merchants & Mfrs Inc
NAS	Nasta International Inc	UNV	Unitel Video Inc
NMS	National Mine Svc Co	UBN	University Bk Natl Assn
NSO	New American Shoes Inc	VRE	Vermont Resh Inc
NZ	New Mexico & Ariz Ld Co	VTK	Viatech Inc
XTX	New York Tx Exmpt Income Fd	VII	Vicon Inds Inc
NLI	Newmark & Lewis Inc	VDT	Voplex Corp
NCL	Nichols S E Inc	VTX	VTX Electrs Corp
NSB	Northeast Svgs Conn Hartford	WID	Wean Utd Inc
NUH	NU Horizons Electrs Corp	WDG	Wedgstone Fincl
NNM	Nuveen NY Muni Income Fd Inc	WC	Weiman Inc
OH	Oakwood Homes Corp	WLC	Wellco Enterprises Inc
OAR	Ohio Art Co	WGA	Wells Gardner Electrs Corp
OLP	One Liberty Pptys Inc	WAE	Wilfred Amern EDL Corp
PPI	Pico Prods Inc	WAE	Winston Res Inc
PAE	Pioneer Sys Inc	ZMX	Zemex Corp
PW	Pittsburgh & W Va RR		

NOTES

1. Victor A. Canto and Robert I. Webb, "The Effect of State Fiscal Policy on State Relative Economic Performance," *Southern Economic Journal* 54, no. 1 (July 1987); and Victor A. Canto, Charles W. Kadlec and Arthur B. Laffer, "The State Competitive Environment, A. B. Laffer Associates, August 8, 1984.

2. Victor A. Canto and Arthur B. Laffer, "A Not-So-Odd Couple: Small-Cap Stocks and the State Competitive Environment," A. B. Laffer Associates, June 24, 1988.

3. Victor A. Canto, "Small Cap and State Competitive Environment: 1988–89 Update," A. B. Laffer Associates, December 15, 1988. At the time of the publication, Connecticut was projected to lower its tax burden. However, that was not the case; taxes were increased during 1989.

4. Stocks listed on the NYSE and AMEX are ranked by capitalization. The stocks in the bottom 10 percent (decile) constitute our sample of small-cap stocks. The locations of the corporate headquarters of the small-cap corporations were identified by consulting Standard and Poor's *Corporate Register,* Standard and Poor's *Stock Reports,* and Dun and Bradstreet's *Million Dollar Directory.*

5. Canto and Laffer, "A Not-So-Odd Couple," 1988.

6. This section draws heavily from "State Budget Actions in 1989; Legislative Finance Paper #69," September 1989; and "Fiscal Survey of the State," September 1989.

7. These estimates were originally reported in V. A. Canto, "The State Competitive Environment: 1987–88 Update," 1988.

8. Truman A. Clark, "When to Realize Capital Gains," A. B. Laffer Associates, September 26, 1986; Victor A. Canto, "Substitution Effects: Perilous to Ignore," A. B. Laffer Associates, June 9, 1988. See also Chapter 9.

9. Canto, "Substitution Effects," 1988.

10. Truman A. Clark, "Are Small Cap Stocks Still Alive?" A. B. Laffer Associates, October 10, 1985; Mark R. Reinganum, "The January Effect," A. B. Laffer Associates, November 17, 1982; Mark R. Reinganum, "Tis the Season to be Jolly," A. B. Laffer Associates, December 7, 1983.

22

International Stock Returns and Real Exchange Rates

Victor A. Canto

Theory and common experience postulate that differences in domestic economic policies across countries will have a differential impact on national economies. It would seem only natural that differences in domestic economic policies would also elicit corresponding responses on domestic equity values. When a country's tax rates fall relative to the tax rates of other countries, it is likely to experience an acceleration of its economic growth. (Tax rates are broadly defined here to include any distortions generated by national economic policies.) Due to the connection between domestic economic policies (e.g., tax rates) and economic performance, the values of assets located in countries that are altering their policies will fluctuate in a predictable direction. Assets will tend to become more valuable in countries that are cutting tax rates while tax-rate increases will tend to depress asset values.

Consider two identical steel mills, one located in northern Minnesota and the other located just across the border in Canada. If both steel mills sell identical products in the U.S. market, competition will force the mills to sell their products at approximately the same price. Given this situation, consider what would happen if Canada does what it did several years ago: increased tax rates while the United States lowered tax rates. Because the steel market is highly competitive, the Canadian company would not be able pass the tax hike on in the form of higher prices.

Initially at least, the Canadian steel mill would have to absorb all or part of the tax hike through lower after-tax profits. This drop in profits would be reflected by a fall in the Canadian mill's stock prices. Clearly, the U.S. mill would benefit in the short run. The investment implications of these observations are straight-forward: buy the stocks of companies located in countries that are lowering tax rates and sell stocks of companies located in countries that are raising tax rates.

As simple as this strategy is, it is difficult to apply. Because many corporations operate in more than one country, the impact of a particular country's tax changes on the value of the stocks of multinational corporations may be difficult to assess. Nevertheless, the basic strategy will apply to the aggregate domestic stock markets. Hence, the aggregate national stock indexes may be used as the basis of an international portfolio strategy.

THE LINKS: ECONOMIC POLICY, REAL EXCHANGE RATES, AND STOCK RETURNS

Although one cannot claim to anticipate all of the changes in terms of trade between the United States and its trading partners, there are some discrete events, such as tax rate reductions, that will have substantial impact on the real exchange rate and can be analyzed prior to implementation of a portfolio strategy.[1] Other events such as oil shocks may not be easily predictable. Once they occur, however, they could be immediately analyzed and incorporated in the portfolio strategy.

Consider the Tax Reform Act of 1986. It resulted in a reduction in the top personal income tax rate to 28 percent in 1988 from 50 percent in 1986. The increase in after-tax rate of return took place over a two-year period, increasing after-tax home pay in 1987 to 61.5 cents on the dollar from 50 cents on the dollar in 1986, a 23 percent increase in incentives. In 1988, the top rate declined to 28 percent, increasing take-home pay to 72 cents on the dollar from 61.5 cents, a 17 percent increase in incentives.

Everything else the same, the increase in after-tax returns would translate into an appreciation of the U.S. real exchange rate vis-à-vis its trading partners. However, everything else is not the same. In 1987, the terms of trade or real exchange rates were being affected by the tail-end adjustment in real exchange rates generated by the Economic Recovery Act of 1981.[2] We estimate that the process was completed in 1987. Thus, according to the analysis, the effect of the tax rate reduction would lead to a change in terms of trade in favor of the United States (i.e., an appreciation of the real exchange rate).

However, the rise in the real exchange rate would not be uniform across countries. The tax rate changes taking place in the rest of the world would also affect the terms of trade. The real exchange rate appreciation between the United States and those countries that did not reduce tax rates would be 17 percent. In turn, the appreciation against countries that raised their tax rates would result in an appreciation of the U.S. real exchange rate in excess of 17 percent. Finally, for countries that lowered their tax rates, the U.S. real exchange rate appreciation would be less than 17 percent. In fact, if the foreign country's tax rate reduction was large enough, it is conceivable that the U.S. real exchange rate would decline.

During 1987–88, no significant tax rate increases were registered by our trading partners. Therefore, an appreciation of the U.S. real exchange rate vis-à-vis its trading partners in excess of 17 percent is not to be expected. A number of our trading partners, most notably Australia, Canada, Japan, Sweden, and the United Kingdom, have responded to the U.S. tax rate reduction by lowering their own tax rates. For these countries, we have argued that the timing and increase in incentives were such that their actions would nullify and overcome those of the United States. Therefore, we expected that during 1988 and possibly 1989, their terms of trade or real exchange rates would appreciate vis-à-vis the U.S. According to our analysis, these five countries—Australia, Canada, Japan, Sweden, and the United Kingdom—are candidates to be included in the international portfolio.

Estimates of the percent change in the real exchange rate for the first 10 months of 1988 using data reported by *The Economist* are reported in Table 22.1. Consistent with our analysis, the U.S. real exchange rate has declined relative to Australia and Canada, although the U.S. real exchange rate has increased relative to Japan, Sweden, and the United Kingdom. The magnitude of the increase, less than 3 percent, is clearly much less than the changes in real exchange rates versus the other countries where the average appreciation of the U.S. terms of trade exceeds 10 percent.

The real exchange rate changes are clearly consistent with our analysis. The performance of the countries determined to be likely candidates to outperform the United States is also quite satisfactory. All of them—Australia, Canada, Japan, and Sweden—outperformed the United States in 1988 (Table 22.2).

Table 22.1
Percent Changes in 1988 Real Exchange Rates*

Australia	-9.95
Belgium	7.07
Canada	-5.28
France	12.1
W. Germany	12.7
Netherlands	13.7
Italy	10.3
Japan	2.1
Sweden	3.6
Switzerland	14.8
United Kingdom	1.9

* As of November 1, 1988.

A.B. Laffer Associates

Table 22.2
Nominal Return of Stock Market Indexes*

Year	Australia	Belgium	Canada	France	W Germany	Netherlands	Italy	Japan	Singapore	Sweden	Switzerland	United Kingdom	US
1971	3.78	14.90	6.89	-4.73	14.50	1.82	-12.75	46.38	N.A	29.20	N.A	44.73	6.20
1972	33.45	25.75	29.86	17.30	14.85	48.27	11.04	99.67	N.A	24.26	N.A	3.69	13.50
1973	-13.79	2.63	-7.32	4.24	-6.73	-12.04	5.34	-16.92	N.A	-17.46	N.A	-39.36	-17.40
1974	-43.92	-16.92	-26.24	-26.90	13.46	-5.74	-38.03	-16.48	N.A	N.A	0.95	-51.31	-28.00
1975	52.13	9.57	5.06	30.28	24.97	4.54	-10.85	20.90	N.A	N.A	22.23	136.86	41.40
1976	-18.58	-1.23	5.61	-30.20	4.41	-5.69	-37.91	20.25	N.A	-14.90	2.21	-23.37	9.90
1977	15.56	4.36	-4.84	-1.87	17.40	2.10	-23.51	12.83	7.06	-29.86	21.18	46.66	-17.20
1978	14.60	21.37	17.23	54.26	16.66	12.94	27.60	42.42	39.68	19.21	15.40	4.14	-0.80
1979	32.49	7.51	39.91	22.03	-7.12	-11.98	21.90	-20.98	24.91	0.87	7.17	-2.69	4.20
1980	46.10	-30.89	23.62	-3.74	-18.64	-18.16	90.47	23.21	54.73	11.74	-14.06	17.94	11.80
1981	-22.57	-14.91	-16.66	-44.28	-19.70	-18.82	-19.56	6.97	22.38	19.50	-16.39	-9.20	-13.90
1982	-31.06	-8.40	-1.97	-8.50	9.20	24.78	-28.97	-3.26	-14.66	12.46	2.18	0.22	21.00
1983	52.48	16.32	29.68	37.77	22.79	45.83	-0.93	24.69	41.42	52.41	22.70	18.75	19.70
1984	-15.43	3.33	-12.09	1.69	-11.07	-8.83	1.84	16.66	-22.20	-19.45	-19.41	3.13	-3.30
1985	20.15	55.56	14.74	66.87	97.91	62.30	113.00	33.45	-20.35	43.58	72.17	43.90	28.00
1986	44.14	58.46	6.48	69.28	26.91	30.32	76.05	65.10	41.57	51.06	22.71	18.07	23.30
1987	-5.32	10.06	9.59	-13.47	-18.96	-3.19	-19.34	37.32	6.91	3.14	1.63	34.94	2.90
1988	54.53	34.59	10.28	27.71	16.85	20.40	8.03	31.41	9.08	41.10	6.70	2.48	5.88

* 1988 figures are as of November 1, 1988.

REAL EXCHANGE RATES AND STOCK RETURNS: THE EVIDENCE

The Economist reports on a regular basis the national stock market index for the following countries: Australia, Belgium, Canada, France, West Germany, Netherlands, Italy, Japan, Singapore, Sweden, Switzerland, the United Kingdom, and the United States. Using data reported in the *International Financial Statistics* we have calculated the real exchange rate for each of these countries vis-à-vis the United States (Table 22.3). The stock price data from *The Economist* have been used to calculate the relative stock returns.[3]

A number of empirical regularities are evident in Figure 22.1:

- As predicted by our framework, a rise in the U.S. real exchange rate vis-à-vis one of its trading partners is associated with an underperformance of the foreign country's stock market relative to the U.S. stock market.

- In addition to a contemporaneous negative relationship, the change in the real exchange rate appears to lead the relative stock return estimates. From a portfolio strategy point of view, this result is extremely important. It suggests that the real exchange rate may be used to predict relative stock price performance across countries.

- It is apparent from the data reported in Table 22.3 that real exchange rate changes (i.e., deviation from purchasing power parity) tend to persist for a number of years. This is consistent with our view that adjustments to economic shocks are costly, hence the gradual adjustment in real exchange rates and rates of return.

- The fourth effect is that the deviations from purchasing power parity are self-correcting (i.e., mean reverting). This is consistent with our view that once the adjustment process is complete and a new equilibrium is established, the excess rates of return will be eliminated.

These findings provide the basis of an international portfolio strategy that is designed to capture economy-wide changes in the terms of trade or real exchange rates. The results are consistent with our approach to the relationship between real exchange rate changes and differential stock returns among countries. For an explanation of our theoretical framework, please see the Appendix.

PORTFOLIO STRATEGY

If commodities are not perfectly mobile, domestic policy changes or other real economic shocks could alter the "transportation cost band" during the transition to a new equilibrium. The imperfect mobility of goods and factors of production implies that the real returns to immobile physical capital will not be equated during a transition to a new equilibrium. In fact, the real return differential for the economy as a whole will ultimately mirror the real exchange rate. Two versions of the strategy could be implemented. One will be a passive strategy that will only react to changes in the terms of trade. Although this strategy will not capture fully the contemporaneous effects, it will capture the partial adjustments that

Table 22.3
Real Exchange Rate

Year	Australia	Belgium	Canada	France	W Germany	Netherlands	Italy	Japan	Singapore	Sweden	Switzerland	United Kingdom
1970	1.30	1.81	0.91	1.62	1.75	1.92	1.26	1.75	1.31	1.42	2.28	1.52
1971	1.21	1.63	0.91	1.52	1.56	1.69	1.20	1.51	1.27	1.29	2.02	1.36
1972	1.08	1.57	0.90	1.45	1.49	1.60	1.15	1.43	1.25	1.16	1.89	1.43
1973	0.90	1.46	0.88	1.32	1.25	1.38	1.15	1.26	0.98	1.18	1.59	1.40
1974	0.97	1.26	0.88	1.21	1.16	1.24	1.14	1.22	0.82	1.06	1.26	1.33
1975	0.97	1.33	0.89	1.20	1.30	1.31	1.12	1.21	0.94	1.14	1.32	1.35
1976	1.05	1.18	0.87	1.28	1.19	1.17	1.30	1.12	1.00	1.03	1.29	1.46
1977	0.96	1.07	0.93	1.18	1.09	1.09	1.17	0.90	0.99	1.11	1.11	1.20
1978	0.95	0.96	1.00	1.03	0.99	0.97	1.07	0.76	0.94	1.00	0.95	1.12
1979	1	1	1	1	1	1	1	1	1	1	1	1
1980	0.97	1.20	1.05	1.12	1.22	1.19	1.08	0.89	1.01	1.05	1.22	0.90
1981	1.02	1.50	1.03	1.39	1.46	1.43	1.29	1.02	1.01	1.32	1.29	1.11
1982	1.12	1.78	1.02	1.55	1.55	1.52	1.34	1.12	1.06	1.69	1.43	1.28
1983	1.14	2.03	1.01	1.81	1.77	1.78	1.47	1.12	1.10	1.76	1.57	1.40
1984	1.24	2.25	1.07	2.02	2.09	2.09	1.61	1.24	1.14	1.90	1.89	1.75
1985	1.47	1.78	1.12	1.56	1.65	1.65	1.32	1.00	1.14	1.55	1.52	1.37
1986	1.41	1.43	1.09	1.30	1.32	1.33	1.01	0.80	1.21	1.36	1.19	1.31
1987	1.24	1.20	1.02	1.09	1.11	1.12	0.87	0.64	1.15	1.16	0.96	1.03

Source: International Financial Statistics

Figure 22.1
Excess Real Returns versus Percent Change in Real Exchange Rate

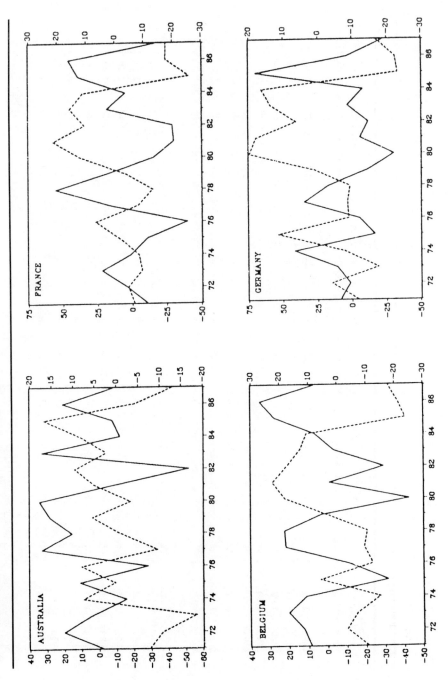

Figure 22.1 (*continued*)

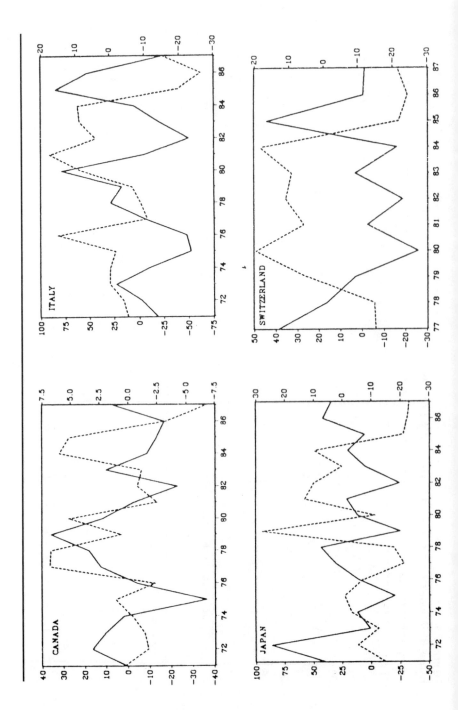

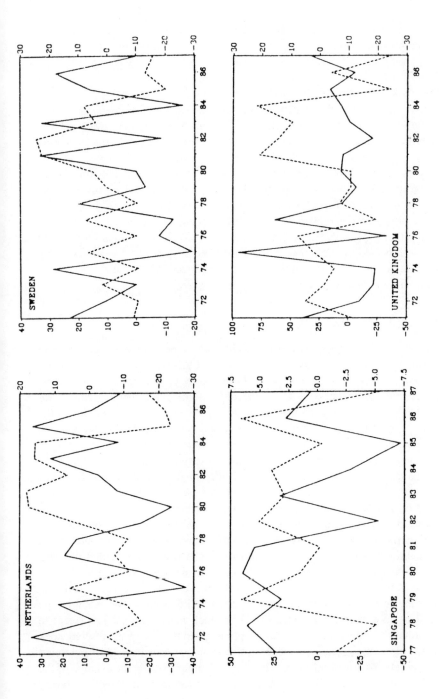

occur subsequent to the change in real exchange rates. If the adjustment process is sufficiently slow, such a strategy could yield a superior return.

The more active and aggressive strategy relates differences in domestic economic policies to changes in real exchange rates. This strategy attempts to reduce the response time of the decision process and, if successful, it will capture some, if not all, of the immediate impact of real exchange rate changes on U.S. stock returns vis-à-vis our trading partners' stock returns. However, changes in the real exchange rate of less than 1 percent are not considered to be significant. The portfolio strategy requires additional information; however, the reward will be the possible higher returns from capturing the initial impact of the economic policies.

Only the perspective of the United States is considered in what follows: all returns from foreign stock markets have been converted into dollar returns (Table 22.2). Further, in order to illustrate the magnitude of the impact of the portfolio strategy, only two positions will be considered: The portfolio will be invested fully in either U.S. securities or in foreign securities. If more than one foreign market is expected to outperform the United States, equal weights will be given to the foreign stock markets. Finally, only the direction of change in the real exchange rate is considered in this analysis.

THE PASSIVE STRATEGY

The empirical evidence indicates that changes in the real exchange rate lead the relative performance of the U.S. stock market vis-à-vis our trading partners. This finding leads to a very simple portfolio strategy: Whenever the U.S. real exchange rate appreciates vis-à-vis one of its trading partners, Germany for example, the U.S. stock market will outperform the German stock market in the ensuing year. In this case, German stocks would not be included in the international portfolio. Similarly, when the real mark/dollar exchange rate declines, in the ensuing year the German stock market is expected to outperform the U.S. stock market and German stocks will be included in the portfolio and U.S. stocks will be excluded. Table 22.4 reports the performance of the passive portfolio strategy on a year-by-year, country-by-country basis.

During 1971, the real exchange rate depreciated against each of the U.S. trading partners (Table 22.3). According to the decision rule, each of the foreign stock markets would be expected to outperform the U.S. stock market in 1972. Hence, domestic stocks would be excluded from the portfolio and all foreign stock markets would be included in the portfolio. The realized excess returns for each of the foreign stock markets are reported in Table 22.4. For example, the Australian stock market exceeded the U.S. stock market by 19.95 percent in 1972 (column 1, row 2). Since equal weight is given to each of the foreign stock markets, the excess return of the portfolio strategy from investing in foreign stock markets for a particular year, 1972 for example, will be the average of the row of entries of 1972 in Table 22.4. The excess return generated by the strategy

Table 22.4
Passive Strategy International Portfolio Selection*

Year	Australia	Belgium	Canada	France	W.Germany	Netherlands	Italy	Japan	Singapore	Sweden	Switzerland	United Kingdom
1971	-2.42	8.70	0.69	-10.93	8.30	-4.38	-18.95	40.18	N.A	23.00	N.A	38.53
1972	19.95	12.25	16.36	3.80	1.35	34.77	-2.46	86.17	N.A	10.76	N.A	-9.81
1973	3.61	20.03	10.08	21.64	10.67	5.36	23.74	0.48	N.A	-0.06	N.A	0
1974	0	11.08	1.76	1.10	41.46	22.26	0	11.52	N.A	0	N.A	-23.31
1975	0	-31.83	-36.34	-11.12	-16.43	-36.86	0	-20.50	N.A	-19.17	N.A	95.46
1976	0	0	0	20.30	0	0	-14.54	10.35	0	0	0	0
1977	0	21.56	12.36	0	34.60	19.30	0	30.03	0	-12.66	38.38	0
1978	15.40	22.17	0	55.06	17.46	13.74	23.46	43.22	40.48	0	16.20	4.94
1979	28.29	3.31	0	17.83	-11.32	-16.18	17.70	-25.18	20.71	-3.33	2.97	-6.89
1980	0	0	0	-15.54	0	0	82.53	0	0	0	0	6.14
1981	-8.67	0	0	0	0	0	0	20.87	0	0	0	4.70
1982	0	0	-22.97	0	0	0	0	0	0	0	0	0
1983	0	0	9.98	0	0	0	0	0	0	0	0	0
1984	0	0	-8.79	0	0	0	0	0	-18.90	0	0	0
1985	0	0	0	0	0	0	0	0	0	0	0	0
1986	0	35.16	0	45.98	3.61	7.02	52.75	41.80	18.27	27.76	-0.59	-5.23
1987	-8.22	7.16	6.69	-16.37	-21.86	-6.09	-22.24	34.42	0	0.24	-1.27	32.04
1988	48.65	28.71	4.4	21.83	10.97	14.52	2.15	25.53	3.20	35.22	0.82	-3.40

* 1988 figures are as of November 1, 1988.

A.B. Laffer Associates

(i.e., returns from foreign stock markets less U.S. stock market returns) is reported in Table 22.5. In 1972, the strategy outperformed the U.S. stock market by 17.31 percentage points (Table 22.5).

In any year, when a foreign stock market is excluded from the portfolio, no excess return will be realized, and a zero will be entered in Table 22.5. During 1984, the real exchange rate appreciated against the U.S. trading partners. According to the passive strategy decision rule, no foreign stock market was expected to outperform the United States in 1985. Foreign stock markets were excluded from the portfolio in 1985. Therefore, no excess return would be generated in 1985; this is reflected by the row of zeros for 1985 in Table 22.4.

Changes in the real exchange rate also result in a different number of stock markets being included in the portfolio in any given year. During 1988, for example, all foreign stock markets were included, while in 1985 no foreign stock markets were included in the portfolio. During 1983 the decision rule yielded only one foreign market, Canada. In 1987, all but two markets, Australia and Canada, were selected.

Table 22.5
Passive Strategy Excess Return*

Year	Passive Strategy Return	U.S. Return	Passive Strategy Excess Return
1971	14.47 %	6.20 %	8.27 %
1972	30.81	13.50	17.31
1973	-6.78	-17.40	10.62
1974	-19.77	-28.00	8.23
1975	31.80	41.40	-9.60
1976	25.27	9.90	5.37
1977	3.31	-17.20	20.51
1978	24.91	-0.80	25.71
1979	6.74	4.20	2.54
1980	36.18	11.80	24.38
1981	-8.27	-13.90	5.63
1982	-1.97	21.00	-22.97
1983	29.68	19.70	9.98
1984	-17.15	-3.30	-13.84
1985	28.00	28.00	0.00
1986	45.95	23.30	22.65
1987	3.31	2.90	0.41
1988	21.93	5.88	16.05

* 1988 figures are as of November 1, 1988.

A.B. Laffer Associates

The performance of the passive strategy is encouraging. In 1 out of 18 years no foreign stocks were deemed superior (Table 22.5). In the remaining 17 years, foreign stock markets were included in the portfolio. In 13 of those 17 years, the strategy outperformed the U.S. stock market. The results are even more impressive when one compares the cumulative returns of the international strategy. To illustrate, if $1 had been invested in 1971, using a portfolio strategy that would have remained fully invested in domestic stocks (i.e., the U.S. stock market index was bought), the $1 would have grown to $2.92 by November 1988. In turn, if the $1 had been invested following the passive international strategy, the amount would have grown to $7.40 by November 1988, a considerable difference.

THE AGGRESSIVE STRATEGY

Countries adopting progrowth policies that result in above-average growth will experience an appreciation of the real exchange rate and above-average equity returns. The real exchange rate and stock return differentials will change in the expected direction and the movement will persist for some time. Ultimately, the change in the real exchange rate and the stock market return will reverse itself.

Economic analysis of changes in domestic economic policies (e.g., tax rate changes) or other economic shocks (e.g., oil price changes) will identify faster any changes in the real exchange rate. In this case there is no need to allow for the one-year lag between changes in real exchange rates and the foreign stock market selections.

One way to estimate the potential profitability of this strategy is to assume that we have identified and interpreted any changes in terms of trade as they occurred. In this case, the portfolio selection will be made in the year in which the real exchange rate change occurs. The selection of foreign stock markets resulting from this strategy is reported in Table 22.6 and the average excess returns are reported in Table 22.7. The results indicate that the strategy would have remained fully invested in the U.S. market in 2 of the 18 years. During the remaining 16 years, the active strategy would have outperformed the U.S. stock market in 13 years. The cumulative returns of the aggressive portfolio strategy are clearly superior to a fully invested strategy that chooses only the domestic stock market. One dollar invested in 1971 following the aggressive international strategy would have grown to $14.85 as opposed to $7.40 for the passive international strategy and $2.92 for the fully invested domestic strategy.

ADDITIONAL CONSIDERATIONS

The viability of an international portfolio strategy based on real exchange rate changes has been presented only from the perspective of U.S. investors. The analysis, however, is sufficiently general to be modified to incorporate the perspective of foreign investors.

Table 22.6
Aggressive Strategy International Portfolio Selection*

Year	Australia	Belgium	Canada	France	W Germany	Netherlands	Italy	Japan	Singapore	Sweden	Switzerland	United Kingdom
1971	-2.42	8.70	0	-10.93	8.30	-4.38	-18.95	40.18	N.A	23.00	N.A	38.53
1972	19.95	12.25	-16.36	3.80	1.35	34.77	-2.46	86.17	N.A	10.76	N.A	0
1973	3.61	20.03	0	21.64	10.67	5.36	23.74	0.48	N.A	0	N.A	0
1974	0	11.08	0	1.10	41.46	22.26	-10.03	11.52	N.A	28.95	N.A	0
1975	0	0	0	-11.12	0	0	-52.25	-20.50	N.A	0	0	0
1976	0	-11.13	-4.29	0	-5.49	-15.59	0	10.35	0	-7.69	N.A	0
1977	32.76	21.56	0	15.33	34.60	19.30	-4.31	30.03	0	0	38.38	63.86
1978	15.40	22.17	0	55.06	17.46	13.74	28.40	43.22	40.48	20.01	16.20	4.94
1979	0	0	0	17.83	0	0	17.70	0	20.71	0	0	-6.89
1980	34.30	0	0	0	0	0	0	11.41	0	0	0	6.14
1981	0	0	-3.76	0	0	0	0	0	0	0	0	0
1982	0	0	0	0	0	0	0	0	0	0	0	0
1983	0	0	9.98	0	0	0	0	0	0	0	0	0
1984	0	0	0	0	0	0	0	0	0	0	0	0
1985	0	27.56	0	38.87	69.91	34.30	85.0	5.45	-48.35	15.58	44.17	15.90
1986	20.86	35.16	-16.82	45.98	3.61	7.02	52.75	41.80	18.27	27.76	-0.59	-5.23
1987	-8.22	7.16	6.69	-16.37	-21.86	-6.09	-22.24	34.42	4.01	0.24	-1.27	32.04
1988	48.65	0	4.4	0	0	0	0	25.53	0	0	0	0

* 1988 figures are as of November 1, 1988.

A.B. Laffer Associates

Table 22.7
Aggressive Strategy Excess Return*

Year	Aggresive Strategy Return	U.S. Return	Aggressive Strategy Excess Return
1971	14.40 %	6.20 %	8.20 %
1972	33.83	13.50	20.33
1973	-6.71	-17.40	10.69
1974	-12.81	-28.00	15.19
1975	13.44	41.40	-27.96
1976	14.26	19.90	-5.64
1977	10.75	-17.20	27.95
1978	24.39	-.80	25.19
1979	16.54	4.20	12.34
1980	29.08	11.80	17.28
1981	-17.66	-13.90	-3.76
1982	21.00	21.00	0
1983	29.68	19.70	9.98
1984	-3.30	-3.30	0
1985	56.84	28.00	28.84
1986	42.51	23.30	19.21
1987	3.61	2.90	0.71
1988	32.07	5.88	26.19

* 1988 figures are as of November 1, 1988.

A.B. Laffer Associates

Very strong and restrictive assumptions were made in order to illustrate, in a simplified manner, the viability of the strategy. A relaxation of these assumptions could move the strategy from the realm of theoretical curiosity to a practical and useful strategy. For example, the decision to allocate the funds among the different markets was based exclusively on signs of change in real exchange rates (whether the change was positive or negative). The 1973 and 1974 changes in real exchange rates versus Belgium were −7.12 and −15.10 percent respectively. In turn, the changes in real exchange rates versus Canada were −1.42 and −0.37 percent (Table 22.3). It is apparent that the magnitude of the change is quite different for the two countries.

A sensible money manager will interpret the U.S.-Belgium real exchange rate as significant and the U.S.-Canada real exchange rate as statistically insignificant. The outcome would not invalidate the judgment: The Belgian stock market outperformed the U.S. stock market during 1973 and 1974, while the relative performance of the Canadian stock market was mixed (Table 22.2). The results suggest that the magnitude of the changes in the real exchange rate should be incorporated in the analysis to reflect the confidence of the forecast.

There is no reason to expect that in practice the selection of foreign stock markets should be an all-or-nothing choice. It seems reasonable to assume that the proportion of the allocation to the different markets should be based on the confidence level (i.e., magnitude) of the percent change in the real exchange rate between the United States and the particular market. Also, there is no reason to assume that all of the industries in a particular foreign stock market will be equally affected by the real exchange rate. The impact of the change will depend on the degree of tradability of the industries. Therefore, differential industry effects will also be present in each of the national markets. The international strategy should be modified and extended to take advantage of these industry effects.

APPENDIX

Theoretical Framework: Purchasing Power Parity

Imagine an idealized situation where all economic factors—either man-made barriers such as taxes or natural barriers such as transportation costs—are absent. In such a fictitious world, prices for goods and services would be set in the world market. As a result, the dollar prices of such things as a ton of steel and machine tools would be identical wherever they were sold, whether in Canada, Germany, or any other country. If the dollar prices were not the same, profit opportunities would arise. Entrepreneurs would purchase the steel where the dollar price was lower (i.e., the steel would be exported from the lower-price country) to sell in the country where the dollar price was higher (i.e., the steel would be imported by the higher-priced country.) As the supply decreased, prices in the exporting country would go up. Symmetrically, an increased supply would produce a price decline in the importing country. This process would continue until prices in the two countries were equalized and all profit opportunities were fully exploited. The price of each commodity would be determined by world demand and supply conditions. In equilibrium, purchasing power parity (PPP) will hold.[4] Algebraically, PPP can be expressed as

$$P_{US} = E \times P_f$$

where P_{US} denotes the dollar price of a ton of steel in the United States; E denotes the exchange rate between the U.S. dollar and a foreign currency; and P_f denotes the price of a ton of steel in the foreign currency.

The analysis may be extended to all commodities, in which case the above relationships will apply to the domestic price levels. It can be shown that purchasing power parity implies

$$\pi_{US} = e + \pi_f$$

where π_{US} denotes the U.S. inflation rate; e denotes the percentage change in the exchange rate; and π_f denotes the foreign inflation rate.

The Real Exchange Rate. The terms of trade or real exchange rate measures the value of goods produced in one country (e.g., the United States) in terms of goods produced in another country (e.g., Germany). The real exchange rate is calculated by first converting the foreign CPI into dollars by multiplying it by the exchange rate. Then the dollar-denominated foreign CPI is divided by the U.S. CPI to obtain the real exchange rate. In a frictionless world where purchasing power parity holds, the dollar price of a German ton of steel will be the same as the dollar price of a ton of steel produced in the United States. Alternatively stated, in a frictionless world where purchasing power parity holds, the real exchange rate or terms of trade will be a constant.

Migration and Factor Returns. The movement of capital and labor can be analyzed using this approach. People would migrate in order to arbitrage persistent differences in their salaries. Similarly, owners of capital would locate production where the opportunity to earn high returns is the greatest and avoid locating where the opportunity to earn high returns is the least. Therefore, in equilibrium the wage level and the rate of return on capital would be equalized across states and nations.[5]

Interest Rate Parity. Under these idealized conditions of no transportation costs or other trade frictions, interest rate parity will hold. The dollar yield of similar classes of assets will be the same anywhere in the world. Hence

$$i_{US} = e + i_f$$

where i_{US} denotes the nominal dollar return; e denotes the percent change in the U.S./mark exchange rate; and i_f denotes the nominal foreign (i.e., German mark's) return.

The Equalization of Real Rates of Return. The Fisher equation postulates that nominal returns equal the real rate (r) plus the expected inflation rate (p). Algebraically the expression is expressed as

$$i = r + \pi$$

substituting the Fisher equation into the interest rate parity relation yields

$$(r_{US} + \pi_{US}) = e + (r_f + \pi_f)$$

where r_{US} denotes the U.S. inflation rate; e denotes the percentage change in the exchange rate; and π_f denotes the foreign inflation rate.

Subtracting the equation relating the two countries' inflation rates from the previous equation yields

$$r_{US} = r_f$$

Implications for Market Efficiency. The above equation indicates that, absent transportation costs and trade barriers, the trade in goods and assets will equalize the real rate of return on physical capital across countries. This will occur even when capital does not move across national boundaries. In such an idealized world, the world economy will be fully integrated and national boundaries will be irrelevant from an investment perspective. In such a world, a location parameter (alpha) and a dispersion parameter (beta) are the only determinants of asset prices. Additional parameters attempting to capture national/country effects will not add any value to the portfolio selection technique.[6]

Although aware that factors may limit the degree of integration among different economies, proponents of the fully integrated view argue that reliable and timely information on these factors is not readily available. Furthermore, since, a priori, there is no reason to expect any empirical regularity, the impact of these unknown factors will not affect the expected returns. Hence, the appropriate framework of analysis is that of a fully integrated economy, in which case an international portfolio strategy will not result in expected risk-adjusted excess returns.

Deviations from Purchasing Power Parity

Transportation costs introduce a band within which it is uneconomical to arbitrage price differences. Transportation costs are broadly defined to include shipping costs, border taxes, and real adjustment costs that cause factors to adjust slowly in response to changes in incentives. Hence, the price levels will differ by the amount of the transportation costs and PPP will not hold. The deviation from purchasing power parity will be reflected as changes in the terms of trade or real exchange rate. The change in the exchange rate will equal the increase in the transportation costs. That is

$$e_{real} \equiv \pi_{US} - e - \quad \pi f = t_c$$

where e_{real} denotes changes in the real exchange rate and t_c denotes the transportation costs.

In a world where transportation costs are present, commodities will be imported only when domestic prices exceed foreign dollar prices by enough to offset transportation and other trade-related costs. For each commodity, there exists a band in which the domestic price of a good can move relative to its exchange-rate-adjusted foreign price without eliciting repercussions in the form of exports or imports. This band represents the sum total of all trading costs whether natural or induced. Within that band there will be absolutely no tendency for purchasing power parity to hold. The transportation cost band denotes the degree to which the domestic commodity is protected from foreign competition.[7]

Different commodities may well have bands of differing widths surrounding their purchasing power parity points. Those commodities whose bands are the narrowest are the most tradable. Those with the widest bands are the least tradable. The magnitude of the bands determines the upper bound by which the industry's rates of return in one country will differ from the rates of return of another country.

Sources of Real Exchange Rate Changes. During the last two decades, the world economy has been subjected to major economic shocks that have significantly affected the differential performance of national economies. The shocks include major fluctuations in gold prices and three oil shocks. Evidence of changes in the national economies' competitive position will be reflected in deviations from purchasing power parity. During the 1970–87 period, significant fluctuations were observed in the real exchange rate between the United States and its trading partners.

Fluctuations in the real exchange rate can emanate from economic shocks outside the country, such as abrupt oil price increases. In other cases, changes in the terms of trade are the result of domestic economic policy. For example, the U.S. tax rate reductions explain a great deal of the exchange rate variation in the 1980s. However, the fact that the terms of trade did not change in an identical fashion against our trading partners is due to the differences in domestic economic policies abroad. Many of our trading partners enacted tax rate reductions of their own.[8] Irrespective of their origins, fluctuations in the real exchange rate alter the rate of return from doing business in the country in question. Consequently, differences in stock market returns will also be observed.

Economic Response to Changes in the Real Exchange Rate

Consider the effect of an increase in the U.S. real exchange rate. On the demand side, the appreciation of the real exchange rate will make the purchase of U.S. goods less attractive to foreign consumers. The foreign demand for U.S. goods will decrease, as will exports as a percent of GNP. The appreciation of the real exchange rate also will decrease the quantity demanded for all domestically produced goods. Both foreign and domestic purchasers will substitute U.S.-produced goods for the relatively less expensive foreign goods.

The story does not end here, however. Looking only at the demand-side responses misses an important point. The real exchange rate decline also has supply-side effects. If one unit of a domestic good acquires more units of foreign goods, domestic producers wil' increase output. Production of traded goods increases while domestic and foreign consumption decreases. As a result, exports as a percentage of GNP will decrease, too. Simultaneously, the rest-of-world production of traded goods and hence the exports of those goods, will also decrease.

An appreciation of the real exchange rate means that every unit of a domestic good is now capable of acquiring more foreign goods than before. This implies that the real rate of return of domestically located assets will increase relative to assets in the rest of the world. The higher real rate of return in the U.S. economy

will increase productive activity in the United States relative to the rest of the
world. Domestic asset values will increase relative to asset values in the rest of
the world, and the United States will experience an inflow of capital. Given a
floating exchange rate system, the balance of payments is always zero, and the
trade balance mirrors the capital account. Thus, the deterioration in the trade
balance will mean an improvement in the capital account.

The approach predicts that an appreciation of the real exchange rate will result
in an increase in domestic production, higher domestic asset values, and a
decrease in both imports and exports as fractions of GNP. However, since there is
a net capital inflow, the trade balance must deteriorate. Hence, the increase in
exports will be less than the increase in imports. The U.S. experience of the
1980s is entirely within this view.[9]

NOTES

The valuable comments and suggestions of Rudolph Hauser and Michael Banton are
greatly appreciated.

1. The real exchange or terms of trade rate measures the value of goods produced in one
country (e.g., the United States) in terms of goods produced in another country (e.g.,
Germany). The real exchange rate is calculated by first converting the foreign CPI into
dollars by dividing it by the exchange rate (foreign currency units per dollar). Then the
dollar-denominated foreign CPI is divided by the U.S. CPI to obtain the real exchange
rate.

2. See Chapter 16.

3. The relative stock return is calculated as follows: The domestic percent change in the
stock price index is converted into dollars; these calculations are reported in Table 22.2.
From the dollar-denominated foreign stock markets, the U.S. stock price performance is
subtracted. This gives rise to the foreign stock market nominal excess return. Subtracting
the U.S. inflation rate yields the real rate of return between each of the foreign countries
and the United States.

4. There is an extensive academic literature on the conditions under which factor prices
may equalize factor returns. See, for example, Paul A. Samuelson, "International Trade
and the Equalization of Factor Prices," *Economic Journal* 58 (June 1948), pp. 163–84.
For the effect of factor mobility in the equalization of factor prices, see Robert A.
Mundell, "International Trade and Factor Mobility," *American Economic Review* 47, no.
3 (June 1957), pp. 321–35.

5. See R. A. Mundell, "International Trade and Factor Mobility."

6. See, for example, Moshe Hagigi, "Industry Versus Country Risk in International
Investments of U.S. Pension Funds," *Financial Analysts Journal*, September/October
1988, pp. 70–74.

7. Arthur B. Laffer, "Minding our Ps and Qs: Exchange Rates and Foreign Trade,"
A. B. Laffer Associates, April 14, 1986.

8. Victor A. Canto and Arthur B. Laffer, "Great Britain Moves to the Supply-Side,"
A. B. Laffer Associates, November 2, 1988. See also Chapter 16.

9. Ibid.

Index

About the Contributors

JAMES BALOG is Chairman of 1838 Investment Advisors in Philadelphia and of Lambert Brussels Capital Corporation in New York. He has had a lifelong involvement with the U.S. health care industry, both as an industry analyst and as a policy expert. In 1981 Mr. Balog was Committee Chairman for the White House Conference on Aging, and he was appointed by President Reagan to the Pepper Commission in January 1989.

VICTOR A. CANTO is President of A. B. Laffer, V. A. Canto & Associates in La Jolla, California, an economic research and financial consulting firm. His previous works include *Supply-Side Portfolio Strategies* (coauthored with Laffer; Quorum, 1988) and *Currency Substitution: Theory and Evidence from Latin America* (coauthored with Gerald Nickelsburg). He also coauthored with Arthur B. Laffer *The Financial Analyst's Guide to Fiscal Policy* (Praeger, 1985) and *The Financial Analyst's Guide to Monetary Policy* (Praeger, 1986).

ARTHUR GRAY, JR., is President and CEO of Dreyfus Personal Management in New York.

HARVEY B. HIRSCHHORN is a Principal and Chief Economist of Stein Roe & Farnham in Chicago.

ARTHUR B. LAFFER is Chairman of A. B. Laffer, V. A. Canto & Associates and was a member of President Reagan's Economic Policy Advisory Board. Among his books are *Foundations of Supply-Side Economics* (coauthored with Victor A. Canto and Douglas H. Joines) and *International Economics in an Integrated World* (coauthored with Marc A. Miles). He also authored *Private*

Short-Term Capital Flows and *The Phenomenon of Worldwide Inflation* (co-edited with David Meiselman).

MARTIN G. LAFFER is President of Martin G. Laffer, an accountancy firm in Beverly Hills, California.

JOHN E. SILVIA is Vice President and Economist at Kemper Financial Services.

ALEX WINTERS is a Vice President of A. B. Laffer, V. A. Canto & Associates.